GOD LOVES YOU INFINITELY!

May the unbounded love of God shine ever in your life and in the lives of all who are dear to you! Pray also for me!!
Andrew.

Andrew Keogh Ph.D.

Dr. A. Keogh Ph.D
905-726-1396
a-ok@sympatico.ca

Copyright © 2010 by Andrew Keogh Ph.D.
Cover design by Peter Billings
www.creedoflove.com

ISBN:	Softcover	978-1-4415-5636-3

All rights reserved. No part of this book may be reproduced or transmitted in any form or by any means, electronic or mechanical, including photocopying, recording, or by any information storage and retrieval system, without permission in writing from the copyright owner.

This book was printed in the United States of America.

To order additional copies of this book, contact:
Xlibris Corporation
1-888-795-4274
www.Xlibris.com
Orders@Xlibris.com

GOD
*so loved the world
that he gave his only Son,
so that everyone who believes
in him may not perish.*

++++++

John 3:16

+++++

*To Mary
Most Holy
Beloved Daughter
of the Father
Chosen to Bring
into this World
His Eternal Son
as its Saviour
and Redeemer*

+++++++

CONTENTS

1. The Question of Faith 15
   Questions #1 .... *31*
2. The Origins of the Creed 33
   Questions #2 .... *46*
3. God the Father Almighty 48
   Questions #3 .... *62*
4. The Creator of Heaven and Earth 64
   Questions #4 .... *87*
5. And in Jesus Christ 89
   Questions #5 .... *104*
6. Conceived by the Spirit 106
   Questions #6 .... *124*
7. He Suffered under Pontius Pilate 126
   Questions #7 .... *141*
8. Was Crucified 143
   Questions #8 .... *160*
9. He Died 162
   Questions #9 .... *180*
10. And was Buried 182
    Questions #10 .... *199*
11. On the Third Day 201
    Questions #11 .... *220*
12. Ascended into Heaven 222
    Questions #12 .... *236*
13. He Will Come Again 238
    Questions #13 .... *257*
14. The Holy Spirit 259
    Questions #14 .... *273*
15. The Giver of Life (i) 275
    Questions #15 .... *296*

16. The Giver of Life (ii) 298
    Questions #16 .... *319*
17. Soul of the Church 321
    Questions #17 .... *335*
18. I Believe in the Church 337
    Questions #18 .... *354*
19. The Holiness of the Church 356
    Questions #19 .... *372*
20. The Catholicity of the Church 374
    Questions #20 .... *391*
21. The People of God 393
    Questions #21 .... *407*
22. The Communion of Saints 409
    Questions #22 .... *424*
23. A Holy Communion 426
    Questions #23 .... *439*
24. Mary, Mother of the Church 441
    Questions #24 .... *460*
25. Devotion to the Saints 462
    Questions #25 .... *475*
26. The Mystery of Iniquity 477
    Questions #26 .... *490*
27. The Divine Forgiveness 492
    Questions #27 .... *507*
28. I Shall Rise Again 509
    Questions #28 .... *522*
29. Eternal Happiness 524
    Questions #29 .... *535*

FOREWORD

++++++++

The title of the present work *God Loves You Infinitely* is the simplest expression of a very profound truth that God is *totally* love and that *Infinite Love* flows into every channel of creation. It was the apostle John himself who gave us this fathomless definition of our Creator: *God is love*! His very essence is love and creation is the outward expression of that love. Yes. God loves us infinitely! It is the only way that God, an infinite being, can love. Love lies at the very heart of the Godhead and from it sprang the Spirit of Love, the Holy Spirit. From that same love flowed the entire complex of creation, from the first realm of the purest spirits, the angels, to the lowest rung of our material existence, the earth and all that is in it to the furthest reaches of the universe. It is difficult for fallen man to grasp this sovereign truth of our faith. However, in the loves and desires of fallen man there are echoes of that spiritual reality. There is even a song that I recall from a distant childhood entitled: *Love makes the world go round!* That song rings so truly in depths and distances that the composer never even dreamt of.

It is into such a context that the reader or student must place all that follows. The author has chosen the Creed, and in particular, the Apostles' Creed, as a point of departure. This is evident in the first half of the text, but then it involves parts of the Nicene Creed and other related topics. No human work, no matter how eloquent or profound, can ever do justice to the wonders of infinite love. Here the author has simply attempted to push open the door so that all who take this book in hand may catch a glimpse of the staggering depths of God's loving action in their lives. Perhaps, they might even come to realise, in some measure, what Francis Thompson seeks to convey in his marvellous poem, the *Hound of Heaven*. Therein he expresses the pitiful ignorance and blindness that beset our best and highest efforts to love the *God of All Love*.

Alack, thou knowest not
How little worthy of any love thou art!
Whom wilt thou find to love ignoble thee,
Save Me, save only Me?

A.K.

The Apostles' Creed

* * *

*I believe
in God, the Father Almighty,
Creator of heaven and earth,
and in Jesus Christ,
His only Son, Our Lord,
who was conceived
by the power of the Holy Spirit
and born of the Virgin Mary.
He suffered under Pontius Pilate,
was crucified, died and was buried.*

*He descended into hell
and on the third day he rose again.
He ascended into heaven
and is seated at the right hand
of the Father.*

*Thence he shall come to judge
the living and the dead!*

*I believe
in the Holy Spirit
the Holy, Catholic Church,
the communion of saints
the forgiveness of sins,
the resurrection of the body
and life everlasting.
Amen*

1. THE QUESTION OF FAITH

* * *

Introduction:
                     Dr Viktor Frankl

(a) In Search of Meaning
- 1. The Meaning of Life?
- 2. Modern Scepticism
- 3. Science and Religion

(b) Christian Faith
- 1. What is Faith?
- 2. Faith is a Gift
- 3. An Affair of the Heart!
- 4. Searching for God

(c) The Reasonableness of Faith
- 1. Our Human Need
- 2. The Motives of Credibility
- 3. Faith and Freedom

(d) Growing in the Faith
- 1. Faith and the Creed
- 2. Faith and Tradition
- 3. A Living Faith!

1. The Question of Faith

* * *

Introduction

VIKTOR FRANKL (1905-1997)[1]

As an introduction to the subject of faith it would be of considerable interest to probe the wartime experience of Dr Viktor Frankl, an Austrian psychiatrist. He was a professor of Neurology and Psychiatry, the author of 32 books, including *Man's Search For Meaning*. This book is considered to be a classic. A survey done by the Library of Congress declared it to be among the top 10 influential books in America to date.

In September of 1942, a young doctor, Viktor Frankl, with his new bride, his mother, father and brother, were arrested in Vienna and taken to a concentration camp in Bohemia. When released in 1945 he was the only survivor, save for a sister who happened to be living in Australia. It was events that occurred there and at three other camps that led the young doctor—*prisoner #119,104*—to realize *the significance of meaningfulness in life*. One of the earliest events to drive home the point was the loss of a manuscript—his own life's work—during the transfer to Auschwitz. He had sewn it into the lining of his coat, but was forced to discard it at the last minute. He spent many later nights trying to reconstruct it, first in his mind, then on slips of stolen paper. This inner tension gave both a goal and a purpose to his survival.

As a prisoner in concentration camps he found himself stripped down to the level of pure survival. Gone were the supports of family and colleagues and all the props that living in society provides. For him and for all the inmates of these camps existence was reduced to the lowest level of existence. The question naturally surfaces in the mind of the reader: How could these virtually lost souls—every possession gone, every human value destroyed, suffering from hunger, cold and brutality,

---

[1] **Viktor Emil Frankl** M.D., Ph.D. (March 26, 1905-September 2, 1997) was an Austrian neurologist and psychiatrist as well as a Holocaust survivor. Frankl was the founder of logotherapy, which is a form of Existential Analysis, the "Third Viennese School of Psychotherapy".

hourly expecting extermination—how could they find in such a life anything worth preserving?

> *For too long we have been dreaming a dream from which we are now waking up: the dream that if we just improve the socio-economic situation of people, everything will be okay, people will become happy. The truth is that as the struggle for survival has subsided, the question has emerged: survival for what? Ever more people today have the means to live, but no meaning to live for.*
>
> The Unheard Cry for Meaning

Despite the secular basis and thrust of his work its spiritual implications are enormous. When he said *The meaning of our existence is not invented by ourselves, but rather detected*. He opened the door to religion, which supplies the ultimate meaning to our existence in this world. Especially when he finds the primary motivation of love as the mainspring of our existence there is the inevitable leap of the soul to God's love as the only thing that can account for man's existence here.

(a) In Search of Meaning!

1. *The Meaning of Life?*

What is it that marks us (mankind) off from the animals in this world? The animal world is driven primarily by *instinct*. It is instinct that drives their search for food, to hunt, to mate and procreate. It also seeks survival in its nests and dens and protection from other species. In all this the animals do not *question* their existence. They do not seek for *meaning* in their lives. Man alone does. Man is restless in his search for *meaning* in his existence. He has conquered so much of the world around him, climbed mountains, sailed the oceans and launched into the conquest of space! But the one question that haunts him relentlessly is *what is the purpose of it all?* Despite the most amazing discoveries of our times, despite all the wealth and power that it is possible to imagine or accumulate, there is still a profound emptiness in the human heart. In that emptiness there echoes the inevitable questions: *Why do I exist? What is the purpose of it all?* Increasingly psychiatrists and psychotherapists are besieged by clients who have lost any sense of meaning in their lives.

Victor Frankl learned from his own harrowing experience that only those who had meaning and purpose in their lives had the *inner* resources for surviving and enduring the horrors of their existence. He came to write of it later:

> *Effectively an ever-increasing number of our clients today suffer from a feeling of interior emptiness—which I have described as existential emptiness—a feeling of total absence of meaning to existence.*

Long before Victor Frankl, however, another great thinker had found his answer to our modern restlessness and its lack of inner meaning:

> *Thou has made us for thyself O God*
> *and our hearts are restless*
> *until they rest in thee!*
>
> St Augustine

2. Modern Scepticism

Faith, *human faith,* is a fundamental fact of our existence. It is a necessary component of human living: it is a fact of life. My every day existence is governed, mostly unconsciously, by *human* faith. Whatever I do, whatever I read or hear on TV, I have to accept, largely on human faith. I walk down the street and I am assuming that I will not be assaulted by a passer-by, nor become a victim of a drive-by shooting. That is *human* faith. I have no *absolute guarantee* of personal safety wherever I go! Virtually every phase of my life is dogged by this existential doubt and uncertainty. Even though it is apparent that faith is a component of ordinary living, when it comes to God, there appears to be an about-face in the sceptics' thinking. Belief in God is distrusted. It is questioned and rejected. Some might even hold it to be *irrational!*

There is the common objection that *religious* faith or belief is somehow an imprisonment of the mind! To submit to God or to his Church is tantamount to handcuffing the mind, and waving farewell to any meaningful argument or rational discussion. It is possible to hear such specious arguments as follows:

Just look at the progress that we have made in the twenty-first century. The world has become a global village with the astonishing advances of technology. We are reaching out to all parts of the world via the Internet. Man has landed on the moon. Astronomy is probing the furthest reaches of the universe, seeking its origins. Religion is now irrelevant to the noblest aspirations of the human spirit. It is a drag on our human destiny. Why hamper our inevitable progress by hanging on to antiquated notions of God and out-of-date religious beliefs that are forever dragging down the human spirit?

What is remarkable in all this litany of technological *advances,* is the assumption that mankind is *on the up and up*! There are, apparently, no limits to the evolutionary spiral of human progress. We are getting *better and better.* Education is all that is needed to achieve *the brave new world* lying there, gleaming and shining at the end of the rainbow of human hopes. The persistence of these mirages and illusions of human progress and betterment is remarkable in an age that has seen more slaughter and mayhem than at any time in human history. Within the last hundred years—*and for the first time in history*—mankind has been plunged into two world wars. This bears repeating—*TWO WORLD WARS!* And now, we teeter on the brink of a *third* one, haunted by the fears of a nuclear holocaust or biological self-annihilation. And we still call this *progress!*

3. Science and Religion

There is also the much used suggestion that religion must be forever locked in conflict with science. This arises, in particular, with the *Book of Genesis*. It must be noted, however, that both religion and science start from different premises. Science does not claim to have a lien on *absolute* truth! On the contrary, its basis is the *search for truth,* through constant *research* and *experimentation*. Its research flows from one *hypothesis* to another in the elaboration of *theories* and so-called *laws*, which may be valid for a time and, in time, they are discarded in the light of further research. It is a *perpetual* challenge which whets the appetite of devoted researchers. Religion, however, has a totally different perspective. It starts with one sole *absolute* truth, with God himself! It deals with *the existence of God*, who is the very *truth* in himself! Theology flows from an investigation into the ramifications of this given, *the Truth itself.* God is the author of both *science* and *theology*. There can be no conflict in their encounter with each other, for *divine Truth* cannot contradict *human 'truth'*. The Catechism, quoting Vatican II, states this very clearly:

> *Though faith is above reason, there can never be any real discrepancy between faith and reason. Since the same God who reveals mysteries and infuses faith, has bestowed the light of reason on the human mind. God cannot deny himself, nor can truth ever contradict truth.*
>
> (#159)[2]

Divine faith frees us from the feeble fetters of *human* hopes and *human* illusions. God alone is the bedrock of all our hopes and desires. How many times must we be told that man has a basically *fractured nature*, beset by ungovernable passions that are so easily unleashed, unless restrained by some higher purpose. This purpose can only come from *outside* of man. It cannot emerge from the *élan* of his own nature. It has been truly said that left to his own resources man is usually hell-bent on self-destruction. It was to avert such a disaster that God took it upon himself to intervene in human affairs. He did so by sending his own Beloved Son to come amongst us and show us the way to salvation.

(b) Christian Faith

1. What is Faith?

As defined by the First Vatican Council (1870):

> *Faith is a supernatural virtue, by which, under the inspiration of and with the aid of God's grace, we hold for true what God has revealed, not because we have perceived its intrinsic truth by the natural light of reason, but on the authority of God himself as its revealer, who can neither deceive nor be deceived.*

---

[2] These numbers refer to the numbers in the Catechism of the Catholic Church.

The Council's *expose* of faith can hardly be bettered. We can probe each element of this definition and see how it applies so clearly to every aspect of the grounds for divine faith. We can think about any particular article of faith. We can examine it in detail by way of answering possible objections. Reason can even produce a stream of flawless arguments to buttress its truth. This is still *human* effort and *human* reasoning, done, perhaps, even under the impulse of the Holy Spirit, but it is still not *divine* faith. We have just reached the portals of the *Temple of Faith*. God must still grant us entrance to its inner sanctum.

Faith, moreover, is a confession of our need for God. It is the answer to our poignant cry for help, for help in conquering the very weaknesses of our nature. But faith also demands a *surrender*! It is not a surrender in the sense of being a defeat of reason, or a blind capitulation to what is incomprehensible, but rather a *surrender* in the sense of being a *loving acceptance* or an *embrace* of the truth. As the Catechism points out, faith must be *freely given*. It cannot be coerced. Jesus himself gave overwhelming evidence of the truth of his claims to be divine. He wrought countless miracles and innumerable healings, even raising the dead to life. But the Scribes and the Pharisees refused this divine testimony to his claims, and sought to destroy him and his message. That same testimony provokes the same response in many today. Religious faith, on the other hand, is by its very nature a confession of our own true nature. As we have already shown human faith is an ingredient of our very existence. Only God can give us the answers to the meaning of life, and enlighten us as to why we exist at all. That is why faith gives us an indispensable orientation that takes us beyond the here and now. In Christian terms, it is that by which we are justified and considered righteous in God's sight.

2. Faith is a Gift!

> *And without faith it is impossible to please God,*
> *for whoever would approach him must believe that he exists*
> *and that he rewards those who seek him.*
> **(1 Corinthians 15:18)**

It is important to stress that faith is a gift, a divine gift. It is wholly gratuitous on God's part. We cannot earn it. Otherwise, it would cease to be a gift, and become something to which we are entitled. Now, of course, it is legitimate to ask *where do prayer and study come in? What about all the arguments that lead up to this conclusion?* Prayer, humility, the desire to learn and the effort to study are all helpful. But they are only preparatory. From an intellectual standpoint I can produce a flawless chain of arguments to prove the existence of God. But the spiritual acceptance of that fact in faith ***is God's work.*** Given our human capacity for error and failure, we can appreciate what is said in Sheed's marvellous work, *Theology and Sanity:*

> *It is pleasant . . . . to know that we can stumble towards the light. Given the rarity of powerful intellects, it is fortunate that sure faith can be had by imperfect intellects. The light is the fact. The believer cannot always prove, that is, state a flawless logical case for his faith, very much as a man in a lighted room might have no clear notion how electricity works. But he has no doubt about the light. He is living in it! That is why faith carries with it a kind of certainty which no chain of argument can produce.*[3]

The importance of faith is spelled out by the First Vatican Council

> *Faith is the beginning of human salvation, the foundation and root of justification, without which it is impossible to please God and to enter the fellowship of his Son.*

From the very fact that it is supernatural we see that it is God's work on the human soul. This work is attributed primarily to the Holy Spirit. Faith is the first and most important of the gifts of the Spirit. It is the very foundation of Christianity. It is the gift by which I accept those truths which God has revealed and I do so, not because those truths are *self-evident,* but simply because *God has revealed them.* All this means that faith is a gift of God. Note it is *a gift!* We cannot earn it; we cannot buy it. It is solely the gift of God's love for his creatures. How then does it come about? We are dealing here with *mystery,* because we are dealing with the action of God on the human soul.

---

[3] Frank Sheed: *Theology and Sanity* (Sheed and Ward) 1960 p. 299

St Thomas defines it *as an act of the intellect giving its assent to a divine truth*. This assent springs from a movement of the will which in its turn is moved by God's grace. This urges the intellect to give its assent. Notice that there is an apparently circular movement here in which God is at work. God gives us the gift of faith and, in accepting it we give it back to him.

3. An Affair of the Heart!

Our faith is *an affair of the heart*, and not simply of the mind. It is unfortunate that the phrase *"I Believe"* conjures up an aura of simple possibility when it prefaces the essential faiths of the Creed. They, thereby, fall into the category of beliefs or things which one may or may not accept. This in turn conjures up the synonyms of uncertainty, doubt, suspicion and notions of opinion, sentiment, feelings and impressions. All these can easily wash over all that follows, i.e. the basic tenets of the faith, reducing them to options of *possibility* instead of proclaiming them as the bedrock principles of Christianity.

It must, therefore, be underscored that the phrase needs emphasis on the tiny preposition *'in'*. *I Believe in* introduces us to profound statements of faith. It echoes in the heart with overtones of personal conviction *in* unshakeable truth. This is brought home by *Faustus of Riez*, a bishop of the fifth century, when he writes about *belief in God*:

> *To believe in God is to seek him in truth, to hope piously in him, and to pass into him by a movement of choice. When I say that I believe in him, I confess him, I offer him worship, I adore him and I give myself over to him wholly, and transfer to him all my affection.*

Moreover, the words *'I believe'* are, in fact, a rather feeble translation of the original word *'Credo'*. This word is derived from two Latin words *cor* meaning *'heart'* and *do* meaning *'I give'*. Combined they become *cor-do*, subsequently transposed into **'credo'**. These words *'I believe'*, therefore, give me a clue to the strength of my belief. They mean *'I give my heart'* to these truths that follow! In other words: *I am profoundly convinced, without any reservation whatsoever, of the truth and the power of these articles of faith, and, if necessary, I am prepared to die for them!*

While giving up one's life, or the prospect of martyrdom, may seem somewhat remote today, fidelity to the faith can, in its daily demands, be a long drawn out form of martyrdom! Hence, it is easy to understand the prayer of St Paul:

> *I pray that the God of our Lord Jesus Christ, the Father of glory,*
> *may give you a spirit of wisdom and revelation*
> *as you come to know him,*
> *so that, with the eyes of your heart enlightened,*
> *you may know what is the hope to which he has called you,*
> *what are the riches of his glorious inheritance among the saints,*
> *and what is the immeasurable greatness of his power for us who*
> *believe, according to the working of his great power.*
> **(Ephesians 1:17-19)**

4. Our Search for God

> *(He) dwells in unapproachable light,*
> *whom no one has ever seen or can see;*
> *to him be honour and eternal dominion. Amen.*
> **(1 Timothy 6:16)**

Any search for God must be one of humble attention and desire. We cannot approach God as if he were a mathematical problem or a geometrical theorem that must be tackled and conquered! Faith is not involved in the *solving* of such questions. Faith itself is not a self-evident truth in the order of *two and two make four*. God is not to be approached, nor can he be approached, as if he were the subject of scientific investigation. True, philosophy can advance reasons for his existence, but God will only reveal himself to those who are truly humble of heart. This is what the prophet Isaiah assures us in God's own name:

> *All these things my hand has made, and so all these things are mine, says the LORD. But this is the one to whom I will look, to the humble and contrite in spirit, who trembles at my word.*
>
> **(Isaiah 66:2)**

It is obvious that the *Eternal God,* the Creator of all things, cannot be grasped in the normal run of human reasoning. Only the humble prostration of the spirit and a profound reverence for *the Truth,* can open the mind, for as one author suggests:

> *The data of faith are not the kind of things*
> *the scientific method can discover or prove . . .*
> *God does not fit into a test tube.*
> *He is not visible to the eye, only to the mind*
> *(when it is wise) and the heart (when it is holy).*[4]

(c) The Reasonableness of Faith

1. Our Human Need

Faith, of itself, is a confession of our need for God to save us from ourselves. It is a poignant cry for help, for help in conquering the very weaknesses of our nature. But faith demands surrender. As the Catechism points out, our consent must be *freely* given. It cannot be coerced. Jesus himself gave overwhelming evidence of the truth of his claims to be divine. We have already seen that they wholly rejected his claims. This same testimony provokes a similar response in many today. It is, therefore, wholly reasonable, that on what St Paul calls the *'things not seen',* those things that far exceed our human understanding, we should accept God's word, the *divine* word, on all that pertains to him! God has far greater credentials than any human being. By the very fact that he is God, he is the very foundation of all truth. He is *truth* itself, and, therefore, wholly incapable of deceiving us or leading us astray. The Catechism assures us of the absolute certainty of this supreme virtue:

> *It is more certain than all human knowledge because it is founded on the very word of God who cannot lie. To be sure, revealed truths can seem obscure to human reason and experience, but 'the certainty that the divine light gives is greater than that which the light of natural reason gives'. (St Thomas Aquinas).*
>
> (#157)[5].

---

[4] Peter J. Kreeft: *Catholic Christianity* (Ignatius Press, San Francisco, 2001) p.11.
[5] These numbers refer to the numbers in the Catechism of the Catholic Church.

In reaching beyond the levels of human understanding it is evident that revealed truths do not appear as *self-evident* or *intelligible* to the light of our reason. I am surrounded with mystery even on the natural order. There is so much even about myself that I do not understand. Reason itself is very limited. I have only to consider the limits of my own knowledge and the limits of my own capacity to understand. There are things I shall never know, and there are things that I shall never understand. No matter how great the range of human genius to be found in the whole of history, there are still things that go far beyond the capacity of human reason to grasp and comprehend. By the very fact of being created, the human mind is thereby limited! So it is not unreasonable to accept what is far beyond any level of human understanding regarding matters of *religious* faith. Such faith enables me to go beyond the frontiers of purely human understanding.

2. *The Motives of Credibility.*

Nevertheless, God does give us what are called *'motives of credibility'*, that is, reasons or arguments that *suggest* or *compel* belief. In these we find, for example, the marvellous teaching of Jesus, his miracles, his Resurrection, the remarkable lives of those who have professed belief in Christianity, the extraordinary example of the saints and the overwhelming witness of countless martyrs throughout its history. All these clearly manifest that *'the assent of faith is by no means a blind impulse of the mind'* (#156). However, it is also natural to assume that *faith seeks understanding*. Underlying this principle, first expressed by St Anselm, a Doctor of the Church, is the assumption, or better, the conviction, that faith can never be at odds with reason. The latter's reach has so limited a range, even in the most brilliant intellects. Man, however, *created in the image of God,* instinctively searches to know more about him. So we naturally reach out to know more about the truths of faith, to get to know more intimately the very foundation of all faith and belief. Faith and reason complement each other. This is expressed by St Augustine:

I believe in order to understand;
and I understand the better to believe. (#158)

3. Faith and Freedom

The issue of authority in matters of faith raises the spectre of the so called *enslavement* or the shackling of man's intellect or reason to such apparently incomprehensible ideas of *salvation* and *redemption*. In response to this common conception of faith as a blight on our sanity, let us return to the definition of faith. *It's a supernatural virtue that enables us, with God's help, to accept those truths he has revealed, not because they are amenable to the light of human reason, but because they have been revealed by God himself.*

God reveals them, and has revealed them to his chosen channel of communication, the *Church*. It is the Church that passes them on in what is called *'deposit of faith'*. The Church does not, nay, it cannot *invent* so-called new doctrines. It cannot succumb to some fashionable idea or a passing whim that strikes the public fancy. If it declares a certain truth to be a dogma or a doctrine of the faith, that truth or dogma must have already existed, explicitly or implicitly, in the *deposit of faith.*

It is disingenuous to suggest that the Church *imposes* or *inflicts* dogma on its faithful as if it were nowadays some *bright idea!* The truths it has inherited from the past are mysteries of the faith that have been revealed and entrusted to it. Left to ourselves we cannot, nor could not, even guess at their existence. We accept them because God has revealed them, and it is impossible for him to deceive us. However, I am still *free* to accept or reject them. That is possible because of the gift of free will and the absence of coercion one way or the other. The Second Vatican Council made this abundantly clear in its *Declaration on Religious Freedom* where it says:

> It is one of the major tenets of Catholic doctrine that one's response to God in faith must be free. No one is to be forced to embrace the Christian faith against his (or her) own free will.

(d) Growing in the Faith

1. Faith and the Creed

Growing in the faith demands more than a vague intellectual assent. It has somehow to be expressed. This expression comes, first of all, in a *creed* and a creed is usually associated with religion. The word *religion* itself is derived from the Latin *religare*, which means *to bind or fasten*. Hence, religion denotes basically an *attachment* or an *allegiance* to a particular cause or faith. Throughout the ages religion has been variously defined as *a system of beliefs* proper to a particular culture, such as Hinduism or Buddhism. In the present context, however, it refers to a special relationship with a God who chose to reveal himself in time to a particular people, and who sent his Son to bring them the Good News of salvation and redemption.

Ultimately, religion implies the three C's—*Creed, Code and Cult*. The *Creed* reflects *what I believe*. In the present instance, this is the *Apostles' Creed*, the summary of Christ's teaching and its fulfilment in the life of the Church. The *Code* dictates *how I behave*. This is to be found in the *Decalogue* or the Ten Commandments. Finally, the *Cult* determines *how I worship*. Here we come to the sacramental system, especially in the Eucharist and in the attendance at Mass. In sum, how I behave and worship rests on what I believe. This means that the most fundamental element in the mix is the Creed, as the *object of faith,* since it concerns the very foundation of belief. This is distinct from the *act of faith* or the acceptance of the data of belief into one's life. For this acceptance we depend on the teaching and guidance of the Church. Here the Catechism summarises this role of the Church as follows:

> *It is the Church that believes first, and so its bears, nourishes and sustains my faith. Everywhere, it is the Church that first confesses the Lord. "Throughout the world the holy Church acclaims you". as we sing in the Te Deum; with her and in her, we are won over and brought to confess; "I Believe". It is through the Church that we receive faith and new life in Christ by Baptism.*
>
> *In the Roman Ritual, the minister of Baptism asks the catechumen; "What do you ask of God's Church?" And the answer is "Faith". "What does faith offer you? And again the answer is "Eternal life!.*[6]

---

[6] Catechism of the Catholic Church #168. This Catechism is also known by the 3 C's—CCC

2. Faith and Tradition

Throughout the Creed reference is often made to scripture as confirmation for some particular point of doctrine. The Second Vatican Council, however, utters a caveat on this point in saying:

> *the Church does not derive her certainty
> about all revealed truths from holy Scripture alone . . . .
> Both Scripture and Tradition
> must be accepted and honoured.*[7]

The word *Tradition* means literally *"a handing on"*. It comes from the Latin *tradere*, to *deliver* or *pass on*. What this means, in our present context, is that the body of revealed truths held by the Church has been handed on to posterity by the apostles and their successors, and from them to successive generations. This was spelled out by the Council of Trent. It proclaimed that Tradition contains both Scripture and the unwritten oral traditions that give life to Scripture. The teaching of Trent was reinforced by the Second Vatican Council, when it stated:

> *It is clear that sacred tradition, sacred Scripture and the teaching authority of the Church, in accord with God's most wise design, are so linked and joined together that one cannot stand without the others, and that all together, and each in its own way, under the action of the one Holy Spirit, contribute effectively to the salvation of souls.*[8]

All this insistence on the role of *Tradition* is the response to Luther's insistence and the current Protestant belief that rejects anything that is not *explicitly* stated in scripture. This belief is aptly and succinctly expressed in the Latin phrase, *"sola scriptura"* as the Protestant canon of theological certainty. Against such a canon the following may be stated:

1. *Such a canon does not exist in scripture!*

---

[7] *Dei Verbum* (the Constitution on *Divine Revelation*) n 9
[8] ibid. n 10

2. It has never existed in the Church's history prior to the sixteenth century.
3. An infallible scripture can only come from an infallible Church, its promoter and its guardian.
4. "Sola scriptura" is a divisive principle since it leads to private interpretation.
5. This divisive canon generates a multiplicity of churches and denominations

3. A Living Faith

Although faith is a gift and so can be accepted or rejected at any time, it is still necessary for salvation. This may sound either paradoxical or puzzling, since it prompts the question: *how can what is essentially a free gift be ultimately necessary for our salvation?* The words of scripture are clearly unambiguous on the issue:

> ***Without faith it is impossible to please God, for whoever would approach him must believe that he exists and that he rewards those who seek him***
>
> **(Hebrews 11:6)**

Faith demands perseverance, and perseverance always demands a constant struggle against the demands of our lower nature and the seductive appeals of the world around us. This unremitting conflict can easily take its toll on our faith. So we can understand why St Paul wrote these words to his young protégé, Timothy:

> *I am giving you these instructions, Timothy, my child, in accordance with the prophecies made earlier about you, so that by following them you may fight the good fight, having faith and a good conscience. By rejecting conscience, certain persons have suffered shipwreck in the faith.*
>
> **(1 Timothy 1:18-19)**

What is so precious about this gift of faith that it merits this constant vigilance against the siren call of the world? It is precious because it holds out to us the promise of eternal life. At issue in this earthly battle is our eternal happiness, the promise of beholding God face to face and sharing his eternal love forever! As St Basil assures us

> *When we contemplate the blessings of faith even now, as if gazing at a reflection in a mirror, it is as if we already possessed the wonderful things which our faith assures us we shall one day enjoy.*[9]

Now, however, *we walk by faith and not by sight*[10] as St Paul tells us in his letter to the Corinthians. In this walk of faith we are inspired by the example of the saints, those mighty champions of the faith and especially by Abraham *"our father in faith"*[11] of whom St Paul wrote:

> **Hoping against hope, he believed that he would become "the father of many nations," according to what was said, "So numerous shall your descendants be."**
> **(Romans 4:18)**

++++++++++++++++++

Prayer for Faith[12]

* * *

Let us, most beloved, pray in this way:

Lord, I believe. I want to believe in you.
Lord, make my faith complete, without reservations,
and let it penetrate my thoughts,
my way of judging divine and human things.
Lord, make my faith a free act;

---

[9] St Basil in his work on the Holy Spirit, *De Spiritu Sancto*.
[10] 2 Corinthians 5:7
[11] These words occur in the Liturgy of the Mass.
[12] From the introduction to Paul VI's *Credo of the People of God*, 1976.

*let it accept the renunciations
and the duties which it imposes
and let it express the culminating point
of my personality:
I believe in you, Lord.*
          Pope Paul VI.

Questions #1

* * *

1. *God alone can give meaning to our lives. Discuss!*

2. *Why do some people reject all idea of God or religion?*

3. *Is there a fundamental or inevitable conflict between science and religion?*

4. *What is divine faith and how does it differ from human faith?*

5. *What does the Council of Trent say about divine faith?*

6. *"Faith is an affair of the heart!" What does this mean?*

7. *What do you understand about 'motives of credibility'?*

8. *What are the three C's of religion?*

9. *The Church does not proclaim a dogma of faith simply on a whim. Explain!*

10. *What do you understand about 'sola scriptura' and its conflict with tradition?*

11. *What do you understand by the term 'living faith'?*

12. *Have you any personal questions or problems concerning faith?*

2. THE ORIGINS OF THE CREED

* * *

(a) Proclaiming the Faith
    —1.   Salvation History
    —2.   The 'kerygma'
    —3.   The Power of the 'kerygma'
    —4.   The Response to the 'kerygma'

(b) From the 'kerygma' to the Creed
    —1.   The Birth of the Creed
    —2.   The Baptismal Creed
    —3.   The Creed as Symbol
    —4.   The Creed in the Liturgy

(c) The Apostles' Creed.
    —1.   What's in a Name?
    —2.   The Growth of the Creed
    —3.   The Rule of Faith
    —4.   The Creed as Doxology

2. The Origins of the Creed

* * *

(a) Proclaiming the Faith

1. *Salvation History*

Salvation history is the history of God's special dealings with mankind from the beginning of creation until the end of time. It is concerned especially with the consequences of the fall of our first parents, in their failure to respond to God's loving concern for their welfare. The subsequent record of God's special dealings with man are recorded in what we know as the *Old Testament*. The long drawn out process of redemption that began with the call of *Abram* ended with the birth of the *Messiah*, Jesus. With the latter salvation history enters a newer and more dramatic phase, one in which God's plan of redemption emerges far more clearly. It casts its light back and illumines much of the prophetic elements of the past. We can now see more clearly how central was Jesus to the whole drama of redemption. This new facet of salvation history embodies two phases in the presence of Jesus.

(i) First of all, there is the *bodily* presence of Jesus seen as a man, walking amongst us, teaching, preaching, proclaiming the Father's message of redemptive compassion and love. He entrusted that message to a chosen band of faithful followers and, finally, offering up his life as the ultimate seal of that message!

(ii) The second phase emphasises his subsequent *spiritual* presence through the gift of the Holy Spirit. This presence is manifested especially in the Church he founded to carry on his work. This second phase will culminate in Christ's *Second Coming* in glory to judge the living and the dead. It is particularly in this second phase that we come to understand the *kerygma*.

2. *The 'kerygma'*

This term *kerygma* is a Greek word that means *'preaching'* or *'proclaiming'*. It is more than a simple message. It must be *proclaimed!* The *Gospel* or *the Good News* must be broadcast from the house tops! It is only in such a context that we can understand the authorisation of the apostles to go forth to the ends of the earth! Investing them with *the plenitude of his authority* he commanded them to go forth in his name:

> ***All authority in heaven and on earth has been given to me. "Go therefore and make disciples of all nations, baptising them in the name of the Father and of the Son and of the Holy Spirit, and teaching them to obey everything that I have commanded you. And remember, I am with you always, to the end of the age."***
> **(Matthew 28: 18-20)**

This Great Commission, given to the apostles by Jesus, epitomises their future mission. We note, in passing, that this commission is an *oral* one. The whole time of their apprenticeship in his presence was one of *oral* instruction. Jesus is recorded of writing only once, and that was in the sand, in the presence of the accusers of the adulterous woman.

The apostles imitated their Master in giving oral instruction to their disciples. Only a minority of them confided some of the essential elements of that message in writing. To our modern generation, the product of systems of universal education, this emphasis on an *oral* message may sound strange, perhaps, even abnormal. However, to the general population of the time it was quite normal. By our standards, they were *uneducated*. They could neither read nor write. Such accomplishments were the privilege of a few, the educated elite. Hence, the necessity of the *kerygma*, the *oral* proclamation of the Good News!

3. The Power of the 'kerygma'

> *For I am not ashamed of the gospel;*
> *it is the power of God for salvation to everyone who has faith,*
> *to the Jew first and also to the Greek. For in it the*
> *righteousness of God*
> *is revealed through faith for faith; as it is written,*
> *"The one who is righteous will live by faith."*
> **(Romans 1:16-17)**

For Paul the proclamation of the Gospel or the *kerygma* was, essentially, *the power of God!* There is a power intrinsic to the message itself. It called for *proclamation!* Because of that innate power *it had to be proclaimed,* and he was a willing servant of that proclamation. Paul here represents the other half of the *kerygma,* as a work that must be undertaken by *man.* God's work, therefore, demands participants. Paul enumerates the many ways that this can be accomplished:

> *The gifts he gave were that some would be apostles, some prophets, some evangelists, some pastors and teachers, to equip the saints for the work of ministry, for building up the body of Christ,*
> **(Ephesians 4:11-12)**

The mystery attached to the *Good News* is that it is so often rejected. St Paul also noted this mystery of rejection, when he said "***But all have not received the Gospel***"**(Romans 10:16).** The Gospel, however, bears witness to itself. It does not need justification from any other source. It can be clouded by heresy, by denial, by sin, by indifference. But, like the sun, which, although it can be obscured by the clouds, it is always there, because it is *the power of God always at work for our redemption!*

4. Our Response to the 'kerygma'

It is important to underscore that in the *kerygma* the *primary* agent is *God's call.* God is *calling* and giving us a message that he wishes us to proclaim. The *secondary* element is man's response to that call. It is a response that comes in faith! This, in its turn, raises certain questions. St Paul poses some of these questions in his letter to the Romans:

> *But how are they to call on one in whom they have not believed?*
> *And how are they to believe in one of whom they have never heard?*
> *And how are they to hear without someone to proclaim him?*
> *And how are they to proclaim him unless they are sent?*
> **(Romans 10:14-15)**

He then proceeds to provide an answer to these questions:

> *So faith comes from what is heard,*
> *and what is heard comes through the word of Christ.*
> **(v.17)**

The imperative of evangelisation is that Christ's message must be *proclaimed*! If there is no proclamation, it cannot be heard. As one author so beautifully expresses it:

> *Faith in the resurrection blossoms*
> *in the presence of the word proclaiming it.*[13]

It is important to note that, because of its intrinsic power, the *word* is not an *empty* word. It is not something that can be ignored or explained away or subjected to empty speculation. It is far more than some passing event in history! It is the proclamation of power and authority. Belief in the resurrection, for example, is not belief in an *empty tomb*, but rather, belief in the *Risen Christ!* That is what must be proclaimed!

(b) From the kerygma to the Creed

1. The Birth of the Creed?

From all the foregoing it is evident that the creed is a summary of the principal truths held by the Church. At first, these truths were handed on by word of mouth. It is a process that we call *tradition*, or *the handing on of the faith!* Later, and inevitably, it was written down for the sake of both accuracy and uniformity. From the book of *Acts* it is apparent that a profession of faith was demanded before baptism. We see this in the case of Philip the Deacon's encounter with the *eunuch of Candace*. When the latter was asked, as a prelude to baptism, *if he believed with all his heart what Philip had told him*, he answered:

> **I believe that Jesus Christ is the Son of God.**
> **(Acts 8:37)**[14]

We have seen that the Creed had its origins in the primitive *kerygma*. However, if we are looking to pinpoint its very first expression, it is to be found in that brief but pregnant phrase: "Jesus **is Lord**"! Against

---

[13] Raniero Cantalamessa: *Life in the Lordship of Christ* (Sheed & Ward, 1990) p. 79

[14] *This is taken from the Douay-Rheims version of the Bible.*

the *polytheism* of pagan Rome and the *divinization* of the Caesars, Christianity proclaimed this simple and very basic belief that there is only *one God, one Lord of all creation.* From that simple truth there emerged a number of related truths to which new converts had to subscribe, truths that were proclaimed as a basic reality to be either accepted or rejected. This proclamation we must emphasise, was primarily oral in what we call *tradition*, or the handing on of the Gospel message—the *Good News* of God's love and man's redemption. This is what St Paul refers to in the conclusion to his letter to the Corinthians:

> *For I handed on to you as of first importance what I in turn had received: that Christ died for our sins in accordance with the scriptures, and that he was buried, and that he was raised on the third day . . . .*
> **(1 Corinthians 15:3-4)**

2. The Baptismal 'Creed'

It is evident that new converts, especially in the Gentile world, had to have some basic instruction prior to the reception of baptism. Various formulas were employed in the course of time. Since most of the baptisms were administered to adults, a series of questions were put to them. By the end of the second century, about the year 200 A.D, we have the *sacramentary* of St Hippolytus which details this interrogation prior to baptism: This interrogatory is basically the Creed in question and answer form as well as a series of directions:

> *Do you believe in God, the Father Almighty*
> *And he who is to be baptised shall say, 'I believe'*
> *Let him forthwith baptise him at once, having his hand laid*
>   *upon his head.*
> *And after this let him say: 'Do you believe in Christ Jesus the Son*
>   *of God,*
> *who was born of the Virgin Mary, who was crucified in the days*
>   *of Pontius Pilate etc'.*
> *And when he says 'I believe' let him be baptised the second*
>   *time . . . .*

In all there were *three* baptisms in the name of each person of the Trinity. This is the Creed in its original *interrogatory* form, as an integral part of the rite of baptism, and as a profession of personal faith. It is obvious that it is but a simple step to its formulation as a synopsis of the essentials to which any catechumen had to learn by heart in the preparatory instruction in the Christian faith. This, in brief, is how the baptismal form of question and answer, or the *interrogatory* form of the Creed, was transformed into a *declaratory* form that simply stated the essentials of belief

3. The Creed as Symbol

It was the custom among the early Fathers of the Church to refer to the liturgical creeds as *symbols*. This referred to the various statements of faith or collections of beliefs, *'brought together'* in the questionnaires that preceded baptism. They are summaries of the basic Christian truths to which the catechumens gave their assent: *I Believe!*

The origin of the word lies in the Greek *symbolon*, which literally means a seal or signet ring which applied the seal. From this it was but a step to apply the term to legally sealed documents, such as a bond or warrant. St Cyprian, Bishop of Carthage (3rd century), also writes of baptising with the *symbol!* By which he meant the liturgical interrogation of the catechumens prior to their baptism.

The Latin word for this summary of the faith became known as the *symbolum*[15] Thus the Apostles' Creed was called the *Symbolum Apostolicum. Rufinus of Aquileia* (d.410 A.D.) in his commentary on the subject says that the word symbolum was borrowed from the military. The *"symbolum"* was also a password by which a soldier could distinguish himself from an enemy. In the Christian context it meant that the believer had now transferred his allegiance from the ranks of Satan to the army of Christ. Knowledge of the *"Symbolum"* was now

---

[15] *Symbol* is ultimately derived from the Greek verb *symballein* = to throw or bring together. This suggests a collection of the basic truths to which the catechumen subscribed.

the password for entry into Christ's army and, ultimately, into eternal life!

The finished Creed was, however, more than a simple *summary* of Christian belief, it was also the abbreviated *story* of salvation. In the tradition of the Old Testament, it was an act of *remembrance*, a calling to mind of God's involvement in the giant rescue operation known as *man's redemption*! It echoed the sentiments of the psalms, for example, that recalled the miracles of the *Exodus* and the miraculous intervention of Yahweh in the history of the Chosen race. Eventually it found its way into the liturgy, not only as a profession of belief, but also as an act of *praise and thanksgiving* in the liturgy of the Word.

4. The Creed in the Liturgy

> *Let us approach with a true heart in full assurance of faith,*
> *with our hearts sprinkled clean from an evil conscience*
> *and our bodies washed with pure water.*
> *Let us hold fast to the confession of our hope without wavering,*
> *for he who has promised is faithful.*
>
> **(Hebrews 10:23)**

It was the *Nicene Creed*[16] that was first incorporated into the liturgy of the east by *Peter the Fuller*, Bishop of Antioch. The Orthodox Church chose to follow the Nicene Creed in order to emphasise the *divinity* of Christ, taking issue with the heresiarch, *Arius,* and his followers who denied it. The Emperor Justin II ordered it to be sung everywhere throughout the Byzantine Empire. By the sixth century, the Creed found its way into the eucharistic liturgy in the West. The practice of reciting the Creed in the *Latin Mass* began in Spain, and spread to Gaul. This was due to the Council of Toledo (589 A.D.), taking its cue from the Orthodox ritual. It was extended throughout the Frankish Empire by order of the Emperor Charlemagne in the eighth century.

---

[16] The so-called *Nicene* Creed is strictly speaking the *Nicene-Constantinopolitan*. The work of the Council of Nicaea (325) was completed and promulgated by the Council of Constantinople in 381.

However, it was another two centuries before it was introduced into the Roman liturgy. It is also a point of interest to note that the Creed was sung sometimes at Baptisms, thus recalling its catechetical origins. Throughout it all, there was the guiding hand of the Holy Spirit that inspired the Church. This profound conviction of divine inspiration is best expressed by St Cyril, Bishop of Jerusalem (346-386 A.D.) who wrote:

This synthesis of the faith was not made in accord with human opinions, but rather, what was of the greatest importance was gathered from all the scriptures to present the one teaching of the faith in its entirety.

(c) The Apostles' Creed

1. *What's in a Name?*

Why should the Creed be called after the *apostles?* An ancient legend has it that the apostles, before responding to the Great Commission, met after Pentecost to decide the basic truths of the Master's message. Each of the Twelve, under the inspiration of the Holy Spirit, made a personal contribution to the text. Peter said:

I believe in God the Father Almighty, maker of Heaven and earth.

Andrew followed: *and in Jesus Christ his Son, our only Lord!* And so it went on down to the last, Matthias, who concluded with *'eternal life'*. While it is true that the whole scenario sounds like some pious fiction, it would appear incontrovertible, from the history of the *kerygma,* that it bears the imprint of *apostolic authority.* Even if the eastern tradition is firmly attached to the *Nicene Creed,* it can be argued that the *Roman* tradition, based on Peter and Paul, argues, ultimately, for *apostolic* authority. All this indicates that there was a remarkable tenacity in the early Church to be faithful to what was passed on, from generation to generation, in the teaching of the apostles, crystallised ultimately in the Old Roman Creed, known as the Apostles' Creed. In the ancient Roman liturgy, and in the Eucharistic canon, the celebrant prays:

for all who hold and teach the Catholic faith that comes to us from the apostles.

Moreover, the Nicene Creed, formulated at the Council of Nicaea in 325 A.D. would appear to follow a pre-existing pattern of beliefs, in making this profession of faith *in the One, Holy, Catholic and Apostolic Church.*

2. The Growth of the Creed

(Jesus) said to them, "But who do you say that I am?"
Simon Peter answered, "You are the Messiah,
the Son of the living God."
And Jesus answered him, "Blessed are you, Simon son of Jonah!
For flesh and blood has not revealed this to you,
but my Father in heaven".
(Matthew 16:15-17)

While it is impossible to trace the Creed back to any one particular individual, it is possible to discern a pattern of development through the *catechesis* of the early Church. If one were to pinpoint the starting point for the genesis of the Creed one might pick this seminal passage from the Gospel of Matthew. Peter's confession of faith could serve both as inspiration and as model for the more informative *symbols* that were used and developed in the various churches. Each of the churches adopted and adapted the nucleus of the apostolic faith and tradition to their own local circumstances. They all agreed on the essentials of the faith for their catechesis, with special emphasis on *the death and resurrection of Jesus*. It must be remembered that these early catecheses were oral and in Greek, since Greek was the *koine*[17] of the Mediterranean seaboard. The creeds were committed to memory. St Jerome tells us explicitly:

The Symbol (Creed) of our faith and hope is not written in pen and ink but (is inscribed) on the tablets of our hearts![18]

---

[17] the *koine* means the common language of communication at the time, somewhat like English today, the universal language of commerce. By the 4th century Greek had been supplanted by Latin.

[18] see Schaff: *The Creeds of Christendom*, vol.1 (Baker Books, 1996) p. 18

This oral tradition was also known as the *Discipline of the Secret*. In an age when the faith was subjected, at times, to ferocious persecution, the passing on of the faith by word of mouth was a safeguard against betrayal, either by incriminating documents or through the presence of *agents provocateurs!* The most complete and most popular forms of the Creed were to be found in the major churches of Rome, Aquileia, Milan, Ravenna, Carthage and Hippo. While there was little difference among them, it was the Roman version that eventually prevailed and gained general acceptance throughout the western Churches. But it was only in the beginning of the eleventh century that it found its way into the Roman liturgy.

3. The Rule of Faith

We also constantly give thanks to God for this, that when you received the word of God that you heard from us, you accepted it not as a human word but as what it really is, God's word, which is also at work in you believers.
(1 Thessalonians 2:13)

There is one development in the history of the Creed that needs to be emphasised, since it is pertinent to the catechetical process. This is the Creed as a test of *orthodoxy* or as *the rule of faith*. It was about the year 200 A.D. that the Creed was considered as a summary of the Christian message and as a safeguard against the assaults of heresy. There was a general agreement that the *Trinitarian* formula expressed the essence of the message that Christ had commanded his apostles to preach and teach to the world. The Church was ever mindful of the words of St Paul to his protégé, Timothy:

If you put these instructions before the brothers and sisters, you will be a good servant of Christ Jesus, nourished on the words of the faith and of the sound teaching that you have followed.
(1 Timothy 4:6)

And as Irenaeus urged, it was the *prime* responsibility of the bishops, as successors of the apostles, to safeguard the unity of the Church and the authenticity of Christ's message, by seeing that their teaching conformed to *the rule of faith* in the Creed. More than that, the Creed, as *the rule of faith*, became the norm for the interpretation of the Scriptures, and for the discernment of those traditions that should be maintained.

4. *The Creed as a Doxology*[19]

The Creed is a *doxology*, or a *hymn of praise to God*. As a hymn it is also a prayer. St Thomas Aquinas ranks it with the Our Father and the Hail Mary as one of the great prayers of Christendom.[20] It is a proclamation of God's sovereign goodness and of his mighty work of creation and redemption. It is a summary that is a constant reminder to us of God's infinite love. It is also the embodiment of our fundamental indebtedness to God's infinite mercy and his plan of redemption in the sacrifice of his beloved Son on our behalf. St Paul brings all this to mind when he writes:

> *The word is near you, on your lips and in your heart, that is, the word of faith that we proclaim; because if you confess with your lips that Jesus is Lord and believe in your heart that God raised him from the dead, you will be saved.*
> **(Romans 10:8-9)**

This confession of faith is, therefore, a clarion call to the world and to all peoples that we are all part of his mighty work of salvation. Hence, the creed should resound in the world as a paean of gratitude for God's immeasurable bounty, a hymn of undying gratitude that the almighty and transcendent God should concern himself so lovingly with his own creation. We can now understand why St Augustine urges us to recite it frequently:

> *Say the Creed daily!*
> *When you rise,*
> *when you compose yourself to sleep.*
> *repeat your Creed!*

---

[19] doxology is based on the Greek *doxa*, meaning *glory*
[20] St Thomas Aquinas: *The Three Greatest Prayers:* Commentaries on the Lord's Prayer, the Hail Mary, The Apostles' Creed (Sophia Institute Press, 1990)

> *Render it to the Lord, remind yourself of it.*
> *be not irked to say it over and over.*[21]

The Creed, *this synthesis of the faith*, is our Christian heritage. It has been passed down from generation to generation, like some family heirloom. We, in our turn, must pass it on to posterity, unsullied and untarnished. Its constant repetition, therefore, should not be a burden. Its recitation is an affirmation of our commitment to the faith. It is a constant reminder of our baptism and of the obligations that the reception of this sacrament entails. It reaffirms our spiritual identity and the goal of all our efforts in this passing world. As St Cyril of Jerusalem (348-386 A.D.) remarks:

> *This synthesis of faith was not made in accordance with human opinions, but rather, what was of the greatest importance was gathered from all the Scriptures, to present the one teaching of the faith in its entirety. And just as the mustard seed contains a great number of branches in a tiny grain, so too this summary of the faith encompasses in a few words the whole knowledge of the true religion contained in the Old and New Testaments.*[22]

++++++++++

"Christ, sent by the Father,
is the source of the Church's whole apostolate";
thus the fruitfulness of apostolate for ordained ministers as well
as for lay people clearly depends on their vital union with Christ.
In keeping with their vocations,
the demands of the times and the various gifts of the Holy Spirit,
the apostolate assumes the most varied forms.
But charity, drawn from the Eucharist above all,
is always "as it were, the soul of the whole apostolate."[23]

---

[21] St Augustine in *Sermon 58* (quoted in Kelly's *Creeds* p.370)
[22] Quoted in the Catechism of the Catholic Church #186. (St Cyril is noted for his catechetical instruction).
[23] Catechism of the Catholic Church #864
   Note all references to the word *Catechism* refer to this official source.

Questions #2

* * *

1. *What do you understand by the phrase salvation history?*

2. *Jesus lies at the heart of salvation history. Explain!*

3. *What does the word kerygma mean and what are its origins?*

4. *The origin of the Creed lies in the rite of baptism. Explain!*

5. *Why is the Creed called the Apostles' Creed?*

6. *What is meant by calling the Creed a Symbol?*

7. *What do St Jerome and St Augustine say about the Creed?*

8. *How do you explain the origins of the various creeds?*

9. *Why is the Creed called the rule of faith and a doxology?*

10. Who or what are the following: a. St Hippolytus; b. St Cyprian; c. Peter the Fuller; d. the Council of Toledo; e. the 'Discipline of the Secret'?

11. What, in summary, does St Cyril of Alexandria say about the Creed?

3. I BELIEVE IN GOD, THE FATHER ALMIGHTY

* * *

(a) The Denial of God!
  —1. The Need for Faith
  —2. Atheism
  —3. Agnosticism
  —4. Indifferentism

(b) In Search of God
  —1. The Witness of Creation
  —2. The God of Philosophy
  —3. The God of Revelation

(c) The Nature of God
  —1. God's Covenant with Abraham
  —2. The Mosaic Covenant
  —3. The Fatherhood of God
  —4. God is Love!

3. I believe in God the father almighty

* * *

(a) The Denial of God!

1. The Need for Faith

When we come to express our faith in God's existence, the virtue of faith is already present. Strictly speaking, therefore, the profession of the creed is not an *act of faith*. It already *presupposes* the act of faith firmly rooted in the heart, before it is outwardly expressed. This conviction of heartfelt faith does not rest on any *human* opinion but on the truth of *God's own word*. The reality of this faith, moreover, gives substance, meaning and purpose to my existence here on this earth. The first *Vatican Council (1870)* expressed this faith as follows:

> *Faith, which is the 'beginning of man's salvation', is a supernatural virtue whereby, inspired and assisted by the grace of God, we believe that what He has revealed is true, not because the intrinsic truth of things is recognised by the natural light of reason, but because of the authority of God Himself who reveals them, and who can neither err nor deceive. For faith, as the apostle testifies, is 'the assurance of things hoped for, the conviction of things not seen'.*
>
> **(Hebrews 11:1)**

As a basic expression of the truth the Creed is based on Christ Himself Who is the Truth.

> *I am the way, and the truth, and the life.*
> *No one comes to the Father except through me.*
> **(John 14:6)**

These words are as relevant today as when they were said to the apostle Thomas. In fact, they are more necessary today when *relativism*, both moral and intellectual, abounds. By that we mean that there is in our culture a denial—either *open* or *covert*—of any such thing as *absolute truth*! From this there arises the popular notion that *one religion is as good or as true as another.* So often, however, this tired, worn-out cliché is simply a cloak for denying God's existence.[24]

2. Atheism

> *Many of our contemporaries either do not at all perceive, or explicitly reject, this intimate and vital bond of man to God. Atheism must, therefore, be regarded as one of the most serious problems of our time.*[25]

These words of the Second Vatican Council highlight the spiritual blight of our times, *atheism,* or the denial of God's existence. Although atheism is but a minority opinion in the history of religion, it has even seen, in our own time, the creation of governments devoted to its propagation. The enforcement of this perverted *credo* through policies of terror and persecution in godless regimes created untold numbers of martyrs to religion.

Therein is dramatised the immortal words of the Scottish poet, Robbie Burns:

> *'Man's inhumanity to man*
> *Makes countless thousands mourn'*

When God is cast out man loses his dignity! Yes, atheism, in all its forms, results in the *brutalising* and *dehumanising* of man. In the past century there has been ample evidence of this in the history of atheistic communism. While we deplore such violations of God's rights and man's dignity, there is also a species of *atheism* that is, perhaps, just as deadly and subversive. It does not consist in any *open* denial of the existence of God, but life is lived *as if He did not exist, as if he was irrelevant to our*

---

[24] We shall return to commenting on this saying under the section dealing with *'Indifferentism'*.
[25] Gaudium et Spes 19 #1

world of today. Vatican II puts the fundamental and supernatural nature of *man* in its *eternal* perspective:

> *Without the Creator, the creature vanishes!*
> (Gaudium et Spes #36)

This mentality abounds in the culture of our age, in the media, in entertainment, in popular music and in our laws and governmental attitudes. We see it in the loss of values and the moral relativism that is all around us. There lies in all of this an implicit denial of God's existence, of religion's transcendent values, and of any claim they might have on our allegiance.

3. Agnosticism

Agnosticism is either an explicit philosophy or an attitude of mind that proclaims a certain religious neutrality. It says, in effect, that *God may exist or he may not. We can never be sure! God is too remote, and, therefore, wholly irrelevant to the task of living here on earth.* All knowledge is thereby reduced to what I experience here and now. It is evident that agnosticism reduces all knowledge to the evidence of the senses and to our emotional responses. Man must confine himself, therefore, to his own practical experience in the world and be content with that. A popular way of expressing this is to say: *I only believe in what I can see and hear!*

One exponent of this *materialist* philosophy was the Englishman, Thomas Huxley, who expressed the notion that our intellects are *incapable* of knowing anything spiritual or immaterial, especially any idea of God, of the human soul and its ultimate destiny. These things are beyond human ken! These ideas have been popular among those scientists who trumpet the advances of science and technology as the panacea for all man's evils and woes! It was about such ideas that the Vatican Council spoke, when it said:

> *No doubt today's progress in science and technology can foster a certain exclusive emphasis on observable data, and as agnosticism about everything else. For the methods, which these sciences use, can be wrongly considered as the supreme rule for discovering the whole truth.*
>
> (Gaudium et Spes 57)

It is evident that agnostics define truth in extremely narrow terms. Logically and inevitably such a point of view fails lamentably to account for our notions of *love, truth* and *beauty*. Life lived on such narrow terms would be a very limited and deprived existence! In practice, however, our agnostic differs very little from our *practical atheist*.

4. Indifferentism

In contrast to *atheism* and *agnosticism*, there exists a mindset that thinks of God as purely an *option* in our lives. Such a point of view cuts a broad swathe through so many people for whom God and religion are simply a matter of taste and choice! Affiliation to this or that religion is just like choosing to belong to this club rather than another. It is all a matter of *personal* preference. Another way of framing this indifferentism is saying: *one religion is as good as another! Again, it is all a matter of taste!* The logic of saying that one religion is as *good* as another is the same as saying that one religion is as *bad* as another! If one religion is as *true* as another then one religion is as *false* as another. All this follows when one denies the existence of *absolutes*. Another aspect of *indifferentism* is to look on God as, somehow, an enlargement of ourselves! This may come, in part, from illustrations that depict God as a venerable, and perhaps, doddery old man with a flowing beard. This results in a terrible diminution of the true nature of God. This is what one author has to say on the subject:

> *To the influence of this same image we may trace two of the principal modern tendencies about God, the tendency to treat Him as an equal, and the tendency to treat him as an extra. Neither tendency could abide for one instant the light of the true idea of God's nature and person.*[26]

Treating God as an *equal* leads people to complain about the nature of the world and all that is in it, and pontificate on how God could have made a better job of creation itself. While this may appear a harmless occupation, there is a far more serious consequence of this diminishing

---

[26] F.J. Sheed: *Theology and Sanity* (Sheed and Ward, 1960) p. 23-24

of the stature of God. There is the loss of the sense of *sin*, arising from the notion that I have no special obligation to observe the commands of a Creator! However, treating God simply as an *extra* on the stage of life has a far wider appeal. Religion, it is felt, is something that you can accept or reject. It is a purely personal decision like taking up golf or going on a holiday. In some quarters it might be considered an impediment in the world of business. But, it is asserted, going to church or talking to or about God is a purely individual affair. It is nobody else's business—a vast error, and a terrible illusion!

> *Error about God cannot be a private affair. It can only lead to a diminished and distorted life for everyone. God's will is the sole reason for our existence; be wrong about his will and we are inescapably wrong about the reason for our existence; be wrong about that and what can we be right about?*[27]

(b) In Search of God

1. The Witness of Creation

> **The heavens are telling the glory of God;**
> **and the firmament proclaims his handiwork.**
> **(Psalm 19:1)**

Just as the foundation of any building is its most important component, so is the existence of God the foundation of Christianity. All the articles of the Creed rest on this as their firm support, and derive their force and obligation from this sovereign fact. The Catechism spells this out:

> *"I believe in God": this is the first affirmation of the Apostles' Creed and the most fundamental,. The whole Creed speaks of God, and when it also speaks of man and the world, it does so in relation to God. All the articles of the Creed depend on the first . . . . The other articles help us to know God better as he*

---

[27] *ibid. p.25*

> revealed himself progressively to men. "The Faithful first profess their belief in God."
>
> (#199)[28]

Our Catholic tradition recognises that our knowledge of God comes in two ways, through *natural* or *divine* revelation. From the viewpoint of *natural* revelation, there is an instinctive recognition on the part of mankind in general that there is a God responsible for creation and all its marvels. St Paul echoes the words of the psalmist in his letter to the Romans. When speaking of the Gentiles he says:

> ***For what can be known about God is plain to them, because God has shown it to them. Ever since the creation of the world his eternal power and divine nature, invisible though they are, have been understood and seen through the things he has made. So they are without excuse; for though they knew God, they did not honour him as God or give thanks to him, but they became futile in their thinking, and their senseless minds were darkened***
>
> **(Romans 1:19-21)**

2. The God of Philosophy

God, nevertheless, is *not*, and *canno*t be, an *object* of human experience. His existence is not *immediately* evident. So how can it be *proved* or *demonstrated*? This has been the great challenge to philosophy for on the answer a great deal depends. Its solution has a bearing on the meaning and purpose of our existence here on earth. If God does *not* exist, then man is a law unto himself and can determine his own destiny. But, if God *does* exist, then man must acknowledge his essential dependence on a creator, and serious consequences follow.

In his famous theological work, the *Summa Theologica*, St Thomas[29] asks the question whether the existence of God can be

---

[28] This last sentence is a quotation from the *Roman Catechism*

[29] St Thomas Aquinas (13th century) was probably the greatest philosopher-theologian of the Middle Ages. He exercised a profound influence on all subsequent students right down to modern times.

demonstrated. Since the existence of God is not self-evident, it can only come from the evidence of things that already exist. Arguments based on the latter are called arguments *'a posteriori'*, or arguments that deduce a cause from its effect. St Thomas set forth five ways in which the principle of causality is evident, Notice he does not call them strictly *proofs*, but *'ways'* (viae) or *approaches* to solve the problem at hand.

The structure of the five ways is the same. Each begins with a fact of experience, a self-evident truth, which leads to the conclusion of an infinite and independent being that alone can account for the existence of the fact or self-evident truth. The following is an outline of the basic arguments.

a. *The Uncaused Cause*
   Everything created has a cause, so there must be a *beginning* without a cause!
b. *The Unmoved Mover*
   Everything is in motion so there must *'Someone'* immovable to start it off!
c. *The Infinite Designer*[30]
   Everything has a design, so there must be an ultimate *Designer* we call God.
d. *The Necessary Being*
   Everything is contingent (dependent on another). There must be an end to this chain of dependency in One completely independent, self-sufficient and necessary.
e. *The Grades of Perfection*
   There are degrees of morality, goodness and virtue etc there must be *'Someone'* who is the *ultimate* of all these!

The five ways can all be reduced to this one statement:

> *A limited or contingent being can only be understood in the context of an infinite or self—existing Being, that we call God.*

---

[30] The principle of design is embedded in all scientific research. Scientists base their work on the unearthing or the discovering of the laws that govern the activities of the world and everything in it!

3. The God of Revelation

Against all claims to the contrary the first affirmation of the Creed is a trumpet call to proclaim that *God truly exists,* that He is very much alive! The recognition of God is *essential*, not only to our personal growth and our progress in the spirit, but even to our political economic well-being and in the mundane affairs of human existence. No matter how deeply we probe the wonders of this world nor scan the furthest reaches of the universe, God always eludes us! It was because of our weakness of will and darkness of intellect that he took pity on us and gradually unfolded knowledge of himself in different stages of our history.

The first major step in history was in the call of Abraham and his choice of a Chosen race, with whom he established a covenant of the Old Law, which was to serve as guide in the moral life of the nation. In addition, there was the promise of a future Messiah, a Redeemer, and a constant reminder to the Chosen people of their faults and betrayals through a succession of prophets, who worked wonders and miracles to buttress their warnings of tragedy and misfortune for the people's violation of the covenant. However, *"in the fulness of time"*, the promised Messiah appeared in the person of the *Word made flesh*. God became one of us! He walked among us and spoke to us. Finally he died for us! It was the complete realisation of all the prophecies, made to the ancestors of the Chosen People that lay strewn across the millennia of their history. Let us now trace more in detail this process of divine revelation to man.

(c) The Nature of God

1. God's Covenant with Abraham

Since the problem is, basically, that we cannot comprehend or reach out to God's nature by ourselves, any intimate knowledge of him must come from the revelation of Himself to us. God slowly lifted the veil to reveal Himself in His covenants with Noah and Abraham. It was to the latter that he initiated a covenant[31] that established a special relationship

---

[31] The term covenant usually means an agreement between two people. In scriptural terms it is used for God's special interventions in human history.

with a man called *Abram* from the city of Ur in Mesopotamia. Changing his name to *Abraham* God said:

> *"I am God Almighty; walk before me, and be blameless.*
> *And I will make my covenant between me and you,*
> *and will make you exceedingly numerous."*
> **(Genesis 17:7)**

Notice God describes himself as *'Almighty*'! This means that God allocates to himself power that is supreme and unquestionable. In virtue of that power he promises to Abraham to make him the ancestor of a people that will be *as numerous as the stars of heaven!* As a sign of that covenant he prescribes the rite of circumcision for them. It would be a constant reminder of the covenant. Moreover, as a test of Abraham's faith and trust in his promise God asked him to sacrifice his son. Since Abraham was quite prepared to do so God re-affirmed the covenant in the strongest terms:

> *By myself I have sworn, says the LORD: Because you have done this, and have not withheld your son, your only son, I will indeed bless you, and I will make your offspring as numerous as the stars of heaven and as the sand that is on the seashore.*
> **(Genesis 22:17)**

The faith of Abraham in God's promises became the touchstone of Christian fidelity to St Paul when he wrote:

> *Therefore his faith "was reckoned to him as righteousness." Now the words, "it was reckoned to him," were written not for his sake alone, but for ours also. It will be reckoned to us who believe in him who raised Jesus our Lord from the dead.*
> **(Romans 4:22-24)**

It is God alone who here takes the initiative, despite the immense disparity between God and man. It is from the Hebrew word *berith* that we get the word *covenant* or *testament* in English.

2. The Mosaic Covenant

The most famous of the ancient covenants was the *Mosaic* covenant. This fact alone merits further consideration and detail about Moses himself. Destined for death as an infant he was rescued from drowning in the Nile by Pharaoh's daughter and was raised by her as an Egyptian until he later discovered his true identity. Involved in a quarrel he killed an Egyptian and was forced to flee from the wrath of Pharaoh to the land of Midian, where he lived and married and had a family. Years later while tending his father-in-laws flocks he saw a burning bush and was curious about the fact that it was not being consumed by the fire. From out the burning bush God spoke to Moses and identified himself as the God of Moses' ancestors:

> *"I am the God of your father, the God of Abraham, the God of Isaac, and the God of Jacob." And Moses hid his face, for he was afraid to look at God.*
>
> **(Exodus 3:6)**

God then charged him with returning to Egypt and delivering his own people from the slavery imposed on them by Pharaoh. At the same time he assured him that all those who sought his life were dead. Moses, however, was extremely reluctant to go and said:

> *"If I come to the Israelites and say to them,*
> *'The God of your ancestors has sent me to you,'*
> *and they ask me,*
> *'What is his name?' what shall I say to them?"*
> *God said to Moses, "I AM WHO I AM."*
> *He said further, "Thus you shall say to the Israelites,*
> *'I AM has sent me to you'."*
>
> **(Exodus 3:13-14)**

Here God reveals that *his very essence is existence itself, the very source of all that is—eternal, infinite, immortal! YAHWEH—he is the One Who Is, the One who must necessarily BE!* [32] This sacred name of God

---

[32] The Hebrew letters are JHWH., often referred to as *Tetragrammaton*, or the 4-letter word. By combining with the vowels of the Hebrew

was so revered by the Jews that they never pronounced it. It was only uttered once in the year by the High Priest in the Holy of Holies. God's *Self-revelation* continues throughout the Old Testament in the prophets and in the psalms. It culminates in the stunning fact of the Incarnation, when God stepped on to the stage of human history in the person of Jesus Christ. God became one of us!

> *'For God so loved the world that he gave his only Son,*
> *so that everyone who believes in him may not perish*
> *but may have eternal life'.*
> **(John 3:16)**

Here, at last, we have the inner clue to the very nature of God. It is summarised in the immortal phrase of St John himself: '**God is love!**'*(1 John 4:16)* Here is the culmination of God's Self-revelation. He, whose very essence is existence, is an *all-consuming fire of eternal love*. The history of salvation is essentially an epic drama of God's unique *love affair* with mankind! God loves us—*infinitely!* It is the only way that he can love! It is this that leads us to call him—*Abba! Father!*

3. The Fatherhood of God!

> *For God so loved the world that he gave his only Son,*
> *so that everyone who believes in him may not perish*
> *but may have eternal life.*
> **(John 3:16)**

Alone among the monotheistic religions of the world Christianity holds that God, although *One* in nature, is in reality a community of persons, a *Tri-unity* or *Trinity* of Father, Son and Holy Spirit. So incomprehensible is this notion of the Trinity to human understanding that it had to be revealed to us by God Himself. In one sense the title *'Father'* can be used of *all* the persons in the Trinity. Through the example of Jesus Himself it is appropriated to one, the *First Person* of the most Holy Trinity. In the Old Testament God as *'father'* appears in only eleven

---

word for Lord ADONAI we get the bastardised, if popular version of JEHOVAH.

places. However, it is never used as a form of address. Typical of such rare references is the one in the prophet Isaiah:

> *'Yet, O LORD, you are our Father; we are the clay,*
> *and you are our potter; we are all the work of your hand'.*
> **(Isaiah 64:8)**

In the New Testament, however, God is revealed in a special loving relationship to His creatures. This revelation from God Himself gives new depths and more profound insights to the idea that God is truly *Our Father!* This title is derived from the prayers and the teaching of Jesus Himself. Moreover, we get a glimpse in the early life of Jesus of this special relationship between Him and His Father. The former was just twelve years old when he said:

> *Why were you searching for me?*
> *Did you not know that I must be in my Father's house?*
> **(Luke 2: 49)**

The word *'Father' is* constantly on Jesus' lips. It is recorded 170 times in the Gospels and on one special occasion when the disciples asked to teach them how to pray, he gave us the greatest prayer on how to address God as *"Our Father, Who art in Heaven . . . ."*

4. God is Love!

However, it is with Jesus himself that we get the greatest insight into God's relationship with man. God himself enters into the very fabric of creation by becoming man! As John tells us so succinctly in his Gospel:

> *And the Word became flesh and dwelt amongst us*
> *and we have seen his glory, the glory as of a father's only son,*
> *full of grace and truth.*
> **(John 1:14)**

When asked by Philip to show him the Father Jesus made that immortal response:

> *Have I been with you all this time, Philip, and you still do not know me? Whoever has seen me has seen the Father. How can you say, 'Show us the Father'? Do you not believe that I am in the Father and the Father is in me?*
> **(John 14:9-10)**

Why God chose to manifest himself in this way is both mind boggling and mysterious. Why he should go to such lengths to win our love and allegiance, when we so often reject his advances, only compounds the mystery. There must be a key to somehow solve this conundrum of God's unfailing persistence in seeking to conquer man's sinfulness and break down the barriers of his incredible selfishness. The answer lies in the very nature of God himself. The apostle John supplies the answer in giving the key to penetrate the mystery of God's relentless pursuit of sinners! He tells us that **God is love.** (1 John 4:8) His very nature is love. He cannot NOT love! In light of all this we can say in the words of the Catechism:

> *No one is father as God is Father!*
> **(#239)**

Questions #3

* * *

1. *What is divine faith and what does the Letter to the Hebrews say about it?*

2. *"Everything is relative!" What do you understand about moral relativism?*

3. *What is the difference between atheism and agnosticism?*

4. *What do you understand about indifferentism?*

5. *"One religion is as good as another!" How would you answer this objection?*

6. *What do you mean by the God of Philosophy?*

7. *What are the stages of God's revelation to man and its climax?*

8. *What does the title of El Shaddai mean and why is it in the Creed?*

9. *Jesus is the manifestation of the Father to us! What does this mean?*

10. *What should be our response in faith to God's love and how do you measure up personally?*

11. *"No one is father as God is Father!" What does this mean?*

4. THE CREATOR OF HEAVEN AND EARTH

* * *

(a) The Creator
 —1. Creation: the Basic Question?
 —2. Creation *'out of Nothing'!*
 —3. God's Conservation & Providence
 —4. Why then did God Create?

(b) of Heaven
 —1. The Angelic Universe
 —2. Ministers and Messengers
 —3. Our Guardian Angels!
 —4. The Fallen Angels!

(c) and Earth
 —1. The Beauty of Creation
 —2. The Crown of Creation!
 —3. God's Co-creators!
 —4. The Guardians of Creation

(e) The Fall of Man
 —1. You will be like God!
 —2. The Consequences of the Fall
 —3. Man's Fundamental Alienation
 —4. The Fall of All Creation!

++++++++++++++++

Postscript: *Creation and Evolution*

4. The Creator of Heaven and Earth[33]

* * *

(a) The Creator

1. Creation: the Basic Question?

There is a fundamental question that often arises in respect of man's existence: *Why are we here? What is the point of living on this earth for so short a span of years and then dying? Is existence nothing but a collection of memories for future generations?* Such questions as these have bedevilled thinkers of all ages. *Why are we here?* Philosophers of all ages have grappled with these questions. It is possible to reduce them all to the most basic question posed by the existentialist philosopher, Martin Heidegger: *Why is there something rather than nothing?*[34]

Some sceptics have sought to answer this question of existence in various forms of *nihilism*. This is the total rejection of all religious and moral principles in society. All forms of appeal to the higher principles of self-sacrifice and devotion to some *Supreme Being* or to a universal Church are deemed totally vain and foolish. Living here on earth itself is wholly pointless! The futility of man's existence was eloquently expressed by the poet:

> *One Moment in Annihilation's Waste,*
> *One Moment, of the Well of Life to taste—*
> *The Stars are setting and the Caravan*
> *Starts for the Dawn of Nothing—Oh, make haste!*[35]

Nevertheless, despite our doubts and misgivings, there is an instinctive urge or desire of the human spirit to find an answer. It is an answer that the psalmist seeks to give us:

---

[33] It is strongly urged that the reader read the opening chapters of *Genesis* before reading the text!

[34] Martin Heidegger; *Introduction to Metaphysics,* (New Haven and London 1959)

[35] Edward Fitzgerald: *The Rubaiyat of Omar Khayyam* (Selfridge & Co Ltd, 1910) #38.

> *Hear, O my people, and I will speak, O Israel, I will testify against you.*
> *I am God, your God. Not for your sacrifices do I rebuke you; your burnt offerings are continually before me.*
> *I will not accept a bull from your house, or goats from your folds.*
> *For every wild animal of the forest is mine, the cattle on a thousand hills.*
> *I know all the birds of the air, and all that moves in the field is mine.*
> *If I were hungry, I would not tell you, for the world and all that is in it is mine.*
>
> **(Psalm 50:7-12)**

This same assurance comes also from the Catechism itself in telling us:

> *Human intelligence is already capable of finding a response to the question of origins. The existence of God the Creator can be known with certainty through his works, by the light of human reason, even if this knowledge is often obscured and disfigured by error. This is why faith comes to confirm and enlighten reason in the correct understanding of the truth:*
>
> > *"By faith we understand that the world was created by the word of God, so that what is seen was made out of things which do not appear".*
> >
> > **(Hebrews 11:3)** [36]

2. Creation 'out of Nothing'! [37]

> *In the beginning*
> *God created the heavens and the earth.*
>
> **(Genesis 1:1)**

---

[36] *Catechism* #286

[37] The phrase *'Creation out of nothing'* is a literal translation of the Latin *'creatio ex nihilo'*, an expression used by the the Fourth Lateran Council in 1215 in defining the matter in hand.

This opening statement of the Bible introduces us, with startling brevity, to the concept of *creation from nothing!* The word *'created'* is rather ambiguous in English. We speak glibly of the *creative* efforts of artists and musicians. Michelangelo, we say, was the *creator* of the *Pieta* and the statue of *David*. However, the efforts of all the artists that have ever existed, no matter the greatness of their skill, cannot make a single work of art *out of nothing!* The artist depends on his paints and canvas and the sculptor on his stone and tools.

Turning back to the original scriptural text we find that there is absolutely no ambiguity in the word for *creation*. The Hebrew language has a unique word *'bara'*, to *create*, which can only be used of God himself. *He alone can give existence!* Therefore, the term *creation*, in the present context, means the bringing into existence something or someone that has no right or title to that existence. It had no form in any previous existence, no substratum of potential being. This means that *'in the beginning'* God created the world out of *nothing*, or, as theologians are wont to say, *'ex nihilo'* (Lateran Council IV. A.D. 1215).

Divine creation, therefore, is the simple act of *willing into existence* things that were never there before. Creation, in this sense, is essentially a mystery, in that it is made *'out of nothing!'* That word *'nothing'* boggles the mind, for it cannot conceive of *nothing*! As one author aptly remarks:

> *It is the measurelessness of infinite power that it can make a universe with no material at all. If we honestly focus our minds upon the act of creation, really and honestly consider what is meant by making something out of nothing, we find it totally baffling.*[38]

From all eternity God has willed to share His life with other beings. As a community of love the Trinity, the three persons of the Godhead, decided to share that love with other beings who had *no right* to existence and *no right* to be loved. From that decree there issued a creation that was neither the product of any *inner necessity* nor the result of *blind*

---

[38] Frank Sheed: *Theology and Sanity* (Sheed and Ward, New York, 1960) p.85

chance. As the twenty-four elders of *Revelation* sang to the *One* who sat upon the throne:

> *"You are worthy, our Lord and God, to receive glory and honour and power, for you created all things, and by your will they existed and were created."*
> **(Revelation 4:11)**

St Paul says something similar, when speaking in his letter to the Romans of the God of Abraham, he says

> *'the God in whom he (Abraham) believed, who gives life to the dead and calls into existence the things that do not exist.'*
> **(Romans 4:17)**

The Catechism makes this very point :

> *The order and harmony of the created world results from the diversity of beings and from the relationships that exist among them. Man discovers them progressively as the laws of nature. They call forth the admiration of scholars. The beauty of creation reflects the infinite beauty of the Creator and ought to inspire the respect and submission of man's intellect and will.*
> (#341)

3. Conservation & Providence[39]

In speaking of creating things *out of nothing*, we noted how God's actions differ totally from human ones. The latter needed some pre-existing materials, the former did not. We have also noted that human works of art survive independently of their creators. But that is not the case with God's creation. Since it was created *out of nothing*, it still needs the sustaining hand of God to keep it in existence. God cannot walk away, so to speak, and leave His creation to survive on its

---

[39] *Conservation refers to the general presence of God and his support of the entire universe. His Providence refers to his concern and support for man's material and spiritual welfare.*

own. It still needs the support of His *conserving* power, to prevent it disappearing into nothingness! St Paul made this abundantly clear to the Athenians:

> ***For in him we live and move and have our being.***
> **(Acts 17 : 28)**

The *Providence* of God extends, primarily, to his *earthly* creation, both natural and supernatural. This divine solicitude is both *concrete* and *immediate.* It extends to the smallest and even to the most apparently trifling aspects of life.

> ***Are not two sparrows sold for a penny? Yet not one of them will fall to the ground apart from your Father. And even the hairs of your head are all counted. So do not be afraid; you are of more value than many sparrows.***
> **(Matthew 10: 29-31)**

St Augustine, in his *Confessions,* is also eloquent on the same subject

> *For you (O God) love all things that exist, and detest none of the things that you have made; for you would not have made anything if you had hated it. How would anything have endured, if you had not willed it? Or would anything, not called forth by you, not been preserved? You spare all things, for they are yours, O Lord, you who love the living.*

The conclusion to all this is that God is no further away than our very thoughts! Reflect just for a moment that the place in which you are at this moment is filled with sounds and images flooding in from all over the world. Yet you can neither *hear* them nor *see* them. But if you had a finely tuned radio or TV you could easily capture them. Likewise you have to fine tune your *spiritual sensitivity* to God's all-pervasive presence and bask in His loving presence!

> *'Therefore do not worry, saying, 'What will we eat?' or 'What will we drink?' or 'What will we wear?' For it is the Gentiles who strive for all these things; and indeed your*

> *heavenly Father knows that you need all these things. But strive first for the kingdom of God and his righteousness, and all these things will be given to you as well.'*
>
> **(Matthew 6:31-33)**

4. Why then did God create?

> *"For who has known the mind of the Lord? Or who has been his counselor?" "Or who has given a gift to him, to receive a gift in return?" For from him and through him and to him are all things. To him be the glory forever. Amen.*
>
> **(Romans 11: 34-36)**

Here we return to our basic question of man's purpose and destiny. From the very fact that creation is the work of a Creator there arises the question of its purpose. *Why did God create?* The beauty of God's handiwork and the intricacy of design give evidence of a destiny. There must be a goal towards which this mighty enterprise is directed. God did not *need* to create. There was no compulsion on his part to exercise his power. It added nothing to his own glory nor to the inner life of the divinity. *The world was made for the glory of God!* This is the fundamental truth of existence. St Paul expresses it in its most meaningful terms:

> *He (Jesus) is the image of the invisible God, the firstborn of all creation; for in him all things in heaven and on earth were created, things visible and invisible, whether thrones or dominions or rulers or powers—all things have been created through him and for him. He himself is before all things, and in him all things hold together.*
>
> **(Colossians 1:15-17)**

God gains nothing from creation itself. It adds nothing to his divinity. John points out the very definition of God is *Love*:

> *Beloved, let us love one another, because love is from God; everyone who loves is born of God and knows God. Whoever does not love does not know God, for God is love.*
>
> **(1 John 4:7-8)**

Love is the mainspring of creation! Even if he had nothing to gain from creation itself, he opened the door for the creatures of his creation to enter into his embrace of eternal happiness. If God gains nothing, man gains everything! All this is borne out in the Catechism, where it states:

> *We believe that God created the world according to his wisdom. It is not the product of any necessity whatever, nor of blind fate or chance. We believe that it proceeds from God's free will, he wanted to make his creatures share in his being, wisdom and goodness:* **'For you created all things, and by your will they existed and were created'.**[40] *Therefore the Psalmist exclaims:*
>
> *'O Lord, how manifold are your works! In wisdom you have made them all' and 'The Lord is good to all and his compassion is over all that he has made.'*
>
> (#295)

From that decree there issued a creation that was neither the product of any *inner necessity* nor the result of *blind chance*. As the twenty four elders sang to the *One who sat upon the throne*:

> *You are worthy, our Lord and God, to receive glory and honour and power, for you created all things, and by your will they existed and were created.*
>
> (Revelation 4:11)

(b) of Heaven

1. The Angelic Universe

> *In the beginning God created the heavens and the earth.*
>
> (Genesis. 1:1)

---

[40] Compare in Wisdom *With you is wisdom, she who knows your works and was present when you made the world; she understands what is pleasing in your sight and what is right according to your commandments.* **(Wisdom 9:9)**

This opening verse of the Bible points to the simultaneous creation of a *spirit* world as well as the *material* universe. The term *'heaven'* can be used to designate some place or state wherein dwells the special presence of God. This is alluded to in the prayer that Jesus taught us; *'Our Father, Who art in Heaven'*. It can also refer to the *material* universe visible either to the naked eye or to the most sophisticated telescopes. But it also refers to those beings who share the special presence of the Almighty, the *angelic* creation. In addition, there is the universe of the *fallen angels* who rebelled against the Almighty. As the new universal Catechism which states:

> *The existence of the spiritual non-corporeal beings that Sacred Scripture usually calls 'angels' is a truth of faith. The witness of Scripture is as clear as the unanimity of Tradition.*
>
> (#328)[41]

There is reference to them in the book of Job:

> **'Where were you when I laid the foundation of the earth? . . . .**
> **when the morning stars sang together and**
> **all the heavenly beings shouted for joy?'**
> **(Job 38: 4,7)**

These spiritual beings reflect in varying degrees the splendour of the perfections and majesty of their Creator. Their occasional assumption of human form in apparitions is to enable them to communicate with human beings. The term *'angel'* does not refer to their *nature* but to their *mission* as *messengers* of God. The word comes from the Greek *angelos*[42] meaning *a messenger*. There are traditionally *nine* choirs of angels. This number is culled from Isaiah, Ezekiel and from St Paul *(Colossians 1:16 & Ephesians 1:21)*. A threefold classification gives us, first, the *Seraphim, Cherubim*, and *Thrones*. Then come the *Dominations, Principalities* and *Powers*. And finally, *the Virtues, Archangels* and *Angels*. Christ stands far above the angelic universe, as is evident from the letter to the Hebrews:

---

[41] As we have already noted, these numbers refer to the universal Catechism.

[42] from the Greek *angellein* = *to deliver a message*.

> *And again, when he brings the firstborn into the world, he says,*
> *"Let all God's angels worship him."*
> *Of the angels he says, "He makes his angels winds,*
> *and his servants flames of fire."*
> **(Hebrews 1: 6-7)**

2. Ministers & Messengers

> *St Augustine says "Angel is the name of their office, not of their nature. If you seek the name of their nature, it is 'spirit'; if you seek the name of their office, it is 'angel'. With their whole beings the angels are servants and messengers of God. Because they "always behold the face of my Father who is in Heaven" they are "the mighty ones who do his word, hearkening to the voice of his word."*
> (#329)

These angels were also the ministers of God's covenant with mankind. It was an angel who stayed the hand of Abraham in the act of slaying Isaac. It was an angel that led Lot forth from the destruction of Sodom and Gomorrah. It was an angel who brought the message of redemption to a virgin named Mary. Angels sang the first *Gloria* at the birth of Christ. They are, we dare to say, the very first *evangelists!* Three in particular are singled out in scripture:

> Michael (= *Who is like to God?*),
> Raphael (= *the healing of God*)
> Gabriel (= *the messenger of God*)

They are, therefore, powerful *intercessors* and worthy of our veneration as *friends* of God and his divine messengers. An everlasting hymn of praise arises from the angels before the throne of God, as is evident from the testimony of Revelation and from the prophet Isaiah.

> *In the year that King Uzziah died, I saw the Lord sitting on a throne, high and lofty; and the hem of his robe filled the temple.*
> *Seraphs were in attendance above him; each had six wings: with two they covered their faces, and with two they*

covered their feet, and with two they flew. And one called to another and said: "Holy, holy, holy is the LORD of hosts; the whole earth is full of his glory."

(Isaiah 6:1-3)

3. Guardian Angels

It is a longstanding Catholic tradition that each person has a *Guardian Angel* who is entrusted with the care and guidance of that person throughout life. There is an angelic companion for every person on earth. This is not a defined article of faith but is closely allied to it, or as is said theologically *'proxima fidei'* (very close to faith). Jesus himself inferred as much when he said:

Take care that you do not despise one of these little ones; for, I tell you, in heaven their angels continually see the face of my Father in heaven.

(Matthew 18:10)

St Basil the Great *(born circa 330 A.D.)*, one of the fathers of the Church, concluded from these words of Jesus himself that:

Beside each believer stands an angel as protector and shepherd leading him to life.

There have been many stories of the timely intervention of angels on behalf of the faithful who invoked their aid. Many saints and holy people have had regular contact with their guardian angels, as, for example, St Frances of Rome, and Padre Pio. All this confirms what the angel of *Revelation* said to St John:

I am a fellow servant with you and your comrades who hold the testimony of Jesus.

(Revelation 19:10)

4. The Fallen Angels

Like our first parents the angelic hosts of heaven also endured a trial before being admitted to the Beatific Vision. The nature of this test is unknown, although it has been suggested that it involved the worship of *Christ the God-Man!* Whatever the test, a number of them failed. As it says in the Book of Job:

> *'Can mortals be righteous before God? Can human beings be pure before their Maker? Even in his servants he puts no trust, and his angels he charges with error.'*[43]
>
> **(Job 4:17-18)**

These fallen angels have a leader to whom Jesus refers when he talks of the **Devil and his angels** *(Matthew 25:41)*. This leader is usually referred to as *Satan*, a Hebrew word meaning *adversary or accuser*. Translated into Greek it becomes *Diabolos*, and thence into English as the *Devil*. Strictly speaking, there is only one *Devil*, Satan. His followers are called *demons*. Traditionally, prior to his fall from grace, he is also referred to as *Lucifer, the bearer of light*. He is the embodiment of evil, and he is described by Jesus when denouncing his enemies!

> *You are from your father the devil, and you choose to do your father's desires. He was a murderer from the beginning and does not stand in the truth, because there is no truth in him. When he lies, he speaks according to his own nature, for he is a liar and the father of lies.*
>
> **(John 8:44)**

The expulsion of Satan and his followers from heaven has led to their inveterate hatred of all things divine. In particular, it has made Christ's Kingdom, and his Church on earth, the object of incessant attack and unremitting temptation. The apparent success of his campaigns has led to him being called by Jesus himself as the *Prince or Ruler of this world* (John 14:30). St Paul also describes their relentless warfare in urging Christians to stand firm against their onslaughts:

> *Put on the whole armour of God, so that you may be able to stand against the wiles of the devil. For our struggle is not against enemies of blood and flesh, but against the rulers, against the authorities, against the cosmic powers of this*

---

[43] *"In his angels he found wickedness"* (Douay translation)

present darkness, against the spiritual forces of evil in the heavenly places.

(Ephesians 6:11-12)

(c) and Earth

1. The Beauty of Creation

"O LORD, how manifold are your works!
In wisdom you have made them all".

(Psalm 104:24)

The opening chapters of Genesis detail the creation of the visible world. It is a *'divine work'* of six days and a seventh day of *'rest'*. (#337)[44] This account reveals a hierarchy of being and a delicate interdependence that manifest the workings of a wonderful *Artist-Designer!*

The Catechism also comments:

> *The beauty of creation reflects the infinite beauty of the Creator and ought to inspire the respect and submission of our intellect and will.*
>
> (#341)

The psalmist reflects on the work of the Creator and sings:

> *'You set the earth on its foundations, so that it shall never be shaken.*
> *You cover it with the deep as with a garment; the waters stood above the mountains. At your rebuke they flee; at the sound of your thunder they take to flight . . . .*
> *You set a boundary that they may not pass, so that they might not again cover the earth. You make springs gush forth in the valleys; they flow between the hills, giving drink to every wild animal; the wild asses quench their thirst. By*

---

[44] *These numbers refer to the universal Catechism of the Catholic Church*

> *the streams the birds of the air have their habitation; they sing among the branches."*
>
> **(Psalm 104 : 6-12)**

At each stage of God's creative work scripture records:

> *And God saw that it was good!*

2. The Crown of Creation!

> *And God said "Let us make man in our image,*
> *according to our likeness; . . . .*
> *So God created man in his image,*
> *in the image of God he created them;*
> *male and female he created them'.*
>
> **(Genesis 1: 27)**

In the cycle of creation man and woman stand out as if something really special in the mind of God is about to take place. The immense dignity of *man* is spelled out in Holy Writ. Both man and woman are fashioned in the *image of their Creator.* They stand at the pinnacle of the earthly creation, created, not out of necessity, but out of *love.* Of all that God had created on earth man alone is *'able to know and love His creator'.* [45]

> *Then the LORD God said, "It is not good*
> *that the man should be alone;*
> *I will make him a helper fit for him."*
>
> **(Genesis 2: 18)**

It is to be noted that God *blessed* them. They are singled out *individually* and as *partners.* Individually, they were created in a state of original *holiness* and of *justice* and enjoyed the pleasures of an earthly paradise. As partners in love they were also *to share in His creative work!* Hence, we can understand what the Catechism goes on to say:

---

[45] *Gaudium et Spes* #24 par. 3

> *Man and woman were made for each other—not that God left them half-made and incomplete; he created then to be a communion of persons, in which each can be the "helpmate" to the other, for they are equal as persons ("bone of my bone") and complementary as masculine and feminine.*
>
> (#372)

3. *God's Co-Creators!*

Created in *equality* of respect and dignity, man and woman are, nevertheless, uniquely different in their respective roles as parents. As *co-creators* they reflected the image of the Trinity in their mutual love and the fruit of that love in new life! In complementing each other they were destined to carry on God's *creative* work. In their union they were to bring forth other *beings* who would also share both in an earthly existence and in an eternal destiny.

> *'By transmitting human life to their descendants, man and woman as spouses and parents cooperate in a unique way in the Creator's work'.*[46]

The significance of all this is underlined by J.F. Sheed:

> *The fatherhood of God is shadowed forth to us as it is not to them (the angels) by a fatherhood of our own. And indeed our part in God's creative act—what we call procreation—is man's greatest glory in the natural order, it is the act by which he comes closest to the creative power of God.*

This command of God cuts across the *'culture of death'* that prevails in our day. They proclaim God's word against *contraception*, against *abortion* and *euthanasia* and against everything that promotes the *Gospel of Death* in lieu of the *Gospel of Life!*[47]

---

[46] *ibid.* 50 par. 1
[47] The actual title of John Paul II's encyclical *"Evangelium Vitae"*.

4. The Guardians of Creation

Furthermore, in fulfilment of the Divine command their mission is to make use of the gift of creation and offer it back to the Creator.

> *.... and let him have dominion over the fish of the sea, and over the birds of the air, and over the cattle, and over all the wild animals of the earth, and over every creeping thing that creeps upon the earth.* **(Genesis 1: 26)**

Men and women have both the responsibility of acting as guardians of the Divine bounty. They share in God's *providence*. It is no easy task to respect all things as coming from the hands of God. We are so accustomed to *manufactured* articles that we forget that we are ultimately indebted to the Divine Giver of all the good things that come to us.

> 'In God's plan man and woman have the vocation of "subduing" the earth as stewards of God. This sovereignty is not to be an arbitrary and destructive domination. God calls man and woman .... to share in His providence towards other creatures; hence their responsibility for the world God has entrusted to them.'
>
> (#373)[48]

> *What are human beings that you are mindful of them, or mortals, that you care for them? You have made them for a little while lower than the angels; you have crowned them with glory and honour.*
> **(Hebrews 2: 6-7)**

(d) The Fall of Man!

1. You will be like God!

The life of our first parents in the Garden of Eden, idyllic as it was, had one restriction:

---

[48] CCC

> *You may freely eat of every tree of the garden; but of the tree of the knowledge of good and evil you shall not eat, for in the day that you eat of it you shall die!*
>
> **(Genesis 2: 16,17)**

The tree of *the knowledge of good and evil* is symbolic of a restriction that was placed upon our first parents. It was a trial to test the fidelity of their free will that is alone capable of love and surrender. It is difficult to imagine how Adam and Eve in all the splendour of that primitive creation, endowed with *preternatural* gifts and rejoicing in the grace and *friendship* of their Creator, could have entertained thoughts of disobedience and rebellion against the express command of their Creator. But to Eve, seduced by the blandishments of the serpent, the fruit was *'fair to the eyes and delightful to behold'!* Such is the seduction of all evil!

> *". . . . for God knows that when you eat of it your eyes will be opened, and you will be like God, knowing good and evil." So when the woman saw that the tree was good for food, and that it was a delight to the eyes, and that the tree was to be desired to make one wise, she took of its fruit and ate; and she also gave some to her husband, who was with her, and he ate.*
>
> **(Genesis 3: 5-6)**

Did it all happen exactly as described in Genesis? To answer this question the Catechism makes this comment:

> *The account of the fall in Genesis 3 uses figurative language, but affirms a primeval event, a deed that took place at the beginning of the history of man. Revelation gives us the certainty of faith that the whole of human history is marked by the original fault freely committed by our first parents.'*
>
> (#309)[49]

---

[49] *CCC*

2. The Consequences of The Fall

The failure of Adam and Eve to respect God's command drew in its wake a host of lamentable consequences. The Puritan poet, Milton,[50] describes it:

> *'Of man's first disobedience, and the fruit*
> *Of that forbidden tree, whose mortal taste*
> *Brought death unto the world and all our woe*
> *With loss of Eden . . . .'*

We might ask: *was this fall an historical event?* The Catechism (#309) suggests that the language of Genesis 3 is *figurative* but does allude to some historical encounter involving our first parents in a test of their fidelity. The fall, obviously, cannot be something purely *symbolical* for we are living with its devastating consequences!

These consequences are:

1. The *loss of immortality* with its penalty of *death,* and its bedfellows, *pain, disease, affliction and sorrow.*
2. The *loss of God's friendship* and the intimacy they enjoyed with Him was replaced with fear of His judgments' . . . . **and the man and his wife hid themselves from the presence of the LORD God among the trees of the garden' (Genesis 3:8)**
3. The *loss of integrity;* the resultant weakening of their will opened the floodgates to concupiscence, to covetousness and to a host of illicit desires.
4. The *loss of solidarity* **with others;** through excessive egotism there is an alienation or basic estrangement of affection which becomes manifest, for example, in the slaying of Abel by his brother Cain. Man became extremely *self-centered,* and obsessively so!

---

[50] *Paradise Lost*: Book 1.i.

3. Man's Fundamental Alienation

St Paul felt the full force of our personal alienation from God, when he exclaimed:

> *I see in my members another law at war with the law of my mind, making me captive to the law of sin that dwells in my members. Wretched man that I am! Who will rescue me from this body of death? Thanks be to God through Jesus Christ our Lord! So then, with my mind I am a slave to the law of God, but with my flesh I am a slave to the law of sin.*
>
> **(Romans 7:23-25)**

Like the fault lines that cover the surface of the globe, a fault line runs through man's inner core. There is a latent rebellion of man's lower appetites against his reason and will. In effect, the disobedience of our first parents brought with it the dreadful penalty of a *fallen* nature. With their rejection of God's friendship a deadly poison entered man's spiritual bloodstream. This brought, in its wake, the raging fevers of *pride, lust, covetousness and greed.* Only the antidote of the *Body and Blood* of Jesus can effect a cure of this potentially fatal condition.

How the whole human race became culpable of the sin of its first parents remains something of a mystery. Adam, as the primeval ancestor of the human race, acted not merely on his own behalf but on behalf of *all his descendants.* The Catechism explains it as follows:

> Original sin . . . *is a sin which will be transmitted by propagation to all mankind, that is, by the transmission of a human nature deprived of original holiness and justice. And that is why original sin is called "sin" only in an analogical sense; it is a sin "contracted "and not "committed"—a state and not an act.'*
>
> (#404)[51]

---

[51] CCC

4. The Fall of All Creation!

At the same time, it must not be forgotten that the Fall affected the whole of creation. Nature fell as well. This is one of the more mysterious effects of Adam's sin. When God delivered that primordial sentence:

> **Cursed is the ground because of you;**
> **in toil you shall eat of it all the days of your life.**
> **(Genesis 3:17)**

A fundamental disorder entered into the very fabric of creation. The initial goodness that God saw in all creation was affected by the fall of Adam, its lord and master. In coming to grips with that creation the works of man are dogged by failure and frustration. As one author remarks:

> *The material universe is so closely inter-linked, inter-balanced, that the catastrophe in its highest part spreads downwards through all its parts.*[52]

We can also point to such things as the environmental destruction that is being wrought today and to a technology that appears to be running out of control, as well as to the possibility of massive self-destruction that a nuclear holocaust poses for all mankind.

> **If we say that we have no sin, we deceive ourselves,**
> **and the truth is not in us.**
> **If we confess our sins, he who is faithful and just**
> **will forgive us our sins**
> **and cleanse us from all unrighteousness.**
> **If we say that we have not sinned, we make him a liar,**
> **and his word is not in us.**
> **(1 John 1: 8-10)**

---

[52] F.J. Sheed: *Theology and Sanity (Sheed and Ward. 1960 p.139)*

A Note on Evolution

What is evolution?

As defined, from a biological standpoint, it is a theory that is primarily concerned with the origin of species. A dictionary gives the following definition:

> *It is the theoretical process by which all species develop from earlier forms of life. On this theory, natural variation in the genetic material of a population favours reproduction by some individuals more than others, so that over the generations all members of the population come to possess the favourable traits.*[53]

It is obvious that there are some debatable presuppositions in this definition. It is equally obvious that we are nor talking about the *origin of life*. but rather, about the *origin of species*. The primary impulse of life must be taken for granted, and that can only come from God. In any discussion about evolution there are two philosophical principles that are central to any meaningful discussion.

1. *Nothing comes from nothing!* This seems so obvious that it hardly needs stating, but it is often overlooked in the heat of debate. It is particularly relevant to discussions on *macro-evolution, or* the evolution of one species into another.
2. *Simplicity does not automatically give rise to complexity.* This means that higher forms of life do not naturally emerge from lower forms. Sometimes millions, and even billions, of years are added to the process. This *'maximisation'* of time is wholly irrelevant to the issue in hand.

The challenge of evolution prompted the Church to evaluate its understanding of the Genesis account of creation. In the first place, there is this basic principle that God's revelation cannot conflict with any scientific research, which is based on a genuine pursuit of the truth. The obvious response to the evolutionary thesis of *transformism,* or the

---

[53] Encarta, World English Dictionary.

gradual development of higher forms of life from lower is, theoretically, impossible without divine intervention at the various stages of development. Moreover, some Catholic theologians have stressed that the *primary* message of Genesis was intended to be *theological* and *spiritual* rather than factual or historical. Even granting the possibility, however remote, of the physical evolution of man from lower forms of life, this process of itself cannot explain his *spiritual* life, or the existence of the soul. Only God can create the soul and the spiritual yearnings of the human heart!

The theory of evolution also raised the spectre of *polygenism*, i.e. mankind has had many ancestral lines, quite apart from that of Adam and Eve. Pius XII in his encyclical, *Humani Generis* (1950), rejected this since it was incompatible with man's fallen state, original sin and the need for redemption. John Paul II, in more recent times, stated that, while Catholic teaching did not object to the *theory* of evolution as such, it did object to all those evolutionary theories that sought to reduce man to purely material terms.[54] The Catholic doctrine of creation maintains that the ultimate creator of all things is God. Even if we accept some form of the evolutionary thesis, God must be the initial creative principle and its divine *supporter* through *the continuous creation of his conservative power!* Creation, *in all its dimensions,* rests ultimately in God's hands. Here is what the Catechism says on this vital issue:

> ### God transcends creation and is always present to it.
>
> > God is infinitely greater than all his works: *"You have set your glory above the heavens."* Indeed, God's *"greatness is unsearchable"*. But because he is the free and sovereign Creator, the first cause of all that exists, God is present to his creatures' inmost being: *"In him we live and move and have our being."* In the words of St. Augustine, God is *"higher than my highest and more inward than my innermost self"*. 300

---

[54] In his *Discourse to the Pontifical Academy of Sciences* on October 22, 1996

With creation, God does not abandon his creatures to themselves. He not only gives them being and existence, but also, and at every moment, upholds and sustains them in being, enables them to act and brings them to their final end. Recognising this utter dependence with respect to the Creator is a source of wisdom and freedom, of joy and confidence:

For you love all things that exist, and detest none of the things that you have made; for you would not have made anything if you had hated it. How would anything have endured, if you had not willed it? Or how would anything not called forth by you have been preserved? You spare all things, for they are yours, O Lord, you who love the living.[55] ***301***

---

[55] (CCC301) The Book of *Wisdom* 11:24-26

Questions #4

* * *

1. *Why did God create? Why is there something rather than nothing?*

2. *God created 'out of nothing'! What exactly does this mean?*

3. *What is the difference between these terms: creation, conservation and divine providence?*

4. *Who are the angels? The Fallen angels? And what does the term angel mean? (38)*

5. *What do you mean by the choirs of angels? Which of them are recognised in the Church's liturgical calendar?*

6. *The Crown of Creation and Co-Creators. To what do these terms refer?*

7. *What are the consequences of the Fall?*

8. *What do you understand by Man's fundamental alienation from God?*

9. *"The whole of creation fell in the fall of our first parents"*. *Explain!*

10. *"The Genesis account of creation and the fall of man is really a myth!"*. *Comments?*

11. *What do you understand by the Gospel of Death prevalent in our society today?*

12. *Any Personal reflections?*

5. AND IN JESUS CHRIST, HIS ONLY SON, OUR LORD

* * *

(a) JESUS!
—1. The Incarnation
—2. The Name!
—3. The Reverence for the Name
—4. The Name above All Names!

(b) CHRIST
—1. The Messiah
—2. Its Importance
—3. Understanding versus Misunderstanding!
—4. Our Incorporation into Jesus' Messiahship!

(c) His Only Son
—1. The 'Son of God'
—2. The Only Son of the Father
—3. Children of the Father!

(d) Our Lord
—1. He is Lord!
—2. The Witness of the Early Church
—3. Leader and Shepherd!
—4. Our Submission
—5. The Church as Leader

(a) JESUS

1. *The Incarnation*

This word incarnation is a sober theological term that disguises a bewildering story—the *'enfleshment'* [56] of God! The fact of the existence of Jesus points to the most astonishing event in the whole of history. When Jesus stepped into this world the unthinkable had happened, God had stepped out of eternity into time! He who had no beginning and no end, the immortal God put on our mortality. St Paul summarises the divine drama that followed:

> *Let the same mind be in you that was in Christ Jesus, who, though he was in the form of God, did not regard equality with God as something to be exploited, but emptied himself, taking the form of a slave, being born in human likeness. And being found in human form, he humbled himself and became obedient to the point of death—even death on a cross. Therefore God also highly exalted him and gave him the name that is above every name, so that at the name of Jesus every knee should bend, in heaven and on earth and under the earth, and every tongue should confess that Jesus Christ is Lord, to the glory of God the Father.*
> **(Philippians 2:5-11)**

These words of St Paul are a vivid summary of the whole mystery of the Incarnation. It describes it as *an emptying out*[57] of the Word, not of his nature—*an impossibility!*—but of his dignity. He took *the form of a slave, being born in human likeness*. These words do not mean that Jesus simply took the outward appearance of man, but he was *truly man*, one who walked and talked with disciples, ate and drank with them and endured a criminal's death on a cross. It means that Jesus was truly God and truly man, two natures in the one Person of the Word.

---

[56] *enfleshment* is a neologism or an invented word, to describe God *becoming man!*
[57] The word that Paul uses is the Greek word *kenosis* from the adjective *kenos* meaning *empty* or *destitute*.

2. The Name!

> *And now, you will conceive*
> *in your womb, and bear a son,*
> *and you will name him Jesus.*
> **(Luke 1: 30,31)**

Mary, the virgin from Nazareth, was the first to hear the holy name of *Jesus*. This name above all names bespeaks the very role that *Jesus* was to play, for it means '*Yahweh is salvation*'. This role of *Saviour* was spelled out in the angelic apparition to Joseph who was contemplating putting Mary away:

> **She will bear a son, and you are to name him Jesus,**
> **for he will save his people from their sins.**
> **(Matthew 1:21)**

For the full significance of this *name above all names* let us turn to the Catechism:

> *The name 'Jesus' signifies that the very name of God is present in the person of his Son, made man for the universal and definitive redemption from sins. It is the divine name that alone brings salvation, and henceforth all can invoke his name, for Jesus united himself to all men through his incarnation, so that* **'there is no other name under heaven given among men by which we must be saved.'**
> **(Acts 2 : 21)** (#432)

Here is the focal point of salvation history when God becomes man! Here is the very reason for our existence! St John right at the beginning of his Gospel makes this very clear.

> *And the Word became flesh and dwelt among us . . . .*
> *we have beheld his glory,*
> *glory as of the only Son from the Father,*
> *full of grace and of truth.*
> **(John 1: 3, 14)**

3. Reverence for the Name

The Jews of old never pronounced the name of God—*Yahweh!* It was invoked only once a year by the High Priest in atonement for the sins of Israel after he had sprinkled the mercy seat in the *Holy of Holies* with the blood of the sacrifice. (#433)[58] Moreover, they never attempted to depict God in any material way. But in Jesus the Father draws an image of Himself, as Jesus replied to Philip's request to show him the Father:

> **Whoever has seen me has seen the Father.**
> **(John 14:9)**

In Jesus God became one of us! The world has never been the same since Jesus walked among us and inspired countless generations with his teachings and above all, by his example. As the English writer and poet Caryll Houselander once wrote to the effect that *Jesus entered into the world like a dye that could never be washed out!* This name is the *holiest* of all names and the prayers of the Church are addressed to the Father *'through our Lord Jesus Christ'* (#435). The apostles gloried in the sufferings and persecutions that they endured **for the sake of the name. (Acts 5: 41)** This name is also a name of *power.* The invocation of it could work miracles, as happened at the Beautiful Gate of the temple when Peter healed the cripple.

> *In the name of Jesus Christ of Nazareth, stand up and walk.'*
> **(Acts 3:6)**

4. The Name is Above All Names!

> *Therefore God also highly exalted him*
> *and gave him the name that is above every name,*
> *so that at the name of Jesus every knee should bend,*
> *in heaven and on earth and under the earth,*
> *and every tongue should confess that*
> *Jesus Christ is Lord, to the glory of God the Father.*
> **(Philippians 2: 9-11)**

---

[58] *CCC*

From all that has been said about the name and its association with our redemption it is very evident that this name of Jesus should only be used with the greatest reverence. It should never be used lightly or irreverently. We can well understand how the saints treasured the name of Jesus. **Jesus, Jesus, be to me a Jesus!** This was one of their favoured invocations, a humble supplication to the Saviour of the world to fulfil, in their regard, his saving mission of redemption, *the forgiveness of their sins!*

> *It is the name that the Father Himself bestowed!*
> *It is the name through which we are saved!*
> *It is the name that guards and protects us!*
> *It is a name that is the delight of all the angels and saints!*
> *It is the name that terrorises the spirits of evil and of darkness!*

In view of all this, we can well understand why Paul wrote about this *Name* so eloquently:

> *And whatever you do, in word or deed,*
> *do everything in the name of the Lord Jesus,*
> *giving thanks to God the Father through him.*
> **(Colossians 3:17)**

(b) The CHRIST

1. The Meaning of 'Messiah'

> *But it is God who establishes us*
> *with you in Christ and has anointed us,*
> **(2 Corinthians 1:21)**

As with the name *Jesus* the word *Christ* comes from the Greek. The latter is a translation of the Hebrew *mashiyach* {pronounced *maw-shee'-akh*}, meaning *'the anointed one'. There* are 456 Messianic references in the Old Testament. The prophet Isaiah summarises all these prophetic threads that refer to the future Messiah as the *'Son of Man'*, *'Son of God'* and as the *'Servant of Yahweh'*. Jesus makes reference to himself as their fulfilment in the presence of an unbelieving audience in his home town of Nazareth. When the leader of the synagogue handed him the scroll of Isaiah, he opened it and read the prophetic passage:

> *The Spirit of the Lord is upon me, because he has anointed me to bring good news to the poor. He has sent me to proclaim release to the captives and recovery of sight to the blind, to let the oppressed go free, to proclaim the year of the Lord's favour.*
>
> **(Luke 4:18,19)**

Jesus was anointed by the *'Spirit of the Lord'*. The *theophany*[59] at the River Jordan saw the Holy Spirit descend upon Jesus and a voice from heaven was heard:

> *You are my Son, the Beloved;*
> *with you I am well pleased!*
>
> **(Mark 1: 11)**

2. Importance of the Title

The word *'Christ'* occurs over 500 times in the New Testament. Strictly speaking, it is really a *title*. We find this use in Paul and the Acts where the combination *'Christ Jesus'* is to be found, and means the *Messiah Jesus*. Jesus is the fulfilment of all the prophecies that foretold the coming of a Saviour or a *Messiah* for Israel. This title is also to be found in the oldest forms of the Creed. In the baptismal rite described by Pope St Hippolytus (3rd cent.) the catechumen was asked—before being immersed the second time—*'Do you believe in Christ Jesus, the Son of God?'* Ultimately, it came to be placed after Jesus, almost as if it were a surname. It was Peter who first made the open profession of Jesus as the *Messiah* at Caesarea Philippi, where Jesus put this central and fundamental question to the apostles:

> *But who do you say that I am? Simon Peter answered,*
> *'You are the Messiah, the Son of the living God.'*
>
> **(Matthew 16: 15-16)**

---

[59] This word refers to manifestations of the divine, as on Mt Sinai or the Transfiguration. The final theophany will be the *Second Coming* of the Son of Man.

This same basic question resonates through the centuries. It comes forth in every age and is put to us all *directly* or *indirectly*. The response comes in the lives we lead and the example that we give to others. We are all destined, in one way or another, to respond to that searching question: *who do you say that I am?* We must be prepared to answer!

3. Understanding and Misunderstanding

Despite his miracles and his teachings as one gifted with authority, the notion of Jesus as the *Messiah* ran wholly counter to the popular notion of what the future Messiah was to be. This was reinforced by the fact that he was to be the *'Son of David'* and, therefore, of *royal* lineage. If he was a *king*, then he would be a great leader, a renowned warrior who would rival the exploits of the Maccabees in taking up arms against the hated Romans. But Jesus, as the Christ, was the antithesis of all these earthly fantasies. Yes, he would be a *warrior*, but on a much higher plane. He would wage war against a far greater enemy, a far deadlier adversary—*Satan*—with the weapons of *humility, suffering and death!* It would be a much deadlier conflict, waged without truce or quarter, until the end of time. The man-made nuclear weapons of war have assumed terrifying aspects in modern times, but they are insignificant, even useless on the plane of the Spirit. It is there that we are led by the *King of Kings* in a war that knows no peace, no truce, no conditions of surrender, no end. It goes on and on until the last trumpet sounds!

4. Our Incorporation into Jesus' 'Messiahship'!

We share in the *Messiahship* of Jesus by the very name we bear as *Christians*! It was at Antioch in Syria that the followers of Jesus were first called *'Christians'*. If we glory in that name we are, literally, declaring ourselves to be *followers of the Messiah!* We cannot lay claim to any misunderstanding on the subject. However, we often fail to realise its meaning in our personal lives. The holy oils used in the sacramental rites are a symbol of the descent of the Holy Spirit upon us.

The very word *'chrism'* (holy oil) recalls this sovereign truth that we become incorporated into *Christ—we become one with him!*—in the baptismal rite by the power of the Holy Spirit! Vatican II declared that *through baptism we are formed in the likeness of Christ.*

> *'For in the one Spirit we were all baptised into one body—Jews or Greeks, slaves or free—we were all made to drink of one Spirit.'*
>
> **(1 Corinthians 12:13)**

In this sacred rite, a union with Christ's death and resurrection is both symbolised and brought about.[60]

> **Therefore, if anyone is in Christ, he is a new creation; the old has passed away, behold the new has come. All this is from God, who, through Christ, reconciled us to himself and gave us the ministry of reconciliation; that is, God was in Christ reconciling the world to himself".**
>
> **(2 Corinthians 5:17-19)**

(c) His Only Son!

1. The Son of God!

> *And a voice from heaven said,*
> *"This is my Son, the Beloved,*
> *with whom I am well pleased."*
>
> **(Matthew 3:17)**

The title *'son of God'* was a common one in antiquity in referring to the genealogy of kings. They were reputed to be descended from the gods! In the Old Testament the same title was also given to the angels, and to the anointed kings of the Chosen people. So the Gospel title, *Son of God*, did not necessarily refer to the divinity in itself.(#441)[61] However, the title takes on a wholly different meaning in the confession of Peter at Caesarea Philippi, when Jesus asked the question; *"Who do men say that I am?"* It was Peter who acknowledged the divinity of Jesus, as a result of a special revelation made to him by God Himself:

> *And Simon Peter answered,*
> *"You are the Messiah, the Son of the living God."*

---

[60] Vatican II. *Lumen Gentium* #7
[61] *CCC*

> *And Jesus answered him,*
> *"Blessed are you, Simon son of Jonah!*
> *For flesh and blood has not revealed this to you,*
> *but my Father in heaven".*
>
> **(Matthew 16:16-17)**

The consequences of those words are immeasurable. The Catechism, however, sums them all up very succinctly:

> *From the beginning this acknowledgement of Christ's divine sonship will be the centre of the apostolic faith, first professed by Peter as the Church's foundation.*
>
> (#442)

2. The Only Son

The expression *'only Son'* is to be found in *John 3:16*. However, the adjective *'only"* found its way into the Creed in the second century, in response to *Gnostic*[62] heresies. *Gnosticism* was a loose grouping of heresies and false religious philosophies claiming *special knowledge* of the faith, and insight into its mysteries. In general, they denied the reality of the humanity of Jesus, that He was not really a man, but only a *phantom*! This odd notion arose from the conviction that all matter was evil. More seriously, in denying the humanity of Jesus it denied the central doctrine of the incarnation of *the Word made flesh* and, consequently, Christ's mission of salvation! Jesus made a clear distinction between His own sonship and that of His followers when He referred to **'My Father and your Father'**. In the theophanies of the baptism of Jesus and the Transfiguration the Father claims Jesus as His **'beloved Son'**. The apostle John also makes this clear when he says:

> **For God so loved the world that he gave his only Son,**
> **so that everyone who believes in him may not perish**
> **but may have eternal life.**
>
> **(John 3:16)**

---

[62] *Gnostic comes from the Greek gnosis meaning 'knowledge', referring to some special secretive or mystical knowledge granted to certain chosen souls known as 'the elect'.*

3. Children of the Father

In the surrender of the Son He loved most, and, in a way that passes all comprehension, we get a faint glimpse of the love that *Our Father in Heaven* has for us. And it was done that we might share—in a very real sense—the divine nature of the Godhead itself. This is one of the most astounding facts of our faith! We *share* in the divine sonship of Jesus!!

> *But to all who received him, who believed in his name, he gave power to become children of God, who were born, not of blood or of the will of the flesh or of the will of man, but of God. And the Word became flesh and lived among us, and we have seen his glory, the glory as of a father's only son, full of grace and truth.*
>
> **(John 1:13,14)**

Here, it must be emphasised again, the expression *'children of God'* is not to be taken in a metaphorical or poetic sense. Here God's *almighty love* comes into play and confers on us a participation in the divine nature, as St Paul tells us in 2 Corinthians chapter 5:17. Vatican II emphasises this *reality of our own sonship in* and *through* Christ: Jesus Our Lord:

> *He, who is the image of the invisible God (Col. 1:15), is himself the perfect man. To the sons of Adam He restores the divine likeness which had been disfigured from the first sin onward. For by His incarnation the Son of God has united Himself in some fashion with every person. He worked with human hands. He thought with a human mind, acted by human choice, and loved with a human heart. Born of the Virgin Mary, he has truly been made one of us, like us in all things except sin.*[63]

---

[63] *Gaudium et Spes #22*

(d) Our Lord

1. He is Lord!

Jesus is Lord! This was the most ancient expression of the faith of Christians and their fidelity to it made them martyrs. They would have no part in the idolatry of others. Here we find a renewal of and a transformation of the ancient faith of Israel:

> **Hear, O Israel: The LORD is our God, the LORD alone.**
> **(Deuteronomy 6:4)**

However, the term *Lord* itself has fallen on hard times today. In our democratic and egalitarian societies it has been stripped of all authority and significance. It survives solely as an empty reminder of former glory, a relic of a mediaeval world, when lords and their ladies ruled the political landscape. However, when we affix the article or the possessive pronoun to it—*the* Lord or *Our* Lord—it takes on a completely different aura. We feel as did St John when he saw the Risen Jesus standing on the seashore . . . **It is the Lord! (John 21:7)**.

One of the most remarkable things in the history of the New Testament is the demonic recognition of Jesus as *'the Son of God'* and *'the Holy One of Israel'*. But at the same time, there was no recognition of Jesus as *'Lord'*. To have recognised him as *Lord* would have entailed a relationship of submission to Him! This they could not do, for they were in total rebellion against Him and all that he stood for. To have called Him *Lord* would have entailed an obligation to be at His disposal, to be His slave. However, this is what St Paul, in recognising the Lordship of Jesus, called both Timothy and himself : **the slaves of Christ Jesus! (Philippians 1:1***)*

2. The Witness of the Early Church

> *Therefore, God also highly exalted him*
> *and gave him the name that is above every name,,,,,,*
> *and every tongue should confess that Jesus Christ is Lord,*
> *to the glory of God the Father.*
> **(Philippians 2: 9-11)**

From the very beginning of Christian history there was this implicit conviction that the *lordship* of Jesus took precedence over every other claim. It was recognised that a Christian could not surrender his (or her) personal freedom in an absolute manner to any earthly authority. (#450) In the aftermath of the destruction of Jerusalem in 70 AD Christian captives, men, women and children were martyred for their faith. Their martyrdom took place in Caesarea, Rome's administrative capital in Palestine. As part of the celebrations men and women were crucified in the city's amphitheatre. It was all part of a culture wherein the killing of its victims were all part of the popular entertainment. It was mentality best expressed by an English poet who said they were *"Butchered to make a Roman holiday"*.[64]

What was their crime? They refused to worship Caesar! They refused to worship anyone other than the Lord Jesus. *Jesus is Lord!* Only Jesus is *kyrios*.[65] *Not Caesar, not any man, not any creature!* That ringing proclamation of the *Lordship of Jesus* comes echoing down the centuries to our own times. Even today, in our own times, there have been thousands of martyrs who have laid down their lives for the faith. It all finds an echo today in the *Kingship of Christ.* to whom we owe our allegiance.

3. Leader & Shepherd!

> *But speaking the truth in love,*
> *we must grow up in every way into him*
> *who is the head, into Christ.*
> **(Ephesians 4:15)**

In the New Testament phrases abound that highlight the *lordship (Gr. kyriotes)* of Jesus. In his first Pentecostal sermon Peter refers to Jesus as the *'Author of life'*. He is just as emphatic when he was haled before the Sanhedrin and proclaimed:

> **God exalted him at his right hand as Leader and Saviour**
> **that he might give repentance to Israel**
> **and forgiveness of sins.**
> **(Acts 4:15)**

---

[64] *Lord Byron's "Childe Harold's Pilgrimage" iv. 141.*
[65] *The Greek term for 'Lord' expressing divinity.*

Leadership, in human terms, involves what the term itself implies, someone who *leads* and shows the way. Physically, it is manifested by taking someone by the hand and taking him or her along a certain route. Likewise, the way can be pointed out, or indicated on a map. This is leadership that demands some form of physical presence. However, leadership can also be a matter of *example and inspiration*. Leadership, therefore, can also be manifested in a non-physical way. This is done when someone becomes an inspiration for others to imitate. It often happens that the example of some heroic figure, living or dead, inspires others to follow in his or her footsteps or imitate some aspect of that that appears admirable. There is some pattern in this life that excites admiration and inspire imitation.

In effect, Jesus embodies all these exemplars. The supreme example of Jesus as *leader* is to be found in the parable of the Good Shepherd. In typically Semitic fashion, Jesus the *Good Shepherd*, walks ahead of his flock, endeavouring to guide his flock to the pastures of eternal life.

> *I am the good shepherd. I know my own and my own know me, just as the Father knows me and I know the Father. And I lay down my life for the sheep. I have other sheep that do not belong to this fold. I must bring them also, and they will listen to my voice. So there will be one flock, one shepherd.*
>
> **(John 10:14-16)**

4. Our Submission

> *For whoever was called in the Lord as a slave*
> *is a freed person belonging to the Lord,*
> *just as whoever was free when called is a slave of Christ.*
> *You were bought with a price; do not become slaves of*
> *human masters.*
>
> **(1 Corinthians 7:22-23)**

Once again, the word *'slave'* has a harsh sound to our democratic ears. We do not take kindly to the notion that we are the *property* of anyone. But the Lordship of Jesus is *total* and *absolute*. It extends to everything. When the unbelieving Thomas fell on his knees before the Risen Christ and exclaimed *"My Lord and my God"*, he gave a cry of total surrender, and of loving adoration. No more doubts, no more reservations!! This is as imperative for us today as it was for the unbelieving Thomas! However, it is a slavery in the service of one *who has our best interests at heart!* St Paul makes this point very clearly:

> **We do not live to ourselves, and we do not die to ourselves.**
> **If we live, we live to the Lord, and if we die, we die to the Lord;**
> **so then, whether we live or whether we die, we are the Lord's.**
> **(Romans 14: 7-8)**

The Catechism is at pains to underscore these same sentiments as characteristic of our liturgy:

> *Christian prayer is characterised by the title "Lord" whether in the invocation to prayer ("The Lord be with you!"), its conclusion ("through Christ our Lord"), or the exclamation full of trust and hope: 'Maran atha' ("Our Lord, come!") . . .*
>
> (#451)

There is a passage in the *Book of Revelation* that depicts Jesus riding forth to the judgement of the nations. It pictures in dramatic terms a very sobering, even terrifying, reminder of the supreme dignity conferred on him by His Father:

> **From his mouth comes a sharp sword with which to strike down the nations, and he will rule them with a rod of iron; he will tread the wine press of the fury of the wrath of God the Almighty. On his robe and on his thigh he has a name inscribed, "King of kings and Lord of lords."**
> **(Revelation 19:14-16)**

5. *The Church as Leader*

This was a powerful theme in the guidance of the early Church. And the term *shepherd* itself has survived as *Pastor* in the vocabulary of the Church to this day. However, even though it is evident that Christ is no longer physically present among us, his presence as leader goes far beyond all human parallels. Through the Church, through the sacramental system and the presence of the Holy Spirit, Christ enters the very fabric of our existence.

The Church is much more than its visible hierarchical structure, far more than its buildings and its legal canons. It is the *mystical Body of Christ* communicating his life and love to the world of today. This is the grace that all should seek—to see the face of the Lord Jesus in all the ceremonies of the Church's liturgy. That is what is meant in a comment of the English author, Monsignor Benson, in calling them *'a continuing incarnation'*. Or, as the great French churchman, Bossuet, wrote: The *Church is Christ spread forth and communicated!* Christ has left his imprint upon the Church to the extent that it takes *his* place in the world today.[66]

---

[66] *This theme is explored more fuller in later chapters when dealing with action of the Holy Spirit in the Church.*

Questions #5

* * *

1. 'The Incarnation'. What does this phrase mean?

2. What reverence is due to the name of Jesus, and what is its power?

3. What does scripture say about the Messiah and how does it concern you?

4. What was the popular notion of the Messiah in the time of Jesus?

5. What is the origin of the term Christian? What is its full meaning especially in its consequences for you?

6. The Son of God and Only Son of God! Any difference between these two phrases?

7. I am a 'Child of God' and a Slave of Christ. What do these terms mean?

8. *"Jesus is Lord!" What did this expression mean to the early Christians and what does it mean for you today?*

9. *Our Leader and Shepherd! How is this role of Jesus fulfilled today, and what does it mean to you?*

10. *How does the book of Revelation portray Jesus as Lord?*

11. *The Church is a continuing incarnation! What does this mean?*

6. HE WAS CONCEIVED BY THE POWER OF THE HOLY SPIRIT AND BORN OF THE VIRGIN MARY

* * *

(a) The Fulfilment of Prophecy!
 —1.   In the Fulness of Time!
 —2.   The 'Overshadowing'!
 —3.   In the Fulness of Grace!
 —4.   The God-Man!

(b) Born of the Virgin Mary
 —1.   The Mother of God
 —2.   Mary's Perpetual Virginity
 —3.   The Second Eve
 —4.   The Law of Association

(c) Why did the Son of God become Man?
 —1.   Introduction
 —2.   To Heal the Breach between Man and God
 —3.   To Know God's Infinite Love!
 —4.   Our Model of Holiness
 —5.   'Partakers' of the Divine Nature!

6. He Was Conceived by the Power of the Holy Spirit and Born of the Virgin Mary

* * *

(a) The Fulfilment of Prophecy

1. In the Fulness of Time!

But when the fullness of time had come, God sent his Son,
born of a woman, born under the law,
in order to redeem those who were under the law,
so that we might receive adoption as children.
(Galatians 4:4-5)

The *Incarnation of the Word* is the most stupendous event in the history of the world. No other event or happening in man's tumultuous history can bear even the faintest comparison to this prodigy of prodigies: *God became man!*

And the Word was made flesh!
And dwelt amongst us.
(John 1:14)

Such an event, so marvellous and so astonishing, was predominantly the work of the Holy Spirit, planned with meticulous detail. Over the centuries, nay, over the millennia that stretched from Creation to the Incarnation, God worked out his plan of redemption. The Holy Spirit was manifest in the lives of great men and saints and in the hundreds of prophecies that pointed towards the future Messiah. Through prophecy and through covenants God worked towards this climax of all the prophecies, the entry of Jesus, *the Second Person of the Most Holy Trinity*, into the world!

This is the very point that the Catechism stresses in saying:

The coming of God's Son to earth is an event of such immensity that God willed to prepare for it over centuries. He

> *makes everything converge on Christ: all the ritual and sacrifices, figures and symbols of the "First Covenant". He announces him through the mouths of the prophets who succeeded one another in Israel. Moreover, he awakens in the hearts of the pagans a dim expectation of this coming.*
>
> (#522)

All this is the work of the Holy Spirit, acting in secret, anonymously (so to speak!). And now *the long desired of the nations* was about to bring all prophecy to fulfilment! From the finest strains of a *Chosen Race* God wove an intricate tapestry of divine love to bring to fulfilment the prophecy made at the very dawn of man's creation:

> ***I will put enmity between you and the woman,***
> ***and between your offspring and hers;***
> ***he will strike your head, and you will strike his heel.***
> **(Genesis 3: 15)**

2. The 'Overshadowing'!

This marvel of divine omnipotence—*the Incarnation*! *How was it to to be accomplished?* Through the visit of an angel to an obscure corner of the Roman Empire, to a village of Galilee. He brought God's message to a young Hebrew girl, known as *Miriam*.

> ***The Holy Spirit will come upon you!***
> ***and the power of the Most High will over shadow you***
> **(Luke 1:35)**

These simple words of the evangelist highlight the action of the Holy Spirit in initiating the work of redemption. The *Incarnation,* the most significant event in the history of the world, was wrought by the Holy Spirit in the womb of the Virgin Mary! The words of the Gospel have a powerful biblical resonance! Even in St Matthew's Gospel the fact is stated so succinctly that she was *"found to be with child by the Holy Spirit!"* (1:18) This indicates so clearly this central fact of Mary's relationship with the Holy Spirit. In human terms, the phrases *"will come upon you"* and *"will overshadow you"*⁶⁷ suggests the embrace of the Spirit in a *quasi-conjugal* relationship! However, it has also Pentecostal overtones. Let us recall that in the aftermath of the Resurrection Jesus exhorts his disciples to remain in Jerusalem to await the coming of the Holy Spirit:

> **But you shall receive power when the Holy Spirit comes upon you; and you shall be my witnesses in Jerusalem and in all Judaea and Samaria and to the ends of the earth.**
> **(Acts 1:8)**

Again, the key word in Luke *"overshadow"*. This suggests the hovering of the creative Spirit hovering over the watery wastes of Genesis:

> **And the Spirit of God hovered over the face of the waters.**
> **(Genesis 1:3)**

This was the prelude to the creative action of God when he said: **Let there be light!** We see here the Spirit hovering over the empty womb of Mary and by his action bringing the *Light of the world* into a world lost in the darkness of sin and death. Possibly the most powerful image is that of the glory of God overshadowing the ark in the wilderness. These references, moreover, have given rise to such Marian titles: *Ark of the Covenant* and *Tabernacle of the Most High!*

> **Then the cloud covered the tent of meeting and the glory of the Lord filled the tabernacle.**
> **(Exodus 40:34)**

3. In the Fulness of Grace!

As much as we admire the work of the Holy Spirit in the events leading up to the Incarnation, they all pale in comparison with his work

---

67 *Here let us note the use of the original Greek 'episkiadso'—to throw or envelop in a shadow—referring to the creative energy of the Holy Spirit within the womb of Mary, in the apostles at Pentecost and in the Church especially through the sacramental system.*

in the immediate preparation for the coming of the Second Person of the Most Holy Trinity into this world. Nothing was to be spared in welcoming Jesus into a world that was crying out for his presence! It is on such a point that the Catechism makes the following observation:

> *The mission of the Holy Spirit is always conjoined and ordered to that of the Son. The Holy Spirit is sent to sanctify the womb of the Virgin Mary and divinely fecundate it, causing her to conceive the eternal Son of the Father in a humanity drawn from her own.*
>
> (#485)

To understand the phrase *"to sanctify the womb of the virgin Mary"* let us turn again to the Gospel of Luke:

> **In the sixth month the angel Gabriel was sent by God to a town in Galilee called Nazareth, to a virgin engaged to a man whose name was Joseph, of the house of David. The virgin's name was Mary. And he came to her and said, "Greetings, favoured one! The Lord is with you."**
> **(Luke 1:26-28)**

The mystery of the Incarnation, this pivotal truth of the Christian faith, would automatically suggest that the mother of Jesus was an extremely *holy* person. When the angel greeted her, he did not use her name, he gave her a title that would suggest as much. St Luke uses the Greek term *kecharitomene* in the angelic greeting and it has been translated *Full of grace* or *Highly favoured*, and in the present instance: *Favoured One!*

Traduttore, traditore![68] This is an Italian saying that points to the shortcomings of all translations, and nowhere is this more apparent than in the present instance. The root of *kecharitomene* is the verb *charitao* which can be translated *to gift or endow with grace; to honour with blessings*. Since it is used by the angel as a mode of address it takes on the flavour of a *divinely authorised identification!* The angel, as God's ambassador, addresses her with a *title* which, in this context,

---

[68] *The translator is a traitor!*

defies all adequate translation. However, from the significance of the encounter—*God seeking entry into this world!*—we would presume that the title itself is invested with its profoundest meaning, that Mary was endowed with grace *to the fullest extent of her being*. As one commentator explains it:

> *The Greek (kecharitomene) indicates a perfection of grace. A perfection must be perfect not only intensively but extensively. The grace (or favour) that Mary enjoyed must not only have been 'full' or strong or complete as possible at any given time, but it must have extended over the whole of her life, from conception.*[69]

The angel Gabriel saluted Mary as *"full of grace"*. She was redeemed from the first moment of her conception *"in a more exalted fashion by virtue of the merits of her Son"*.[70] The gift of *sinlessness* in his mother was the greatest gift that the Holy Spirit could offer to welcome Jesus into this world. This was the immense privilege of the *Immaculate Conception*. It is a privilege that even right reason demands. It is unthinkable that the womb that would carry the Saviour of the world for nine months would have been subject to any manner of sin even for a second. Was this not the very reason why Jesus became man—*to dispel sin from the heart of mankind?* Mary was the first fruits of that redemption! Moreover, was not the *first Eve* created *immaculate?* How could anything less be bestowed on the mother of the Second Adam? As a sharer in the latter's work of salvation she was the *Second Eve!*

4. The God-Man

> *The child to be born will be holy;*
> *he will be called Son of God.*
>
> **(Luke 1:35)**

All the foregoing is but a preparation for the Holy Spirit's masterpiece—the holy humanity of the Son of God. The aspirations of

---

[69] *Karl Keating: Catholicism and Fundamentalism (Ignatius Press, 1988 p.269)*
[70] *ibid.*

countless generations of saintly souls are about to reach fulfilment! And the chosen vessel of fulfilment is the womb of Mary.

> *In Mary, the Holy Spirit fulfills the plan of the Father's loving goodness. With and through the Holy Spirit, the Virgin conceives and gives birth to the Don of God. By the Holy Spirit's power and her faith, her virginity became uniquely fruitful.*
>
> (#723)

The consent of Mary to the angel's request brings Jesus on to the stage of humanity. It brings the promise of the fulfilment of God's promise of salvation. In her surrender to the divine will the Messianic prophecies and promises come to life. Once again, the Catechism sums it all up admirably:

> *Filled with the Holy Spirit she makes the Word visible in the humility of the flesh. It is to the poor and the first representatives of the gentiles that she makes him known. Finally, through Mary, the Holy Spirit begins to bring men, the objects of God's merciful love, into communion with Christ.*
>
> (##724 &725)

Jesus is the love of God *incarnated!* He radiated that love to all around him. The mystery is why it was rejected by so many! Mary, too, brings something of this love to us so that *'In him, with him, and through him'* we can begin to glimpse, however feebly, something of God's infinite holiness and his marvellous love for all mankind.

> ***In this the love of God was made manifest among us,***
> ***that God sent his only Son into the world***
> ***that we might live through him.***
>
> **(1 John 4:9)**

(b) Born of the Virgin Mary

1. *The Mother of God!*

> *And why is this granted to me,*
> *that the mother of my Lord should come to me.*
>
> **(Luke 1:43)**

Mother of my Lord! '*Mother of God!*' These words have echoed down the centuries. They rang in the ears of a British statesman when he once visited a church in Italy. It was John Bright, a noted statesman of nineteenth century England, who had just heard a preacher extol the virtues of the *'Madre di Dio!' (Mother of God)*. He was stunned. The phrase haunted him for over twenty years. He constantly asked himself how could any human being lay claim to such an awesome title. *How could any creature born in time lay claim to be the mother of the eternal God?* John Bright is not alone in his concerns. This title of Mary as the *'Mother of God'* always seems to provoke considerable concern, if not outright indignation, on the part of certain Christians.

This concern arises from the notion that it appears to place Mary on a level with the divinity itself. The concern is not new. It arose in the early Church under the heresiarch *Arius* who denied the divinity of Christ, and by extension, this title of Mary as *Mother of God*. It arose again in the following century when a famous preacher from Antioch, *Nestorius* by name, was made Patriarch of Constantinople in 428 A.D. by the emperor Theodosius II. Nestorius raised the issue again when he doubted that the title of *theotokos* or *God-bearer* was appropriate for the mother of Jesus. He maintained that there were two *persons* in Christ, one *human* and the other *divine*. Mary was simply the mother of the human person.

Therefore, Mary should be called *Christokos—Christ-bearer*, and not *Theotokos—God-bearer!* If, however, *Jesus is God*, then Mary is the *Mother of God*, truly *theotokos!* This impeccable logic was the belief of the early Church. One of its many martyrs, St Ignatius, Bishop of Antioch, who died in 106 A.D. is on record as saying:

Our God was carried in the womb of Mary!

This title of *theotokos* was popular among Orthodox believers and especially in the Greek monasteries. On this issue Nestorius was strongly challenged by the Alexandrian church. There Cyril, the Patriarch of Alexandria (412-444), a noted theologian, denounced him in his sermons, writings and letters. At the Council of Ephesus in 431 A.D. the position of Cyril was proclaimed as the tradition of the Church and Nestorius was denounced and deposed from office. He was sent into exile and died in Egypt around the year 450 A.D. Mary's honour was finally and fully vindicated. The importance of the title *Mother of God* lies at the heart of our redemption. As Cardinal Newman so aptly pointed out:

> *We cannot refuse this title to Mary without denying the Divine Incarnation that is the great and fundamental truth of revelation, that God became man!*

The key to Mary's greatness and dignity lies in her *divine maternity*. She is the *Mother of God!* Everything else that can be said about this supremely privileged creature flows from that unique title. She is, as the English poet Wordsworth depicted her, *our tainted nature's solitary boast!* Her role and her position in the economy of salvation is not simply an accident of history, but was something preordained from all eternity in God's salvific will!

2. Mary's Perpetual Virginity

> *Mary's virginity manifests God's absolute initiative in the Incarnation. Jesus has only God as Father.*
>
> (#503)

The *perpetual* virginity of Mary is part and parcel of the deposit of faith. As the Catechism so clearly affirms:

> *The deepening of faith in the virginal motherhood led the Church to confess Mary's real and perpetual virginity even in the act of giving birth to the Son of God made man. In fact, Christ's birth did not diminish his mother's virginal integrity but sanctified it. And so the Church celebrates Mary as* **Aeiparthenos***, 'Ever Virgin'.*
>
> (#499)

It is evident that this title *Ever Virgin* entails, first of all,

> *'the virginal conception of Jesus as a divine work that surpasses all human understanding and possibility'.*
>
> (#497)

While the perpetual virginity of Mary was a firmly held belief in the early Church, it came under attack in the fourth century from a certain *Helvidius* who, quoting the text of scripture on *"the brethren of the Lord"* stated that these were children born to Mary and Joseph after the birth of Jesus. It is an opinion that is even heard of today. St Jerome dubbed these conclusions as *"novel, wicked and an affront to the faith of the whole world"*. He then went on to write a treatise on the perpetual virginity of the Blessed Mary, citing the works of Ignatius, a disciple of the apostle John, St Polycarp, and St Justin Martyr. St Ambrose and St John Chrysostom affirmed the same.

Mary's perpetual virginity is summed up in the classic Latin phrase: *ante partum, in partu et post partum*. Which, literally, means *before childbirth, in childbirth and after childbirth* Mary remained a virgin! Even though the leading Reformers of the sixteenth century, Luther and Calvin, accepted the perpetual virginity of Mary, the heresy of *Helvidius* has been resurrected in modern times. Suffice it to say, this heresy does not survive a careful scrutiny of the Gospel texts. The so-called *"brethren of the Lord"* are in fact *close relatives* or *cousins*[71]. It was a common Semitic practice to label these close relatives as *brothers* and *sisters*. Jesus was an only child who from the Cross confided his mother to John. This would have been, not only *unlawful* but unthinkable, had there been other family members to whom she would have been entrusted.

3. The Second Eve:

"Do not be afraid, Mary, for you have found favour with God.
And now, you will conceive in your womb
and bear a son, and you will name him Jesus".
(Luke 1 : 30-31)

These words are well-known as part of the text of the Annunciation of the angel Gabriel to an obscure virgin of Nazareth. As we have already suggested, the stark simplicity of St Luke's narrative and our

---

[71] *There is no word in Aramaic for the word 'cousin'*

own familiarity with the text tend to obscure the most startling fact in the whole of history. The long awaited fulfilment of the Genesis prophecy was at hand. For that fulfilment the consent of a daughter of Israel was necessary. On this subject the Second Vatican Council makes the following comment:

> *The Father of mercies willed that the Incarnation should be preceded by assent on the part of the predestined mother, so that just as a woman had a share in the coming of death, so also a woman should contribute to the coming of life.*[72]

It is evident that the first Eve shares responsibility with the first Adam for man's fall from grace. Now in the condemnation of the serpent God singles out a *woman* as his special adversary, as a special punishment for his perfidy. The only logical choice for the identity of this woman is Mary, the mother of the Second Adam. In the words of Elizabeth it is this that makes her *the most blessed of all women!* This reference to Mary as the *Second Eve* takes us back to the early Church Fathers who saw in her the fulfilment of God's words to Satan.

**ced*I will put enmity between you and the woman!*
(Genesis 3:15)**

Even as far back as the second century we find Justin the Martyr (c.165 A.D.), a writer and apologist for the faith, suggesting this same thought:

> "Christ became man through the Virgin in order that disobedience which issued from the serpent be destroyed in the same way in which it took its origin . . . . Thus through the intermediation of this Virgin he came into the world . . . through whom God would crush the serpent and others similar to him".[73]

---

[72] *Lumen Gentium 56 (cfr61)*

[73] quoted in George Maloney S.J. *Mary; the Womb of God* (Dimension Books, N.J. 1976)

4. The Law of Association

> **Behold a virgin shall conceive and bear a son,
> and his name shall be called Emmanuel.**
> **(Isaiah 7: 14)**

On the virginity of Mary the universal Catechism of the Church has this to say:

> *The eyes of faith can discover in the context of the whole of Revelation the mysterious reasons why God in his saving plan wanted his Son to be born of a virgin. These reasons touch both on the person of Christ and his redemptive mission, and the welcome Mary gave to that mission on behalf of all men.* (#502)

In that last sentence the Church touches on the *"Law of Association"* in which the *names of Jesus and Mary are inseparably intertwined*. As both Pius IX in his decree on the *Immaculate Conception* (1854) and Pius XII in his decree of the *Assumption* (1950) asserted that the names of *Jesus* and *Mary* are united in one and the same decree of predestination. Jesus was conceived *immaculate* by *right* and *nature*. Mary was conceived *immaculate* by *grace* and *privilege*. Both are called *'the All Holy'*, though on different levels.

> *The Fathers of the Eastern tradition call the Mother of God 'the All Holy'* (**Panagia**) *and celebrate her 'as free from any stain of sin, as though fashioned by the Holy Spirit and formed as a new creature.'*[74] *By the grace of God Mary remained free of every personal sin her whole life long.*
>
> (#493)

(c) Why did the Son of God become man?

1. Introduction.

The *Incarnation*, stated in its simplest terms, is that *God became man*. The *infinite* God entered the *finite* realm of history! *Was it necessary*

---

[74] *Lumen Gentium*

for him to do so? Before launching out into any discussion about the *'necessity'* of the Incarnation, it would be well to keep in mind a certain basic principle dealing with God's relationship with mankind. This is that God is under no obligation to do anything on our behalf! We have no *rights* before him. The only obligation that God has is *to himself, to the glory of his name!* It follows from this that the *Second Person* of the Most Holy Trinity was under no obligation to come down from heaven and live amongst us. But why the *Second Person* and neither the *First* nor the *Third?* The answer to such a question lies in the special relationship that the *Word* had with creation. This is the point made in a sermon by one of the Church fathers, St Peter Chrysologus:

> *The second Adam (Jesus) stamped his image on the first Adam when he created him. That is why he took on himself the role and the name of the first Adam in order that he might not lose what he had made in his own image. The first Adam, the last Adam; the first had a beginning, the last knows no end. The last Adam is indeed the first, as he himself says: I am the first and the last.*[75]

A similar answer can come from scripture, especially from the letters of Paul:

> **He is the image of the invisible God, the firstborn of all creation; for in him all things in heaven and on earth were created, things visible and invisible, whether thrones or dominions or rulers or powers—all things have been created through him and for him. He himself is before all things, and in him all things hold together.**
> **(Colossians 1:15-17)**

Nevertheless, in the final analysis, the most basic answer must come from the overriding consideration of the will of the Father:

> **Everything that the Father gives me will come to me, and anyone who comes to me I will never drive away; for I have**

---

[75] *Sermom117 in the Latin Fathers 520-523*

> *come down from heaven, not to do my own will, but the will of him who sent me.*
>
> **(John 6:37-38)**

2. To Heal the Breach between Man and God!

> *Behold the Lamb of God!*
> *Behold him who takes away the sin of the world!*
>
> **(John 1:29)**

Notice the phrase *'the sin of the world'* and not the sins of the world! The phrase goes deeper than the sum of all men's sins. It refers rather to the fundamental alienation of mankind and all his works from God's loving concerns. There was now an unbridgeable gap between mankind and its Creator! Adam's fall had brought sin into the world and brought it under the thrall of Satan. St Anselm, Archbishop of Canterbury (1033-1109), wrote precisely on this topic in his greatest work *Why did God Become Man?*[76] 'With the fall of our first parents mankind had run up such a debt of sin that it could never be wiped out. Only God himself could make *satisfaction* for this enormous debt of injury to God's majesty. What Jesus, *as both God and man,* faced on our behalf, were the consequences of that fall in his battle with Satan and his empire of sin! In light of this we can comprehend the words of Jesus at the last Supper:

> *Now shall the Prince of this world be cast out!*
>
> **(John 12:31)**

The mighty contest between *Good* and *Evil* was fought out in the drama surrounding the horrors of Calvary. This battle was also necessary to make atonement for the violation of God's love that sin entailed. Only God himself could bridge the gap that the alienation of sin had brought about between God and his creation. Jesus came down to earth to effect a reconciliation between man and God. What Jesus did, in effect, was to take upon himself the entire burden of man's guilt. In his own person he repaid the enormous debt that man owed to God because

---

[76] *The original Latin title is "Cur Deus Homo?"*

of his gross infidelity. Our stricken human nature could never of itself ever hope to repay it!

3. To Know God's Infinite Love!

Nevertheless, it is obvious that there are other forces at work in the drama of redemption. Without Jesus we would never have even glimpsed the depths of God's infinite love.

The Catechism sums this up so succinctly:

> *The Word became flesh so that we might know God's love.*
> (#458)

Or as the apostle John tells in one of his letters:

> **God's love was revealed among us in this way: God sent his only Son into the world so that we might live through him. In this is love, not that we loved God but that he loved us and sent his Son to be the atoning sacrifice for our sins.**
> **(1 John 4:9-10)**

Divine love had created the world. Every thing in this world was but an echo of that love. Sin not only wreaked havoc in man's soul, it also destroyed even his ability either to know it or recognise it. By taking upon himself human nature Jesus renewed man's essential dignity as a beloved child of God. In doing so he also breathed into the whole of creation the breath of God's eternal love. He did so because mankind, blinded by its own passions and burdened with sin, was unable to help itself. Only God could break down the barriers that cut man off from his Creator. So Jesus entered this fallen world and brought into it the light of his Father's loving concern for sinners. In unforgettable terms this is described by the apostle John:

> **For God so loved the world that he gave his only Son, so that everyone who believes in him may not perish but may have eternal life. Indeed, God did not send the Son into the world to condemn the world, but in order that the world might be saved through him.**
> **(John 3:16-17)**

4. Our Model of Holiness

For I am the LORD your God; sanctify yourselves therefore, and be holy, for I am holy. You shall not defile yourselves with any swarming creature that moves on the earth. For I am the LORD who brought you up from the land of Egypt, to be your God; you shall be holy, for I am holy.
(Leviticus 11:44-45)

This command was given to the Chosen People to be holy *as God himself is holy!* Its fulfilment, as an ideal, was impossible for ordinary mortals until the coming of Jesus. Only then in Jesus could it be fulfilled. Only then was there a model for us, not merely to admire, but much more to imitate. Only then could he repeat the same message and the ideal of holiness manifested in Jesus, who also offers himself as a model of holiness.

His words are an invitation to follow his example in life:

Take my yoke upon you, and learn from me;
for I am gentle and humble in heart,
and you will find rest for your souls.
For my yoke is easy, and my burden is light.
(Matthew 11:29-30)

In light of all this no one can plead ignorance of this imperative of holiness for all Christians. Jesus has trodden the same path and lighted the way for us!

I am the Way, the Truth and the Life
No one comes to the Father except through me.
(John 14:6)

5. 'Partakers' of the Divine Nature!

Here we touch the most incredible aspect in this drama of salvation. We are invited to be united, in some vastly mysterious way, with the divine nature of God himself! The more we reflect on this aspect of the spiritual life, the more mind boggling it becomes! Lest we have any doubts on the subject, let us hear what St Peter tells us in one of his letters:

> *His divine power has given us everything needed for life and godliness, through the knowledge of him who called us by his own glory and goodness. Thus he has given us, through these things, his precious and very great promises, so that through them you may escape from the corruption that is in the world because of lust, and may become participants of the divine nature.*
>
> **(2 Peter 1:3-4)**

One author attempts to try and convey to us, by the analogy of a sculptor and his work, this marvel of spiritual transformation:

> *By nature we are created in God's image, or resemblance, as a statue is created in the image of its sculptor. What Christ calls "being born anew" (John 3:3) is like the statue coming to life, to share the image and likeness of the sculptor, but his very life!—like Pinocchio, transformed from a mere wooden puppet to real boy, miraculously sharing the life of a boy: thinking, choosing, talking, playing. In Paul's terms, our destiny is not merely "flesh" (human nature) but "spirit", living off the life of the Holy Spirit. In St Augustine's formula, the Holy Spirit becomes the life of our soul as the soul is the life of the body.*

++++++++++++++++

> *It is no longer I who live, but Christ who lives in me*
> *and the life I now live in the flesh*
> *I live by faith in the Son of God*
> *who loved me and gave himself up for me!*
>
> **(Galatians 2:20)**

The Breastplate of St Patrick

++++++++++

Christ with me
Christ before me
Christ behind me
Christ within me
Christ beneath me
Christ above me!

Christ on my right
Christ on my left
Christ when I lie down
Christ when I sit down
Christ when I arise!

Christ in the heart of every man
who thinks of me,
Christ in the mouth of every man
who speaks of me,
Christ in the eyes of every man
who sees me,
Christ in every ear that hears me!

I arise today
Through a mighty strength,
the invocation of the Trinity,
Through belief in the threeness,
Through the confession of the oneness
of the Creator of Creation.[77]

---

[77] *This is the conclusion of the famous prayer of St Patrick called 'The Cry of the Deer'. It was an invocation of divine protection from the forces of darkness. Known also as the 'Breastplate of St Patrick', because it was a protection against the forces of evil.*

Questions #6

* * *

1. What do you understand by the Pauline phrase "in the fulness of time"?

2. The 'overshadowing' of the Spirit! What does this expression mean?

3. "Greetings, favoured one!" Any comments on this Angelic greeting?

4. "The humanity of Jesus is the masterpiece of the Holy Spirit." Any comments?

5. It is quite absurd to call Mary the 'Mother of God'! How would you answer this objection?

6. "Ever Virgin (Aeiparthenos)" What does this Marian title mean?

7. Why is Mary called the "Second Eve"?

8. What do you understand by the Law of Association?

9. *"It was wholly unnecessary for the Son of God to become man!" Any comments?*

10. *"'Be holy as I am holy!' This command of God is impossible!" Comments?*

11. *We are partakers of the divine nature? You must be kidding! What do you say?*

7. HE SUFFERED UNDER PONTIUS PILATE

* * *

(a) He Suffered
    —1. The Crucial Question
    —2. A Life of Suffering
    —3. The Garden of Gethsemane
    —4. The 'Crucifixion' of Gethsemane

(b) The Necessity of Suffering
    —1. En Route to Emmaus
    —2. The Mystery of Suffering.
    —3. Joy in Suffering!

(c) 'under Pontius Pilate'
    —1. Who is Pontius Pilate?
    —2. In the Context of Salvation History
    —3. The 'Washing of the Hands"
    —4. Behold Your King!

7. He suffered under Pontius Pilate

* * *

(a) He Suffered

1. *The Crucial Question?*

Even to the most casual reader of the New Testament it might appear that the hostility that Jesus experienced in his ministry borders on the irrational. Why would anyone, in his right mind, seek the death of one who was noted for his compassion, for his miracles of healing and for his inspired teaching? Perhaps it was inevitable that his very success should inspire the envy and ultimately the deadly hostility of the establishment. Right from the very start of his public ministry Jesus was pursued by the antagonism of certain elements of the Pharisees, the Sadducees and the Herodians. It was inevitable that they would take offence at this Galilean upstart who would dare to challenge their authority:

> ***And when Jesus had finished these sayings, the crowds were astonished at his teaching, for he taught them as one having authority, and not as their scribes.***
> **(Matthew 7:28)**

His activities and his remarks were apparently at odds with their own way of life. His very success was a reproach to them. They could not rival his inspired teaching, nor his miracles of healing. And did he not dine with tax collectors and sinners? His life was, in effect, the fulfilment of Simeon's prophecy that he would be *"a sign of contradiction"*. All this is summarised in the Catechism:

> *In the eyes of Israel Jesus seemed to be acting against the essential institutions of the Chosen People:*
>
> — *submission to the whole of the Law in its written commandments and, for the Pharisees, in the interpretation of oral tradition;*

— *the centrality of the Temple at Jerusalem as the holy place where God's presence dwells in a special way;*
— *faith in the one God whose glory no man can share.*

(#576)

2. A Life of Suffering

> ***This child is destined for the falling and the rising of many in Israel, and to be a sign that will be opposed so that the inner thoughts of many will be revealed—and a sword will pierce your own soul too.***
>
> **(Luke 2: 34-35)**

This prophecy of the aged Simeon was only too quickly fulfilled. The Holy Family was compelled to flee from the wrath of Herod. They became *refugees* in a foreign land. Finally, they sought obscurity in northern Palestine, in Nazareth of Galilee. During His public life Jesus had to endure the hatred of the Pharisees and the rejection of an establishment that continually sought his life. Even among those who remained faithful He was constantly dogged with incomprehension and misunderstanding. The Gospels record over a dozen times the Master's reproach to his own disciples: ***Do you not yet understand?*** **(Mark 8 :21)**

The culmination of all this misunderstanding, rejection, mistrust and hatred arrived under the administration of the the Roman procurator of Judea, Pontius Pilate. It came to a head in the garden of Gethsemane, when Jesus apparently sank under the weight of mankind's massive sinfulness and he thrice pleaded with the Father for some relief. Added to all this was the treachery and betrayal by one of his own chosen followers, *Judas Iscariot.* Jesus allowed Himself to be handed over to his enemies, to be mistreated by a brutal soldiery, to be flogged and crowned with thorns. *And it all happened at the hands of the very ones that Jesus had come to save!* This is the divine irony in the whole proceedings, and at the same time a wonderful demonstration of God's love and of the divine patience and humility. Whenever we read the Gospel account, given in such matter-of-fact detail, we are still struck by the excess of physical suffering which Jesus chose to endure—the merciless scourging at the pillar, the crowning with thorns and impalement on a cross. The evangelists recount all this in very summary fashion. Rather than dwell on the physical sufferings that would have killed an ordinary man, they tended to dwell on something that they considered more offensive—*the indignities, the buffoonery and insults*—meted out to one who was their Lord and Creator:

> ***Some began to spit on him, to blindfold him, and to strike him, saying to him, "Prophesy!" The guards also took him over and beat him.***
>
> **(Mark 14 : 65)**

3. The Garden of Gethsemane

All of a sudden there is a dramatic change of pace in the historical narrative of the Creed, a leap from birth to death, or to the prelude to that death. There is not a single word on the ministry of Jesus, his teachings or his miracles. It is all passed over so abruptly. We are transported immediately to the *Garden of Gethsemane*[78], the site of betrayal by Judas. It is so sudden that we might easily miss the whole point of the transition. The whole point is that the Creed now focuses on the reason why Jesus came among us—to redeem us by his suffering. In this we reach new depths in the mystery of the incarnation. As expressed by Matthew:

> ***Then Jesus said to them, "I am deeply grieved, even to death; remain here, and stay awake with me." And going a little farther, he threw himself on the ground and prayed, "My Father, if it is possible, let this cup pass from me; yet not what I want but what you want."***
>
> **(Matthew 26:38-39)**

It is a source of perpetual amazement to us that God, *the Second Person of the Most Holy Trinity,* should take it upon himself to become one of us. But our amazement only deepens when we realise that he did so to embrace death, and death in one of its most horrific forms, *crucifixion! And all for our sakes, for our redemption!* To come to terms with this we must go back to the primordial trial of mankind in the

---

[78] *Gethsemane or the 'Oil Press' recalls the fact that there was a grove of olive trees there.*

persons of Adam and Eve. The punishment for their disobedience is suffering and death for them and for all their descendants.

> *Cursed is the ground because of you; in toil you shall eat of it all the days of your life; thorns and thistles it shall bring forth for you; . . . .*
> *By the sweat of your face you shall eat bread until you return to the ground, for out of it you were taken; you are dust, and to dust you shall return.*
> **(Genesis 3:18-19)**

Sorrow, suffering, distress and death entered into the very fabric of our existence. Death is the one inescapable fact of life! No one has been exempt[79]. Famines, murders, suicides, wars, diseases, plagues, old age, have all taken their toll in the wake of that primal curse. Here we might overlook the significance of the place where the *Hour* of Jesus began. It is the *Garden of Gethsemane!* Where did the fall of mankind begin? *In the Garden of Eden!* Sin originated in a garden and the drama of mankind's redemption begins in a garden. Gethsemane means *the oil press* where the olives were crushed. This is also symbolic of the crushing weight of the agony of Jesus, suffering for the sins of the world, from Adam until the end of time!

4. The 'Crucifixion' of Gethsemane!

At this point in the Creed we now come to realise that Jesus came to take that crushing burden of sorrow upon himself. It was not so much the physical pain or the agonies of mankind, but something far more horrific, the root cause of all that pain and unendurable agony—*sin!*—sin in all its manifestations of man's rebellion against God! A tremendous struggle ensued in which Jesus *"began to be greatly troubled and distressed, and he said to them"*

> *'My soul is sorrowful even unto death'.*
> **(Mark 14:34)**

---

[79] *Two notable exceptions are recorded in scripture—Enoch and Elijah.*

The disciples are in a state of shock. They no longer recognise their Master. He, who had worked such astonishing miracles, rebuked the pride and intolerance of the Pharisees and even raised the dead to life, now pleads for the comfort of their company and prayers: **Could you not watch one hour with me? (Mark 14:37).** Finally, he turns to his heavenly Father:

> *'Father, if you are willing, remove this cup from me;*
> *yet, not my will but yours be done . . . .'*
> *In his anguish he prayed more earnestly,*
> *and his sweat became like great drops of blood*
> *falling down on the ground.*
> **(Luke 22 : 42-44)**

This *cup, to which Jesus refers* is a biblical reference to God's wrath in Isaiah:

> **Behold I have taken from your hand the cup of staggering,**
> **the bowl of my wrath.**
> **(Isaiah 51:22)**

Jesus had now to drink this cup to the dregs! It is little wonder that Jesus, bathed in a sweat of blood, sank in utter helplessness to the ground, under the intolerable burden of man's ghastly sinfulness. One author comments upon this:

> *It is important to grasp just what the suffering was from which Our Lord shrank with so much anguish. It was not simply, nor even primarily, the bodily torments that he was to endure. The ground of his anguish lay much deeper . . . . Our Lord, offering himself for the sins of the world, not only took upon himself the punishment those sins have deserved; in some (mysterious) sense, he took the sins themselves, everything of them save the guilt . . . . That was his agony, that was the chalice which he prayed might pass from him. That is the key to the mysterious phrase of St Paul:*

> **He, who knew no sin, God has made sin for us.** [80]
> **(2 Corinthians 5:21)**

---

[80] F.J Sheed: *Theology and Sanity* (Sheed & Ward, London & New York, 1960)

Nevertheless, though the drama of Gethsemane highlights the onslaught of suffering and sorrow in the life of Jesus, it cannot be overlooked that his whole life was an odyssey of misunderstanding, of contradiction, rejection and suffering. Here the crucifixion of Jesus has already begun! However, it was a *spiritual* crucifixion. It was a crucifixion that brought the heart-rending plea of Jesus to his Father that he might be released from this crushing burden of mankind's sinful ways.

(b) The Necessity of Suffering

1. *En Route to Emmaus*

There is a very memorable scene recorded by Luke describing the experience of two disciples, Cleopas and his wife, who had left Jerusalem on that first resurrection day and were on their way to Emmaus. They were depressed and weighed down by the events of the past week and the tragedy that had seen the execution of their beloved Master. *En route* they were joined by a stranger who asked them what they were talking about. What was the topic of their conversation? From the context it would appear that they were talking about the capture and death of Jesus. Nevertheless, they failed to recognise that their travelling companion was Jesus! They expressed great surprise that the latter did not know what had happened in Jerusalem that weekend!

Jesus listened quietly to their tale of tragedy and then said:

> **Oh, how foolish you are, and how slow of heart to believe all that the prophets have declared! *Was it not necessary that the Messiah should suffer these things and then enter into his glory?***
>
> **(Luke 24:25-26)**

Jesus was saying to them, and his words resonate down to us today, that he *had to suffer*. All that had been foretold by the prophets had to be accomplished in his person. The explanation of Jesus would have undoubtedly covered the account of the *Suffering Servant* so prominent in the prophecies of Isaiah.[81]

---

[81] *Of all the Old Testament prophecies relating to the New Testament those of Isaiah hold the lion's share!*

> *Surely he has borne our infirmities and carried our diseases;*
> *yet we accounted him stricken, struck down by God, and*
> *afflicted. But he was wounded for our transgressions,*
> *crushed for our iniquities; upon him was the punishment*
> *that made us whole, and by his bruises we are healed.*
> **(Isaiah 53:3-5)**

Jesus took the very punishment meted out in the primordial trial of Genesis to the entire human race upon himself. He used it as an instrument for our redemption. Henceforward, all our pains and aches and tragedies take on a different hue. They have all been touched by the sufferings of Jesus. This led the apostles and disciples to face the most terrible of deaths in order to follow in the footsteps of the Master. The early history of the Church is drenched with the blood of martyrs. Many of them eagerly sought martyrdom. Their example has been a shining example throughout the centuries right down to our own times. It is, perhaps, no exaggeration to say that this past century has probably seen more martyrs to the faith than all preceding centuries!

2. *The Mystery of Suffering*

In the mystery of human suffering we are constantly confronted with the problem of not wasting it! The question has also been raised—*why do bad things happen to good people?* Behind this question there might be, what we might call, a *Pollyanna theology* that insists that virtue and goodness of life will bring, in its wake, material happiness and prosperity. This is a dangerous illusion! Jesus has taught us to accept the common ills of our humanity. They can be stepping stones to greater holiness. When we unite our setbacks and sufferings to the Cross we fulfil here and now Christ's redemptive mission. Moreover, St Paul tells us of the wider effect of uniting our own sufferings to those of Christ on the Cross:

> *I want to know Christ and the power of his resurrection and the sharing of his sufferings by becoming like him in his death, if somehow I may attain the resurrection from the dead.*
> **(Philippians 3:10-11)**

There is an unfortunate weakness in the human psyche—*part of our fallen nature!*—that prefers to indulge immediate gratification here on earth rather than aspire to the long term gains of the divine friendship and of eternal glory. We need the constant reminder of the goal of which the Cross speaks to us and to which St Paul refers when he says:

> ***I consider that the sufferings of this present time are not worth comparing with the glory about to be revealed to us.***
> **(Romans 8:18)**

The Gospel record of the Passion of Jesus might naturally lead us to take sides. Here is the founder of our Church being tortured and done to death! The immense injustice of the whole proceedings might blind us to the fact that it is we ourselves, in all our wretched sinfulness, who were the real agents of the Passion. The heart-rending dramas of Gethsemane and Golgotha still go on in our own times and in our own lives.

> *"It was not demons who crucified him; it is you who crucified him and you crucify him still, when you delight in your vices and sins".*[82]

These words of St Francis of Assisi pinpoint the far reaching consequences of the sufferings of Jesus. As with the whole redemptive drama they reach out and touch us in the sacramental outreach of the Church. We are all conspirators in the trial and condemnation of Jesus and we all clamoured for his death! Our sins and moral lapses are far more potent than the cries of any enraged and rabble-rousing Sanhedrin. Although these events have passed nigh two millennia ago, their echoes, and still more, their effects, keep ringing down through the centuries. The Catechism elaborates on this same point:

> *And it can be seen that our crime in this case is greater in us than in the Jews. As for them, according to the witness of the Apostle, none of the rulers of this age understood this; for if they had, they would not have crucified the Lord of glory. We, however, profess to know him. And when we deny*

---

[82] *St Francis of Assisi*

him by our deeds, we in some way seem to lay violent hands upon him.

(#598)[83]

3. Joy in Suffering!

> *Let us also lay aside every weight*
> *and the sin that clings so closely,*
> *looking to Jesus the pioneer and perfecter of our faith,*
> *who, for the sake of the joy that was set before him,*
> *endured the cross, disregarding its shame.*
> **(Hebrews 1: 1-2)**

It is related in the lives of the mystics that Jesus embraced his Passion with joy! The joy arises from the prospect of the release of all those made in his image from the grievous threat of everlasting punishment. This joy flows from the love of the Eternal Word for his Father and the fulfilment of the latter's sovereign will in the redemption of stricken humanity. We see a striking reversal of values when we look at the contrast between the way of the world and the *Way of the Cross*. We see what happened in the Garden of Eden when Eve beheld the forbidden fruit. The fruit was *fair to the eyes and delightful to behold*. It held out the seductive promise of happiness and bliss, but it had the taste of death! This is the seduction of the things of this world, described so aptly by Cardinal Newman in one of his *Parochial and Plain Sermons*, entitled *The Cross the Measure of the World!*

> *The world is sweet to the lips but bitter to the taste*
> *It pleases at first but not at last.*
> *It looks pleasant on the outside,*
> *but evil and misery lie concealed within.*[84]

But from our experience we never seem to learn what the *Wise Man*[85] dubbed so long ago as **Vanity of Vanities and all is Vanity!** until we are

---

[83] *CCC*

[84] *J.H. Cardinal Newman: Newman for Everyone* (Alba House, N.Y. 1998) p.122

[85] The Book of Sirach in the Old Testament

forced to confront the reality and the *wisdom of the Cross* of Christ. It is then that we come face to face with the mystery of Gethsemane and Calvary. The sufferings of Jesus bring to the fore the place of suffering in our own lives. This is what the apostle James constantly tells us:

> ***My brothers and sisters, whenever you face trials of any kind, consider it nothing but joy!***
> **(James 1:2)**

These words touch a tender nerve in the human psyche! *'Trials of any kind'* are not usually looked upon as causes for rejoicing! It is a given of our human existence that pain and suffering are to be avoided at all costs. Mankind usually seeks to minimise pain and promote so-called physical and psychological well-being. There are some who even preach that we are well on the way to the abolition of all human woes and affliction in the next millennium! This is all a vast illusion. Pain and suffering are the very warp and woof of the human condition. If we are doomed *to die*, we are destined *to suffer*. It is the one inescapable fact of life. The curse of *Genesis* is branded into our very souls, and will never be erased in this life. Only in eternity will be verified what John tells us in the Book of Revelation:

> ***Death will be no more; mourning and crying and pain will be no more, for the former things have passed away.***
> **(Revelation 21:4)**

So why should we take *joy* in our affliction?! It is because Jesus has touched it, because He has experienced it, because He has, so to speak, embraced it and even immersed Himself in it. Jesus has thereby sanctified it! As part of our own redemption every facet of Christ's Passion has been woven into the warp and woof of our daily existence!

(c) 'Under Pontius Pilate'

1. Who is Pontius Pilate?

Foremost among the characters that emerge in the trial of Jesus is Pontius Pilate. It might appear strange that the name of a pagan ruler should be mentioned in the *Apostles' Creed* alongside that of Jesus and

Mary. However, he is a central figure in the drama of redemption. He alone had the power to order the crucifixion of Jesus. The early Christians were deeply attached to this central historical fact about Jesus that he was crucified *"under Pontius Pilate."* He is mentioned three times in *Acts*. There is, therefore, no disputing the existence of Jesus who was done to death under the aegis of a Roman governor. Moreover, it established the fact that Jesus was not a fictional or mythical figure, and that in the drama of his trial Pilate had made futile attempts to save him. The pagan procurator of Judea, Samaria and Idumaea was of the equestrian or *knightly* class and his name *Pontius* tells us that he was a *Samnite* of the clan *Pontii*. He was appointed by Tiberius to his post in 26 AD. Normally he resided in the administrative capital of Caesarea. But on festive occasions, because of the crowds, he came to Jerusalem. So it came about that he became the prime figure to whom the Sanhedrin brought their treasonable charges against an obscure religious figure from Galilee. The political setting of the trial of Jesus and the mention of a Roman governor puts Jesus in an historical setting. It puts to rest any notion that the history of Jesus and his salvific death belongs to myth or fable. We have seen that Pontius Pilate figured prominently in the primitive *kerygma* of the Church. Paul could write to Timothy:

> *In the presence of God, who gives life to all things,*
> *and of Christ Jesus, who in his testimony before*
> *Pontius Pilate made the good confession*
> *to keep the commandment without spot or blame*
> *until the manifestation of our Lord Jesus Christ.*
> **(1 Timothy 6 : 12-13)**

2. In the Context of Salvation History

> *From then on Pilate tried to release him, but the Jews cried out,*
> *"If you release this man, you are no friend of the emperor.*
> *Everyone who claims to be a king sets himself against the emperor".*
> **(John 19:12)**

The drama of Pilate and Jesus must be set in the much larger context of the Father's salvific will for the redemption of mankind. But this does not mean, however, that the characters in this historic drama were simply pawns in the divine plan. As the Catechism puts it:

> *To God all moments of time are present in their immediacy. When, therefore, he establishes his eternal plan of 'predestination' he includes in it each person's free response to his grace: 'In this city, in fact, both Herod and Pontius Pilate, with the Gentiles and the peoples of Israel, gathered together against your holy servant Jesus, whom you anointed, to do whatever your hand and your plan had predestined to take place.'[86] For the sake of accomplishing his plan of salvation, God permitted the acts that flowed from their blindness.*
>
> (#600)[87]

There are powerful lessons to be gleaned from this encounter of Pilate with Jesus. The first is the utter *abasement* of Jesus. Here is the *King of Kings* and the *Lord of Lords* being put at the mercy of a petty governor. This is an outstanding example of the divine humility of Jesus, who kept silent in the face of so many unjust accusations. Secondly, there is the *apparent* triumph of the world. The Church, which stands as a counterculture to the ways of the world, is often at a disadvantage when it is persecuted and hassled by unjust laws. The Christian must be prepared to follow the Master:

> **Whoever does not carry the cross and follow me cannot be my disciple.**
>
> **(Luke 14:27)**

3. The 'Washing of the Hands'

> **When Pilate saw that he was gaining nothing, but that a riot was beginning, he took water and washed his hands before the crowd saying: I am innocent of this man's blood Look to it yourselves.**
>
> **(Matthew 27:24)**

---

[86] *Acts 4: 27-28*
[87] *CCC*

On the personal level, Pilate was intrigued by Jesus. He was amazed at his silence and his quiet dignity, and was convinced of his innocence. His wife even intervened on Jesus' behalf. But, first and foremost, he was Caesar's representative and, therefore, a civil administrator devoted to keeping the peace. He capitulated to popular clamour and the threat of violence. Moreover, in Pilate's[88] *washing of his hands* we see a striking symbol of all those betrayals to which so many Christians are prone.

We see this especially in politics, where Christian politicians so often capitulate to popular clamour and compromise their religious principles. On a personal level, there are a thousand different ways in which we seek compromise with the world. The attractions of the world are so strong and their siren voices so seductive that, left to our own devices, we can so easily succumb.

At other times, we seek to walk in both camps, attempting the impossible of keeping one foot in the *world* and the other in *heaven*! There is the ever present danger of seeking attractive and comfortable compromises in linking the goods of this world to the promises of Paradise! Such *worldly bargaining* only leave us *spiritual* cripples! The prophet Elijah saw this happening to his own people, the Chosen Race! They sought to blend the worship of Yahweh with the false gods of Canaan. This prefigures the petty bargains we so often try to make in dealing with God! Elijah's reproach to his countrymen is a reproach to us!

> ***"How long will you go limping with two different opinions? If the LORD is God, follow him; but if Baal[89], then follow him."***
>
> **(1 Kings 18: 21)**

---

[88] *Pilate committed suicide 39 A.D. on orders from the Emperor Caligula. His wife, Claudia Proculla, is honoured as a saint in the Eastern Oorthodox tradition.*

[89] *Baal, the false god of the Canaanites, was a fertility god that attracted many Israelites.*

4. Behold Your King!

And Pilate said to the Jews:

> *"Behold your king!" They cried out: "Away with him! Away with him! Crucify him!" "Shall I crucify your king?" The chief priests answered: "We have no king but Caesar"*
> **(John 19:14-15)**

Pilate had brought Jesus out to a place called the Pavement and made him sit on the *bema* or the platform. This was where the members of the tribunal usually sat and where judgements were pronounced by the procurator. There is an astonishing dramatic irony about the whole scene, for it opens the door to a profound theological meaning. Here we have a pagan procurator proclaiming to the Jews their king. The time is also important, for it was about the *'sixth hour'* on the vigil of the Passover, the Day of Preparation. From a spiritual perspective, and this is always the author's primary point of view, it is a proclamation to the Jews of their Messianic King. This fundamental significance is underscored by one author:

> But to John's eyes of faith, this scene forms the summit of the whole Passion story: the proclamation to the Jewish people by the plenipotentiary of Palestine, representing the Emperor, "Behold your king!"; that was the solemn proclamation of the Messianic Kingship of Jesus, as he sat on the tribunal in front of the praetorium.[90]

The response of the Jews was one of total rejection: *"Away with him! Away with him!"* This was an outright rejection of their Messiah. Despite his years of service, despite all of his miracles of healing and of his inspired teaching, Jesus is summarily rejected. His only response was one of silence and in that silence the world stood condemned. For the moment, however, the world triumphed and had its way. Immediately Pilate delivered Jesus over to its wishes. He was now led forth to Calvary where he would mount the throne of his Cross and from it conquer the world!

---

[90] *Ignace de la Poterie: The House of Jesus (Alba House, N.Y. 1989) p.84.*

Questions #7

* * *

1. *What do you mean by the 'Crucial Question'?*

2. *Jesus' entire life was one of suffering. Explain!*

3. *What are the literal and the spiritual meanings attached to Gethsemane?*

4. *In what does the real agony of Gethsemane consist?*

5. *Jesus had to suffer and die! Comments?*

6. *Why is Pontius Pilate mentioned in the Creed?*

7. *What is the spiritual significance of the washing of the hands?*

8. *Here is your king! Spiritual meaning?*

9. How can there be possibly joy in suffering?

10. Christ the King reigns from the throne of the Cross. Meaning?

11. Any personal reflections on Gethsemane?

8. HE WAS CRUCIFIED

* * *

(a) The Sentence of Death
    1. The Origin of Crucifixion
    2. The Horror of Crucifixion
    3. The Reason for Crucifixion
    4. The Site

(b) The 'Hour'!
    1. The Hour of Destiny
    2. The Hour of Darkness!
    3. The Hour of Glory
    4. The Hour of Redemption

(c) The Divine Legacy
    1. The Last Will
    2. Mary's Compassion
    3. Mary's Spiritual Motherhood
    4. The Second Eve

(d) The Mystery of the Cross
    1. The Challenge of the Cross
    2. The Burden of the Cross
    3. The Wisdom of the Cross

8. He Was Crucified

* * *

(a) The Death Sentence

1. The Origin of Crucifixion

Crucifixion was an extreme form of capital punishment common in the Mediterranean world, and it would appear that it originated in Persia and was adopted by the Carthaginians. As a result of the wars it found its way into the Roman system of justice. It was the custom for the condemned criminal to be scourged. Then a crossbeam *(patibulum)* was fastened to his shoulders by ropes and a young lad or slave carried notice of the crime on a placard in front of the procession. At the place of execution the criminal was nailed to the crossbeam and then hoisted on to the upright *(stipes)* which was already in place. This would place the victim about 8' or 9' from the ground. It is wholly a matter of academic debate as to the actual mode of Christ's execution, whether he carried the whole cross or only the crossbeam. By and large, the details of the Gospel narrative conform to historic practices. Obviously, the brutality of the punishment was meant to serve as a deterrent. It is recorded that entire cities were known to surrender immediately when their inhabitants were threatened with crucifixion. In the eyes of Roman law it was considered so shameful that no Roman citizen could be condemned to this form of death[91].

However, the Romans had very few reservations about inflicting this mode of punishment on *non-Romans*. The most notable example of this was the crucifixion, along the Appian Way outside of Rome, of 6000 gladiators who had participated in the revolt of Spartacus *(73 BC)*. But crucifixion was not unknown, even among the Jews. It is found in the *Book of Joshua*[92] where five *Amorite* kings were crucified. In the second century before Christ, the king and

---

[91] *St Paul was beheaded, while Peter was crucified upside down. Paul was a Roman citizen while Peter was not.*

[92] *see J.D.Crossan: The Birth of Christianity (Harper, San Francisco) for a fuller account of crucifixion history, pp 541-545.*

high priest of Judea, Alexander Jannaeus, crucified a few hundred Pharisees! Their right of capital punishment was lost in the Roman conquest of Palestine.

2. The Horror of Crucifixion

> **Crucify Him! Crucify Him!**
> **(Luke 23:21)**

"A most cruel and absolutely terrifying punishment!" [93] That was how a Roman orator and statesman, Cicero, described the horror of the act of *crucifixion*. The word itself means *'impalement'*. It denoted a form of punishment that the Romans had inherited from the Carthaginians in the *Punic*[94] Wars. The Romans used this method of capital punishment until it was abolished in 327 AD by Constantine the Great in deference to the *Cross* of our redemption.

Today we can debate the merits and demerits of capital punishment. Many of us have misgivings about putting another human being to death, whatever the crime that he or she may have committed. The ancient world was apparently never troubled by any such scruples! We are so familiar with the details of the Bible story that we have become inured to the full impact of the reality of what Christ endured for us. The Gospel narrative has become so familiar that our spiritual sensitivity has become deadened to the gruesome horror of all that surrounds *'this most cruel and absolutely terrifying punishment'!* It is important to emphasize that crucifixion was not only a death sentence, it was also a sentence to torture and to the most unspeakable cruelties.

Catholic artists are sometimes upbraided for attempting to depict scenes of the crucifixion in all its grisly detail. But no artist can ever depict the *true* horror of it all. Like the Israelites of old, we are so fickle and wayward in our allegiance to God that we stand in need of constant

---

[93] This is a translation of the original Latin: "Crudelissimum teterrimumque supplicium".

[94] Punic is another term for 'Carthaginian'. It refers to the spoken language of the Phoenicians originating in the Middle East.

reminders of what Jesus, the wholly *Sinless One*, went through and endured for our sakes, for our redemption.

3. The Reason for Crucifixion

> *He was despised and rejected by others; a man of suffering and acquainted with infirmity; and as one from whom others hide their faces he was despised, and we held him of no account. Surely he has borne our infirmities and carried our diseases; yet we accounted him stricken, struck down by God, and afflicted.*
>
> **(Isaiah 53:3-4)**

The prophet, Isaiah, had long ago foretold the ignominious death of the future Messiah. It now fell to the Jewish rulers to fulfill that prophecy! Even though the Sanhedrin condemned Jesus to death for blasphemy, they had no *'ius gladii' (the law of the sword) i.e.* the power to inflict capital punishment. This right belonged to their Roman masters. The Jewish sentence of death was purely *declaratory*. It was devoid of any means of putting the sentence into effect. The Sanhedrin had now, therefore, to convince Pontius Pilate to order the execution of Jesus. They had to adduce *political* motives, that Jesus had *treasonable* ambitions, that he claimed to be a *king* etc. This was all the more necessary since they sought to disguise the real reason for their decision. It was the claim of Jesus to be *divine*, to be the *Son of God*, that had provoked their fury and their decision to seek his death. Nevertheless, although Jesus was tried in three different courts, before Pilate, the High Priest and Herod, he was found to be innocent!

There are so many tragedies surrounding the death of Jesus. There is the tragedy of *Judas*, the tragedy of Pilate, the tragedy of *Peter's* denial and the tragedy of desertion by most of the apostles. But there also is the tragedy of the High Priest and the Sanhedrin. Faced with the irrefutable proofs of Christ's divine mission, blinded by hate, malice or fear, they bayed like bloodhounds for the blood of their victim. The words of the High Priest, Caiphas, fearful of the political fallout of Jesus' popularity, are an unconscious prophecy:

> *You do not understand that*
> *it is better for you to have one man die for the people*
> *than to have the whole nation destroyed.*
>
> **(John 11:50)**

4. The Site

The site of the crucifixion was the hill of Golgotha. The word *Golgotha* comes from the Aramaic. The English term *'Calvary'* comes from the Latin equivalent *'calvaria'* meaning a *skull!* Calvary marks the climax of the *hour* of Jesus, the culmination of the Passion and the *site* of our redemption and a byword for life's agonies and the deepest suffering. It had all been foreseen centuries beforehand. It is implicit, as we have already seen, in the so-called *Fifth Gospel of the Suffering Servant* depicted by the prophet Isaiah:

> *"See, my servant shall prosper; he shall be exalted and lifted up, and shall be very high. Just as there were many who were astonished at him so marred was his appearance, beyond human semblance, and his form beyond that of mortals."*
>
> **(Isaiah 52:13,14)**

It has been said that the very fact of God *becoming man* would have been sufficient to redeem mankind. It is therefore utterly astounding that Jesus should have deliberately chosen this mode of dying on our behalf. That He should have willed to expiate our sins in this horrifying fashion masks the profoundest mystery.

(b) The 'Hour'!

1. The Hour of Destiny

> *I came to bring fire to the earth,*
> *and how I wish it were already kindled!*
> *I have a baptism with which to be baptized, and what stress I am under until it is completed!*
>
> **(Luke 12:49-50)**

Here, at last, is the climax of the *'Hour'* to which Jesus referred so often during his public ministry. He foresaw clearly this *'baptism'* in his own blood, of the suffering and the ignominy to which he was destined. Although the above quotation is from Luke, it is in the Gospel of John that we find the most dramatic references to the *'hour'* of man's redemption. In fact, it is characteristic of this Gospel right from its very beginning, that the entire life of Jesus is focused on this climax of suffering. Even in the very first sign given us by John, Jesus makes the remark that his *hour had not yet come (John 2:4)*. It is particularly in the latter part of John's Gospel that the references to the *'hour'* of redemption abound. There is one remarkable sentence that may serve as a preface to the horrors of Calvary:

> *Now before the festival of the Passover, Jesus knew that his hour had come to depart from this world and go to the Father. Having loved his own who were in the world, he loved them to the end.*
>
> **(John 13:1)**

What emerges from these extraordinary words is that this hour is an *hour of love*! The whole drama of Calvary is to manifest God's infinite love for sinful mankind. But, at the same time, it is also an hour of glory.

> *Father, the hour has come; glorify your Son so that the Son may glorify you,*
>
> **(John 17:1)**

All this boggles the mind! We are so accustomed to associate suffering, in all its forms, its agony, distress and misfortune, that we instinctively consider all the torments surrounding Calvary are to be roundly deplored and condemned outright. Here is a mystery most profound, *the mystery of the Cross*. Here is to be found the climax of a life wholly devoted to goodness, to teaching us the way to *life*, and to healing the afflicted. Yet it all culminated in dying the death of a common criminal on the hill of Golgotha. It lay just outside the city wall, a little rocky mound slightly higher than the surrounding terrain. Hence it would be quite visible from the city itself and serve as a warning to passers-by.

2. The Hour of Darkness

> *"But this is your hour,*
> *and the power of darkness!"*
> **(Luke 22:53)**

So often during his ministry Jesus had eluded the death threats of his enemies. His hour had not yet come. Now with Gethsemane Jesus submits to the power of darkness. He enters the *dark night of the spirit*. Here the words of the prophet Isaiah are to be fulfilled:

> **Surely he has borne our infirmities**
> **and carried our diseases;**
> **yet we accounted him stricken,**
> **struck down by God,**
> **and afflicted.**
> **(Isaiah 53:4)**

Jesus is now prepared to accept immense and overwhelming debt of man's sinful ingratitude and discharge that debt before his Father. He was prepared to accept the full weight of his Father's anger and offer himself up to whatever that anger would dictate. Jesus is now open to bear this immense burden of sin and, in doing so, leaves himself open to the full weight of the Father's wrath. As the psalmist had foretold of the future Messiah:

> **You have put me in the depths of the Pit,**
> **in the regions dark and deep.**
> **Your wrath lies heavy upon me,**
> **and you overwhelm me with all your waves.**
> **(Psalm 88:6-7)**

A tremendous conflict arises in the soul of Jesus, for, in taking upon himself the burden of man's sinfulness he would appear to deprive himself of the love of the Father! This absence of the Father's love is the greatest torment that Jesus can endure.

Fr Cantalamessa comments:

> *God is the cause of his greatest torment, not in the sense that he is responsible, but in the sense that by simply existing he brings sin to light and makes it unbearable. The infinite attraction between the Father and the Son is now thwarted by an equally infinite repulsion. God's supreme holiness clashes with the supreme evil of sin, causing an indescribable upheaval in the Redeemer's soul,*[95]

The mystic, Blessed Angela di Foligno[96], describes this overwhelming grief and sorrow of Jesus:

> *Christ's suffering was indescribable, manifold and mysterious, the greatest suffering that can be imagined, reserved for him by the divine wisdom. In fact, God's will, which the human mind cannot define, and which is eternally united to Christ, reserved the greatest of all suffering for him . . . . It as an agonising, inexpressible suffering given by the divine will, so intense that it cannot be comprehended by the human mind.*[97]

> **I am deeply grieved, even unto death.**
> **(Matthew 26:38)**

3. The Hour of Glory!

> **Father, the hour has come; glorify your Son**
> **so that the Son may glorify you.**
> **(John 17:1)**

This extraordinary prayer of Jesus to his Father casts the light of *glory* upon the events of the Passion and death of Jesus. It is all the more remarkable since we do not normally associate the sufferings of the Passion with glorification. Indeed, nothing would appear to be

---

[95] *Raniero Cantalamessa: Life in the Lordship of Christ (Sheed and Ward. 1990) p.62*

[96] *This saint (1248-1309) known as "The Mistress of Theologoans" was a noted penitent and mystic.*

[97] *Raniero Cantalamessa ibid. p.63*

more alien to the picture of Jesus alone and abandoned in the agony of crucifixion on the hill of Calvary. We normally associate *'glory'* with shouts of victory and triumph rather than an exhibition of the torments convulsing in the utter ignominy of impalement on a cross between two common criminals. As the Catechism states:

> *Jesus' violent death was not the result of chance in an unfortunate coincidence of circumstances, but is part of the mystery of God's plan, as St. Peter explains to the Jews of Jerusalem in his first sermon on Pentecost: "This Jesus [was] delivered up according to the definite plan and foreknowledge of God." This Biblical language does not mean that those who handed him over were merely passive players in a scenario written in advance by God.*
> (#599)

It sounds rather banal to remark that here all human values are cast aside! The Father's will has brought Jesus to this point of a total surrender to disgrace and infamy. This surrender to the agony of Gethsemane, and to the overwhelming anguish of Calvary contribute to Jesus' glory. He has perfectly fulfilled the Father's will, and in doing so he has given glory to his Father. But in pleasing the Father he is also redeeming sinful man. Our road to the Father has now been opened up through the crucified heart of Jesus. We can now truly say that God is *"Our Father"*!

> *And I, when I am lifted up from the earth, will draw all people to myself.*
> **(John 12:32)**

4. The Hour of Redemption

> *For our sake he made him to be sin who knew no sin, so that in him we might become the righteousness of God.*
> **(2 Corinthians 5:21)**

The *divine choice* of crucifixion seeks to convey to us the utter depravity and heinousness of sin, that our sins are so repugnant and opposed to the absolute holiness of God. It was the experience of the saints that the closer they approached the sanctity of God the more wretched did their own sinfulness appear to them. It was in this light St Francis of Assisi considered himself the *world's most miserable sinner!* On the other hand, it conveys to us the overwhelming love of God for us. Nothing reveals so much the depth of God's incomprehensible love for us than the fact of the crucifixion, with all its tortures, and with all the ignominy that surrounds it.

> *In this is love, not that we loved God*
> *but that he loved us and sent his Son*
> *to be the atoning sacrifice for our sins.*
> **(1 John 4:10)**

Jesus was prepared to suffer this most horrible of tortures so that, in expiating the sins of all mankind, heaven's gates would be thrown open wide for all sinners, for us!

> *He humbled himself and became obedient*
> *to the point of death—even death on a cross.*
> **(Philippians 2: 8)**

The Catechism puts it all in perspective:

> *This sacrifice of Christ is unique; it completes and surpasses all other sacrifices. First, it is a gift from God the Father himself, for the Father handed his Son over to sinners in order to reconcile us with himself. At the same time it is the offering of the Son of God made man, who in freedom and love offered his life to His Father through the Holy Spirit in reparation for our disobedience.*
>
> (#614)

The cross of Jesus stands at the very centre of the crossroads of history. Jesus, our king, crowned with thorns, reigns from the throne of the Cross! This appealed so powerfully to St Paul that it became the centrepiece of his apostolic proclamation:

> *May I never boast of anything*
> *except the cross of our Lord Jesus Christ,*
> *by which the world has been crucified to me,*
> *and I to the world.*
> **(Galatians 6:14)**

(c) The Divine Legacy

1. The Last Will of Jesus

> *When Jesus saw his mother*
> *and the disciple whom he loved standing beside her,*
> *he said to his mother, 'Woman, here is your son.'*
> *Then he said to the disciple, 'Here is your mother.'*
> *And from that hour the disciple took her into his own home.*
> **(John 19: 26-27)**

As we behold Jesus in his final agony on the cross we are inclined to think that he has nothing more to surrender. He has surrendered everything to his Father. Stripped of his clothes, of his authority, of his popular appeal, even of the loyalty of his closest followers, he still has one last mission to accomplish, *the surrender of his mother!*

He surrenders her to the only disciple who had remained faithful, the beloved John: *Woman, here is your son!* These words of the dying Jesus confirm the fact that Jesus was an *only son*. Had there been any close relative, he could not have done so under Jewish law of which Jesus was the perfect fulfilment. However, there is a far deeper spiritual message in the words of Jesus. And that is the confirmation of the *spiritual motherhood of Mary* for all the redeemed. John, as the representative of all mankind, accepted this trust of Jesus. Hence Calvary, and the agony of all that surrounds it, represents Mary's pangs of labour in her *spiritual* childbirth. In that spiritual and mystical passion the *motherhood* of the future Church is entrusted to her. Mary is not simply an accident of history, standing forlorn beneath the cross on Calvary, she is destined to play an integral part in God's salvific will in the drama of our redemption.

2. Mary's 'Compassion'

The sword, prophesied by the aged Simeon, was now driven up to the very hilt into Mary's heart! Every mother feels the pain and the suffering of her beloved child. This is no less true of Mary in seeing her beloved Son in the agony of torture and crucifixion. She is not merely a passive spectator. She is united to him in a *mystical* crucifixion that rivets her Immaculate Heart to the Cross! Here we may recall the solemn prophecy of Simeon, who, in predicting Jesus to become a sign of contradiction, made this prophecy concerning his mother!

> **and a sword will pierce your own soul too.**
> **(Luke 2:35)**

The death of anyone is always news, for it represents the sudden end of a life lived in the dimensions of time and space. The dramatic impact of those moments just before death gives an unusual importance to anything said. The words of a dying man gain a special significance. But what must be said of such circumstances when *it is one who claims divinity as "The Son of God" is dying?* His words from the Cross are invested with the utmost solemnity. They are, as it were, *the last will and testament of Jesus to all mankind.* The words, therefore, addressed to Mary and to John take on, in such a solemn context, the most profound Messianic significance. **Woman, behold thy son**! It is, moreover, a remarkable fact that Jesus, the *Son of Mary*, in this most solemn moment of redemption addresses her as *'Woman'!* This has been the source of much misunderstanding. It has often been interpreted as something either *demeaning* or a reproach. Under the circumstances such interpretations must be dismissed as incomprehensible! We must, once again, go back to the primordial trial of Eden, and the curse pronounced on the serpent. Here Jesus seals that solemn prophecy made at the dawn of history, when God promised perpetual enmity between Satan and the *'Woman'*. This is all summed up in the words of Vatican II:

> Thus the Blessed Virgin advanced in her pilgrimage of faith, and faithfully persevered in her union with her Son unto the cross. There she stood, in keeping with the divine plan, enduring with her only begotten Son the intensity of his suffering, joining herself with his sacrifice in her mother's heart, and lovingly consenting to the immolation of this victim, born of her: to be given, by the same Christ Jesus dying on the cross, as a mother to his disciple, with these words: Woman behold your son! [98]
>
> (Lumen Gentium #58)

---

[98] *Lumen Gentium 58 commenting on John 19:26-27*

3. Mary's Spiritual Motherhood

Between the woman, predestined to be the *new Eve*, and Lucifer there would be waged an unrelenting warfare. It is at the foot of the Cross that Mary becomes the new Eve. In her *compassion,* that is in her union with her dying Son, she endures the travail of a spiritual childbirth. It is the birth of the Church flowing from the side of Christ. No words can describe the suffering of any mother who is compelled to watch the agony of a dying son. Likewise, no words can possibly describe the agony of Mary in beholding the terrible sufferings of the dying Jesus. This is already seen in the *Book of Revelation* where Mary, *clothed with the sun* (Rev. 12:1) is depicted in the agony of childbirth:

> **She was pregnant and was crying out in birth pangs,**
> **in the agony of giving birth.**
> **(Revelation 12:2)**

In these birth pangs Mary became the Mother of all those who were being redeemed in the Blood of her Son. This *'woman'* was to be the *new Eve* associated with the new Adam in the re-creation of the fallen world! However, in addressing John, Jesus now uses the term *'Mother'*. The whole human race is confided to Mary in the person of John.

4. Mary, the Second Eve!

The Gospel records that John took Mary *into his own home*. However, the Greek original *eis ta idia* means far more than a purely physical space. It means that Mary became part of his life, an integral part of his *spiritual space!* These words of Jesus, therefore, give us a whole new insight into the role that Mary should play in our own lives, and in the life of the church.

From the second century, from the days of St Irenaeus and of St Justin the Martyr the comparison between Mary and Eve was commonplace. Mary is the *second* Eve, just as Jesus is the *second* Adam. Particularly during the past 100 years it has been repeated time and again by the Supreme Pontiffs of the Church. Eve, as the mother of all the living, finds her spiritual and redemptive counterpart in Mary. They throw light on the active role that Mary played in the drama of redemption by using such terms as *co-Redemptrix, co-operatrix* or *adjutrix*. Beneath the shadow of the *tree of good and evil* Eve prevailed on Adam to savour the *fruit of death* not only for themselves but for all her children. So, likewise, beneath the shadow of the *Tree of the Cross* the second Adam conferred on the second Eve the spiritual maternity of all humanity. This is portrayed beautifully by Pope Pius XII in his encyclical on the Mystical Body:

> *Free from all sin, original and personal, always most intimately united with her Son, as another Eve, she offered Him on Golgotha to the eternal Father for all the children of Adam, sin-stained by his fall, and her mother's rights and mother love included in the holocaust.*
>
> *Thus she who corporally was the mother of the Head, through the added title of pain and glory, became spiritually the mother of all His members . . . . and she continued to show for the Mystical Body of Christ . . . the same mother's care and ardent love with which she clasped the infant Jesus to her warm and nourishing breast!* [99]

(d) The Mystery of the Cross

1. The Challenge of the Cross

The *Wisdom of the Cross* is the secret of the saints and the key to their holiness. As St Louis Grignion de Montfort expressed it:

> *The Cross is, according to my belief,*
> *the greatest secret of the King*
> *—the greatest secret of Eternal Wisdom.* [100]

The *scandal of the Cross* is a constant challenge to the world! Cocooned in the comforts of the twenty-first century, we do not want our lives

---

[99] *Pius XII in "Mystici Corporis" #108*
[100] *God Alone: The Collected Writings of St Louis Grignon de Montfort (Montfort Publications, 1987) p.95.*

of ease and comfort to be disturbed. We, therefore, strenuously resist any attempts to dislodge us from our petty routines and disturb our comfort-zone! The Cross casts a long shadow across these routines of earthly indulgence. Prosperity, it has been said, is bad for religion, for it shuns the Cross! Nevertheless, it is a fundamental fact of life that material things cannot satisfy our innermost yearnings. There is a restlessness in the human spirit that pines for spiritual fulfilment.

St Augustine expressed it so wonderfully:

> *Thou hast made us for Thyself, O God,*
> *and our hearts are restless until they rest in Thee!*

It is but natural for us to flee from the *Cross*. It is unpleasant to be stricken with illness or affliction in any form. We avoid discomfort of any kind and seek feverishly for what is pleasing to the self and the senses. But sensual pleasure soon palls. That is the way of the world which has its eyes very firmly fixed on the here and now. But as the Catechism assures us:

> *Suffering, a consequence of original sin, acquires a new meaning;*
> *it becomes a participation in the saving work of Jesus.* (#1521)

2. The Burden of the Cross

In weighing the balance of reparation, we must go far beyond the fall of Adam and Eve. Jesus had to expiate, not only their sins, but the sins of the whole of humanity, that is, the entire burden of humanity's sinfulness down to the last trespass of the last sinner on earth. There lay the ultimate burden of Gethsemane and the burden of the Cross. It is in the light of that terrible burden that we find St Thomas and the Fathers of the Church unanimous in concluding that Jesus suffered far more than all the martyrs of the Old Dispensation, and far surpassed the sufferings of all those destined to die for the sake of his name! The offering of himself in a *holocaust of suffering* was why he came down from Heaven, for the forgiveness of our sins! It has been said that until we know the full reality of the Cross and penetrate its secret we cannot really claim to know Jesus! When he cried out from the Cross; *I thirst!* for what was he thirsting?

St Laurence Justinian[101] gives us the answer:

> *His thirst arose from the ardour of his love,*
> *from the depth and the abundance of his charity.*
> *He was thirsting for us, thirsting to give*
> *himself to us and to suffer for us!*
> *No wonder that the saints bemoaned our failure*
> *to appreciate the deep love God has for us . . . .*

O Love, how little you are known! (St Mary Magdalene de' Pazzi)
Jesus, my crucified Love, is not loved! (St Francis of Assisi)

3. *The Wisdom of the Cross*

The mystery of the Cross is also a call to the hidden wisdom of the Cross. The shadow of the Cross lies athwart the centuries. Its tragedy is re-enacted in every age, in the sins and failures of countless generations. As the Catechism of the Council of Trent spells it out:

> *Since our sins made the Lord Christ suffer the torments of the Cross, those who plunge themselves into disorders and crimes crucify the Son of God anew in their hearts (for he is in them) and hold him up to contempt. And it can be seen that our crime in this case is greater in us than in the Jews. As for them, according to the witness of the Apostle: "None of the rulers of this age understood this ; for if they had, they would not have crucified the Lord of glory." We, however, profess to know him!*

So why do we search for the secret of *the Wisdom of the Cross?* Wisdom lies in accepting it, nay, in embracing it in the difficulties and trials of life, and in seeing God's hand in our upsets and misfortunes. The whole burden of Christ's messsge is an exaltation of the cross. It can be summarised as follows:

---

[101] *St Lawrence Justinian (1381-1455) Archbishop of Venice 1451, author of several mystical treatises.*

1. *It makes us resemble Jesus Christ, whose name we bear as Christians!*
2. *It makes us more acceptable to the Father who sees the suffering Jesus in us.*
3. *The Cross is a light to the mind and gives us a spiritual insight that no book can give.*
4. *Accepting the Cross is a proof of the deepest love.*
5. *Embracing the Cross opens the floodgates of heavenly delight and consolation.*
6. *Carrying the Cross brings with it a weight of everlasting glory.*[102]

Or, as Paul himself exclaimed so eloquently:

> **For Jews demand signs and Greeks desire wisdom,**
> **but we proclaim Christ crucified, a stumbling block to Jews**
> **and foolishness to Gentiles, but to those who are the called,**
> **both Jews and Greeks,**
> **Christ the power of God and the wisdom of God.**
> **For God's foolishness is wiser than human wisdom,**
> **and God's weakness is stronger than human strength.**
> **(1 Corinthians 1:22-25)**

---

[102] *This is a condensation of the thought of St Louis Grignon de Montfort in "God Alone" op.cit. p.98*

Questions #8

* * *

1. What do you say about crucifixion and its origins and what does Cicero say about it?

2. Why were the public authorities so determined on the crucifixion of Jesus?

3. What do these words signify: the stipes, the patibulum, Golgotha and Calvary?

4. What do you understand about the 'Hour' and how can the Hour of Darkness be also the Hour of Glory?

5. Why did Jesus choose such a terrible and such an ignominious way to die?

6. The Passion of Jesus was a spiritual crucifixion as well as being a physical one. Explain!

7. What was the last will and testament of Jesus?

8. We are all co-conspirators in Jesus' death on the Cross? Comments?

9. What have you to say on these titles of Mary: Co-redemptrix, the Second Eve, our Mother in the Spirit?

10. What do you understand by the "Wisdom of the Cross?"

11. What does Thomas a Kempis say about our attitude to the Cross?

12. What are your own personal reflections on this subject?

9. HE DIED!

* * *

(a) The Death of Jesus
    —1. The Conquest of Death
    —2. The Aftermath of Death
    —3. The Witness of Nature
    —4. "It is Finished!"

(b) The Significance of Christ's Death
    —1. Surrendering to Death!
    —2. Jesus the Second Adam
    —3. "Dying to Sin!"
    —4. Ultimate Love!

(c) Death of the Old Dispensation
    —1. The Transcendence of the Death of Jesus
    —2. The Heart of Jesus
    —3. The Ratification of the New Covenant
    —4. The Obedience of Jesus

(d) Ultimate Meaning
    —1. The Doctrine of Atonement-
    —2. Atonement and Reconciliation
    —3. Atonement and Redemption
    —4. Our Baptism into His Death!

9. He Died!

* * *

(a) The Death of Jesus!

1. *The Conquest of Death!!*

> *Then Jesus gave a loud cry and breathed forth his spirit.*
> **(Mark 15 : 37)**

The Gospel account also emphasises the drama that attended the death of Jesus. This *'loud cry'* so impressed the centurion that he was obliged to confess to the extraordinary character of the victim on the Cross!

> *'Truly this man was God's Son!'*
> **(Mark 15 : 39)**

As one in charge of the execution, and who had witnessed so many crucifixions in the course of his career, the centurion realised that the loud cry of Jesus was not the impotent cry of one in extremity, but one of complete consciousness and control. It fulfilled Jesus' own words:

> *For this reason the Father loves me, because I lay down my life in order to take it up again. No one takes it from me, but I lay it down of my own accord. I have power to lay it down, and I have power to take it up again.*
> **(John 10 : 17-18)**

There is always something dramatic, even riveting, about a person's entry into the world and in his (or her) departure from it. In the case of one dying a special importance is attached to the words that are uttered by the one dying as a final farewell to the world. Jesus also foretold the manner of His death:

> *And I, when I am lifted up from the earth, will draw all people to myself.*
> **(John 15:32)**

Jesus is, in effect, saying that he was going to choose death in one of its most horrifying forms. By the same token *Christ conquered Death!* to use the language of an early Christian hymn. Here lies the divine *paradox!* In freely submitting to *death* Jesus also *conquered* it! We must never forget that Jesus *chose* death, and death in its most terrible form—*crucifixion*!

Moreover, he could have chosen other ways of dying, but he chose one that demonstrated God's divine and infinite love for man, on the one hand, and the horror and the heinousness of sin, on the other. The death of Jesus is, in itself, a proclamation of His full humanity, that He was *truly man*. Moreover, as the first born of all creation He had to show His victory over death by first of all dying. It was the prelude to the resurrection, winning for us all the pledge of eternal life!

> *The last enemy to be destroyed is death.*
> **(1 Corinthians 15:26)**

2. The Aftermath of Death

> *But when they came to Jesus and saw that he was already dead, they did not break his legs. One of the soldiers pierced his side with a spear, and at once blood and water came out.*
> **(John 19:33-34)**

Jesus was spared the *crurifragium*, that is, the traditional *breaking of the legs*, when death was a matter of urgency. In crucifixion the victim was usually able to survive for some time by raising his body on the nails of the feet in order to sustain the effort to breathe. When the legs were broken, this became impossible. The proximity of the Passover demanded death as quickly as possible. The presence of a corpse that was not disposed of before sundown would have polluted the celebrations. The final act of desecration was the piercing of the side of Jesus by *Longinus*. Nevertheless, it was also a precious revelation of the love of Jesus in the shedding of His blood, the price of our redemption, to the last drop. It was also the fulfilment of the Old Testament prophecy:

> *And I will pour out a spirit of compassion and supplication on the house of David and the inhabitants of*

> *Jerusalem, so that, when they look on the one whom they have pierced, they shall mourn for him, as one mourns for an only child, and weep bitterly over him, as one weeps over a firstborn.*
>
> **(Zechariah 12:10)**

3. The 'Witness' of Nature!

> *Then Jesus cried again with a loud voice and breathed his last. At that moment the curtain of the temple was torn in two, from top to bottom.*
> *The earth shook, and the rocks were split.*
>
> **(Matthew 27:50-51)**

As if to underscore the immense significance of Jesus' death, nature itself was convulsed at the death of Jesus. The extraordinary events surrounding this death emphasise the importance of the event and its significance in the economy of salvation. Not only was the visible and material world of the senses covered with darkness, as if nature itself mourned the death of Jesus. There was an earthquake and the nether world of the dead also gave up its prey in homage and recognition of the redemption that was being wrought. We know little else about those who rose from the dead other than what the scripture tells us. But this convulsion of nature points to this central event in mankind's history—*the death of the God-Man!*

As we have already noted, Jesus *deliberately* chose this most infamous mode of dying. He said himself that he had both the power to lay his life down and the power to take it up again! In this he remains the conqueror of death. Here is the climax of God's creative efforts, and the fulfilment of all His promises, fulfilled in the death of the Father's Beloved Son!

> *For I handed on to you as of first importance*
> *what I in turn had received:*
> *that Christ died for our sins in accordance with the scriptures.*
>
> **(1 Corinthians 15 : 3)**

This was all the more important in view of the *Gnostic* heresies that denied the humanity of Jesus. Since matter was evil he could not be truly man! Therefore, Jesus did not *really* die! Here in his letter St Paul is at pains to point out to his converts this central fact of the Gospel and the full meaning of the death of Jesus, *that He died for our sins.* Death was also the necessary prelude to resurrection.

> *But he was wounded for our transgressions,*
> *crushed for our iniquities;*
> *upon him was the punishment that made us whole,*
> *and by his bruises we are healed.*
> **(Isaiah 53:4-5)**

4. "It is Finished!"

> *When Jesus had received the wine, he said, "It is finished."*
> *Then he bowed his head and gave up his spirit.*
> **(John 19:30)**

These mysterious words of Jesus have provoked furious controversy in finding an answer to the question: *What was finished?* It is evident that Jesus' life on earth was finished, for death put an end to his public ministry. But to what does the *'It'* refer to in the phrase *'It is finished'*?

It is possible to hasard a guess that the *work of Redemption* had been completed. The task that the Father had assigned him to do was over. The sovereign will of his Father had ruled his life and was, even now, manifest in his death! Moreover, the long reign of Satan over sinful man was at an end. Man's mysterious subjection to the Devil, that had gone on since the expulsion of Adam and Eve from the Garden of Eden, was finished! The Satanic dominion that had reigned almost unchecked for millennia was over. In his decree *Firmiter* Pope Eugenius IV (15th. century) had said on this topic:

> *No one has ever been liberated from the domination of the Devil*
> *save by the merit of the Mediator, (Jesus)*

The primary effect of Christ's sacrifice on Calvary was to cut the bonds of the *slavery* that had bound Adam and all his descendants. Now Satan's earthly sovereignty was destroyed, and the breach between man and God was now healed. As St John says in one of his letters:

> *Everyone who commits sin is a child of the devil; for the devil has been sinning from the beginning. The Son of God was revealed for this purpose, to destroy the works of the devil.*
> **(1 John 3:8)**

(b) Significance of Christ's Death?

1. Surrendering to Death!

> *Then Jesus, crying with a loud voice, said,*
> *'Father, into your hands I commend my spirit.'*
> *Having said this, he breathed his last.*
> **(Luke 23 : 46)**

Death is a dramatic moment in the life of any individual. Its very finality brings to an end all the hopes, dreams and ambitions of life. It is the entire fate of mankind, and the source of endless tragedy. Our mortality, however, was not part of the humanity of Jesus. He was not subject to this penalty of our human nature, which was part and parcel of the condemnation inflicted upon our first parents. Death was part of God's judgement on Adam and Eve for their disobedience in eating of the tree of the knowledge of *good and evil.* (Genesis 2 : 17)

> *For the wages of sin is death.*
> **(Romans 6:23)**

But Jesus was the *'Sinless One'*. The very fact of the union of His human nature with that of the Divine would have automatically excluded any claims that death might have had upon Him. The Letter to the Hebrews gives us the clue to the answer taking its theme from the Psalms:

> *I know all the birds of the air, and all that moves in the field is mine.*
> *If I were hungry, I would not tell you, for the world and all that is in it is mine.*
> *Do I eat the flesh of bulls, or drink the blood of goats?*
> *Offer to God a sacrifice of thanksgiving.*
> **(Psalm 50:12-14)**

Its author takes this theme and underscores the fruitlessness of all human efforts to appease God's wrath. *What is the point of sacrificing to God created things? They all belong to him in the first place!* So the writer envisages Jesus thinking on the matter!

> ***Consequently, when Christ came into the world, he said, "Sacrifices and offerings you have not desired, but a body you have prepared for me; in burnt offerings and sin offerings you have taken no pleasure." Then I said, "See, God, I have come to do your will, O God in the scroll of the book it is written of me." When he said above, "You have neither desired nor taken pleasure in sacrifices and offerings and burnt offerings and sin offerings" (these are offered according to the law), then he added, "See, I have come to do your will."***
> **(Hebrews 10:-5-9)**

2. Jesus, the Second Adam!

To honour the Father and glorify his name Jesus came among us. Jesus became the *Second Adam, the first born of all creation!* As the new head of the human race that was sorely in need of the restoration of God's friendship, he took upon Himself, freely and willingly, the full consequences of the sin of our first parents. Only the God-man could restore man's original dignity as the friend of God. As *man* Jesus could now do what only man could do, that is, *he could suffer and die!* As *God* He could do what only God could do, that is,

> *he could restore the original supernatural dignity of fallen man!*

Death was part of his *destiny* as our Redeemer! It was therefore most fitting that Jesus should endure the full penalty of all humanity in taking upon Himself the burden of our sins and all their consequences. He took up the Cross, freely, deliberately, and even joyfully, in obedience to the wishes of His Father, surrendering Himself completely to the full gamut of a criminal's cruel death.

> ***The death he died, he died to sin, once for all.***
> **(Romans 6 : 10)**

3. 'Dying to Sin'!

The death of Jesus *'to sin'* is ultimately beyond our comprehension, for we do not fully understand the gravity and the heinousness of sin itself. We are so *immersed* in it as a result of the Fall that we fail to grasp the inner meaning of the Cross. Fulton Sheen endeavoured to put it in perspective when he wrote:

> *To most men the burden of sin is as natural as the clothes they wear, but to Him (Jesus) the touch of that which men take so easily was the veriest agony.*[103]

But it was not merely the *'touch of sin'* that Jesus experienced but He was *immersed* in it. As St Paul himself says: *He became sin itself!* That was Gethsemane's hidden and terrible torment:

> **For our sake he made him to be sin who knew no sin,**
> **so that in him we might become the righteousness of God.**
> **(2 Corinthians 5 : 21)**

We can therefore understand why the universal Catechism makes the point that Jesus not merely died but *'tasted death'* to the full. Every nuance of an agonising death, even to the abandonment by His Father, was undergone for our sakes. It is, therefore, possible, to construe the whole drama of the crucifixion as a form of an immense conspiracy by mankind to execute Jesus! This is the sense of the words of St Francis of Assisi:

> *Nor did demons crucify him, it is you who have crucified him and crucify him still, when you delight in your sins and vices.*[104]

> *By the grace of God Jesus tasted death 'for every one'. In his plan of salvation, God ordained that His Son should, not only 'die for our sins', but should also 'taste death', experience the condition*

---

[103] *Fulton Sheen: The Life of Christ (Doubleday, 1990) p.321.*
[104] *St Francis of Assisi: Admonitio 5,3 (quoted in the CCC #598)*

> *of death, the separation of his soul from his body, between the time he expired on the cross and the time he was raised from the dead. (#624)*[105]

If there is one outstanding lesson in the death of Jesus, it is a glimpse of the enormity of sin as an offence against the *holiness* of God. Mankind had accumulated an enormous and *un-repayable* debt, and, unfortunately, is still adding to that debt before God. Jesus undertook to wipe out that debt in its entirety. *How can we ever repay Jesus for wiping out our mountainous debt of corruption and moral failure?* The answer is obvious. There is nothing in this world, nothing in the entire field of human endeavour, that can repay the debt that mankind has contracted. It is, therefore, all the more imperative that we manifest unfailing gratitude to the Eternal Father for this wondrous gift of redemption in Jesus.

> *No one has greater love than this,*
> *to lay down one's life for one's friends.*
> **(John 15 : 13)**

4. Ultimate Love!

Jesus exemplified in his own person the last extremity of love to which a person would go in order to manifest that love. Jesus died for all men, for all who were sinners. No one was to be excluded from the salvific love of Jesus.

> *For while we were still weak, at the right time Christ died for the ungodly.*
> *Indeed, rarely will anyone die for a righteous person—though perhaps for a good person someone might actually dare to die. But God proves his love for us in that while we still were sinners Christ died for us.*
> **(Romans 5 : 6-8)**

We all instinctively fear death. The fear of death comes as a natural consequence of sin. It is part of the primeval curse. As far as this world

---

[105] CCC

is concerned, death is the greatest of all human tragedies. This is all too apparent when we read the obituaries especially of the young. It appears to sound the death knell of all their dearest hopes and aspirations. In some cemeteries this is symbolised by a broken column, a monument to a life, unfinished and unfulfilled!

But, by the Cross, by submitting to the ignominy of the crucifixion, Jesus robbed death of its power over us. It follows that the Cross, and all that surrounds it, has become an integral part of Christian living. Hence, the Catechism spells out the necessity of following in the footsteps of Jesus on the way to Calvary:

> *The cross is the unique sacrifice of Christ, the 'one mediator between God and men.' (1 Tim. 2:5) But because in His incarnate divine person He has in some way united Himself to every man, ' the possibility of being made partners, in a way known to God, in the Paschal mystery' is offered to all men . . . . In fact Jesus desires to associate with His redeeming sacrifice those who were to be its first beneficiaries. This is achieved supremely in the case of His mother, who was associated more intimately than any other person in the mystery of His redemptive suffering.(#618)*

It goes on to quote a saying of St Rose of Lima:

> *Apart from the cross there is no other ladder*
> *by which we may get to heaven.*

(c) Death of the Old Dispensation

1. The Transcendence of the Death of Jesus!

At that moment the curtain of the temple was torn in two, from top to bottom. The earth shook, and the rocks were split. The tombs also were opened, and many bodies of the saints who had fallen asleep were raised.

(Matthew 27: 51,52)

It is important to keep reminding ourselves that the events of the life of Jesus transcends the boundaries of contemporary history. It is possible to look on Calvary like any other event in history. Historically, that is, it is a *'once for all'* happening that can never be replicated. However, the life of Jesus, his miracles and his teaching, and above all, his Passion and Death are far more than that. They are *transhistorical* or *transcendent*.

They are an integral part of salvation history. This means that the events of his life have consequences that go far beyond immediate and visible results. They resonate throughout the whole of God's dealings with mankind and the Chosen race. The life of Jesus is the culmination of Old Testament prophecy and with his death it all comes to an end. His life and death are now projected into the past for the redemption of all who sinned since the days of Adam and into the future for the salvation of all the generations to come, down to the end of time! Moreover, during His public ministry Jesus had referred to His own body as a temple:

> ***Destroy this temple, and in three days I will raise it up.***
> ***The Jews then said, 'This temple has been under construction for forty-six years, and will you raise it up in three days?'***
> ***But he was speaking of the temple of his body.***
> **(John 2 : 19-21)**

2. The Heart of Jesus

The Temple veil was a massive curtain, some 60' long and 30' wide, that shielded the *Holy of Holies*. It had the thickness of a man's palm. Indeed, it was so massive, that it was said, perhaps with edifying exaggeration, that it took some 300 priests to handle it! The fact that it was torn from top to bottom indicates that it was rent not by the hand of man, but rather by the hand of God! Its sundering has a mystic reference to the death of Jesus, to the rending of His humanity, to the separation of body and soul.

There is also an intimate connection between the rending of the temple veil and the opening of the side of Jesus. The lance of *Longinus*[106] pierced the heart of Jesus, revealing the new *Holy of Holies*, the new *Ark*

---

[106] *It is interesting to note that the Latin name 'Longinus' comes from the Greek word meaning 'lance' or 'spear'. Legend has it that he became a bishop and ultimately a martyr. His feast was held on March 15th.*

of the Covenant of the new dispensation of grace. It is worthy of note that the Passion and Death of Jesus, *the Lamb of God,* coincided with the Great Passover eve when thousands of lambs were slaughtered in preparation for the feast of the morrow. All this recalls the incidents of Exodus when the Israelites were spared the final plague of the death of the first-born by sprinkling the lintels of the doorways of their homes with *the blood of a lamb.* The lamb also recalled the *Pesach* or *Passover* of the destroying angel in Egypt. It was a *passing over* that ensured the safety of the Chosen People. God ordered a perpetual remembrance of it and his will was carried out by Moses in the fulfilling of the Covenant. He erected an altar with 12 pillars. Taking the blood of the sacrifice he poured half on the altar, and the other half on the twelve tribes with these words:

> **See the blood of the covenant**
> **that the LORD has made with you**
> **in accordance with all these words.**
> **(Exodus 24:8)**

3. Ratification of the New Covenant

Here, both at the Last Supper and on Calvary, Jesus now ratifies the New Testament or Covenant with His own blood! The two events are inextricably intertwined in Jesus' own words. This covenant was ratified in the presence of the 12 pillars of the *New Israel,* the apostles, the *patriarchs* of the new dispensation. The Fathers of the Church saw an indissoluble link between *Calvary* and the *Upper Room* where Jesus issued his sacramental command as he offered the chalice to his followers. It must be underscored that it is the Lord's command as a sign of the New Covenant and that the whole purpose is to set man's relationship with God aright.

> ***Drink of it all of you; for this is my blood of the covenant,***
> ***which is poured out for many for the forgiveness of sins.***
> **(Matthew 26:27)**

The *Blood of the Lamb* is the lifeblood of the Church, the *Mystical Body of Christ.* It flows through the sacramental system washing us, cleansing us, protecting us, comforting us, strengthening us in our pilgrimage to the promised land of eternity. In a special way it reminds us of the Eucharist with the transformation of the bread into the Body and Blood of Christ. Moreover, the water that flowed from the heart of Jesus also signified the sacrament of *Baptism*. It all begins in that initial ceremony wherein the newly baptised is incorporated into the body of the Church through the Passion and Death of Jesus.

4. *The Obedience of Jesus*

The Catechism summarises the sacrificial obedience of Jesus:

> (i) *The sacrifice of Christ is unique: it completes and surpasses all other sacrifices.*
>
> *First, it is a gift from God the Father himself, for the Father handed his Son over to sinners in order to reconcile us with himself. At the same time, it is the offering of the Son of God made man, who in freedom and love offered his life to his Father through the Holy Spirit, in reparation for our disobedience.* (#614)
>
> (ii) *Jesus atoned for our faults and made satisfaction for our sins to the Father.*[107] *(#615)*
>
> (iii) *Jesus substitutes his obedience for our disobedience.*

"For as by one man's disobedience many were made sinners, so by one man's obedience many will be made righteous"
                                                      (Romans 5:19)

> *By his obedience unto death, Jesus accomplished the substitution of the Suffering Servant, who makes himself an offering for sin, when he bore the sin of many, and who shall make many to be accounted righteous, for he shall bear their iniquities.*
>   (see **Isaiah 53: 10-12**)

---

[107] *This is a quote from the Council of Trent (1547 to1563)*

d) Ultimate Meaning!

1. The Doctrine of Atonement

The word *atonement* has the unique distinction of being the only word of Anglo-Saxon origin that has theological implications[108]. This word *atonement*, split into its components of *at-one-ment*, conveys the notion of *reuniting* parts that have been broken or separated.

In the Old Testament *atonement* meant the *re-establishment of communion!* The atonement is the work of divine mercy in the acceptance by Yahweh of certain sacrificial offerings[109]. As laid down in the Book of Leviticus, the High priest sacrificed a bull for his own sins and for the sins of the priests. This was the occasion, and the only occasion, that the High Priest was permitted to enter the *Holy of Holies,* and when he sprinkled the blood of sacrifice on the *mercy seat.* For the people a goat was sacrificed and the blood sprinkled in the sanctuary.

All this calls to mind, once again, the author of the letter to the Hebrews. There Jesus is depicted as the new High Priest, *who holds his priesthood permanently* (7:23). In general, it denotes the saving effect that flows from the death of Christ. Here there is also a reference to the opening up of the *Holy of Holies,* the abode of the special presence of God, *to the whole of fallen humanity.* Therefore, the author of Hebrews exclaims:

> *Therefore, my friends, since we have confidence to enter the sanctuary by the blood of Jesus, by the new and living way that he opened for us through the curtain (that is, through his flesh), and since we have a great priest over the house of God, let us approach with a true heart in full assurance of faith, with our hearts sprinkled clean from an evil conscience and our bodies washed with pure water.*
> **(Hebrews 10: 9-22)**

The rending of the veil of the temple was also a portent of catastrophe. As such, it was recorded even by secular historians such as Tacitus and

---

[108] see also New Catholic Encyclopedia vol.1 p.836

[109] *Feast of Yom Kippur or the Jewish Day of Atonement (held in September or October) which recalls the ancient ritual recorded in Leviticus ch.4..*

Josephus, as well as in the *Talmud* itself. However, although it foretells the destruction of the Temple and of the Holy City, it is a sign of the rending of the Old Covenant and the institution of the New. We must not forget the most solemn words of Jesus at the Last Supper when he instituted the sacrament of the Eucharist:

> *This cup that is poured out for you*
> *is the new covenant in my blood.*
> **(Luke 22:20)**

2. Atonement as Reconciliation

> *But God proves his love for us in that while we still were sinners Christ died for us. Much more surely then, now that we have been justified by his blood, will we be saved through him from the wrath of God.*
> *For if while we were enemies, we were reconciled to God through the death of his Son, much more surely, having been reconciled, will we be saved by his life.*
> **(Romans 5:8-10)**

Here St Paul introduces us to atonement as *reconciliation*. The Greek word Paul uses is *katallage*, a word borrowed from the culture of the money traders! It brings to mind the *adjustment of differences*, or *striking a balance*, in a word, *reconciliation!* It is, therefore, the restoration of God's favour to those sinners who repent and put their trust in the saving power of Christ's sacrifice St Paul's words may be taken as a summary of Christ's atonement for our sins and as a reparation of the breach between God and man. Theologically, it emphasises once again the notion of *restoring the relationship* that had been broken by our first parents. Jesus, with his death on the cross, repairs the damage that our first parents had done, and retrieves the divine friendship that had been lost for so long.

However, in pursuing this notion of atonement, one cannot, and must not, isolate the death of Jesus from his life. Fundamentally, the doctrine of the atonement rests ultimately on the fact of the Incarnation. From the first moment that the Word entered the womb of Mary, the work of atonement began. This is the point that St Paul makes when he wrote:

> *But when the fullness of time had come, God sent his Son, born of a woman, born under the law, in order to redeem those who were under the law, so that we might receive adoption as children.*
> **(Galatians 4:4-5)**

It reached its climax on that ignominious death on Calvary, and was sealed with the Resurrection from the dead. Hence the work of the atonement is all of a piece from the first moment of the Incarnation to the last breath of Jesus on the Cross and in his resurrection from the dead. Nevertheless, it is *Calvary* where Jesus breathed his last, and surrendered himself totally to his Father's will, that is, from a purely human standpoint, the most dramatic moment of this doctrine of atonement. Here again St Paul becomes more specific in his letter:

> *Since all have sinned and fall short of the glory of God;*
> *they are now justified by his grace as a gift,*
> *through the redemption that is in Christ Jesus,*
> *whom God put forward*
> *as a sacrifice of atonement by his blood,*
> *effective through faith.*
> **(Romans 3:23-24)**

3. Atonement and Redemption

The word *redemptio* is the Latin Vulgate rendering of Hebrew *kopher* and Greek *lytron* which, in the Old Testament means generally a *ransom-price*. Literally, it means *a buying back!* In the New Testament, it is the classic term designating the *"great price"* which the Redeemer paid for our spiritual liberation. It is to this St Paul refers when he writes:

> *For you were bought with a price;*
> *therefore glorify God in your body.*
> **(1 Corinthians 6:20)**

These words of St Paul gave rise to the idea of redemption as a form of business transaction in which Jesus bought us back from the slavery of Satan. The price paid was the blood of Christ. It is an expressive image, but that of St Peter is even more so!

> *You know that you were ransomed*
> *from the futile ways inherited from your ancestors,*
> *not with perishable things like silver or gold,*
> *but with the precious blood of Christ,*
> *like that of a lamb without defect or blemish.*
> **(1 Peter 1: 18-19)**

All the benefits of Christ's sacrifice and the shedding of his blood would be useless were they not available to us here and now. It would be like people standing on one side of a river where there is a raging famine and all are dying of hunger while on the other side of the river there is an abundance of food and no means of conveying it across! So atonement becomes very personal when we seek to avail ourselves of the fruits of Christ's atonement. The atonement still goes on. And it still goes on in the liturgical and sacramental life of the Church, and in the incessant intercession of Jesus, seated at the right hand of the Father, and pleading with him on our behalf!

> *Consequently he is able for all time to save those who approach*
> *God through him, since he always lives to make intercession for*
> *them.*
> **(Hebrews 7:25)**

4. Our Baptism into His Death!

> *Do you not know that all of us*
> *who have been baptised into Christ Jesus*
> *were baptised into his death?*
> **(Romans 6:3)**

It is evident that atonement has special relevance to the sacrament of Baptism. St Thomas Aquinas in commenting on St Paul emphasises the reality of this *baptism into the death of Jesus!* What he wishes to emphasise is that the sacramental washing in Baptism is, so to speak, a re-enactment of the Passion, Death and Resurrection of Jesus in the life of the one baptised.

> *Hence it is clear that the Passion of Christ is communicated to every baptised person so that he (or she) is healed as if he himself had suffered and died.*

These words of the Angelic Doctor are telling us, in effect, that the untold and yet unborn billions who were destined to be baptised throughout the life of the Church were all *crucified and that they all died* in the Passion and Death of their Lord and Saviour! That is the meaning of Paul's own phrase, *baptised into his death!* Moreover, every time we go to Mass we bring to mind the memory of this astonishing sacrifice that Jesus made for us, for our redemption and salvation. It gives us the opportunity to express our thanks for God's amazing generosity. That is one reason why the ceremony is called the *Eucharist,* the *Thanksgiving!*

> *For as often as you eat this bread and drink this cup, you proclaim the Lord's death until he comes. Whoever, therefore, eats the bread or drinks the cup of the Lord in an unworthy manner will be answerable for the body and blood of the Lord.*
> **(1 Corinthians 11:26-27)**

++++++++++++++

All this is summed up in the Catechism:

> *Because of Christ, Christian death has a positive meaning: "For to me to live is Christ, and to die is gain." The saying is sure: if we have died with him, we will also live with him. What is essentially new about Christian death is this: through Baptism, the Christian has already "died with Christ" sacramentally, in order to live a new life; and if we die in Christ's grace, physical death completes this "dying with Christ" and so completes our incorporation into him in his redeeming act:. (#1010)*

Questions #9

* * *

1. *Did Jesus have to die?*

2. *If Jesus conquered death, why do we still die?*

3. *Nature was convulsed at the death of Jesus! Meaning?*

4. *The last words of Jesus: It is finished! What is finished?*

5. *What is meant by saying that Jesus is the Second Adam!*

6. *Jesus' death is a vivid demonstration of God's ultimate and infinite love! Explain!*

7. *The death of Jesus is a transcendent and a transhistorical event! Meaning?*

8. *Detail the significance of the following:*

    a. *The veil of the Temple was rent in two.*

    b. *The crurifragium*

c. *The piercing of the heart of Jesus, and the meaning of the blood & water flowing from his side.*

   d. *The link between the Upper Room and Calvary.*

9. *What do you understand by atonement, redemption and reconciliation?*

10. *What does St Paul mean in saying that we are baptised into the death of Jesus?*

11. *"We are all guilty of the death of Jesus!" Any comments?*

12. *What should the death of Jesus mean to you personally?*

10. (HE) WAS BURIED.
AND DESCENDED INTO HELL

* * *

(a) He was Buried
  —1. The Puzzle
  —2. A Possible Answer?
  —3. The Entombment
  —4. The Garden of Burial

(b) The Sacramental Answer
  —1. The Humblest part of the Creed!
  —2. A Unique Death
  —3. The Sacramental Burial in Baptism
  —4. The 'Second Day'
  —5. Our Spiritual Entombment

(c) The Burial of the Self
  —1. Newness of Life
  —2. The Challenge
  —3. Death to the Self!
  —4. The Foundation of Humility
  —5. A Balance

(d) He Descended into Hell
  —1. Another Puzzle
  —2. Life after Death (St Peter)
  —3. Preaching to the Dead!
  —4. The Liturgical Response

10. (He) was Buried.
and Descended into Hell

* * *

(a) He was Buried!

1. The Puzzle

Many commentators on the Creed are puzzled by this reference to the burial of Christ. Why should such an obvious consequence of his death be a fundamental matter of faith? The same idea occurs in the Nicene Creed. It would appear to be wholly redundant to emphasise that, after a person had died, he was *buried!* And yet it is to be found in the primitive *kerygma*, as St Paul is at pains to point out in his letter to the Corinthians:

> *For I handed on to you as of first importance what I in turn had received: that Christ died for our sins, in accordance with the scriptures, and that he was buried.*
> **(1 Corinthians 15:3-4)**

Here this fact of Jesus' burial following upon his death is treated as something of prime importance. In his preaching on his apostolic journeys he stresses the same. At Antioch in Pisidia the intrepid apostle, in outlining to the Jews of the *Diaspora* the history of their people, concluded with the life and death of Jesus and uttered the following:

> *Even though they found no cause for a sentence of death, they asked Pilate to have him killed. When they had carried out everything that was written about him, they took him down from the tree and laid him in a tomb.*
> **(Acts 13:28-29)**

Commentators, both ancient and modern, have been intrigued by this emphasis on the *burial* of Jesus in a tomb. However, the emphasis is to be found in scripture itself. The Gospel of Luke relates how Joseph of Arimathea went to Pilate for the release of the dead body of Jesus

> *and he laid it in a rock-hewn tomb where no one had ever been laid.*
> **(Luke 23:53)**

Some have argued that this emphasis on the burial was an answer to the *Docetists* who denied the true humanity of Jesus. They were a branch of the *Gnostics* who, in considering that matter was evil, denied that Jesus was truly man, that he was merely a phantom, a very substantial phantom, but a phantom, nonetheless[110]!

2. A Possible Answer?

He was buried! Here again we have the answer to the *Gnostics* that Jesus was truly a man, now dead and *buried!* Moreover, this stark and utterly prosaic statement points to the apparent failure of the life and message of Jesus. On the one hand, the compelling drama of the public life of Jesus with its marvellous healings and miracles alongside his authoritative and irresistible teachings had seemingly all fizzled out on Golgotha. On the other, the hopes and dreams of the apostles and disciples for an earthly kingdom and a resurgent Jewish nationalism were evidently now buried in the tomb with their beloved master. At the same time one is struck by certain aspects of this ceremony of entombment. The first thing we notice is the absence of the apostles. Save for John, they had all slunk into hiding, and it was two secret admirers of Jesus who now spring into prominence. According to Jewish ritual the body was to be buried on the day of death. But on this occasion, there was the added anxiety of performing the ceremony before sunset when the great feast of the Passover began.

3. The Entombment

Who, then, assisted Mary in the lugubrious task of disposing of the body?
The first was *Joseph of Arimathea*, a wealthy member of the Sanhedrin, and probably a dissenting one(?), who stood by Mary in her hour of sorrow, awaiting the permission of Pilate to dispose of the body. As a man of wealth and influence, he could easily make this request. The Synoptics describe him as one who was *looking for*

---

[110] *The issue of Gnosticism has already been discussed in the birth of the God-Man*

the kingdom of God[111]. In the Gospel of John, however, his quest was, understandably, very prudent and secretive. As a faithful Jew, he was concerned about the law and its decree of burying the body on the day of death. According to standard Roman practice the body of an executed criminal was usually left to hang on the cross to be savaged and devoured by vultures and wild animals. The second to spring to the help of Mary was *Nicodemus*[112] who had once come to Jesus by night in search of the Kingdom of God. He also provided the spices for anointing the body. As John tells us:

> *Nicodemus, who had at first come to Jesus by night, also came, bringing a mixture of myrrh and aloes, weighing about a hundred pounds.*
> **(John 19:39)**

Nicodemus was also the one who openly challenged the Sanhedrin about arresting Jesus:

> *"Our law does not judge people without first giving them a hearing to find out what they are doing, does it?" They replied, "Surely you are not also from Galilee, are you? Search and you will see that no prophet is to arise from Galilee."*
> **(John 7:51-52)**

4. The Garden of Burial

At a critical moment these secret admirers sprang to the fore. Their presence gives another possible answer to the question of why the burial of Jesus played so definite a role in the primitive *kerygma*. Joseph gave up his tomb for the burial of Jesus, and John relates:

> *Now there was a garden in the place where he was crucified, and in the garden there was a new tomb in which no one had ever been laid.*
> **(John 19:41)**

---

[111] *see Mark 15:43 and Luke 23:51*

[112] *A Greek name meaning "conqueor of the people".*

This tomb was close by to where Jesus was crucified. This immediately conjures up two other gardens. The first is the garden of *Eden* where the drama of redemption was born in the promise of a redeemer and that promise is now redeemed. The second garden is that of *Gethsemane* where the sorrows that were laid on mankind in the first were now transferred to the Redeemer. In this respect Bishop Fulton Sheen helps to shed another light on the question:

> *The word 'garden' hinted at Eden and the fall of man, as it also suggested, through its flowers in the springtime, the Resurrection from the dead. In that garden was the tomb in which 'no man had ever been buried'.*
> *Born of a virgin womb,*
> *He was buried in a virgin tomb!*

And as the English poet Crashaw[113] said:

> *And a Joseph did betroth them both.*
>
> *Nothing seems more repelling than to have a Crucifixion in a garden, and yet there would be a compensation, for the garden would have its Resurrection.*[114]

Here, at last, we have the final answer to our original question!

The burial of Jesus sets the stage for the Resurrection!

(b) The sacramental answer

1. "The humblest part of the Creed!"

Do you not know that all of us who have been baptised into Christ Jesus were baptised into his death?

---

[113] *Crashaw, an English poet (1613?-1649)*
[114] *quoted in Fulton Sheen: Life of Christ (Image Books, Doubleday 1990) p.401.*

> *Therefore we have been buried with him by baptism into death, so that, just as Christ was raised from the dead by the glory of the Father, so we too might walk in newness of life.*
> **(Romans 6:3-4)**

The Catechism has this to say about this aspect of Christ's death and burial:

> *The state of the dead Christ is the mystery of the tomb, and the descent into hell. It is the mystery of Holy Saturday, when Christ lying in the tomb, reveals God's great sabbath rest after the fulfilment of man's salvation, which brings peace to the whole universe.* (#624)

One writer, Karl Barth, calls the burial of Jesus 'the **humblest part of our symbol (creed)**'. It is a telling reminder, if one was needed, of the complete humanity of Jesus. This was something that he shared with all the descendants of Adam. He was now truly dead and buried and, in the hopes and plans of all his enemies, so was all that he had stood for. Even his closest friends, for the most part, appeared to think that it was all over! Their beloved Master and Lord was gone for good! They locked themselves away, as if all that he had taught them was also buried and all that remained was a memory of a life and ministry that had apparently come to nought!

2. A Unique Death & Burial

However, the death of Jesus was like no other. We must not forget that it was deliberately chosen. It highlights the indisputable fact that Jesus was truly man. It was an answer to all those who stoutly denied the humanity of Jesus. His death was not an illusion; it was no fiction. Now he was truly buried! It was all part of the divine plan. There was, however, a profound difference from all other burials! The Catechism seeks to put it all into its proper perspective:

> *Christ's death was a real death in that it put an end to his earthly human existence. But because of the union his body retained with the person of the Son, his was not a mortal*

corpse like others, for 'divine power preserved Christ's body from corruption.'[115]

Both of these statements can be said of Christ: 'He was cut off from the land of the living', and 'My flesh will dwell in hope. For you will not abandon my soul to Hades, nor let your Holy One see corruption.'[116] Jesus' Resurrection 'on the third day' was the proof of this for bodily decay was held to begin on the fourth day after death. (#627)

3. The Sacramental Burial in Baptism!

However, a profound sacramental lesson lay in this fact of the burial of Jesus. It had special reference to the sacrament of baptism with the total immersion of the catechumen in the waters of the death and burial of Jesus. Hence Paul could write to the Colossians:

> **You were buried with him in baptism,**
> **you were also raised with him through faith**
> **in the power of God, who raised him from the dead.**
> **(Colossians 2:12)**

It is instructive to consider how the early Church viewed it. St Cyril of Jerusalem (c.315-386 AD), in discussing the meaning of the *'mysteries'*. or sacraments, with reference to those who were newly baptised, refers to what was addressed to the catechumens in the Church of the Holy Sepulchre:

> *You were led to the holy pool of Divine baptism, as Christ was carried from the Cross to the Sepulchre which is before our eyes. And each of you was asked, whether he believed in the name of the Father and of the Son and of the Holy Spirit, and you made the saving confession and descended three times into the water, and ascended again; here also hinting by a symbol at the three days burial of Christ . . . . And at the selfsame moment you were both dying and being born; and that water of salvation was at once your grave and your mother . . . . There*

---

[115] *quoting Thomas Aquinas Summa III 51, 3-5*
[116] *see Acts 2:26*

was a time to die and a time to be born; and one and the same time effected both of these, and your birth went hand in hand with your death.

4. The Second Day

The Second Day *(Holy Saturday!)* of Christ's death marks the final sabbath of the Old Dispensation. God rested on the seventh day from all his labours as it appears in Genesis. Jesus is now resting from all the labours of his ministry. It is a pause in the divine plan of redemption. Now the world gets ready for a new creation which will be launched on the morrow in the Resurrection! Through Baptism we are *incorporated into Christ*. This is not simply a metaphor or a piece of religious poetry. It flows from what Christ endured for us. His sufferings were not imaginary or poetic or symbolic. They were a harsh and terrible reality endured for love of us.

So St Paul could write:

> **I have been crucified with Christ; and it is no longer I who live, but it is Christ who lives in me. And the life I now live in the flesh I live by faith in the Son of God, who loved me and gave himself for me.**
>
> **(Galatians 2:19-20)**

From which St Thomas concludes

> *His sufferings avail for us, as if we had suffered them ourselves*[117].

5. Our Spiritual Entombment!

The *mystical* logic in all of this is that we are now *in the tomb* awaiting the resurrection! We are in the spiritual tomb of death to this world and to all its false values. As St Paul writes:

> **So you also must consider yourselves dead to sin and alive to God in Christ Jesus. (Romans 6:11)**

---

[117] *Summa Theologica III q. 69*

Everything about Christ's life and death is profoundly relevant to us today. It is very tempting to read the events of his life as a wonderful story, and even, as something worthy of approval and praise, however superficial that might be. But, the facts of the life and death of the God-man go far beyond sympathy, admiration or eulogy. They have entered the very fabric of our world and of our existence. They can be ignored; they can be scorned or vilified; they can be treated as irrelevant. Nothing, however, can alter the historical fact that God became man and the world has been forever changed because of that central event. We in our faith can never be the same!

> *Therefore, we have been buried with him by baptism into death, so that, just as Christ was raised from the dead by the glory of the Father, so we too might walk in newness of life. For if we have been united with him in a death like his, we will certainly be united with him in a resurrection like his.*
> **(Romans 6: 4-5)**

(c) The Burial of the Self!

1. Newness of Life

> *We do not live to ourselves, and we do not die to ourselves. If we live, we live to the Lord, and if we die, we die to the Lord; so then, whether we live or whether we die, we are the Lord's.*
> **Romans 14:7-8)**

The death of Jesus and his burial raises issues that are inescapable. St Paul tells us that we must now walk *in newness of life.*(Romans 6:4). The supreme example for this model of newness of life is Jesus himself. The faithful get a start in this newness of life through the sacraments. Baptism opens the door to the life of God in the human soul, and it is nourished through the other sacraments at specific intervals in life. Confirmation brings a special presence of the Holy Spirit.

The Eucharist is the food of angels that sustains us in life's battles, and the sacrament of Reconciliation revives us when we fall wounded.

But in the intervals that lie between this reception of the sacraments, there is the spiritual imperative of living out our lives in the spirit of Christ himself. That is why we are called Christians; we are followers of Christ, and we have to follow him to the Hill of Calvary! That is where the problem begins and where the journey ends!!

2. The Challenge

We are forever dogged by the question of how to live out the sacramental moments that we experience only periodically, and bring them into the workaday world where most of our lives are spent. How do we achieve the abiding presence of Jesus in our lives? How can we reach the goal so briefly and so wonderfully expressed by St Paul:

> *I have been crucified with Christ; and it is no longer*
> *I who live, but it is Christ who lives in me.*
> *And the life I now live in the flesh I live by faith in the*
> *Son of God, who loved me and gave himself for me.*
> **(Galatians 2:19-20)**

Once more we are challenged by the magnificence of the goal and, at the same time, appalled by its terrors. We do not want to be crucified! Far from it, we prefer to get to heaven on our own terms, in comfort! We may be thrilled with the splendour of the Transfiguration and inspired by the Resurrection but we are apt to forget that Calvary lies between them. Every age has faced this challenge of how to imitate the life of Christ. Every aspect of that life is worthy of imitation. Jesus began his ministry by retiring into the desert, and this very fact has inspired thousands in the early centuries to pursue a life of self-denial on the grand scale. We have the example of St Paul, the first hermit, who spent 90 years in the desert, and that of the Abbot, St Anthony, who spent a paltry 60 years there! They were the forerunners of the Desert Fathers, whose stories of incredible self-sacrifice have left an indelible imprint on Christian mysticism. But all who seek to follow Christ, whatever their walk in life, must seek to put to death the incessant demands of our wayward selfishness.

3. Death to the Self!

Even though in the twenty-first century the remarkable stories of the saints of old, may sound more like fairy tales, there lies a common thread that appears to bring the goal much closer to us. This is the death and *burial of the self*. What does this mean? It revolves around the command of Jesus himself. Though he left many commands in relation to the Church, there is one specific command that goes out to every individual. It is the only command that he has asked us to learn from him!

> *Take my yoke upon you, and learn from me;*
> *for I am gentle and humble in heart,*
> *and you will find rest for your souls.*
> **(Matthew 11:29-30)**

Humility is what Jesus commanded us to learn from him, and humility will bring gentleness in its train. It is quite unlikely that we will ever be beheaded like John the Baptist, or that we will be nailed to a cross like Jesus himself. But opportunities will never be lacking for humility and self-denial. Our culture is utterly opposed to the demands of humility. On the contrary, self-promotion is the order of the day. *To get on* I must push myself forward. I must advertise myself, highlight my abilities, my accomplishments and anything else that will propel me up the ladder of success. That is the way of the world, but it does not foster humility!

4. The Foundation of Humility

Humility is the foundation of the spiritual life. There is absolutely no progress without it! Humility, however, runs counter to all our human instincts of self-promotion. However, it is not the inverted type of humility displayed by one of Dickens' characters, Uriah Heep:

> *I'm a very 'umble person . . . . My mother is, likewise. a very 'umble person. We live in a 'umble abode, Master Copperfield, but 'ave much to be thankful for!*

This is what is called *humility with a hook*, because it is, in reality, fishing for compliments! True humility, on the contrary, is a supernatural virtue by which a person is enabled to make a true and just estimate of himself (or herself) and hold his accomplishments in contempt in recognition that all good comes from God alone[118]

St Ignatius calls it a relinquishment of *'self-will, self-love, and self-interest'*.

This is most evident in the parable that Jesus related about *some who trusted in themselves that they were righteous and regarded others with contempt!*

> *Two men went up to the temple to pray, one a Pharisee and the other a tax collector . . . .*
> *But the tax collector, standing far off, would not even look up to heaven, but was beating his breast and saying, 'God, be merciful to me, a sinner!'*
> *I tell you, this man went down to his home justified rather than the other; for all who exalt themselves will be humbled, but all who humble themselves will be exalted.*
> **(Luke 18:10-14)**

Above all, there is the example of Jesus himself who lived a life of poverty and obscurity for thirty years in submission to his parents! In his public life he submitted himself to misunderstanding and persecution, endured the insults and maltreatment of his enemies and, finally, embraced the most horrible of deaths at the very hands of those he had come to save!

5. A Balance

Humility, however, is not a denial of personal gifts or achievements, but a constant recognition of the origin of these gifts and our accomplishments. Therefore, it is a positive outlook in not striving for notice or the seeking of honours. All this, naturally, runs counter to

---

[118] *The Catholic Encyclopedia (Nelson 1986) p.270.*

our human instincts of self-expression and self-promotion. It is at war with the worldly ideals of getting ahead, no matter what the cost, in our fiercely competitive culture. To be truly humble is, in itself, a martyrdom in little things. Spiritually it is *the death of a thousand cuts* to the self that is deathly sick with the venom of pride. Spiritually, humility is the *vaccine* that immunises our spiritual bloodstream against all assaults of the evil one. In one of the stories about the Desert Fathers it is related that the devil met the *Abba*, St Macarius, and complained bitterly against him:

> *"Great is the violence that I suffer from you, Macarius, for when I want to hurt you I cannot. But whatever you do, I do, and more...*
>
> *Only in one thing, are you better than I am and I acknowledge that".*
> "And what is that?" asked Macarius
> *"It is because of your humility alone that I cannot overcome you".*

John the Baptist put the question of humility in a nutshell when he spoke of himself in reference to Jesus, the bridegroom: **He must increase, but I must decrease. (John 3:30)**

(d) He Descended into Hell!

1. Another Puzzle!

The Creed now introduces us to one of the most mysterious and most intriguing elements in this summary of the faith. For one thing it was incorporated into the Creed quite late. For another it introduces us to a dimension of existence that is completely hidden from us, *the afterlife!* Cardinal Ratzinger had this to say about this article of the Creed:

> *Possibly no article of the Creed is so far from present day attitudes of mind as this one*[119].

---

[119] *Joseph Cardinal Ratzinger (now Benedict XVI) Inroduction to Christianity (Ignatius Press 1969) p.223*

Apart from this, there is a discrepancy about the actual translation of the original. The Latin original has two variants—*descendit ad inferos* and *descendit ad inferna,* These variants give us two different translations: **'*He descended to the dead*'** and **'*He descended into Hell*'**. In either case, however, there is a reference to the *underworld*, or the abode of the dead, *Sheol* in Hebrew or *Hades* in Greek. The latter must be distinguished from *Gehenna* or the Hell of the damned:

> *'where their worm never dies,*
> *and the fire is never quenched.'*
> **(Mark 9: 48)**

Where the term *'hell'* is used in the Creed it is explained in the Catechism as follows:

> *Scripture calls the abode of the dead, to which the dead Christ went down, 'hell', . . . because those who are there are deprived of the vision of God. Such is the case for all the dead, whether evil or righteous, while they await the redeemer, which does not mean that their lot is identical, as Jesus shows through the parable of the poor man Lazarus who was received into 'Abraham's bosom'. 'It is precisely these holy souls, who awaited their Saviour in Abraham's bosom, whom Christ the Lord delivered when he descended into hell.'[120] Jesus did not descend into hell to deliver the damned, but to free those who had gone before him.*
>
> (#633)

2. Life after Death

It was common among the Greek fathers to suggest that among those freed in Christ's descent were all those who had hoped and prayed for his coming—the *prophets* and *patriarchs* and all the *just* of bygone ages. There has been much speculation about the life after death, or, as someone has termed it, *"life after life"*! It deals with an entirely different

---

[120] *The Roman Catechism 6, 3-8*

mode of existence. So we move into a dimension of life in death about which the poet Shakespeare has written:

> *The undiscover'd country from whose bourn*
> *no traveller returns*[121]

And even if it *'puzzles the will'*, as the poet continues to say, there are grounds for the belief that, even in death, Christ still continued His ministry of love. At any given point in time the number of the dead far exceeds the number of the living, and so the world of the dead provided for Jesus another field for the Gospel! In this way Jesus will *"fill all things"*, as Paul points out in Ephesians:

> **He who descended is the same one**
> **who ascended far above all the heavens,**
> **so that he might fill all things.**
> **(Ephesians 4:10)**

3. Preaching to the Dead!

> *For Christ also suffered for sins once for all, the righteous for the unrighteous, in order to bring you to God. He was put to death in the flesh, but made alive in the spirit, in which also he went and made a proclamation to the spirits in prison who in former times did not obey, when God waited patiently in the days of Noah, during the building of the ark.*
> **(1 Peter 3 : 18-20)**

On these words of Peter the Catechism makes the following comment:

> "The gospel was preached even to the dead". The descent into hell brings the Gospel message of salvation to complete fulfilment. This is the last phase of Jesus' messianic mission, a phase which is condensed in time, but vast in its real significance, the spread of

---

[121] *Shakesppeare: Hamlet III. i.47*

Christ's redemptive work to all men of all times and of all places, for all who are saved have been made sharers in the redemption.
(#634)

Hence, modern exegesis has given more emphasis to the words of St Peter, who is at pains to point out that even death did not bring closure to the salvific mission of Jesus. The message of salvation must be announced to the dead! Death itself could not prevent the *Word* from preaching to the dead! He singles out specifically those who perished in the flood of Noah's time. There is also a subtext to this creedal affirmation of Christ in *Hades*. As the holder of the *keys of Death and of Hades*, Jesus points to his ultimate destiny as the Lord and Judge of all. The Creed is, furthermore, an affirmation that life goes on even after death. It gives the lie to the very glib remark that death is the end of everything in a person's life. No, the life of the Second Adam goes on even after death, and proclaims that, even after death, there is a life to be lived! As he proclaimed in the gospel of John:

> **For the hour is coming, and now is,**
> **when the dead will hear the voice of the Son of God,**
> **and those who hear will live.**
>
> **(John 5:25)**

4. The Liturgical Response

The liturgical commemoration of this article falls on what we call *Holy Saturday*—a *non-day*, so to speak, since its silence speaks of the *death of God!* In a sense, this strange article echoes uncannily the temper of our times where so many dwell in a life of the non-existence of God. The latter's existence is a quaint notion that is now irrelevant to the new millennium. Nietsche's saying that *God is dead and we have killed him* is so apposite to the lives of all those caught up in the maelstrom of materialism and secularism. This breeds a practical paganism of a life without God! However, there is still a redemptive quality about this paganism of which Karl Adam speaks:

> *So far as paganism is genuine paganism, that is to say, a revolt from the living God, self-deification, or the deification of nature, it has no more resolute foe than Catholicism. But there is more*

> *in paganism than revolt. There break forth even in paganism, from out of the uncorrupted sources of human nature, noble and pure impulses, thoughts and resolves, not only in philosophy and art, but also in religion and morality. The seeds of truth, as the Fathers constantly declare, are to be found everywhere . . . . What we have to do is to free these seeds from the non-Christian growth that chokes them and to redeem them for the kingdom of God.*[122]

The deafening silence of Holy Saturday is a clarion call to all to take time out, and pause and reflect on the faith and its meaning in our lives. An ancient homily for Holy Saturday echoes this call from the past to free us from the deadness of the present:

> *Today a great silence reigns on earth,*
> *a great silence and a great stillness.*
> *A great silence because the King is asleep.*
> *The earth trembled and is still*
> *because God has fallen asleep in the flesh*
> *and he has raised up all who have slept*
> *ever since the world began . . . .*
> *he has gone to free from sorrow Adam in his bonds*
> *and Eve, captive with him . . . .*
> *He who is both their God and the son of Eve . . . .*
> *"I am your God, who for your sake have become your son . . .*
> *I order you sleeper, to awake.*
> *I did not create you to be a prisoner in hell.*
> *Rise from the dead, for I am the life of the dead!" (CCC #635)*

---

[122] *Karl Adam: The Spirit of Catholicism (Franciscan Universsity Press, 1996) p.161.*

Questions #10

* * *

1. Why were commentators puzzled by the inclusion of the following in the Creed:

   (a) the burial of Jesus

   (b) his descent into hell

2. Who came into prominence in the burial of Jesus and why?

3. There was a garden in the place where he was crucified. Comment.

4. What did Karl Barth say about the burial of Jesus?

5. What is the sacramental answer to the question of the burial of Jesus?

6. What mystic symbolism is attached to the burial of Jesus?

7. The corpse of Jesus was not like other corpses! How do you explain this?

8. *Humility is the foundation of the spiritual life. Comment.*

9. *Why did Jesus preach to the dead?!*

10. *What is the liturgical significance of Holy Saturday?*

11. *Any personal thoughts or reflections on the burial of Jesus?*

11. ON THE THIRD DAY HE ROSE AGAIN!

*   *   *

(a) The Third Day
  —1. The Meaning of 'the Third Day'
  —2. The Empty Tomb!
  —3. The Disciples' Disbelief!
  —4. The Enemies of the Resurrection

(b) He Rose Again!
  —1. Christ's New Existence
  —2. The Radiance of the Resurrection
  —3. The Anchor of Our Faith
  —4. The Road to Emmaus

(c) The Remembrance of the Resurrection
  —1. In the Power of the Resurrection
  —2. The Lord's Day!
  —3. The Sunday Eucharist
  —4. Vatican II.

(d) The Glory of the Resurrection
  —1. The Father's Gift
  —2. In Newness of Life
  —3. Our Own Failures!
  —4. In the Hope of the Resurrection!

11. On the Third Day He Rose Again!

* * *

(a) The Third Day!

1. The Meaning of the "Third Day"?

> *The Son of Man must undergo great suffering,*
> *and be rejected by the elders, chief priests, and scribes,*
> *and be killed, and on the third day be raised.*
> **(Luke 9:22)**

Here again we are faced with the obvious queries: *Why this emphasis on the third day?* Numbers played an important part in the religious psyche of the cultures of the Middle East. The number *3* was one of the oldest to be considered sacred or highly significant in the unfolding of affairs. The Israelites were no exception to this mind set in recounting the events in the history of their relationship with Yahweh! We can count about *thirty* references in the Old Testament to the *third day*. *On the third day* something really important was going to be decided. Abraham was asked by God to sacrifice his son Isaac and he set out with his son, and on the *third day* came within sight of Mt Moriah. There after two days of sorrow God blessed Abraham because of his obedience, and Isaac was saved from death *on the third day!*[123] At a crucial point in the wandering of the Jews in the desert God gave very special instructions to Moses relative to *the third day*:

> *"Go to the people and consecrate them today and tomorrow. Have them wash their clothes and prepare for the third day, because on the third day the LORD will come down upon Mount Sinai in the sight of all the people".*
> **(Exodus 19:10,11)**

The prophet Hosea, who lived in the 8th century before Christ, has a telling passage that has a startling parallel to the resurrection story.

---

[123] *see Genesis .22*

> *Come, let us return to the LORD; for it is he who has torn,*
> *and he will heal us; he has struck down, and he will bind*
> *us up. After two days he will revive us; on the third day he*
> *will raise us up, that we may live before him.*
> **(Hosea 6:1,2)**

It is extraordinary how often this motif of *three days* keeps cropping up in the Old Testament. David chose the *three days* pestilence as a penance for his pride. Jonah spent *three days* in the belly of the whale![124] Jesus himself made special reference to this when he said:

> *For just as Jonah was three days and three nights in the*
> *belly of the sea monster, so for three days and three nights*
> *the Son of Man will be in the heart of the earth.*
> **(Matthew 12:40)**

2. **The Empty Tomb!**

> *But on the first day of the week, at early dawn,*
> *they came to the tomb, taking the spices that they had prepared.*
> *They found the stone rolled away from the tomb,*
> *but when they went in, they did not find the body.*
> **(Luke 24: 1-3)**

It is very probable that no incident has provoked more comment and controversy than the discovery of this empty tomb on Resurrection Sunday. As far as *recorded* history goes, this is the only occasion that a tomb had first been sealed and then guards set before it, to ensure that a corpse should not escape! There was also the suggestion that his disciples might come and steal it! St Matthew is at pains to remind us of the efforts of the chief priests and the Pharisees to persuade Pilate to take action against this:

> *Sir, we remember what that impostor said while he*
> *was still alive, 'After three days I will rise again.' Therefore*
> *command the tomb to be made secure until the third day;*

---

[124] *Book of Jonah 1:17*

> *otherwise his disciples may go and steal him away, and tell the people, 'He has been raised from the dead,' and the last deception would be worse than the first.*
>
> **(Matthew 27: 63-64)**

The alleged concern of those who had clamoured for the death of Jesus was that the guards would prevent violence. The seal would ensure that there would be no tampering. Christ's enemies, for the moment, had had their way.

3. The Disciples' Disbelief!

Another group had totally different thoughts. The entombment had been so hastily carried out that the rites of burial had been shortened. So the holy women were up at dawn, hastening to complete the burial ritual with the appropriate spices. They too shared the idea that any notion of resurrection was wholly out of the question. They were more concerned with his death and its rituals. The question of the stone and how to get it off the entrance certainly occurred to them but did not deter them. Apparently Mary Magdalene had preceded the main body of women and on noticing that the stone had been rolled aside, peered in and saw the empty tomb. In excitement and alarm she thought of the apostles and she rushed back to Peter and John with the news:

> **They have taken the Lord out of the tomb, and we do not know where they have laid him.**
>
> **(John 20:2)**

It is obvious that even Mary Magdalene did not entertain any thoughts of a *resurrection*. According to the Mosaic Law, a woman was ineligible to bear witness, Peter and John needed to verify Mary's remarkable news for themselves and they rushed to the tomb. In passing it is worth noting, as Bishop Fulton Sheen remarks:

> *It was a forecast of the way the world would receive the news of the Resurrection. Mary Magdalene and the other women did not at first believe in the Resurrection: they had to be convinced. Neither did the Apostles believe. Their answer was 'You know*

women! Always imagining things'. Long before the advent of scientific psychology, people were afraid of their minds playing tricks on them.

Modern incredulity in face of the extraordinary is nothing compared to the skepticism which immediately greeted the first news of the Resurrection. What modern skeptics say about the Resurrection story, the disciples themselves were the first to say, namely, that it was an idle tale.[125]

4. The Enemies of the Resurrection!

Strange, and even incredible as it may seem, it was the very enemies of Jesus who seemed to give greater credence to the *possibility* of resurrection. As we have already noted, so profound was their concern on this score that the chief priests and the Pharisees even went out of their way to break the Sabbath(!) and approach Pilate with their request to guard and seal the tomb. Here indeed is a spectacle for the gods, if we are to believe our modern skeptics—an armed guard is set over a tomb to prevent a dead man from arising or escaping, or his body being stolen!

Bishop Fulton Sheen sums up the situation:

> *The King lay in state with His guard about Him. The most astounding fact about this spectacle of vigilance over the dead was that the enemies of Christ expected the Resurrection, but His friends did not. It was the believers who were the skeptics; it was the unbelievers who were credulous. His followers needed and demanded proof before they would be convinced.*[126]

At this distance of some two thousand years, it is wholly impossible to grasp the full impact of the Resurrection on contemporaries and especially upon the disciples. At the same time, the story is so well worn that it may provoke apathy or a *'who cares'* attitude on the one hand, and, on the other, in the minds of modern sophisticates a reaction of frank incredulity. As one author so aptly remarks:

---

[125] *Fulton Sheen op.cit. p.409*
[126] *ibid. p.403*

*The full meaning of the resurrection has never been
so fully understood as during apostolic times.*[127]

(b) He rose again

1. Christ's New Mode of Existence!

Jesus rose from the dead! That is the inescapable conclusion in the careful examination of all the evidence confronting us. It is the very scepticism of his closest followers that is the greatest guarantee of its truthfulness. By *resurrection* we mean that it was the resurrection of the whole man, body and soul united, never again to be separated. This sealed the conquest of death! Now corruption and mortality were discarded and the body of Jesus was now invested with *immortality* and *incorruptibility*. It is this that gives us support and hope, as Paul points out to the Corinthians, of our own promise of immortality. He likens our mortality to a tent!

> *For while we are still in this tent, we groan under our burden,
> because we wish not to be unclothed but to be further clothed,
> so that what is mortal may be swallowed up by life.*
> **(2 Corinthians 5:4)**

The Resurrection opens a new phase in the ministry of Jesus. It is a ministry that is no longer hampered by considerations of time and space. Contacts were renewed with his disciples. But he comes and goes at will. He comes to his apostles through closed doors and vanishes as mysteriously as he came. This is not *miraculous* in the terms of this world, but the consequence of the *glorification* of his body. His ministry is a consolidation of what he had already told them in his earthly ministry. He was preparing to leave them definitively, for it was these apostles and disciples who must now continue his work when at last they would be deprived of his presence.

The miracle of the Resurrection now gives point to all that he had said during his earthly ministry. He confers upon them the power to

---

[127] F.X. Durwell: *New Catholic Encyclopedia*, vol 12 p.410.

forgive sins or withhold that forgiveness *(John 20:22-23)*. He opens the scriptures to them to show how his death was inevitable *(Luke 24:45)*. He entrusts them with the Great Commission that was to take them to the ends of the earth!

> *And Jesus came and said to them, "All authority in heaven and on earth has been given to me. Go therefore and make disciples of all nations, baptising them in the name of the Father and of the Son and of the Holy Spirit, and teaching them to obey everything that I have commanded you. And remember, I am with you always, to the end of the age."*
>
> **(Matthew 28:18-19)**

2. **The Radiance of the Resurrection!**

> *Do not be afraid; go and tell my brethren to go to Galilee; there they will see me.*
>
> **(Matthew 28:10)**

The Catechism points out to us these words of Jesus put us on his level. It is not something that we have earned or merited, it is one of God's most glorious gifts to us:

> *We are brethren not by nature, but by the gift of grace, because that adoptive filiation gains us a real share in the life of the only Son, which was fully revealed in the Resurrection. (#654)*[128]

When God declares something *to be*, it becomes a reality! When He said *"Let there be light!"* then, *there was light!* When He declares us to be *his children*, then we *are* his *children*, sharing mysteriously in *his own nature!* St John is quite emphatic about it in his Gospel Prologue:

> *But to all who received him, who believed in his name, He gave power to become children of God, who were born,*

---

[128] *CCC p.128*

> *not of blood or of the will of the flesh or of the will of man,*
> *but of God.*
>
> **(John 1:12-13)**

The light of the Resurrection illumines the whole world! It is not some sort of celestial camouflage. It it not only all around us, it flows through us. It is in the light of the Resurrection that we radiate Christ in our surroundings, proclaiming him to the world by the power of our example. St Peter is so eloquent in proclaiming its consequences for us!

> *But you are a chosen race, a royal priesthood,*
> *a holy nation, God's own people,*
> *in order that you may proclaim the mighty acts of him*
> *who called you out of darkness into his marvellous light.*
>
> **(1 Peter 2:9)**

3. Anchor of Our Faith!

> *If there is no resurrection of the dead, then Christ has*
> *not been raised; and if Christ has not been raised,*
> *then our proclamation has been in vain and*
> *your faith has been in vain.*
>
> **(1 Corinthians 15:13-14)**

Here St Paul is simply telling us that our faith *rises or falls* on the truth of the Resurrection. The miracle of the Resurrection sets the Divine seal on the life and teaching of Jesus. It is an unshakeable confirmation of all that has preceded it. As the Catechism says:

> *The Resurrection, above all, constitutes the confirmation of all Christ's works and teachings. All truths, even those that are most inaccessible to human reason, find their justification, if Christ by His Resurrection has given the definitive proof of the divine authority, which He had promised.*
>
> *(#651)*

St Paul dwells at length on the subject to leave us in no doubt that the Resurrection lies at the very heart of our belief in Jesus. He goes on to say:

> *If Christ has not been raised, your faith is futile*
> *and you are still in your sins.*
> *Then those also who have died in Christ have perished.*
> *If for this life only we have hoped in Christ,*
> *we are of all people most to be pitied.*
> **(1 Corinthians 15: 17-19)**

The Resurrection is proof, above all, of Christ's divinity. It set its seal on his entire ministry, on his teachings and healings. It was the fulfilment of prophecy! This Jesus foretold when He was preaching in the treasury of the Temple:

> *When you have lifted up the Son of Man,*
> *then you will realise that I am He,*
> *and that I do nothing on my own,*
> *but I speak these things as the Father instructed me.*
> **(John 8:28)**

It is for that very reason that the Resurrection is subject to constant attack. The most elaborate arguments and the most convoluted exegesis are often employed by the enemies of the Resurrection to demonstrate that it never happened!

4. The Road to Emmaus!

We see this transformation in the encounter of Jesus with the two disciples who were on the way to Emmaus. They were saddened and dispirited by the events of the previous week. They are the prototypes of all those who experience deep discouragement in their walk of faith.

The very words they use bespeak a sense of extinguished hopes and vanished dreams:

> *But we had hoped that he (Jesus) was the one to redeem Israel*
> **(Luke 24:21)**

Jesus, *(all the while listening to them!)* upbraided them in these words:

> *Oh, how foolish you are, and how slow of heart to believe all that the prophets have declared! Was it not necessary that the*

> *Messiah should suffer these things and then enter into his glory? Then beginning with Moses and all the prophets, he interpreted to them the things about himself in all the scriptures.*
> **(Luke 24:25-27)**

At the evening meal the two disciples recognised Jesus *in the breaking of the Bread.* Reflection brought home to them how His presence had raised their spirits and heartened them to the extent that they immediately returned to Jerusalem and spread the Good News:

> *Were not our hearts burning within us while he was talking to us on the road, while he was opening the scriptures to us?*
> **(Luke 24: 32)**

Likewise the resurrection speaks to us across the centuries as a message of hope and consolation. Without it we are lost, as Paul himself proclaimed to his converts in Corinth:

> *If Christ has not been raised, your faith is futile and you are still in your sins. Then those also who have died in Christ have perished. If for this life only we have hoped in Christ, we are of all people most to be pitied.*
> **(1 Corinthians 15:17-19)**

Jesus is still with us even though we only see or recognise Him with the eyes of faith.[129] Moreover, the Resurrection of Jesus points to our own resurrection. His Resurrection prefigures our own resurrection. As the Catechism points out:

> *Finally, Christ's Resurrection—and the risen Christ Himself— is the principal source of our future resurrection.*
> (#655)

Hence, the Resurrection is not merely an historical event, its meaning *transcends* history. It reaches back to the dawn of creation and

---

[129] *The term Resurrection implies a new level of existence and this would explain, to some extent, how some fail to recognize him as did the two disciples on the road to Emmaus.*

stretches forward to the end of time and on into eternity. It is a perpetual challenge to our faith, because it is the ultimate mystery of Christ's life here on earth. Above all, it is the supreme confirmation of the *divinity* of Jesus. It sets its seal on the validity of his message and of the reality of his Church and its mission to mankind!

(c) Remembrance of the Resurrection!

1. In the Power of the Resurrection!

> *If the Spirit of him who raised Jesus from the dead dwells in you, he who raised Jesus from the dead will give life to your mortal bodies also through his Spirit who dwells in you.*
>
> **(Romans 8:11)**

What Paul is telling us is that Jesus is raised from the dead by the Father through the power of the Holy Spirit. The resurrection, as we have already noted, is the gift of the Father to his beloved Son who endured the horrors of Gethsemane and of Calvary in fulfilment of the former's will. In the virtue and the power of that resurrection Jesus is now established as King and Lord of all. As Paul says elsewhere, he was

> *designated as Son of God in power according to the Spirit of holiness by his resurrection from the dead, Jesus Christ our Lord. through whom we have received grace and apostleship to bring about the obedience of faith for the sake of the name among all the nations.*
>
> **(Romans 1:4-5)**

Paul is revealing to us the power of the resurrection, first given to Jesus, and then given to himself in *"grace and apostleship"*. This so overwhelmed the Apostles of the Gentiles that it became the *leitmotif* of his ministry. It was that same power that inspired him to endure the trials and afflictions of that ministry, the rejections of his own people, the floggings, the shipwreck and ultimately death. Hence he could exclaim with considerable passion:

> *For his sake I have suffered the loss of all things and*
> *count them as refuse . . .*
> *that I may know Christ and the power of his resurrection.*
> **(Philippians 3:8,10)**

The key phrase he offers us is to *"know Christ"*. What Paul is expressing and yearning for in his ministry was the *knowledge* of the interior power of the resurrection. This interior power was not simply to know about it intellectually, but to *experience it, to possess it, to be overwhelmed by it.* He wanted to radiate to others the glory of the Christ that he had encountered on the road to Damascus. That was the vision that he held out to his converts, and it is the same vision that he holds out to us, almost two millennia later. So we are not to be satisfied about accepting the resurrection as just a fact of history, but as a living reality that should shine forth in our lives, that Christ has truly risen in our times and in our world.

2. The Lord's Day!

The resurrection of Jesus comes to a *re-creation* of the world; raising *fallen* man to walk anew in friendship with God, just as Adam and Eve once did. This first day of the week became known as the *Lord's Day*. This tradition is enshrined in the various romance languages, wherein it is known as *domenica, domingo* and *dimanche*. Even the English word *Sunday* (German *Sonntag*), the day of the *Sun*, recalls Jesus as the *Sun of Justice*. His light illumines the whole world both in time and eternity. St Eusebius of Caesarea wrote in the same vein:

> *It was on this day that at the time of creation when God said 'let there be light' there was light; and on this day also the Sun of Justice arose in our souls.*

What also emerges in the history of this tradition was, that with the cessation of persecution in the 4th century, an effort was made to honour the Lord's day in a more public manner. Sunday was a normal working day throughout the Roman empire. Hence the Emperor Constantine decreed the venerable *'day of the sun'* as a weekly holiday—except for farmers whose work could not be interrupted. The first recorded church law with regard to the Sunday rest dates from the end of the fourth century.

The synod of *Laodicea* (c. A.D. 380) advised the faithful to abstain from work as far as possible. The general law of the Church forbidding '*servile work*' or manual labour dates from the 13th century. Many church fathers, however, also spoke of servile work as being understood figuratively, that is, as *sinning*. The Sunday rest was, above all, a day for abstaining from sinful activities!

3. The Sunday Eucharist

> *For I handed on to you as of first importance what I*
> *in turn had received: that Christ died for our sins in*
> *accordance with the scriptures, and that he was buried,*
> *and that he was raised on the third day*
> *in accordance with the scriptures.*
> **(1 Corinthians 15:3-4)**

The Catechism makes this very succinct comment on this passage of St Paul's:

> *The Apostle speaks here of the living tradition of the Resurrection which he had learned after his conversion at the gates of Damascus.*
> (#639)

In other words, the *living tradition*, of which Paul speaks, points to the reality of a *Sunday* observance which emphasised the importance of the Resurrection. In fact, St Paul, writing about the year A.D. 56, refers to this event *"of first importance"*. It lay, therefore, at the very heart of the *kerygma* or the Christian message. Moreover, the connection between Sunday and the Eucharist is fairly obvious, since it is *the Body of the Risen Lord* that we receive in communion. Hence, Christians felt obliged, from the very urgency of the Lord's command, to gather *on the Lord's day* and celebrate the Eucharist. But the whole point of the Sunday Eucharist becomes all the more evident from the action of Christ himself in his encounter with the two disciples on the way to Emmaus. The latter recognised the Lord *"in the breaking of the Bread"!* This brings home to us today the importance of the Sunday Mass in which we too recognise the Lord in *the breaking of the bread. His* Passion and Death are renewed in accordance with His command to repeat the covenant of the Last Supper *in a perpetual remembrance!*[130]

4. Vatican II

Sunday is above all a day for rejoicing in *memory* of the *Good News* which is celebrated in the *Liturgies of the Word* and of *the Eucharist.* Habit and routine tend to obscure their profound significance, and dull the impact that they should have on our lives. It is for this reason that the second Vatican Council recalls to us what the *'Lord's Day'* should mean in our lives:

> *By a tradition handed down from the apostles, which took its origin from the very day of Christ's resurrection, the Church celebrates the Paschal mystery every seventh day, which day is appropriately called the Lord's day or Sunday.*
>
> *For on this day Christ's faithful are bound to come together into one place. They should listen to the word of God and take part in the Eucharist, thus calling to mind the passion, resurrection, and glory of the Lord Jesus, and giving thanks to God who 'has begotten them again, through the resurrection of Jesus from the dead, unto a living hope'* (1 Peter 1:3).
>
> *The Lord's day is the original feast day, and it should be proposed to the faithful and taught to them so that it may become in fact a day of joy and freedom from work. Other celebrations, unless they be truly of the greatest importance, shall not have precedence over Sunday, which is the foundation and kernel of the whole liturgical year.*[131]

---

[130] *This perpetual remembrance (or the 'anamnesis', lit. the non-forgetting) is reflected in the words of the celebrant: "Father we celebrate the memory of Christ, your Son etc."*

[131] *The Constitution on the Liturgy (Sacrosanctum Concilium) #106.*

(d) The Glory of the Resurrection!

1. *The Father's Gift!*

In the light of salvation history it is easy to look upon the Resurrection from the human standpoint of our redemption, that it set its seal on the whole life and message of Jesus. We are apt to forget the central aspect of *the will of his beloved Father*. It was primarily in response to the Father's will that Jesus took flesh and came among us. Jesus was the Father's gift of love to a wayward humanity. John so aptly expresses it:

> *For God so loved the world that he gave his only Son,*
> *so that everyone who believes in him may not perish*
> *but may have eternal life. Indeed, God did not send the Son*
> *into the world to condemn the world,*
> *but in order that the world might be saved through him.*
> **(John 3:16-17)**

Jesus, having faithfully fulfilled the Father's will even to his death on the Cross, is now *raised up* by the Father and *rewarded* in the Resurrection for his fidelity! This is, of course, a very awkward but human way of attempting to understand this profound object of our faith. Herein is wrought a transcendent intervention of the Almighty in the affairs of men! The Catechism seeks to express the result as follows:

> *The Father "raised up" Christ his Son, and, by doing so, perfectly introduced his Son's humanity, including his body, into the Trinity. Jesus is conclusively revealed as the "Son of God" in power, according to the Spirit of holiness by his Resurrection from the dead.*
>
> (#648)

2. *In Newness of Life!*

> *Do you not know that all of us who have been baptised into Christ Jesus were baptised into his death? Therefore we have been buried with him by baptism into death, so*

> *that, just as Christ was raised from the dead by the glory of the Father, so we too might walk in newness of life.*
> **(Romans 6:3-4)**

The Resurrection of Jesus has blazed a trail for redeemed humanity. The embrace of the humanity of Jesus in the bosom of the Trinity, has opened the door for us to that same embrace! The wonder of that destiny means that through the sacraments, particularly through baptism, the same wonderful goal is presented to us. There is an obvious danger that the phrase *"newness of life"* be taken as some form of poetry or literary metaphor. Far from it! It is not, as Luther maintained, an *external* act of vindication by which the righteousness of Jesus was simply *imputed* to the believer. The reformers likened it to the *purely judicial* act of a divine court by which the merits of Christ were said to cover over or cloak the *leprosy* of our sins and sinful nature. One Protestant theologian expresses it thus:

> *Justification is a forensic act imputing the righteousness of Christ to the believer; it is not an actual infusing of holiness into the individual. It is a matter of declaring a person righteous, as a judge does in acquitting the accused. It is not a matter of making the person righteous or altering his or her actual spiritual condition.*[132]

The Catholic teaching of the Church rejects this purely *legalistic* view outright. On the contrary, *justification* denotes a spiritual reality whereby I participate in the divine life itself through *filial adoption*. Through this divine life I become truly a *brother* or *sister* of Christ Himself. As He told the holy woman near the empty tomb:

> *"Do not be afraid; go and tell my brethren to go to Galilee; there they will see me."*
> **(Matthew 28:10)**

My brethren! This is the expression used by Jesus himself. He does not say *my disciples*, nor *my followers*, but *my brethren*, as if we were all members of the *same family*! As the Catechism points out to us, these

---

[132] *Millard J. Erickson: Christian Theology (Baker Book House. 1986) vol.3 p.956.*

words of Jesus put us on a level with Jesus Himself. It is not something that we have earned or merited. Far from it, it is one more proof of God's *infinite* love in sharing this most glorious gift with us:

> *We are brethren not by nature, but by the gift of grace,*
> *because that adoptive filiation gains us a real share*
> *in the life of the only Son, which was fully revealed in the Resurrection.*
> (#654)[133]

3. Our Own Failures!

The wonder of our spiritual destiny prefigured by the Resurrection is so easily lost in the humdrum activity of daily existence. In one sense, we act like his own followers, in practical disbelief! It is easy to understand the hostility of the Jews towards Jesus in his claim to divinity. What is more difficult to grasp is the lack of understanding by his closest followers with regard to the prophecies Jesus made about himself. Though he constantly reminded his disciples of what was going to happen to him, he was dogged by misunderstanding and incomprehension. In our own lives we can easily merit the reproof that Jesus meted out to Peter:

> **Are you also still without understanding?**
> **(Matthew 15: 16)**

In our own personal failures to live up to Christ's message, in our sins and moral lapses, we deny, in practice, the Resurrection of Christ! Serious sin involves the loss of the justification that he won for us at so dear a price. We also merit the same reproof that, we too, are still *without understanding*. Finally, in assessing the full meaning of the Resurrection we cannot ignore it as the work of the Most Holy Trinity. The whole thrust of the Gospel narrative concentrates upon Jesus. But he is responding to the will of his Father who raised him from the dead and now welcomes his humanity into the bosom of the Trinity. The Holy Spirit is also at work as the Spirit of holiness who co-operates in the raising of Jesus from the dead.

---

[133] *CCC*

4. In the Hope of the Resurrection

We have already noted that in his quest for souls Paul experienced the full gamut of disappointment and failure. But that did not quench his spirit. Far from it! He seemed to relish it!

Once again he expresses his unquenchable optimism:

> *More than that we rejoice in our sufferings,*
> *knowing that suffering produces endurance,*
> *and endurance produces character, and character*
> *produces hope,*
> *and hope does not disappoint, because God's love*
> *has been poured into our hearts through the Holy Spirit.*
> **(Romans 5:3-5)**

Why, despite the litany of trials in his life, does Paul speak of *hope*? Because of the Resurrection! This is something that he has in common with Peter who also tells us in his first letter abut the *'living hope'* of the resurrection:

> **Blessed be the God and Father of our Lord Jesus Christ!**
> **By his great mercy we have been born anew to a living hope**
> **through the resurrection of Jesus Christ from the dead.**
> **(1 Peter 1:3).**

The Catechism defines this virtue of hope as follows:

> *Hope is the theological virtue by which we desire the kingdom of heaven and eternal life as our happiness, placing our trust in Christ's promises, relying not on our own strength, but on the grace of the Holy Spirit.*
>
> (#1817)

While all this may sound very prosaic or matter-of-fact, it goes on in far more lyrical terms quoting the letters of Paul:

> Hope is the "sure and steadfast anchor of the soul . . . that enters . . . . where Jesus has gone as a forerunner on our behalf."
>
> *(Hebrews 6:19-20)*

Hope is also a weapon that protects us in the struggle of salvation:

> "Let us . . . put on the breastplate of faith and charity, and for a helmet the hope of salvation." (1 Thessalonians 5:8) It affords us joy even under trial. "Rejoice in your hope, be patient in tribulation." (Romans 12:12)
>
> (#1820)

Peter's *'living hope'* should permeate our lives, and all these visions of hope should draw their life from the Resurrection of Jesus who still walks among us in his Church and in his sacraments, especially in the Holy Eucharist. It was this vision of *'resurrected hope'* that transformed the apostles from skulking cowards into intrepid witnesses to Christ's message of salvation. It is this same hope that gives point to our existence here in this world. Without it we would wither away. When hope, even in its most natural human manifestations, is absent the will to live perishes and suicide is often its most natural conclusion. Christian hope, however, animated by the Risen Christ, gives life and meaning to our existence. *Hope* is the gift of the Resurrection. Christ is ever rising from the tomb and rising in our lives, giving us the wondrous light that allows us to see and follow him into eternity. With John we can still behold the vision of Jesus standing on the shores of our lives and exclaim:

It is the Lord!
(John 21:7)

++++++++++++++++++++++

Questions #11

* * *

1. What is the significance of the phrase "on the third day"?

2. Comment on the following statements:

    (a) "No one actually saw the Resurrection, it's a myth!"

    (b) "The Resurrection was the product of overwrought imaginations on the part of Christ's devoted disciples!"

    (c) "Christianity rises or falls on the truth of the Resurrection!"

3. "The Resurrection was the beginning of a new life for Jesus". Comment!

4. 'The Road to Emmaus'! What is the significance of this incident?

5. What do you understand by 'the Radiance of the Resurrection'?

6. The Resurrection is 'the Anchor of our Faith!' What does this mean?

7. Why did the first day of the week become the new Sabbath?

8. *What does Vatican II say about Sunday?*

9. *'Newness of life' is a reality and not a figure of speech! Any comments?*

10. *What do you understand by the power and the hope of the Resurrection?*

11. *What profound personal reflections arise from your study of the resurrection?*

12. HE ASCENDED INTO HEAVEN AND IS SEATED AT THE RIGHT HAND OF THE FATHER

* * *

(a) He Ascended into Heaven
—1. The Mystery of the Ascension
—2. "When I am Lifted Up!"
—3. A Time of Expectancy
—4. The Gift of the Ascension

(b) He is Seated
—1. The Assumption of Authority
—2. The New Presence of Jesus
—3. The Lordship of Jesus
—4. The Delegation of Authority

(c) At The Right Hand of the Father
—1. The Crown of the Creed!
—2. The Messianic Kingdom
—3. The Father's Gift

12. He Ascended into Heaven and is seated at the Right Hand of the Father

* * *

Do not let your hearts be troubled,
and do not let them be afraid.
You heard me say to you,
'I am going away, and I am coming to you.'
If you loved me, you would rejoice
that I am going to the Father,
because the Father is greater than I.
(John 14:27-28)

* * *

(a) He Ascended into Heaven

1. *The Mystery of the Ascension*

Nevertheless I tell you the truth:
it is to your advantage that I go away,
for if I do not go away, the Advocate will not come to you;
but if I go, I will send him to you.
(John 16:7)

In the Ascension we reach the *third* dimension in the life of Jesus! First, he comes to live among us, born in Bethlehem and died on Calvary, or as the saying goes:

Born in a stranger's cave
Buried in a stranger's grave!

Then he went *down to Hell* to perform some mysterious ministry. Now he goes *up to Heaven!* These are mind boggling affirmations of mystery, but nevertheless the Ascension is both a mystery and an object of our faith. At first leap, however, it appears to add little, if anything, to the life and message of Jesus. Somehow, it seems a trifle superfluous and rather irrelevant to the redemptive message. Such a point of view would appear to be suggested by the words of the angels to the disciples who were left gazing heavenwards:

> *Men of Galilee, why do you stand looking up toward heaven? This Jesus, who has been taken up from you into heaven, will come in the same way as you saw him go into heaven.*
> **(Acts 1:11)**

From St Luke's Gospel it would appear that the Resurrection and the Ascension occurred on the same day![134] However, in his *Acts of the Apostles* he gives us a specific time frame for these events. The Ascension took place *forty* days after Easter, and *ten* days later came the feast of Pentecost. There had to be an official closure to the life of Jesus here on earth. This earthly existence had two components—a *natural* and a *glorified* existence. There was an official closure of the *natural* on the mount of Calvary, and now there was to be an official closure of the *glorified* existence on the mount of the Ascension.

2. *When I Am Lifted Up!*

It is evident that the Ascension is highly relevant in the story of salvation, both with regard to Jesus Himself, and then to all believers. It gives new meaning to the prophecy of Jesus:

> *And I, when I am lifted up from the earth, will draw all people to myself.*
> **(John 12:32)**

It is customary to interpret this saying of Jesus as referring to his *crucifixion*. However, the origin of such phrases as '*being raised*' or '*being lifted up*' is etymologically interesting. They come from the Greek *hypoun* which found its way into Jewish apocalyptic literature. Although it was used in everyday language to denote *"being wakened"* or *"roused from sleep"*, here in this literature it was used specifically to denote a transition from one state of existence to another. This casts a whole new light on the

---

[134] *cfr Luke 24:50*

subject, illuminating these words of Jesus. In sum, the Ascension points to a new state of existence for Jesus in his *exaltation and glorification by the Father*. He now goes to claim the crown of victory. And now the Father will set his seal on a name that will be for ever a name of hope, a prayer and the source of undying inspiration to all believers. This is the point that St Paul makes in writing to the Philippians:

> *Therefore God also highly exalted him*
> *and gave him the name that is above every name,*
> *so that at the name of Jesus every knee should bend,*
> *in heaven and on earth and under the earth,*
> *and every tongue should confess*
> *that Jesus Christ is Lord,*
> *to the glory of God the Father.*
> **(Philippians 2:9-11)**

3. A Time of Expectancy

We are now living in a time of waiting, a period of expectancy. The question asked by the apostles before the Ascension has still to be answered:

> *Lord, is this the time*
> *when you will restore the kingdom to Israel?*
> **(Acts 1:6)**

The apostles were still mentally locked in to the notion that the kingdom, of which Jesus constantly spoke, was an *earthly* one, one in which they hoped to play a prominent role. The Kingdom of Heaven which Jesus promised was far removed from such earthly ideas. In a sense, we can understand their misguided thinking. What Heaven is like baffles the human mind. We are so hemmed in with notions of time and space and constricted in our ideas of things that have had no beginning and no end that the simplest solution is either to ignore them or deny them. The notion of everlasting happiness is so far removed from all our imaginings that some have gone so far as to dub it as *pie in the sky!* The Ascension of Jesus into Heaven is a powerful invitation for us to follow him! The gates of Heaven have been thrown open to us. A man has now entered where no man has gone before! The gates of eternity now stand open! We are all invited to enter!

> **For those whom he foreknew he also predestined
> to be conformed to the image of his Son,
> in order that he might be the firstborn among many brethren.**
> **(Romans 8:29)**

4. The Gift of the Ascension

It must never be forgotten that the Ascension forms part of Christ's eternal sacrifice. His death on Calvary, the Resurrection and the Ascension are are all part of that sacrifice. After his victory over Satan and all his forces, Jesus now triumphally enters into glory to take his seat at the right hand of the Father! This is also apparent in the prayers of the Church. In the *anamnesis* or memorial of the first Eucharistic prayer she says:

> *Father, we celebrate the memory of Christ, your Son,*
> *We your people and your ministers, recall his passion,*
> *his resurrection from the dead, and his ascension into glory . . .*

These three elements form, so to speak, a complete *package*! They are the gift of Jesus to his Eternal Father. Like the sacrifice of Abel it is accepted. To quote the words of St Paul Jesus rises as **a fragrant offering, a sacrifice acceptable and pleasing to God**[135]. The presence of the disciples at the mount of the Ascension is the public and human witness to the Father's acceptance of the gift! It is also a dramatic reminder that just as he left us, so one day he will return! And in the same way he will lead the blessed into the Kingdom of his Father. The Catechism puts the Ascension in this perspective:

> *Christ's ascension marks the definitive entrance of Jesus' humanity into God's heavenly domain, whence he will come again; in the meantime, this humanity hides Him from the eyes of men.*
> *(#666)*[136]

---

[135] *see Philippians 4:18*
[136] *CCC*

Moreover, it is not too much to say that the Ascension of Jesus also marks out the path to glory, which is destined for all true believers. It is a dress rehearsal—a dramatic foreshadowing—of the sequel to the final judgement on humanity. This is the point that the Church makes in its prayer for the feast of the Ascension:

"God, our Father, make us joyful in the
ascension of your Son Jesus Christ.
May we follow Him into the new creation,
for His ascension is our glory and our hope."

This, therefore, is our hope that one day we too might join the glorious throng of the saints who accompanied Jesus in that first Ascension into heaven. As the psalmist says:

You ascended the high mount, leading captives in your train and receiving gifts from people, even from those who rebel against the LORD God's abiding there.
(Psalm 68: 18)

++++++++++++++++++++++++++++

Too late have I loved you,
O Beauty, ever ancient, ever new!
And behold you were within, and I abroad, and there I searched for You.
Deformed I plunged amidst those fair forms which You had made.
You were with me, but I was not with You!
Things held me far from You, which, unless they were in You,
were not at all!
You called, You shouted, and You burst my deafness!
You breathed Your fragrances, and I drew breath and panted for You!
I tasted both hunger and thirst.
You touched me and I burned for Your peace!
from The Confessions of St Augustine

(b) And is Seated

1. Assumption of Authority

Let us run with perseverance the race that is set before us,
looking to Jesus the pioneer and perfecter of our faith,
who for the sake of the joy that was set before
him endured the cross, disregarding its shame,
and has taken his seat at the right hand of the throne of God.
(Hebrews 12:1-2)

Christ as the first born of all creation is now the *second Adam* in the spiritual re-creation of fallen man. Even though He took His seat at the right hand of the Father that does not mean that He is no longer interested in us. Far from it! His ministry takes on a new meaning in a far reaching operation on behalf of all mankind through the power of the Holy Spirit. As St Paul says in his letter to the Romans:

For to this end Christ died and lived again, so that he might
be Lord of both the dead and the living.
(Romans 14:9)

Stephen, the first martyr, enraged his persecutors when he cried out in their presence:

"Look," he said, "I see the heavens opened and the Son of Man
standing at the right hand of God!"
(Acts 7:56)

The expressions either of being seated, or standing, might provoke queries about whether any real difference is intended. Such queries are really irrelevant. What either word is intended to convey is that Jesus is totally accepted by the Father and is now in a position of power. It is a confirmation of what Jesus had already told the apostles in the closing verses of Matthew's Gospel:

All power is given to me in heaven and on earth!
(Matthew 28:18)

2. The New Presence of Jesus

In departing physically from this world Jesus renewed His promise of a far richer presence through the operations of the Holy Spirit. St Leo the Great makes this very point in saying that:

> *Christ became more fully present as God on the day he became less present as man!*

Hence the Ascension was the prologue, so to speak, the inauguration of a new and special presence of Jesus through the ministry of the Holy Spirit. It was to be a much more profound and a far more fruitful presence than a purely physical presence could ever have been.

> ***Consequently he is able for all time to save those who approach God through him, since he always lives to make intercession for them. For it was fitting that we should have such a high priest, holy, blameless, undefiled, separated from sinners, and exalted above the heavens.***
> **(Hebrews 7:25-26)**

Salvation is not only the repayment of a debt contracted by Adam before God, but a *re-creation of humanity* in the very image and life of Jesus as the *second Adam*. This re-creation was to be a *transformation* of the whole of humanity in new life in Christ.

> ***For those whom He foreknew He also predestined to be conformed to the image of His Son, in order that He might be the firstborn of many brethren.***
> **(Romans 8:29)**

3. The Lordship of Jesus

The title *"Lord"*, in translation from either Hebrew or the Greek, meant *"Master"*. It was a title for anyone in authority. In the New Testament it is used as synonym for *God*, as when Jesus addresses his Father: **'Lord of Heaven and earth!'**

After the Resurrection this title is given to Jesus in recognition of his universal sovereignty. When the Beloved Disciple saw Jesus on the shore of Lake Galilee, he said to Peter: **It is the Lord!** Taking his seat at the right hand of the Father, Jesus now exercises His power as Lord of all creation.

> *Christ's Ascension into heaven signifies His participation, in His humanity, in God's power and authority. Jesus Christ is Lord: He possesses all power in heaven and on earth. He is 'far above all rule and authority and power and dominion', for the father 'has put all things under His feet'. Christ is Lord of the cosmos and of history. In Him human history and indeed all creation are 'set forth' and transcendently fulfilled.*
>
> (#668)

During Christ's earthly existence His disciples addressed Him as *Lord*, but, for the most part, it simply meant that He was the master, the great *Rabbi* or *Rabbouni*. That first Easter experience transformed their perceptions, as we witness in both Thomas and John. The former made that profound profession of faith that has resounded down through the centuries:

> **My Lord and my God!**
> **(John 20:28)**

This Lordship proper to Jesus is a hidden one as far as this world is concerned. It is now exercised through His Church of which He is the Head. The Catechism makes this very point:

> *As Lord, Christ is the Head of the Church, which is His Body. Taken up to heaven and glorified after he had thus fully accomplished his mission, Christ dwells on earth in His Church. The redemption is the source of the authority that Christ, by virtue of the Holy Spirit, exercises over the Church.*
>
> (#669)

4. *The Delegation of Authority*

This authority has been delegated to his Church! Here on earth it is wielded by Peter and the apostles and by their successors. We are now living in *the acceptable time* and in *the day of salvation!* This enables Jesus, in the meantime, to exercise through the Holy Spirit his Lordship of mercy! As the letter to the Hebrews states:

> ***Consequently he is able for all time to save those who approach God through him, since he always lives to make intercession for them.***
> **(Hebrews 7:25)**

Jesus still continues His redemptive work; He still pleads our cause before the Father; His dying prayer *'Father forgive them, for they know not what they do!'* still echoes within the portals of Heaven, pleading before the throne of our Father who is in Heaven. It is evident that this heavenly ministry of mercy demands a response from us and it is given voice in the letter of St Paul to the Colossians:

> *"So if you have been raised with Christ, seek the things that are above, where Christ is, seated at the right hand of God."*
> **(Colossians 3:1)**

(c) At the right hand of the Father

1. *The Crown of the Creed!*

Here we reach the crown of the Creed!

> *It is the enthronement of Jesus at the right hand of the Father!*

The *right* side not only denotes the side of precedence and courtesy, it also signifies the position of authority and of special trust. To sit at one's *right hand* is to confer the highest honour. We see this in the case of Bathsheba, the Queen-Mother, who came before Solomon. He had a throne brought and placed her on his right hand. This was to give due honour to the *gebirah* (Queen Mother) when she interceded for her son Adonijah. *(2 Kings 2:19)*. Hence the Catechism clarifies for us the importance of it all in relation to Jesus:

> By 'the Father's right hand' we understand the glory and honour of divinity, where He who exists as Son of God before all ages, indeed as God, of one being with the Father, is seated bodily after He became incarnate and His flesh was glorified.
>
> (#663)[137]

The total submission of Jesus to the will of the Father in every aspect of His life—*the hidden life at Nazareth, the public ministry in Galilee and Judea, the Passion and Death on the Cross*—all now receive their reward and crown in the place of highest honour in Heaven.

2. The Messianic Kingdom

All the foregoing points to the establishment of the Messianic Kingdom that had long been prophesied under the Old Law. Being seated at the Father's right hand signifies the inauguration of the Messiah's kingdom, the fulfilment of the prophet Daniel's vision concerning the Son of Man:

> **To him was given dominion and glory and kingship, that all peoples, nations, and languages should serve him. His dominion is an everlasting dominion that shall not pass away, and his kingship is one that shall never be destroyed.**
>
> **(Daniel 7:14)**

This dominion is a theme that runs through the letters of St Paul. In fact, the title of Jesus as *Lord* occurs 130 times in the Pauline letters. However, there is little in scripture to rival what Paul wrote in the following:

> **God put this power to work in Christ when he raised him from the dead and seated him at his right hand in the**

---

[137] This quote is from St John of Damascus (his birthplace). He ranks as the greatest theologian of the 8th century and is considered as the last of the Fathers of the Church.

> *heavenly places, far above all rule and authority and power and dominion, and above every name that is named, not only in this age but also in the age to come.*
> **(Ephesians 1:20-21)**

Here is the focal point of the entire life of Jesus. Everything is subordinated to the will and glory of the Father. And because of that devotion to His Father, the Father, in turn, gives Him the highest place in Heaven. He also confers on Him the name above all names, *Kyrios* or *Lord* of the whole of creation. In fact, Jesus had already announced his supreme authority in commissioning his apostles to go forth to the ends of the earth:

> *All power is given to me in Heaven and on earth.*
> **(Matthew 28:18)**

3. The Father's Gift

In sum, it is important to remember that the life of Jesus and his sacrifice is not only the gift of the Father to mankind it is also, first and foremost, Jesus' own gift to his heavenly Father! It is the nature of sacrifice, as gift, that it not only be *offered* but that it also be *accepted*. Hence, in this context, as we have already detailed how *Calvary, the Resurrection and the Ascension* are all of a piece in Jesus' sacrifice. The Father, in the miracle of the Resurrection, accepted the offering of Jesus on the Cross. The frailty of his *(and our)* humanity is transformed into immortality and incorruptibility. Finally, in the Ascension, Jesus is accepted publicly, in full view of his followers, and placed at the Father's right hand. Humanity, if faithful, will follow at the appointed time! And so we find in the last book of Holy Writ the angel of the seventh trumpet inaugurating the Messianic reign of Christ:

> *Then the seventh angel blew his trumpet, and there were loud voices in heaven, saying, The kingdom of the world has become the kingdom of our Lord and of his Messiah, and he will reign forever and ever.*
> **(Revelation 11:15)**

Heaven rings throughout with the triumph of Jesus and the glory that he brought to the throne of his Father:

> *And the twenty-four elders and the four living creatures fell down and worshipped God who is seated on the throne, saying, Amen. Hallelujah! And from the throne came a voice saying, Praise our God, all you his servants, and all who fear him, small and great.*
>
> (Revelation 19:4-5)

These verses of Revelation inspired Handel in his immortal *Hallelujah Chorus*. But the exuberant joy of heaven, and our own, is tempered by the sight of the armies of Heaven riding forth under the Lordship of Jesus to the judgement of the nations!

> *From his mouth comes a sharp sword*
> *with which to strike down the nations,*
> *and he will rule them with a rod of iron;*
> *he will tread the wine press of the fury*
> *of the wrath of God the Almighty.*
>
> (Revelation 19:15)

* * *

> By the miracle of the Resurrection,
> God at once shows
> His acceptance of the Priest
> as a true priest of a true sacrifice and perfects
> the Victim offered to Him,
> so that, whereas it was offered mortal and corruptible,
> it has gained immortality and incorruptibility.
> By the Ascension God accepts the offered Victim
> by actually taking it to Himself.
> Humanity, offered to God in Christ the Victim,
> is now forever at the right hand of the Father.[138]

---

[138] F.J. Sheed: *Theology and Sanity* (Sheed and Ward, London & New York. 1946) p.190

The Possession of Faith!

* * *

Faith is, above all, a possession!
The believer already possesses some supreme truths
deriving from the word of God;
he is already the guardian of some revelations
which enter into his life and dominate it,
and he is already happy in his certitude
which gives to his spirit a fulness,
a strength, a joy, a desire to express it and celebrate it,
which nourishes within him a marvellous interiority.

For the believer, it is, as if in the obscurity
and the confusion of his interior life,
a light has been enkindled.
He sees the light, that is to say, the divine realities
which have entered into his spirit; and,
in virtue of this light, he sees himself, his conscience.
And not only that, he also sees whatever surrounds him,
his position in the world and the world itself.

(Now) everything acquires a meaning;
everything appears as it really is.
It cannot be denied that this first vision is magnificent,
however much it may uncover inaccessible heights,
the depths of an abyss, and even humble things
which are concrete and already known,
but recognised now in new and real dimensions—
that is to say, however much the sense of mystery is enlarged,
precisely on the basis of this initial discovery
of the realities of our daily life
in the midst of which is discovered
our fear-ridden existence.[139]

---

[139] *Paul VI. Allocution in the General Audience July 10 1968.*

Questions #12

* * *

1. What is the significance, if any, and the relevance of this mystery in the Creed?

2. When I am lifted up ... What meanings can be attached to these words of Jesus?

3. "We are living in an era of expectancy." What does this mean in this context?

4. Christ became more fully present as God on the day he became less present as man. What does this mean?

5. The Lordship of Jesus is manifested (and delegated!) in what ways?

6. What is meant by saying that Jesus is seated at the right hand of the Father?

7. Why is the Ascension called the Crown of the Creed?

8. *In the Ascension is planted the seed of the Messianic Kingdom! Explain!*

9. *What do you understand by "the Gift of the Ascension"?*

10. *What does this mystery mean to you personally?*

13. HE WILL COME AGAIN TO JUDGE THE LIVING AND THE DEAD

* * *

(a) He Will Come Again
    —1.   The 'End Times'!
    —2.   The Great Question: When?
    —3.   The Signs of the End Times!

(b) To Judge
    —1.   In the Old Testament
    —2.   In the New Testament
    —3.   In the Present!
    —4.   The Ultimate answer

(c) The living and the dead
    —1.   Christ the Judge
    —2.   Dissent
    —3.   The Mystery of Salvation
    —4.   The Final Vision

(d) Purgatory
    —1.   The Particular Judgement
    —2.   The Ultimate Forgiveness
    —3.   The Conformity to Christ, the Firstborn!
    —4.   The Maccabees

13. He Will Come Again to Judge the Living and the Dead

* * *

(a) He Will Come Again

1. The 'End Times'!

> *Children, it is the last hour!*
> *As you have heard that antichrist is coming,*
> *so now many antichrists have come.*
> *From this we know that it is the last hour.*
> **(1 John 2:18)**

This last section of the Creed launches us into a consideration of the *'end times'* which involves notions of *death, judgement, hell* and *heaven*. The Greek word *eschaton*, meaning *last*, with its plural *ta eschata*, gives us the English equivalent of *the last things*. It is also called *'the end times'*, that is, those days which immediately precede Christ's return from Heaven and the establishment of the Messianic kingdom in the wake of the final judgement. Hence, the word *eschatology* is a term that means 'the *teaching of the last things'*. On this rather sobering subject the Catechism of the Catholic Church notes the following:

> *Since the Ascension God's plan has entered into its fulfilment. We are already at 'the last hour'. Already the final age of the world is with us and the renewal of the world is irrevocably under way; it is even now anticipated in a certain real way, for the Church on earth is endowed already with a sanctity that is real but imperfect. Christ's kingdom already manifests its presence through the miraculous signs that attend its proclamation by the Church.*
>
> (#670)

The *Second Coming* of Jesus is the climax of the drama of the Incarnation. It is commonly called by the Greek term the *'parousia'*. In secular usage it pointed to *a presence* or *a coming*. In particular, it referred to the ceremonial visit of a ruler to a city or country. The New Testament writers adopted the term and gave it *apocalyptic* overtones. Hence it was used rather widely to refer to the *'Second Coming'*, the *'Day of the Lord'*, the *'Gathering of the Elect'*, the' *Last Judgement'*, or the *'End of the World'*. More precisely, it refers to *the coming of Christ in glory*. He will come when the Great Commission given to the apostles is accomplished:

> *Go into all the world and proclaim*
> *the good news to the whole creation!*
> **(Mark 16:15)**

In the *'parousia'* are summed up the hopes and desires of all Christians that are now summoned before the throne of judgement. It represents the fullness and the completion of mankind's salvation history. In the *parousia* is played out the final chapter in the economy of divine grace. It is the advent of entry into an eternal union with Christ in the glory of the Father's Kingdom.

2. *The Great Question; When?*

We have been given a warning of the great trials that must precede the *parousia*. These trials centre around the coming of **the Antichrist**. There is considerable debate about whether the term refers to a single person, an idea, or a group of persons who are opposing or intend to oppose Christ as manifested in the teachings of the Church. In the sense of either *opponents* or *persecutions* there have been many *antichrists* in the history of the Church. What this all adds up to is that the *Second Coming* of Christ is imminent. As St John says *"it is the last hour"!* We are prone to interpret these terms of *'imminent'* and *'the last hour'* from a purely human perspective. There have also been many false prophets who have even given us precise dates for the *Second Coming* of Christ!

Some fifty years ago an Australian persuaded hundreds of his fellow countrymen to buy seats in an outdoor theatre facing the entrance to Sydney harbour. There they would have ringside seats, so to speak, and have the privilege of getting a close-up view of the Second Coming! It is such follies that tend to trivialise the solemn warnings that Scripture gives. The antics of these would-be prophets rob them of the seriousness and the urgency they deserve. They must be judged, as St Peter himself warns us, in the light of eternity:

> *But do not ignore this one fact, beloved,*
> *that with the Lord one day is like a thousand years,*
> *and a thousand years are like one day.*
> *The Lord is not slow about his promise,*
> *as some think of slowness, but is patient with you,*
> *not wanting any to perish, but all to come to repentance*
> **(2 Peter 3:8-9)**

3. Signs of the End

When Jesus was asked about the restoration of the kingdom of Israel he made this enigmatic reply:

> *It is not for you to know the times or the seasons*
> *which the Father has fixed by his own authority.*
> **(Acts 1:7)**

This has been generally interpreted as referring to the end of the world and to the *Second Coming* of Christ for judgement. At the same time, if the exact moment of this coming is unknown, its coming will be heralded by certain events which would indicate that it was coming soon! It is customary for commentators to list the following as signs of the Last Judgement:

(i). The Universal Reach of the Gospel to all Nations:

Our Lord's own words are pertinent when he responded once again to the Apostles' query:

> *Tell us when this will be and what will be the sign of your coming and of the close of the age? . . . . This gospel must be preached throughout the whole world, as a testimony to all the nations, and then the end will come.*
> **(Matthew 24: 3,14)**

(ii). The Great Apostasy

However, *"before Christ's second coming the Church must pass through a final trial that will shake the faith of many believers"*. (#675) This is very evident from the Gospel of Matthew, especially in the 24th chapter where there is depicted a great crisis in the Church:

> *Then many will fall away, and they will betray one another and hate one another. And many false prophets will arise and lead many astray.*
> *And because of the increase of lawlessness, the love of many will grow cold.*
> *But the one who endures to the end will be saved.*
> **(Matthew 24:10-13)**

St Paul in Thessalonians is even more precise:

> *Let no one deceive you in any way; for that day will not come unless the rebellion comes first and the lawless one is revealed, the one destined for destruction.*
> *He opposes and exalts himself above every so-called god or object of worship, so that he takes his seat in the temple of God, declaring himself to be God.*
> **(2 Thessalonians 2:3-4)**

(iii). The Overthrow of the Man of Lawlessness

At the same time Paul prophecies the overthrow and destruction of this enemy of Christ:

> *And then the lawless one will be revealed, whom the Lord Jesus will destroy with the breath of his mouth, annihilating him by the manifestation of his coming.*
> **(v.8)**

Scripture also mentions the **Antichrist** and it is difficult to identify any relationship between it and *the man of lawlessness*. We can only make *educated (?)* guesses on matters that are buried in the future, and seek to enlarge on the rather cryptic references that scripture offers here and there. The Catechism has this to say about the same:

> "*The persecution that accompanies her (the Church's) pilgrimage on earth will unveil the 'mystery of iniquity' in the*

form of a religious deception offering men an apparent solution to their problems at the price of apostasy from the truth. The supreme religious deception is that of the Antichrist, a pseudo-messianism by which man glorifies himself in place of God and of His Messiah come in the flesh".

(#675)

(iv). The Conversion of the Jews

As a Jew himself, and as a Pharisee, Paul held the welfare of his people so close to his heart. He even wished himself to be *anathema!* for their sakes, if only they could be won to Christ! On this issue he says:

> *So that you may not claim to be wiser than you are, brothers and sisters, I want you to understand this mystery: a hardening has come upon part of Israel, until the full number of the Gentiles has come in. And so all Israel will be saved; as it is written, Out of Zion will come the Deliverer; he will banish ungodliness from Jacob.*
>
> **(Romans 11:25-26)**

The exact meaning of this passage has been disputed and the *'salvation of Israel'* has been interpreted in various ways. However, it would appear from Paul's words that *"Israel"* somehow figures in the end times! Many evangelicals today consider the establishment of the modern state of Israel as heralding the end times!

(v). The Calamities of War and the Convulsions of Nature

We return again to Matthew 24, and also to Luke 21 where Jesus says:

> *And you will hear of wars and rumours of wars; see that you are not alarmed; for this must take place, but the end is not yet. For nation will rise against nation, and kingdom against kingdom, and there will be famines and earthquakes in various places: all this is but the beginning of the birth pangs.*
>
> **(Matthew 24:6-8)**

> *There will be signs in the sun, the moon, and the stars, and on the earth distress among nations confused by the roaring of the sea and the waves. People will faint from fear and foreboding of what is coming upon the world, for the powers of the heavens will be shaken. Then they will see 'the Son of Man coming in a cloud' with power and great glory.* (Luke 21:25-27)

(b) To Judge!

1. In the Old Testament

The dramatic language to be found in the Gospels might give the impression that what is described is unique and awe-inspiring. It may be awe-inspiring but hardly unique. This basic theme, that nations and individuals are accountable before God for their actions, runs through the Old Testament. At times it would appear that rewards and punishments are allotted in this life. Justice was done when Israel's enemies were defeated and the Chosen People were triumphant. Judgement, however, seemed to be confined to the national or corporate level rather than to that of individuals. This type of language is to be found in Jewish apocalyptic literature, to which Jesus himself made reference when questioned by the High Priest. When the latter asked him whether he was the Messiah, Jesus replied by quoting the prophet Daniel.

> *But I tell you, From now on you will see the Son of Man seated at the right hand of Power and coming on the clouds of heaven.*
>
> **(Matthew 26:64)**

The *Book of Daniel*[140] was written in the second century before Christ in the days of the Maccabees. In chapter seven the author

---

[140] *There is considerable dispute about the authorship of this book. The traditional view is that it relates to the prophet Daniel whose name means 'God is my Judge.' The view expressed here is that of the 4th century philosopher Porphry.*

describes Daniel's dream of four monstrous beasts emerging from the sea. They represented the successive empires of the Babylonians, the Medes, the Persians and the Greeks. Judgement was passed on them by *the Ancient One*!

The visionary also saw:

> *One like a son of man coming on the clouds of heaven, when he reached the Ancient One and was presented before him, he received dominion, glory and kingship; nations and peoples of every language serve him. His dominion is an everlasting dominion that shall not be taken away; his kingdom shall not be destroyed.*
> **(Daniel 7:13-14)**

All this prefigures a future and final judgement upon the world! It is in line with what is to be found in the New Testament. The prophet Joel calls it the *Day of the Lord* (Joel 2:31). The same phrase is also found in Ezekiel (13:5). Similarly, in the prophet Isaiah we read:

> *For the Lord of hosts will have his day against all that is proud and arrogant, all that is high will be brought low . . . And the Lord alone will be exalted on that day!*
> **(Isaiah 2:12,17)**

2. In the New Testament

> *And just as it is appointed for mortals to die once, and after that the judgement, so Christ, having been offered once to bear the sins of many, will appear a second time, not to deal with sin, but to save those who are eagerly waiting for him.*
> **(Hebrews 9:27-28)**

What is prefigured in the Old Dispensation is even more clearly demonstrated in the New. It can truly be said that there are few truths so openly proclaimed as that of a *General Judgement* at the end of time. Jesus himself dwells on it at considerable length in the Gospel of Matthew:

> *When the Son of Man comes in his glory, and all the angels with him, then he will sit on the throne of his glory. All the nations will be gathered before him, and he will separate people one from another as a shepherd separates the sheep from the goats.*
>
> **(Matthew 25: 31-32)**[141]

In this context judgement rests upon the sovereign rule of charity. Sentence depends on the acts of kindness and charity done or denied to others. Apart from this there is not much further detail. It would appear that these works of charity are taken as a measuring rod or as representative of a wider spectrum of virtue and *conformity* or *nonconformity* with God's will while here on earth. But judgement will be complete in the sense that all present will see their own actions within the context of community and the overarching concerns of God's divine will and providence. Then the whole world will see before its eyes the marvellous pattern of God's plan for creation and his redemptive work. Then, in the words of one author:

> *At last we shall see the shape and bearing of all things.*[142]

3. In the Present!

It is far too easy to assume that *judgement* is something that has not yet happened. It belongs to some far-off distant event that will emerge in some hazy future. This is a common but fatal illusion! *Judgement is an ever present and a very personal reality!*

Ever since the Garden of Eden mankind has been living under judgement, the judgement of original sin! That first trial cast a pall over us all, condemning us to live in the shadow of the infidelity of our first parents. It was to bring *light* into this darkness that Jesus, *the Light of the World,* came among us.

---

[141] *See here chapter 24 of Matthew's Gospel*
[142] *Sheed op.cit. p.258*

> *But God proves his love for us in that while we still were sinners Christ died for us. Much more surely then, now that we have been justified by his blood, will we be saved through him from the wrath of God.*
> **(Romans 5:8-9)**

In the light of Christ's redemption we live under the continuous judgement of God. Whether for good or ill we respond to it under the impulse of the grace won for us. If for ill, then God's judgement is a destructive one. Nevertheless, there is always the invitation to *repentance*, which will cancel out the evil done. This is the *judgement of mercy* that tempers God's action. Of course, the sinner is incapable of repentance on his own. He (or she) must be drawn by God to consider the disorder of his (or her) life and be led to reject it. There is still one aspect of judgement that needs to be emphasised. It is that it is *very personal*! This is also pointed out in the Catechism:

> *By rejecting grace in this life, one already judges oneself, receives according to one's works, and can even condemn oneself for all eternity, by rejecting the Spirit of love.*
> **(#679)**

My actions for good or bad are *my* actions! As such they entail consequences, and these consequences also are *mine!* In a sense, therefore, I have passed judgement on myself and condemned myself in the choices I have made. It is this very point that St Paul wishes to make, in a letter to the *Corinthians,* to those who approach the table of the Lord unworthily:

> *Whoever, therefore, eats the bread or drinks the cup of the Lord in an unworthy manner will be answerable for the body and blood of the Lord: Examine yourselves, and only then eat of the bread and drink of the cup. For all who eat and drink without discerning the body, eat and drink judgement against themselves.*
> **(1 Corinthians 11:228-29)**

4. The Ultimate Answer

Then the king will say to those at his right hand,
Come, you that are blessed by my Father,
inherit the kingdom prepared for you
from the foundation of the world.
(Matthew 25: 34)

These chapters 24 and 25 of Matthew are the *locus classicus* on this subject of the Last Judgement. Here is conjured up a magnificent panorama of the angels and saints, the whole host of Heaven, gathered with Jesus in glory. Before them are assembled all the nations of the earth arrayed for judgement. The Catechism summarises the Gospel message in the following words:

> *In the presence of Christ, who is the Truth itself, the truth of each man's relationship with God will be laid bare. The Last Judgement will reveal even to its furthest consequences the good each person has done or failed to do during his earthly life.*
> (#1039)

These words underscore the ultimate lesson implied in the Gospel narrative and in the words of Christ. All our actions, and even our very thoughts, have eternal consequences. Even a cup of cold water has its eternal reward. All this brings into sharp relief a radical perspective that should give us pause, especially in the light of Jesus' own words:

Truly I tell you, just as you did it to one of the least of these who are members of my family, you did it to me:
(Matthew 25:40)

It is so easy to dismiss such a spiritual outlook as quite irrelevant in the rough and tumble of modern daily living. We tend to lose any sense of the *divine* in our lives. There is an ingrained myopia of the spirit when it comes to assessing the long term consequences of our actions. But the solemn scenario conjured up in Jesus' own words should give us pause. Although the details of the *Last Judgement* are at best sketchy, one thing is clear in the mind of our Judge; the sentence to be delivered will rest upon the works of charity done or refused by us. At the same time it will become abundantly evident to all of the true value of their actions here on earth. These latter will be seen and assessed within the scope of God's pattern of creation and redemption. Hence, while death marks the peak of our earthly existence, the Last Judgement sets its seal upon it when body and soul are united in the presence of our Judge. Here, at last, is the final answer to all of life's fundamental questions:

Why am I here? Why was I created?

(c) . . . the Living and the Dead

1. *Christ the Judge*

On this subject the Catechism depicts the role of Jesus:

> *Christ is Lord of eternal life. Full right to pass definitive judgement on the works and hearts of men belongs to him as redeemer of the world. He acquired the right by his cross. The Father has given all judgement (John 5:22) to the Son. Yet the Son did not come to judge, but to save and to give the life that he has in himself.*
>
> (#679)

By shedding his precious Blood on the Cross Jesus earned his right to judge the whole of mankind. It is fairly obvious, even today, that not all accept this right. His triumph, the triumph of his Kingdom, has not yet been accomplished. The parable of *the weeds and the wheat* shows that God tolerates the existence and even the temporary triumph of evil, but there comes, ultimately, a day of reckoning:

> **Let both of them grow together until the harvest; and at harvest time I will tell the reapers: collect the weeds first and bind them in bundles to be burned, but gather the wheat into my barn.**
>
> **(Matthew 13:30)**

His judgement scans the whole of mankind's history. It is the final verdict on the choices that we have made in life. Matthew has given us a very graphic picture of it all, with the *goats* on one side and the *sheep* on the other. It is fairly obvious that the *'goats' (weeds)* represent those condemned to everlasting punishment, and the *sheep (wheat)* are those destined for glory!

2. *Dissent*

Nevertheless, there are not lacking those critics who, indulging in some form of mental and academic gymnastics, seek to discount these very unpleasant aspects of the Gospel, or attempt to explain them away as being purely *figurative* or *metaphorical*. The words and phrases of the evangelist are robbed of their most frightening aspects and reduced to purely human dimensions. Their efforts remind us of one Scottish nobleman in the sixteenth century who described all references to Hell as *"a bogie to flee bairns!"*[143] Others have simply denied the existence of hell as wholly incompatible with the notion of an infinitely merciful and loving God. One author has gone so far as to refer to it as

the barbarous doctrine of an eternal hell![144]

God, it is said, is far too compassionate, far too loving, to permit any of His creatures to suffer an *eternity* of torment. Such thinking has led to the heresy of *apokatastasis*[145], or the doctrine of *universal* salvation, that, ultimately, everyone will be saved! True, God is all-merciful and all-loving, but He is also infinitely *just*. How divine justice and divine love are to be reconciled is a profound mystery. As with everything surrounding God, and with everything that touches his nature, there is a barrier of impenetrability to all human reasoning.

For who has known the mind of the Lord?
Or who has been his counselor?
(Romans 11:34)

---

[143] *This Scottish dialect may be translated: "a bogey man to frighten children!"*
[144] *see also John Macquarrie's Principles of Christian Theology (Charles Scribner & Sons, New York 1977) p.361.*
[145] *apokastastasis; a Greek word that means 'the reconciliation of the restoration of all things in Christ'.*

3. The Mystery of Salvation!

The mystery of redemption, in its ultimate terms, still remains a mystery. God dwells in a totally different dimension of existence, wholly immune to every attempt we can make to reduce Him to our own human terms of understanding. However, as He is the *eternal* truth, the *ultimate* truth, what He says must be taken *very seriously!* So we must note that Hell is mentioned over *twenty* times in the New Testament:

> *Where their worm dieth not*
> *and the fire is not extinguished.*
> **(Mark 9:48)**

These so explicit terms of the *One,* who is *the Truth*, must certainly give us pause. The whole concept of an *eternity* of punishment is far too terrible for the human mind even to invent, never mind to contemplate. But that is the reality of the Gospel. We can only take refuge in the words of Jesus Himself. His message is all too stark for verbal casuistry!

> *If your hand or your foot causes you to stumble, cut it off and throw it away; it is better for you to enter life maimed or lame than to have two hands or two feet and to be thrown into the eternal fire.*
> **(Matthew 18:8)**

The solemnity of these words gives the lie to any sloppy thinking on the subject. To empty them of any real significance or even to play down their meaning is, in the last resort, a diminishing of the life and teaching of Jesus. It causes us to throw doubt on the whole point of the *Passion and Death of Jesus,* and the extremity of His suffering.

> *Why was it at all necessary if, ultimately,*
> *nobody is damned forever in Hell?*

The drama of Holy Week and the horror of the Passion become trivialised in the wake of such reductionist thinking. It has been truly said that *love* and *justice* meet and kiss on the Hill of Calvary! Here lies the message of the Good News! And we can begin to appreciate how *good the Good News really* is when we stop for a moment to consider *how bad* the *bad news* is! And the *really bad news* is that there is *a hell and an eternity of punishment for sinners!*

> *I saw under the altar the souls of those who had been slaughtered for the word of God and for the testimony they had given; they cried out with a loud voice, Sovereign Lord, holy and true, how long will it be before you judge and avenge our blood on the inhabitants of the earth?*
> **(Revelation 6: 9,10)**

4. *The Final Vision*

At that moment all the answers that countless generations have sought will come to the fore. On the one hand, our sins and vices, our dishonesty, greed and immorality are unmasked. But on the other hand, so are our good deeds and virtues. Once again the second Vatican Council puts it all in perspective:

> *Mindful of the Lord's saying: 'By this shall all men know that you are my disciples, if you have love for one another' (John 13:35), Christians cannot yearn for anything more ardently than to serve the men of the modern world even more generously and effectively. Therefore, holding faithfully to the Gospel, and benefiting from its resources, and united with every man who loves and practises justice, Christians have shouldered a gigantic task demanding fulfilment in this world. Concerning this task they must give a reckoning to Him, who will judge every man on the last day.* [146]

While the eyes of faith hold fast to this vision of eternity, it is imperative to keep our feet firmly planted on this earth. The Council again, in the Catechism, makes this point clear:

> *Far from diminishing our concern to develop this earth, the expectancy of a new earth should spur us on, for it is here that the body of a new human family grows, foreshadowing in some*

---

[146] *Vatican II's Gaudium et Spes #39 par.1.*

way the age which is to come. That is why, although we must be careful to distinguish earthly progress clearly from the increase of the kingdom of Christ, such progress is of vital concern to the kingdom of God, insofar as it can contribute to the better ordering human society.[147] (#1049)

++++++++++++++

Note: *We now turn to a topic that might appear to be out of place here. It is a topic that might be more appropriately dealt with under the Communion of Saints, as the Church Suffering. We do so because it is here that it is placed in the Catechism of the Catholic Church.*

(d) Purgatory

1. The Particular Judgement

> **If the work is burned up, the builder will suffer loss; the builder will be saved, but only as through fire.**
> **(1 Corinthians 3:15)**

Here the reference is to the teaching of St Paul wherein judgement is referred to as a *consuming fire*. From the very nature of the subject, it is obvious that much that can be said about the final judgement of mankind is necessarily obscure. However, if the details are obscure, the substance of the reality is not. This reality, as revealed by scripture, is that there will come a time when all the actions of everyone, whatever their status in this life, will be judged. The coming of Jesus, referred to in the Creed, deals with the *General* Judgement. However, it has already been preceded by the *Particular* Judgement. This is the judgement that follows immediately after death, and is, in a sense, an anticipation of the General Judgement. The latter is a confirmation of the former. The Church also declares that there is an intermediary state for those who have died and still preserve some attachment to sin. Catechism defines this as follows:

---

[147] *Diaogues 4,41 PL, 396 (Pope Leo the Great is quoted here).*

> *The Church gives the name Purgatory to this final purification of the elect, which is entirely different from the punishment of the damned. The Church formulated her doctrine of faith on Purgatory, especially at the Councils of Florence (1439) and Trent (1563). The Tradition of the Church, by reference to certain texts of Scripture, speaks of "a cleansing fire". As for lesser faults, we must believe that before the Final Judgement, there is a purifying fire. He who is truth says that whoever utters blasphemy against the Holy Spirit will be pardoned neither in this age nor in the age to come. From this sentence we understand that certain offences can be forgiven in this age, but certain others in the age to come.*[148]
>
> (1031)

2. *The Ultimate Forgiveness*

This reference of Jesus to forgiveness in the next world also occurs in the parable of the unjust steward who had not forgiven his fellow servant despite the forgiveness of his colossal debt of ten thousand talents. The lord's words are revealing:

> *You wicked slave! I forgave you all that debt because you pleaded with me. Should you not have had mercy on your fellow slave, as I had mercy on you?' And in anger his lord handed him over to be tortured until he would pay his entire debt.*
>
> (Matthew 18:32-34)

In this lesson of forgiveness the words *until he would pay his entire debt* reveal that there is a possibility of forgiveness in the punishment meted out to the delinquent slave! So the particular judgement is an encounter with Christ wherein is weighed our merit and our degree of service and love, as well as the burden of guilt in our sins. This judgement, in effect, revolves around how well we have endeavoured to follow in the footsteps of Jesus.

---

[148] *ibid.*

3. Conformity to Christ, the Firstborn!

We know that all things work together for good for those who love God, who are called according to his purpose. For those whom he foreknew he also predestined to be conformed to the image of his Son, in order that he might be the firstborn within a large family.
(Romans 8: 28-29)

If we are to be conformed to the image of *'his Son'* we have to confess our own innate inadequacy. It is inevitable that we always fall far short of our ideals and principles in this life. Right to our very last breath we carry within ourselves this heavy burden of human inadequacy and imperfection. It is the heavy burden of our weakness and attachment to the things and persons of this world.

God's love and infinite mercy provides a remedy for all this. For those souls that have died in a state of grace but are still far short of that purity and perfection needed for the grace of the beatific vision there is a remedy. It is an intermediate state of purgation in which departed souls atone for unforgiven venial sins and remit the temporal punishment due to mortal sins that have been forgiven in the *Sacrament of Reconciliation*. The centre of the Church's teaching on the subject of Purgatory is also to be found in the Council of Lyons II (1274):

> *Because if they die truly repentant in charity before they have made satisfaction by worthy fruits of penance for (sins) committed and omitted, their souls are cleansed after death by purgatorial or purifying punishments . . .*

4. The Maccabees

The existence of an intermediate state of purgation can be readily inferred from scripture. In the account of the wars of the Maccabees in the 2nd century B.C. It is related that *Judas Maccabaeus* discovered idols among his followers who had been slain, and he made a sin-offering on their behalf:

> ***In doing this he acted very well and honourably, taking account of the resurrection. For if he were not expecting that those who had fallen would rise again, it would have been superfluous and foolish to pray for the dead.***
> **(2 Maccabees 12:43-44)**

As with so much of the future life after death, we know so little of the nature of Purgatory. It is an *intermediate* state, a *transitional* state, a period of waiting where the soul is prepared for the wonderful experience of God's glory and infinite love! Here suffering is *lovingly* and *joyfully* accepted as a price for the cleansing of the soul from all that would be an impediment to the divine embrace. Only the *absolute* purity of heart and soul can endure the vision of God. The soul must be purged of all those attachments that bound and tied it to the superficial and passing delights of this world. It must not be forgotten that these souls in purgatory are still members of the mystical body of Christ. They need our prayers and sacrifices. For this reason the Church commends *prayers, almsgiving, indulgences* and *works of penance* undertaken on behalf of the dead.

Questions #13

* * *

1. What do you understand by the parousia and the 'End Times'?

2. What are the signs that herald the Second Coming of Jesus?

3. What does the Judgement mean in the Old Testament?

4. And the Judgement in the New Testament?

5. Where is to be found the locus classicus of the Last Judgement?

6. What do you understand by (a) continuous and (b) personal judgement?

7. How has Christ earned the right to judge the living and the dead?

8. How can anyone subscribe to "this barbarous doctrine of an eternal hell"?

9. *What is the Particular Judgement and its scriptural warranty?*

10. *What are the rational and scriptural bases for the doctrine of Purgatory?*

11. *The doctrine of Purgatory is obviously based on right reason! Comments?*

I Believe in the Holy Spirit

14. THE HOLY SPIRIT

* * *

Introduction

++++++++

(a) The Most Holy Trinity
 —1. The Mystery of Mysteries!
 —2. God—a Communion of Persons!
 —3. St Augustine
 —4. Appropriation and Mission

(b) He is Lord!
 —1. The Divinity of the Holy Spirit
 —2. The Spirit of Love
 —3. The Spirit of Truth
 —4. The Spirit of Sanctification

(c) The 'Holy' Spirit
 —1. The 'Paraclete'
 —2. The Spirit of Holiness
 —3. The Goal of 'Christification'
 —4. The Greatest Gift!

14. THE HOLY SPIRIT

* * *

Introduction

The first part of the Creed dealt with the Father and the Son. Now in the final section of the Creed we are confronted with a rather enigmatic 'person' called the Spirit. Who is this Spirit? To answer this question we must first attempt to probe the great mystery of God in the Trinity. True, this mystery of the Trinity is the most incomprehensible of all mysteries, but that should not deter us from attempting to explore what both scripture and tradition offer us on the subject.

(a) The Most Holy Trinity

1. *The Mystery of Mysteries!*

It is well to keep repeating, in seeking to come to terms with this mystery, that our words are limited by their very origin. They are human, *very* human and by that very fact, they are shot through with limitation. They are weighted down with all the biases of human thought and experience. But, faith seeks understanding in its probing of revelation, and in endeavouring to come to terms with what ultimately eludes all human comprehension. Human reason has obvious limitations, so it is equally obvious that there exists truths that far exceed its capacity to grasp. But we still seek assurance that, although this truth is above reason, it is not against reason! Hence, theologians seek clarification; they seek to enlighten and dispel the apparent contradictions in the data of revelation. Our minds were created for seeking the truth!

When we come to this mystery of the Trinity we touch the most unfathomable of all the mysteries of faith and yet it is the very foundation of the Christian faith. This is the doctrine of the *Tri-unity* or the most profound of all the mysteries of the faith, the existence of the Most Holy Trinity. So impervious to human reason is this doctrine that it had to be revealed to us by God himself. Inevitably, the human mind struggles to comprehend the *incomprehensible!* The Catechism summarises the doctrine of the Trinity in these words:

> ***The mystery of the Most Holy Trinity is the central mystery of Christian faith and life.*** *It is the mystery of God in himself. It is therefore the source of all other mysteries of faith the light that enlightens them. It is the most fundamental and essential teaching in the 'hierarchy of truths of faith'. The whole history of salvation is identical with the history of the way and the means by which the one true God, Father, Son and Holy Spirit, reveals himself to men and reconciles and unites with himself those who turn away from sin.* (#234)[149]

2. God—A Communion of Persons!

Alone, therefore, among the monotheistic religions of the world, Christianity maintains this startling and mind-boggling truth that the Godhead is a *communion of Persons!* We can well imagine how revolutionary must have been this idea to the apostles and disciples of Jesus. As Jews devoted to the Torah, they must have wrestled with Jesus' claim to be God, and how this fitted into their traditional monotheistic worship of the One God, *Yahweh*. And Jesus still insisted that not only was he God but that there was also a third person in the divinity!

In this community there is a *First Principle*, the *Father*, from whom *proceeds* the Son. This word *proceeds* gives us the theological term *procession*. This first *Procession* is called *the generation of the Son*, the Second Person of the Trinity. This Son is the Word spoken by the Father and is the image of the Father! The second procession is called a *breathing* or *spiration*[150]. This is the action of the loving union of Father and Son that breathes forth the Third Person, The Holy Spirit. The conclusion to this reasoning about the Processions of the Trinity is that there are three *Persons* subsisting in One nature and essence.

Stating this all as succinctly as possible, we might say that:

---

[149] *CCC*

[150] *It is from this that we get the word 'Spirit'.*

> ***God is absolutely One in nature and essence and
> relatively Three in Persons, Father, Son and Holy Spirit.***

3. St Augustine

Traditionally, the explanation offered by St Augustine has been used as an analogy to help us to throw light on this most baffling of mysteries. It is called the *psychological theory*. Starting with the premise that we have been created in the image of God, it is possible to detect something of the nature of God from that image. We might liken it to a detective, who, seeing a footprint in the sand, begins to speculate on the kind of person who made that print! The distinctive characteristic of man, what marks him off from the rest of creation, is his *mind* or reason. If we analyse the thought processes of that mind they revolve around the *triadic formula* of *willing, thinking* and *remembering*. The mind in its will to know brings forth an idea. This idea *generates* a word or a thought which is then named, acknowledged and embraced!

These thought processes give a very faint idea of the divine *processions*. By procession we mean *an issuing or going forth*. We speak of the coming forth of the Word as a *generation* or a begetting and of the Holy Spirit as *spiration*, a breathing forth *from the Father and the Son*.

4. Appropriation and Mission

Once again we approach the problem of analysing the operations of the Most Holy Trinity. It is our wont to analyse and dissect a problem since it is the usual and the only way to come to terms with it.

So in considering divine things and divine operations we attribute certain qualities, names and proceedings to one or other of the divine persons. This attribution is called *appropriation*. Hence we appropriate *creation* to the Father, *redemption* to the Son and *sanctification* to the Holy Spirit. This does not mean that these operations are confined to the one Person involved, since all three are involved. It is our human way of attempting to grapple with those things that concern God's dealings with mankind. The Catechism makes this abundantly clear in saying:

> *The whole divine economy is the common work of the three divine persons. For as the Trinity has only one and the same nature, so too does it have only one and the same operation: "The Father, the Son and the Holy Spirit are not three principles of creation, but one principle."[151] However, each divine person performs the common work according to his unique personal property.*
>
> (#258)

Closely linked to *appropriation* is the term *mission*, or *a sending forth!* In relation to the economy of salvation it refers to the *sending forth* of the Son for the redemption of mankind, and to the *sending forth* of the Spirit to carry on that redemption in the work of sanctification of the Church and its members. The mission then flows into the *Great Commission* when the apostles are sent forth to evangelise the world.

(b) He is Lord!

1. The Divinity of the Holy Spirit

We come to the inevitable conclusion that the Holy Spirit is the *Third Person* of the Most Holy Trinity. Nevertheless, it has endured constant attack. Just as Arius had earlier denied the divinity of Jesus so others began to deny the divinity of the Holy Spirit. This was especially so in the latter part of the fourth century, when the Patriarch of Constantinople, *Macedonius*, denied that the Spirit was divine. Those who followed him were hence called *Macedonians*. They were also known as *pneumatomachoi*, a Greek word meaning *Spirit-fighters* or *'enemies of the Spirit'!* In 381 A.D. at the Council of Constantinople this Macedonian heresy was officially condemned. This decision was ratified by Pope Damasus in 382 A.D. and the divinity of the Spirit was inserted into the Nicene[152] Creed:

---

[151] Here the Catechism is quoting the words of the *Council of Florence* (1442)

[152] This is the popular title, although, strictly speaking, it should be called the *Nicene-Constantinopolitan Creed*

> *We believe in the Holy Spirit, the Lord, the Giver of Life, who proceeds from the Father and the Son. With the Father and the Son he is worshipped and glorified.*

It is important to note that in reference to the Trinity we use the term *Person* to denote that each has the perfection of an individual personality. In that revelation we behold the *First* Person, the *Father* contemplating himself and knowing himself. In that knowledge of himself is *generated* the *Second* Person, the *Son*, who is the perfect image or reflection of the Father. Then both Father and Son embrace in the ecstasy of eternal love, producing *a state of Lovingness within the Divine Nature of the Godhead.*

> *Into this Lovingness, Father and Son pour all that They have and all that they are, with no diminution, holding nothing back. Thus this Lovingness within the Godhead is utterly equal to the Father and the Son, for they have poured Their all into it. There is nothing They have which their Lovingness does not have. Thus Their Lovingness too is Infinite, Eternal, Living, Someone, a Person, God.*[153]

2. *The Spirit of Love!*

The Holy Spirit, therefore, is the fruit of the love of the Father and the Son. In this Trinitarian relationship there exists a unique community of love, a total *self-giving* of each to the other. This love then spills out into creation.

> **In the beginning God created the heavens and the earth. The earth was a formless wasteland and darkness covered the abyss, while the spirit of God swept over the waters.**
> **(Genesis 1:1)**

Further along in the sacred text we witness the marvellous spectacle of God's self-giving to his creatures, whom he created in his own image! This image, besmirched by original sin, is restored by the outpouring of

---

[153] Frank Sheed: *Theology and Sanity*, (Sheed and Ward, 1960) p. 67

the Holy Spirit at Baptism and is constantly renewed by the wonders of the sacramental life.

This love is the key to the Kingdom of God. This love also shines forth in the first and greatest of all the commandments. However, the term used by Scripture in alluding to *love* is *agape*, a Greek word that has a specialised meaning that, unfortunately, is lost in translation. It means *unconditional* love! It is used in the new Testament 120 times. The corresponding verb form *agapan* is used 130 times. So the concept of *unconditional love* is to be found in the New Testament 250 times. This fact alone should alert us to its supreme importance in the Christian faith, in our walk with the Spirit of *agape*!

The Spirit of Love is especially the Spirit of *agape!* It is a love that knows no borders, boundaries or conditions. It is a love that embraces everyone including, in particular, our enemies and those we dislike! This is the burden of the famous parable of the *Good Samaritan,* an oxymoron to its first audience! To them there was no such thing as a *Good Samaritan!*

Love is the perfect image of the Holy Spirit since it reflects its divine origin in the heart of the Trinity. When love is in the soul *there is the Holy Spirit!* This love has guided countless saints in their earthly pilgrimage. It was the vocation of St Therese, the *Little Flower,* just as it must serve as a guide for us in our walk with the Spirit of Love! All things in the spiritual life pave the way for the reign of the *Spirit of Love.* St Paul has given us an immortal hymn to *agape* in the letter to the Corinthians. It is also a hymn to the Spirit of Love

> *If I speak in the tongues of men and of angels,*
> *but do not have love,*
> *I am a noisy gong or a clanging cymbal . . . .*
> *And now faith, hope, and love abide, these three;*
> *and the greatest of these is love.*
> **(1 Corinthians 13:1-13)**

3. *The Spirit of Truth*

It is Jesus himself who gives us this title. It is at the Last Supper that he gives this comforting assurance that his disciples would always have someone at their sides to assure them of the *truth*, that they would never go astray. No, far from straying into error the Holy Spirit would guide them *'into all the truth'!*

> *When the Spirit of truth comes, he will guide you into all the truth; for he will not speak on his own, but will speak whatever he hears, and he will declare to you the things that are to come.*
> **(John 16:13)**

In a world awash in moral relativism, in times of crisis about the claims of the Church to speak the *Truth*, Peter's question echoes in the presence of the Holy Spirit among us; *'Lord, to whom can we go?'* It may be fashionable to deny the existence of an *absolute truth* that demands *unconditional* allegiance. It is trendy or *'hip'* or to be *with it,* that is to say, to be tolerant of conflicting views and questionable life-styles. This moral relativism is sometimes called *"Situation Ethics"* about which the *Congregation of the Holy Office (*1956) stated that such a system that depends on *"some internal judgement and illumination of the mind . . . . is contrary to the truth of reality and the dictates of sound reason".*

4. *The Spirit of Sanctification*

> *In him (Jesus) the whole structure is joined together and grows into a holy temple of the lord; in whom you also are built together spiritually into a dwelling place for God.*
> **(Ephesians 2:21-22)**

The transforming power of the Holy Spirit on the individual soul is called the process of sanctification. By the power of the Holy Spirit we are grafted on to the vine that is Christ. However, a constant battle is being waged within us against the spirit of the world and all its seductive values. All that is opposed to the spirit of Christ is outlined in unmistakable terms by St Paul in his letter to the Galatians. Therein he warns his converts against the idolatry and the gross immorality that surrounds them.

> *Now the works of the flesh are obvious: fornication, impurity, licentiousness. idolatry, sorcery, enmities,*

> *strife jealousy, anger, quarrels, dissensions, factions, envy, drunkenness, carousing and things like these. I am warning you, as I warned you before; those who do such things will not inherit the kingdom of God.*
> **(Galatians 5: 19-21)**

It is superfluous to say that these warnings of Paul are as relevant today as they were then. We stand in need of the Holy Spirit as our ally against the forces of evil. His help is so desperately needed if we are to realize the goal of Jesus coming to our aid:

> *I came that that they may have life and have it abundantly.*
> **(John 10:10)**

This promise of abundant life comes from John's parable of the Good Shepherd. Jesus, himself the Good Shepherd, laid down his life for his sheep and won for us the right to lay claim to this abundant life. Through the presence of the Holy Spirit, especially in the sacraments of the Church, this 'abundant life' flows into the lives of all those who seek it.

One of the greatest hymns in Christian hymnody is the Veni Creator Spiritus. The author of this timeless hymn is reputedly a monk of the 8th century, Rabanus Maurus. In it he captures the longing and the spirit of the first Pentecost. It echoes the constant cry of the Church:

> *Come Holy Spirit, Creator come*
> *From thy bright heavenly throne.*
> *Come take possession of our souls and*
> *make then all thy own*!

(c) The Holy Spirit

1. The Paraclete

There is a special name given to the Holy SpIrit in scripture. He is called the *Paraclete*, a term derived from the Greek *parakletos*. It means a person who is summoned to the help of someone in trouble and in need of comfort, assurance and advice. All this portrays the Holy Spirit as the *helper* of the faithful. Nothing could be more fitting than the use of such a term to define the role of the Holy Spirit in the life of the Church. There is, however, no precise equivalent in the English language. We have either to resort to such terms as *Comforter, Advocate* or *Helper,* or simply keep the original term in *Paraclete.* The term *Advocate* has legal overtones. This comes from the fact that the *parakletos* was the friend of the accused or prisoner. He was the one who bore witness to his friend's character when the latter most needed such a defence. In this sense Christ is also our *parakletos* since he pleads with the Father on our behalf! This is the point of the author of the letter to the Hebrews who points to Jesus as always living to make intercession on our behalf. *(Hebrews 7:25)* as if underscoring at the same time, the role of the Holy Spirit as one who pleads our cause in the courts of Heaven!

The title of *Comforter* suggests that of *Consoler,* but in its original meaning, it points rather to that of *Strengthener,* a more fitting term for the One who helps us to endure the inevitable trials and travails of Christian fidelity. There is one final aspect of this elusive term that is derived from the Greek root verb *parakalein,* meaning to address, exhort or entreat. It was used in particular by a general speaking to his troops on the eve of battle urging them on to victory!

> Life is always calling us into battle and the one who is able to make us stand up to the opposing forces, to cope with life and to conquer life is the parakletos, the Holy Spirit, who is none other than the presence and the power of the Risen Christ.[154]

2. *The Spirit of Holiness*

There is a special title attached to the Paraclete in that he is known as the *Holy* Spirit. Holiness is the characteristic of the three Persons of the Trinity. But it is attributed to the Spirit in a special way, since it is the

---

[154] William Barclay: *New Testament Words* (The Westminster Press, Philadelphia, 1974) p.222

lot of the Spirit to convey this holiness to the Church. This emerges very clearly in the letters of St Paul and in the Catechism when he says

> *No one can say 'Jesus is Lord' except by the Holy Spirit.*
> *(1 Corinthians 12:3)*

> *God has sent the Spirit of his Son into our hearts crying 'Abba Father!'*
> *(Galatians 4:6)*

The Catechism also spells this out in the clearest possible terms:

> *This knowledge of faith is possible only in the Holy Spirit: to be in touch with Christ we must first have been touched by the Holy Spirit. He comes to meet us and kindles faith in us. By virtue of our Baptism, the first sacrament of the faith, the Holy Spirit in the Church communicates to us, intimately and personally, the life that originates in the Father and is offered to us in the Son.*
> (#683)

3. The Goal of Christification

There has to be some rationale for this divine bounty. The answer lies in the goal of the workings of the Holy Spirit within us. This goal entails a process of Christification, of making us more like Christ, or other Christs! The priest, in virtue of his sacerdotal ordination, is called an *alter Christus* (another Christ). Something similar takes place in the sacrament of baptism. In this sacrament the newly baptised is united in some mysterious way to the priesthood of Jesus. In fact, by the very title of becoming a Christian we bear witness. It is a process, by this very title, entailing a solemn undertaking to strive to become more like Christ himself! The Catechism points out:

> *The grace of the Holy Spirit confers upon us the righteousness of God. Uniting us by faith and Baptism to the Passion and the Resurrection of Christ the Spirit makes us sharers in his life.*
> (#2017)

One author, Frank Sheed, has sought to shed some light on this magnificent process:

> *The moral for us is simple: in our approach to God we are helped enormously by seeing him in our nature; and for the mind this means a continual study of Christ whereby the apostles' experience of him becomes our own personal experience; their intimacy become our intimacy. We cannot always analyse intimacy; but there is no mistaking it; we know the person quite differently. You do not learn intimacy, or reap the fruit of someone else's. You grow into it.*[155]

4. The Greatest Gift

As our soul's most welcome guest the Spirit honours us with a whole battery of gifts that are commensurate with his divinity. Generous beyond all measure his gifts reflect his title of Paraclete, a title that struggles for translation into English. Such titles as *Advocate*, *Counselor* and *Comforter*, scarcely do it justice. St Peter, in his first Pentecostal sermon, quotes the prophetic words of the prophet Joel:

> **And in the last days it shall be, God declares, that I will put out my Spirit upon all flesh, and your sons and your daughters will prophesy, and your young men will see visions, and your old men shall dream dreams; yea, and on my menservants and my maid servants in those days I will pour out my Spirit; and they shall prophesy.**
>
> **(Acts 2:17-18)**

This magnificent promise points to a pouring out of the Spirit and his gifts on future generations, especially on the last days. The biblical use of the word 'pour' is a tribute to the amazing generosity of our Father in heaven. It is a generosity that is echoed in the letters of Paul:

---

[155] *op.cit. 49*

> *Blessed by the God and Father of our Lord Jesus Christ.*
> *who has blessed us in Christ with every spiritual blessings*
> *in the heavenly places*
>
> **(Ephesians 1:3)**

It is evident that the gifts of the Spirit are most manifest in the sacramental life of the Church. The Spirit brings the gift of eternal life in the sacrament of Baptism, when the priest breathes into the face of the one being baptized and says: *"Go out from him unclean spirit, and give place to the Holy Spirit!"* a gift that is renewed in the sacrament of Confirmation. Through this *"free gift of righteousness"* (Romans 5:17) it is impossible to do justice to the divine generosity and liberality. Not only do we receive the gifts of *faith, hop*e and *charity,* but a whole array of supernatural gifts are made available to us— *"every spiritual blessing in the heavenly places".*

* * *

> *When the Advocate comes,*
> *whom I will send to you from the Father,*
> *the Spirit of truth who comes from the Father,*
> *he will testify on my behalf.*
>
> **(John 15:26)**

++++++++++++

Jesus and the Spirit

++++++++++++++

> *Then Jesus, filled with the power of the Spirit,*
> *returned to Galilee, and a report about him*
> *spread through all the surrounding country.*
> *He began to teach in their synagogues*
> *and was praised by everyone.*

> *When he came to Nazareth,*
> *where he had been brought up,*
> *he went to the synagogue on the sabbath day,*
> *as was his custom. He stood up to read,*
> *and the scroll of the prophet Isaiah was given to him.*
> *He unrolled the scroll and found the place*
> *where it was written:*
>
> *"The Spirit of the Lord is upon me,*
> *because he has anointed me to bring good news to the poor.*
> *He has sent me to proclaim release to the captives*
> *and recovery of sight to the blind,*
> *to let the oppressed go free,*
> *to proclaim the year of the Lord's favor."* [156]
>
> *And he rolled up the scroll,*
> *gave it back to the attendant, and sat down.*
> *The eyes of all in the synagogue were fixed on him.*
> *Then he began to say to them,*
> *"Today this scripture has been fulfilled*
> *in your hearing."*
>
> (Luke 4:14-21)

---

[156] **Isaiah 61:1**

Questions #14

* * *

1. *What does the Catechism say about this central mystery of the Christian faith?*

2. *What do you mean by saying that the Trinity is a Communion of Persons?*

3. *Why did the disciples have such trouble accepting what Jesus said on this subject?*

4. *What do these terms mean in their present context?*

    Procession and Appropriation

    Mission, Spiration and Generation

5. *How does Augustine try to help us "understand" this mystery?*

6. *The entire life of Jesus as the Messiah was dominated by the Spirit. Explain!*

7. *Why is the Holy Spirit called the Spirit of Love and Truth?*

8. *The Spirit of Truth is utterly opposed to Situation Ethics or moral relativism! Why?*

9. *What do you understand by the term 'Paraclete'? Why is it said to be untranslatable?*

10. *The Goal of the Spirit is our Christification! Meaning?*

11. *"The Greatest Gift!" Why is this title given to the Holy Spirit?*

15. THE LORD—
THE GIVER OF LIFE (I)

* * *

(a) The Sacramental System
 —1. Christ: the Eternal High Priest
 —2. Christ—the Sacrament of the Church
 —3. Channels of Divine Life
 —4. God's Masterpieces

(b) The Sacrament of Baptism
 —1. The Divine Command
 —2. "In Water and in Blood!"
 —3. A New Creation
 —4. The Character Of Baptism

(c) The Sacrament of Confirmation
 —1. The Consuming Fire!
 —2. The Seal of the Spirit

(d) The Sacrament of the Eucharist
 —1. The Incredible Truth!
 —2. The Sacrament of Sacraments
 —3. The Breaking of the Bread
 —4. The Eucharistic Sacrifice

15. The Giver of Life (i)[157]

* * *

(a) The Sacramental System

1. Christ; the Eternal High Priest

> *For it was fitting that we should have such a high priest, holy, blameless, undefiled, separated from sinners, and exalted above the heavens. Unlike the other high priests, he has no need to offer sacrifices day after day, first for his own sins, and then for those of the people; this he did once for all when he offered himself.*
> **(Hebrews 7:26-27)**

This letter to the Hebrews makes the very valid point that Christ is a high priest far superior to the high priests of the Old Law. The latter as sinners themselves stood in need of redemption. Christ did not. As both *Priest* and *Victim* his sacrifice is wholly unique. He offered himself *once for all* (Romans 6:10) and from this unique sacrifice flows the power of the sacraments of the Church. Mankind stood sadly in need of redemption and for this Christ had to suffer. He had to endure the scandal of the Cross, as the price of man's deliverance:

> *Christ redeemed us from the curse of the law by becoming a curse for us!*
> **(Galatians 3:13)**

It is also evident that this *curse*, embraced by Christ for our sakes, is not a simple historical drama rooted forever in the past. It is a *transhistorical* or *transcendent* event that reaches back to the Garden of Eden and stretches forward to the Last Judgement! Christ's sacrifice and his complete submission to his Eternal Father is an abiding reality that is wholly relevant to the life of the Church today. Even now he is our Priest in Heaven still offering himself and His Blood poured out

---

[157] *This title "Giver of Life" comes from the Nicene Creed.*

from Gethsemane to Calvary. This was the vision witnessed by John in Revelation, when he beheld the Lamb of of God *"as though it had been slain" (Revelation 5:6)* worshipped by the four living creatures and the twenty four elders who sang a new song:

> **You were slaughtered and by your blood you ransomed for God saints from every tribe and language and people and nation; you have made them to be a kingdom and priests serving our God, and they will reign on earth."**
> **(Revelation 5: 9-10)**

It is but a truism to say that we cannot touch or reach out to our Great High Priest who dwells in unapproachable light, *whom no one has ever seen or can see.* (1 Timothy 6:16). But we can reach out to him through the Church, through the sacramental system.

> *For this reason we have the Church, with all its external apparatus of law, teaching authority and liturgy, through which we can come into bodily contact with our Mediator-Priest to receive from him, in the human fashion that the Incarnation implies, the law of grace and the word of life and so participate in his sacrifice.*[158]

2. Christ—the Sacrament of the Church

Christ's earthly existence was a matter of some 33 years and then he left behind a band of chosen followers to carry on his work. His life was the climax of interventions in the life of the Chosen People who ultimately rejected him.[159] However, he left behind a group of apostles whom he charged to bring his message of redemption to the whole of humanity!

> ***Go therefore and make disciples of all nations!***
> **(Matthew 28:18)**

---

[158] *Colman E. O'Neill O.P. Meeting Christ in the Sacraments (Alba House, N.Y. 1991) p.21*

[159] *Christ will always be a source of conflict of acceptance and rejection.*

How was this great Commission to be carried out? True, scripture assures us that Jesus' concern was reinforced by prayer on behalf of his followers in Heaven where *he ever lives to make intercession for them.* (Hebrews 7:25) His presence was assured in the Church he left behind to carry on his work. He told his grieving followers at the Last Supper that it was expedient that he should leave them!

> **If I do not go away, the Advocate will not come to you;**
> **but if I go, I will send him to you.**
> **(John 16:7)**

Jesus, in effect, is telling them that he is going to die. It is necessary for him to fulfill the will of the Father. In doing so he becomes the Head of the Church, the new People of God. It is here that St Augustine's comment is so appropriate:

> *Christ dies that the Church may be born.*[160]

Christ promised his apostles that he would be with them to the end of time. It is through the sacraments in particular that he manifests this presence. That of the Eucharist is a striking example. Just as Mary became fertile with Jesus through the embrace of the Holy Spirit, so through the action of that same Spirit the sacraments become efficacious channels of the divine life in us. It is this that the catechism states so forcefully:

> *Celebrated worthily in faith, the sacraments confer the grace*
> *that they signify.*
> *They are efficacious because, in them, Christ himself is at work;*
> *it is he who baptises, he who acts in the sacraments*
> *in order to communicate the grace that each sacrament signifies.*
> (#1127)

---

[160] *The original Latin is more striking: 'Moritur Christus ut fiat Ecclesia!'*

3. Channels of Divine Life

From the foregoing it follows that the sacraments are the primary channels of the divine life. The power of the sacrament resides in three essential elements:

(i) *It must be instituted by Christ himself.*
(ii) *Sanctifying grace is conferred through the requisite matter and form.*
(iii) *It is conferred by a minister acting on behalf of the Church.*

The Church was *conceived* when Christ became man and was *born* in Pentecost when the Holy Spirit came down in the guise of a mighty wind upon Mary and the apostles at Pentecost. The Church, therefore, is this *Mystical Body of Christ* as first conceived in the womb of Mary in the embrace of the Holy Spirit sent by the Father. Seen in this light it can be said that the Church is a prolongation of the Incarnation and dispensing the fruits of redemption to all generations. As the fruit of all this the Church became the instrument of the Father's will here on earth.

Matter and *form* are said to be of the essence of a sacrament. *Matter* refers to the outward sign of the physical elements used in the administration of the sacrament. This outward sign can be the material used (for example *water* in baptism) or the action observed. The *form* refers to the words and signs that are used in conjunction with the matter.

It must be emphasised that the Church has no power to *institute a sacrament*. This is Christ's sole prerogative. He gave his apostles a mandate to carry out his wishes. In doing so, they are said to act *'in his name'* and with his supreme authority. By force of that authority the sacraments are said to confer grace *'ex opere operato'*.[161] This means that grace is conferred *in virtue of the rite itself that is now being administered*[162]. The

---

[161] *The Latin means 'from the work done'.*
[162] *This emphasis on the act itself is a blow to the Donatist heresy that maintained that the validity of the sacrament depended on the spiritual condition of the one ministering the sacrament.*

minister thus expresses the mind of the Church in fulfilling the wishes of Christ himself. The Catechism expresses this as follows:

> *From the moment that a sacrament is celebrated in accordance with the intention of the Church, the power of Christ and his Holy Spirit acts in and through it, independently of the personal holiness of the minister. Nevertheless, the fruits of the sacrament also depend on the disposition of the one who receives them.*
>
> (#1128)

4. God's Masterpieces

> *Sacraments are 'powers that come forth' from the Body of Christ which is ever-living and life-giving. They are the actions of the Holy Spirit at work in his body, the Church. They are the masterpieces of God in the new and everlasting covenant.*
>
> (#1117)

The whole sacramental system centres around this astonishing goal of the offering of God's infinite love to us sinners who are wholly unworthy of that love! It is within this context that the drama of salvation is played out.

The whole liturgical life of the Church revolves around these sacraments, of which there are seven, *Baptism, Confirmation, Eucharist, Penance, Anointing of the Sick, Holy Orders and Matrimony.* At the same time, one cannot help marvelling at how the list of the sacraments echoes in the natural development of the lives of the faithful. Here is how one author, Frank Sheed, views it:

> *Observe how precisely this system of sacraments corresponds to the shape of man's natural life. Ordinarily, we can count upon four determining points in human life; a man is born, a man dies; in between he grows up and marries—or, if he be Catholic, he may choose the direct ministry of God. For these four points with their five possibilities there are five sacraments.*
>
> *A man is reborn by Baptism, by which he gets a place in the Kingdom; for growing out of childhood there is Confirmation, by which he gets a function in the Kingdom; for marriage there is Matrimony. for ministry there is Holy Orders, this latter being*

a fuller function in the Kingdom; for death there is the last Anointing. As life flows normally from one point to the next, there are two other needs, for daily bread and for healing in sickness. In the supernatural life there are sacraments for these two, completing the seven. The Blessed Eucharist provides our daily bread, the sacrament of Penance our healing in the soul's sickness.[163]

(b) Baptism

1. The Divine Command

All authority in heaven and on earth has been given to me. Go therefore and make disciples of all nations, baptizing them in the name of the Father and of the Son and of the Holy Spirit.
(Matthew 28:18-19)

There are few words in all the Gospels that are so explicit and forthright as these words that conclude the Gospel of Matthew. These are the words of the Great Commission that express the imperative of conversion. It is reflected again in the response of Peter to those of his hearers who, in the aftermath of Pentecost, asked him what they should do:

> ***"Repent, and be baptized every one of you in the name of Jesus Christ so that your sins may be forgiven; and you will receive the gift of the Holy Spirit.".***
> **(Acts 2:38)**

It is through Baptism, the most important of all the sacraments, that mankind is delivered from the deadly contagion of original sin. As the *Epistle of Barnabas*[164] describes it:

> *We descend in to the water laden with sins and filth and we emerge from it bearing fruit with the fear (of God) in our heart and the hopes of Jesus in the soul.*

---

[163] *Frank Sheed: op.cit. pp216-217*
[164] *This refers to an apocryphal letter of thre first century.*

Baptism forgives all sins, both original and personal. However, the specific target of Baptism is original sin, the sin inherited from our first parents, Adam and Eve. This sin epitomises the *'sin of the world'* that expresses our total estrangement from God.

This estrangement from God is expressed by St Paul:

> *Therefore, just as sin came into the world through one man, and death came through sin, and so death spread to all because all have sinned.... For just as by the one man's disobedience the many were made sinners, so by the one man's obedience the many will be made righteous.*
> *(Romans 5:12,19)*

2. In Water and in Blood!

> *Very truly, I tell you, no one can enter the kingdom of God without being born of water and Spirit.*
> **(John 3:5)**

In *Genesis* there is a close identification of water with God's creative action wherein the sacred author tells us that the Spirit of God was moving over the waters *(Genesis 1:2)*. Water is one of the necessities of life and in that sombre fact there is prefigured the role that water has to play in the founding of the Church. On this very subject the Catechism remarks:

> Since the beginning of the world water, so humble and wonderful a creature, has been the source of life and fruitfulness. Sacred Scripture sees it as 'foreshadowed' by the Spirit of God at the dawn of creation. Your Spirit breathed on the waters, making them the wellspring of all holiness.
> (#1218)

Water, therefore, was destined to become a symbol of God's creative action on the human soul. This symbolism is heightened considerably in the Baptism of Jesus in the River Jordan. There we see the heavens opened and the Spirit of God descending upon him while the voice of the Father is heard:

> *"This is my Son, the Beloved, with whom I am well pleased."*
> **(Matthew 3:17)**

This baptism of water is ultimately sealed in the sacrifice of Calvary. The Jordan is but a foreshadowing of the Messiah's mission. It still has to be consummated on Calvary. The greater baptism of Jesus is in the blood of his sacred Passion, about which Jesus himself exclaims:

> *I came to bring fire to the earth, and how I wish it were already kindled! I have a baptism with which to be baptized, and what stress I am under until it is completed!*
> **(Luke 12:49-50)**

It is this that prompts the apostle Paul to pose the rhetorical question

> *Do you not know that all of us who have been baptized into Christ Jesus were baptized into his death?*
> **(Romans 6:3)**

3. A New Creation

From all the foregoing it follows that this sacrament is the very foundation of our participation in the divine life. Even the Greek original of this word baptism—*baptizethai*—conveys the notion of *drowning!* Symbolically it conveys the idea of a deep transforming and a radical cleansing of the soul.

This is forcibly expressed by Pope St Leo the Great in one of his sermons:

> *At the new birth of each one of us the baptismal water becomes the mother's womb. For the same Holy Spirit which filled the Virgin, fills the font as well so that sin, which in her case was eliminated by her sacred conception, is here blotted out by a mystical washing.*

The thought here expressed goes far beyond the notion of *'membership'* that was once current in Catholic thought. This is the idea of rebirth or *incorporation*. It was revived by the Second Vatican Council to reflect the reality of new life in Christ[165]. It must be stressed that every true Baptism brings the baptised into the Body of Christ. From the gift of the Holy Spirit an indelible seal is imprinted on the soul of the newly baptised signifying this union with the Body of Christ. This incorporation through baptism normally signifies membership in one true Church. The Catechism summarises all this in saying:

> *Baptism not only purifies from sin, but also makes the neophyte a 'new creature' and adopted son of God, who has become a 'partaker of the divine nature'[166] a member of Christ and co-heir with him, and a temple of the Holy Spirit.*
>
> (#1265)

However, it is an unfortunate reality that the Church of today is splintered into various denominations, *Catholic, Orthodox, Anglican, Lutheran* and innumerable *Christian sects*. In general, the Protestant view is that the Church is an *invisible* reality. Its focus is on the inner world, known only to God, wherein the baptised *is united to Christ in sincerity and truth*. The Catholic view is that the Church is a *visible and recognisable reality* that traces its legitimate lineage back to the apostles chosen by Christ himself. Baptism is an initiation, tangible and visible, into this visible reality. As the Council itself states:

> *They are fully incorporated into the society of the Church, who, possessing the Spirit of Christ, accept her entire system and all the means of salvation given to her.*[167]

Implicit in Baptism is the call to holiness of life. If the complete forgiveness of sins is to have any meaning in the future life of the recipient. It entails a life focussed on Christ, on a spirit of repentance and the imperative of sincerity and righteousness in life.

---

[165] *Decree of the Second Vatican Council 'Lumen Gentium'.*
[166] *Here the Catechism is referring to Paul's letters" 2 Cor. 5:17 and Gal. 4:5-7.*
[167] *Lumen Gentium 14:2.*

4. The Character of Baptism

In this context the term *'character'* has a specialised meaning. a mysterious and indelible seal or mark impressed upon the soul of the newly baptised. This seal entitles the recipient to a share in the priesthood of Christ. It confers the status of a special relationship to the Body of Christ, a status that is renewed in the sacrament of Confirmation:

> *This configuration to Christ and to the Church, brought about by the (Holy) Spirit is indelible; it remains for ever in the Christian as a positive disposition for grace, a promise and a guarantee of divine protection and as a vocation to divine worship and to the service of the Church.*
>
> (#1121)

There remains the danger of considering this initial sacrament as purely symbolic. Such was the extreme view of some of the reformers of the sixteenth century Reformation, such as Zwingli,[168] held. The explicit command of Jesus himself cannot be taken as purely symbolic. It underscores the fact that the recipient is entitled to bring Christ into liturgical actions and to act effectively at the level of visible Church functions. One author expresses this fundamental aspect:

> *The baptismal character might be thought of as the key which opens the door to the sacramental or visible life of the Church, or it could be considered as something like the plug of an electrical appliance; it makes the connection between the sanctifying activity of the Christ in the visible structure of the Church and the spiritual life of the faithful.*[169]

The terms *key* and *plug* may be very *earthy* terms but they seek to convey a profound *spiritual* reality, the reality of the presence of Christ

---

[168] *Ulrich Zwingli (1484-1531) a Swiss and radical 'reformer' killed at the Battle of Kappel.*

[169] *Colman O'Neill op.cit. p.114*

in the congregation. This goes far beyond the simple responses, the singing and the acclamations of those present. They echo the reality of a divine presence. Here, where the Church is in action, the Body of Christ is present!

(c) Confirmation

1. The Consuming Fire!

> *Then Elijah arose, a prophet like fire,*
> *and his word burned like a torch.* **(Sirach 48:1)**

Fire, as the source of illumination and warmth, is a symbol of *zeal and dedication*. The ancient Greeks spoke of such dedication as *enthusiasm* as of one *possessed by a god!*[170] We also speak of persons being *on fire* for a special cause. In the Old Testament we get a glimpse of its power in the ministry of the prophet Elijah. In the New Testament it is again echoed in the ministry of John the Baptist. He went before the Lord in the spirit and the power of Elijah, proclaiming the message and mission of the Messiah:

> *"I baptize you with water; but one who is more powerful than I is coming; I am not worthy to untie the thong of his sandals. He will baptize you with the Holy Spirit and fire."*
>
> **(Luke 3:16)**

Jesus himself emerged from the anonymity of Nazareth in proclaiming the fulfilment of the prophecy of Isaiah in his own person:

> *The spirit of the Lord GOD is upon me, because the LORD has anointed me; he has sent me to bring good news to the oppressed, to bind up the broken-hearted, to proclaim liberty to the captives, and release to the prisoners.*
>
> **(Isaiah 61:1)**

---

[170] *from the Greek 'enthousiasmos' meaning 'one possessed by a god'!*

At his Ascension he told his disciples to await the coming of the Spirit:

> *"But you will receive power when the Holy Spirit has come upon you; and you will be my witnesses in Jerusalem, in all Judea and Samaria, and to the ends of the earth."*
> **(Acts 1:8)**

The promise of Jesus was fulfilled on the feast of Pentecost:

> *And suddenly from heaven there came a sound like the rush of a violent wind, and it filled the entire house where they were sitting. Divided tongues, as of fire, appeared among them, and a tongue rested on each of them. All of them were filled with the Holy Spirit and began to speak in other languages as the Spirit gave them ability.*
> Acts 2:2-4)

2. *The Seal of the Spirit*

The essential effect of the sacrament of Confirmation is to bring to perfection the gifts of the Holy Spirit that have been received in Baptism. Where Baptism delivers from sin and confers new life the sacrament of Confirmation highlights these gifts in exhorting the recipients to give to the world the authentic witness of what being a Christian really means.

As followers of the Messiah, whose name they bear, they must go forth and be examples of true Christian living. Christians are called to service and bear witness. The very name they bear—*Christian*—is derived from the Greek translation of *Messiah* that is *Christos, Anointed One!* Hence, the very name Christian that we bear brings with it the responsibility of honouring that name by a life of good example and devotion.

There are obvious questions that can be raised on this issue of 'being confirmed'. *Is this sacrament really necessary? Isn't Baptism alone sufficient? Isn't Christ sufficient?* The main answer is to be found in the descent of the Holy Spirit at Pentecost. This was the urgent message of Christ himself as he prepared to ascend to Heaven:

> *And see, I am sending upon you what my Father promised;*
> *so stay here in the city until you have been clothed*
> *with power from on high.*
>
> **(Luke 24:49)**

The descent of the Holy Spirit transformed the apostles and disciples. From being skulking cowards and very ordinary fishermen they became the intrepid messengers of the Gospel to the furthest reaches of the Roman Empire and beyond. In pre-Vatican days it used to be said that Confirmation was an enlisting in the army of Christ. The recipients were now *'soldiers of Christ'*! This military vocabulary, however, is no longer popular, but it best expresses the purpose of the sacrament.

All the foregoing are aptly summarised in the Catechism:

> *it roots us more deeply in the divine Sonship of Christ;*
> *it strengthens our relationship with the Father (Abba! Father!)*
> *it deepens and increases the gifts of the Holy Spirit within;*
> *it reinforces the bond with the Church, the Body of Christ;*
> *it empowers the recipients, under the influence of the Holy Spirit, to be truly witnesses, and even martyrs, to the cross of Christ!*
>
> (see #1303)

Moreover, the need for a fresh influx of spiritual power becomes necessary where infant baptism is the norm. It is an opportunity for the recipient to make that personal commitment to Christ which he or she was unable to make as a child or baby. Confirmation seals the baptismal covenant. It confers the power to live a life of holiness in a world that is often at war with the Gospel of Christ. Christianity, by its very creed, is countercultural.

(d) The Eucharist

1. The Incredible Truth

> *Very truly, I tell you, unless you eat the flesh of the Son of Man and drink his blood, you have no life in you. Those who eat my flesh and drink my blood have eternal life, and I will raise them up on the last day; for my flesh is*

> *true food and my blood is true drink. Those who eat my flesh and drink my blood abide in me, and I in them.*
> **(John 6:53-56)**

These dramatic words uttered by Jesus to his audience in Capharnaum were the climax of a series of events that began in the miraculous multiplication of loaves in the desert. In the context of that miracle there was an obvious allusion to the historic feeding of the people of Israel with manna during their flight from Egypt to the Promised Land. What Jesus is telling to a largely incredulous audience was that he was the new Manna of the New Covenant. It was a claim that fell on deaf ears! It is recorded that many took offence at it and simply got up and left him. Jesus made no attempt to stop them. He did not attempt to explain or qualify, but turned to his apostles and asked if they too wanted to go. He wanted their trust and an avowal of their faith in him. It was Peter that gave it in words that have resounded down the centuries:

> *Lord to whom shall we go?*
> *You have the words of eternal life!*
> **(John 6:68)**

That drama of assertion and denial has repeated itself countless times in the course of history of the Church. Just as Christ was a source of division so has belief in his Real Presence in the Eucharist throughout the centuries. This reality is one of history's ironies that what was intended to be a source of unity became a source of conflict and disunity. The same sense of incredulity that greeted Jesus himself echoes and re-echoes down the centuries to the present day:

> *How can this man give us his flesh to eat.*
> **(John 6:52)**

This sacrament is such a marvel of God's love that, on a very human level one can understand, to some extent, the misgivings of unbelievers. Yes, purely on human terms it is utterly incomprehensible. In addition, the most convoluted arguments are advanced to explain away the obvious meaning of what Jesus said. We get lost in a meaningless labyrinth of misinterpretations all endeavouring to explain what Jesus really meant!

The life of Jesus was too short in human terms, just over 30 years! In this sacrament he found a way to stay with us in a way that only infinite love could devise. FOR GOD LOVES US INFINITELY! Only infinite love could have devised this means of perpetuating Christ's presence here on earth. This was the real Presence of Jesus in the Eucharist. We can only marvel at the depth of such love that *'imprisons'* itself in our tabernacles, where it is so often treated with disrespect and neglect. But Jesus was prepared to submit even to such in order to satisfy his burning love and thirst for our salvation. St Thomas Aquinas penned a marvellous hymn to the wonders of divine love:

> *Godhead here in hiding, whom I do adore*
> *Masked by these bare shadows, shape and nothing more!*
> *See, Lord, at thy service low lies here a heart*
> *Lost, all in wonder at the God thou art*

2. The Sacrament of Sacraments

> The Eucharist is the *'source and summit of the Christian life.'* The other sacraments, and indeed all other ecclesiastical ministries and works of the apostolate, are bound up with the Eucharist, and are oriented towards it. For in the blessed Eucharist is contained the whole spiritual good of the Church, namely Christ himself, our Pasch.
>
> (#1324)

Christ as *'our Pasch'* is a reference to the Jewish feast of Passover, the first great feast of the liturgical year. The Passover commemorated the saving of the Israelites from the avenging angel when the blood of a lamb was sprinkled on their door posts. The reference to Jesus here is the fulfilment of the antitype in Jesus as the *'Lamb of God'* sacrificed on Calvary for the salvation of all humanity. This sacrament, therefore, is a special link with the Passion, Death and Resurrection of Jesus. These events lie at the very heart of the Christian message, which is why the Vatican Council called the Eucharist *"the source and summit of the Christian life"*. This sacrament rests fully on the authority of Christ himself, whose words are recorded in all the synoptic gospels.

> *Jesus took a loaf of bread, and after blessing it he broke it, gave it to the disciples, and said, "Take, eat; this is my body." Then he took a cup, and after giving thanks he gave it to them, saying, "Drink from it, all of you; for this is my blood of the covenant, which is poured out for many for the forgiveness of sins."*
>
> **(Matthew 26: 26-28)**

It is but a truism to assert that all the actions, gestures and words of Jesus are laden with mystery, since he is the God-Man. From this union of two natures, the divine and the human, flows the inevitable consequence that the divine invades every aspect of what Jesus says and does. And when the occasion is so momentous, as here in the celebration of the Passover, what he says and does is invested with the profoundest significance, not merely for one instance but for all time. Here in this most solemn moment of the *'hour'* of Jesus, he takes a loaf of bread, blesses it and breaks it and gives it to his disciples with the most solemn injunction:

> *Do this in remembrance of me!*
> **(Luke 22:19)**[171,172]

3. The Breaking of the Bread!

> *They devoted themselves to the apostles' teaching and fellowship, to the breaking of bread and the prayers.*
> **(Acts 2:42)**

The Breaking of the Bread! All the synoptics record and emphasize this simple and homely gesture. It is this fact of record that prompts the question: Why did Jesus break the bread? Beyond the fact that it is a gesture of convenience for the sake of distribution, there is a profound symbolism that made it a synonym for the Eucharist. The bread recalls the manna of the desert years in the days of Moses. Now it is the new

---

[171,172] *This repetition of the Lord's command only emphasises that every Mass is a fulfilment of that divne command!*

manna of the new covenant. But far more than that it represents Jesus himself. No, more than that, it *is* Jesus!

The breaking symbolises his complete submission to his Father's will. That will dominated his whole life. It culminated in the Passion and Death of Jesus. The struggle that it involves emerges in the heart-rending prayer of Jesus:

> *"Father, if you are willing, remove this cup from me; yet, not my will but yours be done." Then an angel from heaven appeared to him and gave him strength. In his anguish he prayed more earnestly, and his sweat became like great drops of blood falling down on the ground.*
> **(Luke 22:42-44)**

There is an unbreakable link between the Passover of the Upper Room and the Crucifixion of Calvary. It witnessed the titanic struggle of Jesus coming to terms with all that the Father desired for the redemption of mankind. The breaking of the bread speaks to us of that terrible combat between good and evil, culminating in the ultimate surrender of Jesus :

> *When Jesus had received the wine, he said, "It is finished." Then he bowed his head and gave up his spirit.*
> **(John 19:30)**

In its turn this brokenness of the bread also speaks to us of our need to surrender to God's holy will in our own drama of redemption. That surrender to God's holy will is the supreme end of our existence. Nothing is more sanctifying and nothing holier than complete submission to God's will:

> *Consequently, when Christ came into the world, he said, "Sacrifices and offerings you have not desired, but a body you have prepared for me; in burnt offerings and sin offerings you have taken no pleasure. Then I said, 'See, God, I have come to do your will, O God' in the scroll of the book it is written of me."*
> **(Hebrews 10:5-7)**

4. The Eucharistic Sacrifice

Through the command of Jesus to *"do this in remembrance of me"* the celebration of the Eucharist became a permanent institution of the Church. It was a perpetual reminder of the death and resurrection of Jesus. So we get set formulas of remembrance of which that of St Hippolytus, a second century Pope, is typical:

> *"In memory of his death and resurrection,*
> *we offer you, Father, this life-giving bread"*

This is called the *anamnesis*[173], a Greek word which reminds us that the Mass was said in Greek in the early centuries. Its meaning is more elusive than the simple translation of *remembrance*. It recalls the sense of a memorial to the past, but goes beyond that of a simple representation. It evokes the literal sense of the latter in *'making present'* the events of the past in accordance with the will of Christ himself.

> *The anamnesis interprets the mystery of the Mass, tying it to the events of salvation history; it serves to bring out a basic aspect of the Mass that it is a memorial of Christ and his salvific acts . . . but it also represents these acts sacramentally, so that the worshipping community enters effectively into the everlasting sacrifice of the risen Lord, which is made present on earth*[174].

In conjuction with anamnesis we also have the special appeal to the Holy Sprirt to bring about the miracle of the Eucharist. This is called *epiclesis*, a Greeek word meaning *'invocation'*. This is part of the elements that are to be found in the Mass. There are four in all:

1. *The invocation of the Father*
2. *A plea for him to the Holy Spirit.*

---

[173] *A reminder of the relevance of scriptural history to our modern world/*
[174] *The full theological import of the concept of 'anamnesis' may be further strengthened in the reading of the relevant article in the New Catholic Encyclopedia Vol. 1.*

3. A prayer to the Holy Spirit to change the gifts into the Body and the Blood of Christ.
4. A prayer that the Body and Blood of Christ may bring life and grace to the faithful.

In light of all this we can come to understand the richness of the sacrament in the variety of words and phrases that are used to describe it as follows:

> *The Eucharist or Thanksgiving*
> *The Eucharistic Assembly (the 'synaxis')*—the visible manifestation of the Church.
> *The Memorial of the Lord's Passion, Death and Resurrection* (manifested in the acclamations after the consecration; Christ has died, Christ is Risen, Christ will come again!)
> *The Holy Sacrifice (*in which Christ is the Priest)
> *The Divine Liturgy*
> *The Sacred Mysteries*
> *The Most Blessed Sacrament*
> *Holy Communion*
> *The Bread of Angels*
> *The Medicine of Immortality!*
> *The Holy Mass*[175]

Hence we can understand the comment of one author:

> *God performs a miracle in each Mass. In fact there never has been a miracle as great as this anywhere on earth for almost two thousand years. And it happens in every Catholic Church every day.*[176]

No words can ever do justice to the importance and significance of the Holy Eucharist in the life of the Church. It remains a matter of utter astonishment when we consider the lengths to which divine love

---

[175] *All these titles can be explored in the CCC #1328-#1332.*
[176] *Peter Kreeft: Catholic Christianity (Ignatius Press, San Frrancisco, 2001) p.127.*

will go in order to win our fickle allegiance and our volatile devotion. It is sadder still, and a matter of profound regret, that this amazing and wholly sublime gift is so often treated with so much indifference and neglect. Too often we merit this sad reproach that Jesus uttered so often to his own disciples:

> *Are you still without understanding?*
> **(Matthew 15:16)**

Therein lies the divine challenge to our modern world which seeks to challenge God's will and eternal love with its feeble dismissals of everything that does not fit into its limited vision of reality.

Questions #15

* * *

1. *The Eucharist is pre-eminently the sacrament of God's love. Explain!*

2. *The ultimate reason for the creation of the universe is the Eucharist. Comments?*

3. *How is the Eucharist connected with the Jewish feast of Passover?*

4. *Why is the Eucharist called the heavenly manna?*

5. *Where and how does the Eucharist figure in the Gospel of John?*

6. *The words of institution must be taken in a spiritual sense? Answer this objection!*

7. *Among the names and titles of the Eucharist which one (or ones) appeal to you?*

8. *What is the symbolism of the "Breaking of the Bread"?*

9. *What do you understand by transubstatiation?*

10. *What do the following terms in the Mass mean: 'epiclesis' and 'anamnesis'?*

11. *What part should the Eucharist play in your life?*

16. THE LORD THE GIVER OF LIFE (II)

* * *

(a) The Sacrament of Reconciliation
—1. The Denial of Sin
—2. Repentance
—3. Reconciliation
—4. Confession

(b) The Sacrament of Matrimony
—1. Its Importance
—2. Its Indissolubility
—3. The Sacramental Effects

(c) The Sacrament of Holy Orders
—1. Christ the High Priest
—2. The Episcopate
—3. The Presbyterate
—4. The Diaconate

(d) The Anointing of the Sick
—1. The Fruit of Disobedience
—2. Christ—the Healer!
—3. The Sacrament of the Sick

16 (b) The Giver of Life

* * *

(a) The Sacrament of Reconciliation

1. *The Denial of Sin*

That there is wholesale moral disorder in the world is far too evident. The graphic evidence of pornography on the Internet, the personal testimony of its victims and the public approval of divorce, abortion and gay marriages—the list goes on and on—are striking indications of a massive breakdown in the moral order. What springs to mind is that there is a profound malaise in society in particular and in the world in general, that is wholly inimical to this particular sacrament of the Church! The sacrament of Reconciliation presupposes the reality of sin. However, we live in an environment that virtually denies its very existence. Such a frame of mind becomes understandable in a materialist climate that denies the existence of God. If there is no God, then any acknowledgement of sin against him becomes not merely superfluous but laughable.

What, however, is less credible is that this mentality can even be found among people who would consider themselves *spiritual* and even *religious!* It is astonishing that when you tell them that they are a *sinful* lot, that, fundamentally, they are sinners in need of redemption, they wonder what you are talking about. *Oh, no we are good people, kind people and obliging people, even if we are not paragons of virtue!*

Such futile protestations cannot disguise the overwhelming reality of sin. Unfortunately, despite widespread and wholesale denials, sin does exist. We cannot be a law unto ourselves for we do not have within ourselves a rationale for our very existence here on earth. Only God can give the answer to all of life's questions. Denials of God's existence cannot make him disappear. To ignore him is only to deepen our mortal misery for, without him, life has no meaning. We are born to worship and to adore. If we do not worship God, and honour his place in our lives, then we simply replace him with other worldly idols, the idols of wealth, power, pleasure and prestige.

Nevertheless, this spiritual climate of denial has an unlikely ally—our human nature. There is an instinctive repulsion within us to admit our faults, still less our sins to another human being. We want others to think the best of us. So, the thought of baring our souls to the scrutiny of another person, just like ourselves, is inherently nauseating. It even raises the question within us: why did Christ institute this apparently difficult mode of reconciliation with God? On the other hand, and, especially in the instance of grievous falls from grace, there is a fundamental need in the human psyche that cries out for forgiveness. This is a profound sense of *guilt* that calls for an inner cleansing. This is most manifest where others have been hurt or devastated by these sins.

2. Repentance

> *Interior repentance is a radical reorientation of our whole life, a return, a conversion to God with all our heart, an end of sin, a turning away from evil, with repugnance toward the evil actions we have committed. . . . This conversion of heart is accompanied by a salutary pain and sadness which the Fathers called animi cruciatus (affliction of spirit) and compunctio cordis (repentance of heart).*
>
> (#1439)

Repentance is the human response to the action of the Holy Spirit where there is a turning away from sin. This has been called *metanoia*[177], a Greek term that signifies an about turn in the sinner's psyche, or conversion of heart. In this sense we can understand the reaction of the crowd in Acts when St Peter accused them of crucifying Jesus:

> **Now when they heard this, they were cut to the heart**
> **and said to Peter and to the other apostles,**
> **"Brothers, what should we do?"**
> **Peter said to them, "Repent!"**
>
> **(Acts 2:37-38)**

---

[177] *The original Greek 'metanoien' means to 'to change one's mind' or 'to reverse one's way of thinking'.*

Notice that the crowd *were cut to the heart*! This is the *compunctio cordis, 'pricking of the heart,'* to which the Catechism refers. A sincere sorrow is an essential part of repentance. It is not merely the acknowledgement that we have done wrong, but deeply regret that we have done so. Especially when we look at the crucifix and glimpse what Jesus endured to free us from our sins and the depths of the torments to which he subjected himself to save us from ourselves! The other side of the coin is that we are prepared to accept God's condemnation and judgement, that we deserve his punishment. These were the sentiments and mindset of King David who repented of his adultery with Bathsheba and the murder of her husband, as expressed in one of the most enduring and most memorable expressions of true repentance:

> *Have mercy on me, O God, according to your steadfast love; according to your abundant mercy blot out my transgressions. Wash me thoroughly from my iniquity, and cleanse me from my sin. For I know my transgressions, and my sin is ever before me. Against you, you alone, have I sinned, and done what is evil in your sight so that you are justified in your sentence and blameless when you pass judgement.*
>
> **(Psalm 51)**

One of the basic problems confronting us is that we do not understand sin as an offence against God's sovereign goodness. On the one hand, we fail to recognise who God really is and the depths of his eternal love for us. On the other, this failure echoes the corresponding failure to grasp how he is offended. The Catechism underscores this human dimension in saying:

> *The confession (or disclosure) of sins, even from a simply human point of view, frees us and facilitates our reconciliation with others. Through such an admission man looks squarely at the sins he is guilty of, takes responsibility for them, and thereby opens himself again to God and to the communion of the Church in order to make a new future possible.*
>
> (#1455)

3. Reconciliation

God responds to our crying need for forgiveness by instituting the sacrament of forgiveness or the sacrament of Reconciliation, as it has been called. In the Old Dispensation God's forgiveness was mediated by the High Priest on the feast of *Yom Kippur*, the Day of Atonement. The High Priest of the New Law, Jesus Christ, replaced all this in his role as both Priest and Victim in his Passion and Death on the cross. As St Paul tells us

> *So if anyone is in Christ, there is a new creation: everything old has passed away; see, everything has become new! All this is from God, who reconciled us to himself through Christ, and has given us the ministry of reconciliation; that is, in Christ God was reconciling the world to himself, not counting their trespasses against them, and entrusting the message of reconciliation to us.*
> **(2 Corinthians 5-17-19)**

By his perfect obedience to his Father's will Christ made up for the disobedience of our first parents and for all the sins that flowed from that primal act of rebellion against God's infinite love. Christ is thus the supreme Mediator for all mankind and is ever living to make intercession for us before the throne of our Father who is in heaven. This is the very point that St Paul emphasises to the converts of Colossae:

> *And when you were dead in trespasses and the uncircumcision of your flesh, God made you alive together with him, when he forgave us all our trespasses, erasing the record that stood against us with its legal demands. He set this aside, nailing it to the cross.*
> **(Colossians 2:13-14)**

In virtue of Christ's sacrifice and its power before the Father, the role of mediation on behalf of sinners was passed on to the Church. It was a role that was passed on, first of all to the apostles and from them to their successors. It is fitting to recall the circumstances since they seem so much in harmony with the whole saga of redemption. The day is the day of the Resurrection. The apostles are cowering behind closed doors, *"the doors being shut"* as John describes it for us. They are in disarray, wholly shattered by the events of the past few days and then are baffled by word of an *'empty tomb'*. All of a sudden, on the evening of that day Jesus came and stood among them and said:

> *"Peace be with you. As the Father has sent me, so I send you."*
> *When he had said this, he breathed on them and said to them,*
> *"Receive the Holy Spirit. If you forgive the sins of any,*
> *they are forgiven them; if you retain the sins of any,*
> *they are retained."*
>
> **(John 20:21-23)**

In the peace of Christ there is a powerful remedy for all our spiritual ills, for all those moral failures and lapses that speak of the loss of baptismal innocence and the forfeiture of God's grace. It is the sacrament of Reconciliation. It can be so easily called the *Sacrament of the Resurrection,* or the sacrament of divine Forgiveness! This power of forgiveness was passed on to the successors of the apostles, to the bishops and their close collaborators in virtue of the sacrament of Holy Orders. In this way we are infallibly assured of forgiveness.

4. *The Sacrament of Confession*

> *Since therefore Christ suffered in the flesh, arm yourselves also with the same intention (for whoever has suffered in the flesh has finished with sin), so as to live for the rest of your earthly life no longer by human desires but by the will of God.*
>
> **(1 Peter 4:1-2)**

The four conditions that are necessary for the validity of this sacrament are *contrition, confession, satisfaction* and *absolution*. The matter is the sins confessed and the form is the words of absolution. Contrition is the basic sorrow for having offended an all-loving God and violating his laws. We have already dealt with it at length under Repentance. Here we would add that this sorrow must be spiritual, and not merely the natural shame of having made a fool of ourselves. What is the most basic spiritual mode of contrition? It is said to be the fear of going to hell. This is called *attrition* or an imperfect contrition that still suffices for the validity of the sacrament. Although Confession is presumed for serious lapses from grace, the Church also recommends the confession of *venial* sins or minor lapses in charity, the everyday failures that are associated with human weakness. It is very humbling, at the same time very salutary to acknowledge our weaknesses. Sacramental satisfaction is the penance given us by the confessor. It is usually given in the form of prayers, almsgiving or acts of charity to expiate the temporal punishment due to sin.

It is important to stress that confession is the open acceptance of Christ's offer of forgiveness, and is, therefore, a humble prostration of the penitent before him in the person of the priest. The latter is only the mediator of God's forgiveness, which in virtue of the sacrament is infallibly given. It is never easy to admit that we are sinners. But that is the whole basis of salvation history and the fundamental acceptance that we are sinners in need of redemption. To entertain seriously such thoughts of personal rectitude of sinlessness is to wallow in the most dangerous of spiritual illusions. It is against such a mindset that St John warns us:

> *If we walk in the light as he himself is in the light,*
> *we have fellowship with one another,*
> *and the blood of Jesus his Son cleanses us from all sin.*
> *If we say that we have no sin,*
> *we deceive ourselves, and the truth is not in us.*
> **(1 John 1:7-8)**

It is presumptuous for us to maintain that we can decide for ourselves how sin must be forgiven. That is God's prerogative alone. He alone can decide how we are to be restored to fellowship in his Church. As one author puts it:

> *The way God chose to remit sins through confession fulfills, after all, the very natural and deep need of the human psyche to free itself from what is oppressing it just by giving expression to it. Psychoanalysis itself is based on this fact and involuntarily confirms it. Experience shows that the abandonment of confession always leads to a progressive loss of sensitivity toward sin and of spiritual fervour.*[178]

---

[178] Cantalamessa, Raniero: *Life in the Lordship of Christ* (Sheed and Ward, Kansas City MO 1990) p. 129.

(b) The Sacrament of Matrimony

1. *Its Importance*

> *So God created humankind in his image, in the image of God he created them; male and female he created them. God blessed them, and God said to them, "Be fruitful and multiply, and fill the earth."* (Genesis 1:27-28)

Marriage emerges from the pages of Genesis as a divine institution. Man and woman reflect the very image of God himself. It is in this very image that God chooses to continue his creative power in the generation of children: *Be fruitful and multiply!* This creative and delegated power is the very *foundation of society*, as Vatican II was at pains to stress. It goes on to say:

> *The family is a a kind of school of a deeper humanity. But if it is to achieve the full flowering of its life and mission, it needs the kindly communion of minds and the joint deliberation of spouses, as well as the painstaking co-operation of the parents in the education of their children*[179].

The conclusion to all this is that there are three persons in a marriage: *man, woman and God!* It is no exaggeration, however, to assert that the institution of marriage is under serious attack on many fronts. There is a spurious *egalitarianism* abroad that denies any difference between the sexes. On the one hand it engenders a rampant *feminism* that seeks to merge the roles and identities of male and female in society. On the other it seeks to propagate an *individualism* that is destructive of the complementary roles that are instinctive in husband and wife. It is on these issues that one author wisely remarks:

> *The divinely revealed truth about the nature of man and woman fundamentally contradicts all three popular alternatives*

---

[179] *Vatican II: The Pastoral Constitution of the Church in the Modern World* #52.

> *found in our society: chauvinism which denies natural equality, unisexism which denies their natural difference; and the individualism which denies their natural complementarity.*[180]

In a secular society, where God is considered as *dispensable,* and even openly attacked as *irrelevant* to the human condition, it comes as no surprise that marriage, even as a secular institution, is on the rocks. Divorce is rampant, single families abound and children are often abandoned. Where God is ignored or denied, the family inevitably suffers.

There is, therefore, a culture of death abroad in society which is wholly inimical to the living out of family life as God intended. In a culture, absorbed with the rights of man and the individual, the building block of society, the family, is under a withering attack. The solvent of *"situation ethics"* and the gospel of personal *'happiness'* have been profoundly destructive of family life as God intended. The Church stands for the indissolubility of marriage and the sacredness of the gift of life. From the very nature of marriage, as willed by God, it must do battle against all those forces that threaten to destroy it. Inevitably, it must clash with the rising tide of promiscuity, divorce, abortion, and marital infidelity.

2. Indissolubility

The Church insists that marriage is a covenant between baptised persons and that it has been raised by Christ himself to the dignity of a sacrament. From this sacramental dignity there flows God's grace and the sacred presence that graced the marriage feast of Cana.

> *Christ dwells with them, gives them the strength to take up their crosses and so follow him, to rise again after they have fallen, to forgive one another, to bear one another's burdens, to be subject to one another out of reverence for Christ and to love one another with supernatural, tender, and fruitful love.*
>
> (#1642)

---

[180] *Peter Kreeft: op.cit. p.352.*

It is presumed that marriage springs from the profound love that the couple share. The acid test of that love comes in the sacrifices that they are willing to make. True love, as it says in the Song of Songs, is *"as strong as death"*, that is, it is irrevocable! St Paul's hymn to love says much the same Love never ends!(1 Cor. 13:8) It is not that marriage is devoid of sacrifice, for it is precisely in sacrifice that the marriage bond is sealed: In sickness and in health until death do us part! From all this emerges the indissolubility of marriage, for it is God's covenant and not man's. The presence of Jesus at the marriage feast of Cana underscores the sanctity of the married state. And if there were any doubt on this score, Jesus reaffirmed this in his answer to the Pharisees on the subject of divorce:

> ***Have you not read that the one who made them at the beginning 'made them male and female,' and said, 'For this reason a man shall leave his father and mother and be joined to his wife, and the two shall become one flesh'? So they are no longer two, but one flesh. Therefore, what God has joined together, let no one separate.***
> **(Matthew 19:4-6)**

There are some who complain of the *intransigence* of the Church on this issue of the indissolubility of marriage. *Surely the Church could bend a little in difficult cases! Look at all the annulments that have been granted since Vatican II!* However, the Church cannot go against Christ's own command. It has no power to grant divorce. As for the question of *annulments*, these are granted when there are serious reasons to believe that there was no real marriage in the first place."[181]

3. *Sacramental Effects*

The sacrament of matrimony, therefore, sets its seal on the marriage bond. The Catechism spells this out as follows:

---

[181] *As would be the case where there was a previous marriage, or a close blood relationship, or even overwhelming family pressures. These are known as 'diriment impediments'.*

> *The consent by which the spouses mutually give and receive one another is sealed by God himself. From their covenant arises an institution, confirmed by the divine law . . . even in the eyes of society. The covenant between the spouses is integrated into God's covenant with man. Authentic married love is caught up into divine love.*
>
> (#1639)

It is evident that the marriage bond imposes *fidelity* on the spouses. Having made a solemn commitment to each other, they renounce all thoughts of seeking sexual pleasure *outside of the marriage bond*. This is even a prohibition of the natural law: *Thou shalt not commit adultery* and *Thou shalt not covet thy neighbour's wife!* Marriage also reflects the self-giving of the Most Holy Trinity! In the latter there is a fruitful surrender in the love of the Father and the Son in the Holy Spirit. Likewise, husband and wife surrender to each other in the procreation of children. The latter are the fruit of their love and God's blessing on that union. In light of this we can understand the words of the Council: Children are the supreme gift of marriage and contribute greatly to the good of the parents themselves. God himself said: "It is not good for man to be alone: and "from the beginning he made them male and female"; wishing to associate them in a special way in his own creative work, God blessed man and woman with the words: Be fruitful and multiply!" The presence of children in a marriage is a great blessing. However, it also imposes the obligation of bringing them up in the faith by word and example.

> *Thus the home is the first school of Christian life and "a school for human enrichment." Here one learns endurance and the joy of work. fraternal love, generous—even repeated—forgiveness, and above all, worship in prayer and the offering of one's life.*
>
> (#1657)

For all these reasons the family home has been called the 'domestic Church', a miniature community of prayer and grace and a school for Christian living! In this respect, a Christian family fulfills the Gospel maxims in being the *salt of the earth* and a *light to the world!*

(c) The Sacrament of Holy Orders

1. *Christ, the High Priest*

> *For it was fitting that we should have such a high priest, holy, blameless, undefiled, separated from sinners, and exalted above the heavens.*
>
> **(Hebrews 7:26)**

All that has been said previously about Christ as the Eternal High Priest applies particularly to the sacrament of Holy Orders. The priesthood of the Old Covenant prefigured Christ in the New. Abraham encountered the priest Melchizedek, *"priest of the Most High God"*, prefiguring Christ in the Eucharist with his offering of bread and wine. The Mosaic Law established the Levitical priesthood which was responsible for the Temple worship and its ritual sacrifices. All this was but a type of the sacrifice of the New Law, centred on Christ. Herein Christ was both priest and victim, being immolated on the Cross to his heavenly Father for the forgiveness of sins.

> **But when Christ had offered for all time a single sacrifice for sins, "he sat down at the right hand of God," and since then has been waiting "until his enemies would be made a footstool for his feet." For by a single offering he has perfected for all time those who are sanctified.**
>
> **(Hebrews 10:12-14)**

It is from the priesthood of Christ, the Head of the Church, that both the *ministerial* priesthood of the clergy and the *common* priesthood of the faithful is derived. Here we are concerned with the ministerial priesthood, of which St Thomas Aquinas writes:

> *Christ is the source of all priesthood:*
> *the priest of the Old Law was a figure of Christ.*
> *and the priest of the New Law acts in the place of Christ.*[182]

---

[182] *Quoted in Vatican II's "Gaudium et Spes" #50 (1)*

Christ completed and fulfilled the priesthood of the Old Covenant. At the same time he completely transformed it by being both Priest and Victim. In doing so he ushered in the New Covenant wherein he extended his saving grace to the whole of humanity. He did so in ordaining his chosen band of apostles to carry on his work. In this way we can say that the Catholic priesthood is simply an extension of Christ himself. As one author so graphically expresses it:

> *Priests are Christ's own hands and lips!*[183]

Christ's choice of apostles inevitably created a hierarchy of service. First and foremost, the successors to the apostles were the bishops, who alone express the fullness of Christ's priesthood. They, in their turn, ordained helpers or co-workers, known as *priests*, and finally, under the power conferred on them the apostles ordained *deacons*. So, essentially, there are three degrees of special or ordained ministry: the *episcopate*, the *presbyterate* and the *diaconate*, so constituted by the rite of Holy Orders, also called the rite of Ordination.

2. The Episcopate

Although all the faithful share in the priesthood of Christ, Jesus chose a select body of his followers to lead his disciples. After his resurrection from the dead, He chose twelve men, the apostles, to instruct and shepherd the faithful. This is so evident from the Great Commission wherein Christ, after his Resurrection, conferred apostolic powers on the apostles:

> *All authority in heaven and on earth has been given to me.*
> *Go therefore and make disciples of all nations,*
> *baptizing them in the name of the Father*
> *and of the Son and of the Holy Spirit,*
> *and teaching them to obey everything*
> *that 1 have commanded you. And remember,*
> *1 am with you always, to the end of the age.*
> **(Matthew 28: 18-20)**

---

[183] *Kreeft op.cit. p.365*

It is impossible to stress too much these final verses of St Matthew's Gospel. The authority they confer is overwhelming and this should always be borne in mind that it is God himself who has conferred this authority upon the Church. It is passed on from generation to generation in the rite of Ordination. This rite of Ordination consists on *the laying on of hands*, with the appropriate consecratory prayers that go back to the days of the apostles and ensures the succession of bishops and validates the claim of apostolic succession. In virtue of that claim the bishops are empowered to teach and to rule over their flocks as true shepherds. In our own days, because of the primacy of Peter, the lawful ordination of bishops requires the permission of the Bishop of Rome, the principle of unity and the bond of union with Christ. Moreover, the Church teaches that in the episcopate resides the fulness of the priesthood of Christ.

> *The Second Vatican Council teaches . . . that the fulness of the sacrament of Holy Orders is conferred by episcopal consecration, that fulness namely which, both in the liturgical tradition of the Church and in the language of the Fathers of the Church, is called the high priesthood, the acme (summa) of the sacred ministry.*
> (#1557)

Each bishop has the pastoral care of a particular church or diocese entrusted to him. But as a successor of the apostles, he shares with his brother bishops throughout the world a solicitude for all the churches of the world. The Great Commission gave the apostles a mission to all the nations and that is of interest to every bishop.

3. The Presbyterate

> **Do not neglect the gift that is in you, which was given to you through prophecy with the laying on of hands by the council of elders.**
> **(1 Timothy 4: 1 4)**

Priests are the Bishop's co-workers. They are ordained by him in order to assist him in the shepherding of the faithful. In ordination the priest makes a promise of obedience to his bishop and so is subject to him in his ministry. As presbyters they also share in the priestly office of the bishop and lay their hands on the man being ordained a priest. The prime function of the priest stands in relation to the Eucharist. Vatican II makes this abundantly clear in stating:

> *Though all the faithful can baptise, the priest alone can complete the building up of the Body in the Eucharistic Sacrifice. Thus are fulfilled the words of God, spoken through his prophet: From the rising of the sun, even to its setting, my name is great among the nations; and everywhere they bring sacrifice to my name and a pure offering.*

The title of *'Father'* by which the priests are known and addressed speaks of the familial relationship that exists between him and his flock. He marries their parents and baptises their children and buries their dead. And in Christ's name he forgives them their sins! It is also through the priest that the bishop keeps in touch with the faithful throughout the diocese. It is this intimate relationship that prompted the Cure of Ars to say that *"The Priesthood is the love of the heart of Jesus!"* The immense dignity of the priesthood and the sacrifices that its ministry entails have been given classical expression by Jean-Baptiste Lacordaire:

> *To live in the world without wishing its pleasures;*
> *to be a member of each family, yet belonging to none;*
> *to share all suffering; to penetrate all secrets; to heal all wounds;*
> *to go from men to God and offer him their prayers,*
> *to return from God to men to bring pardon and hope;*
> *to have a heart of fire for charity and a heart of bronze for chastity;*
> *to teach and to pardon, to console and bless always—*
> *what a glorious life! And it is yours, O Priest of Christ!* [184]

4. The Diaconate

The diaconate is the first of the major orders, but the lowest in the hierarchical order of the Church. The term *'deacon'* literally means *servant* and it expresses the special ministry of service to which the deacon is dedicated. In the ordination service only the bishop lays hands on the candidate to signify the latter's attachment to the bishop in the tasks

---

[184] *Lacordaire, a famous Dominican preacher in France in 19th century.*

of his special service, such as a ministry in the prisons or as a hospital chaplain. It is in Acts that the institution of the diaconate first appears when the apostles decided to ordain seven deacons for service to the faithful, in order that they would be free for their work of evangelisation. St Paul includes the deacons in his letter to the Philippians:

> *To all the saints in Christ Jesus who are in Philippi,*
> *with the bishops and deacons:*
> **(Philippians 1:1)**

He also gives advice to his protégé Timothy:

> *Deacons likewise must be serious, not double-tongued,*
> *not indulging in much wine, not greedy for money; they must*
> *hold fast to the mystery of the faith with a clear conscience.*
> *And let them first be tested; then, if they prove themselves*
> *blameless, let them serve as deacons.*
> **(1 Timothy 3::8-10)**

The rank of permanent deacon disappeared in the West but survived in the East. It was revived in the West by the Second Vatican Council. Its special functions are laid out in the General Instructions of the Roman Missal: At Mass he has his own functions; he proclaims the Gospel, sometimes preaches God's word, leads the general intercessions of the faithful, assists the priest, gives communion to the faithful (in particular, ministering the chalice and sometimes gives directions to the congregation). The deacon can also administer baptism, and, when authorised to do so, bless marriages in the name of the Church, administer sacramentals and officiate at funerals and burial services.

(d) The Anointing of the Sick

1. The Fruit of Disobedience

> *The LORD God took the man and put him in the garden*
> *of Eden to till it and keep it.*
> *And the LORD God commanded the man, "You may*
> *freely eat of every tree of the garden; but of the tree of the*
> *knowledge of good and evil you shall not eat,*

> *for in the day that you eat of it you shall die."*
> **(Genesis 2:14-16)**

The threat of death did not deter our first parents from disobeying God's command. In the subsequent trial the sentence of death was carried out. Of course, it was not carried out immediately, but it was inevitable!

> *By the sweat of your face you shall eat bread until you return to the ground, for out of it you were taken; you are dust, and to dust you shall return.*
> **(Genesis 3: 19)**

That primal curse of toil and frustration in eking out a living was ultimately to end in the separation of body and soul. But that end was also the result of a gradual disintegration of bodily powers and a weakening of the body's hold on life. Sickness and disease are all a part of that bodily disintegration. As the psalmist exclaims:

> *There is no soundness in my flesh because of your indignation; there is no health in my bones because of my sin.*
> **(Psalm 38:3)**

These biblical threats involving God's indignation and his threats of punishment give point to the oft-repeated complaints about their apparent conflict with the belief in God's inherent goodness and his omnipotent love. *Why does God permit all these terrible evils and misfortunes if he is all-loving?* The stock reply is that we have brought all these evils upon ourselves by our constant betrayals of God's covenant of love. It started with the rebellion of our first parents in the Garden of Eden. Nevertheless, our world of tragedy and misfortune has been radically transformed by the incarnation of the Word in Jesus and redeemed by his death and resurrection.

> *By his passion and death on the cross Christ has given a new meaning to suffering; it can henceforth configure us to him and unite us with his redemptive Passion*
> *(1505)*

2. Christ the Healer!

The ministry of Jesus on earth was marked by miracles of healing. Everywhere he went he was besieged by crowds seeking his healing touch:

> ***Many crowds followed him, and he cured all of them.***
> **(Matthew 12:15)**

The Catechism comments as follows:

> *Christ's compassion towards the sick and his many healings of every kind of infirmity are a resplendent sign that God has visited his people, and that the Kingdom of God is close at hand. Jesus has the power not only to heal, but also to forgive sins.*
> (#1503)

The bodily healings point to a much more profound healing, the healing of the soul, the ultimate goal of redemption. Christ, the Sinless One, was not subject to the bodily infirmities that are man's normal lot. Nevertheless, he took upon himself to endure the most terrible torments in order to win redemption for mankind. In doing so he gave point to all suffering:

> *On the Cross Christ took upon himself the whole weight of evil and took away the sin of the world of which illness is only a consequence. By his passion and death on the cross Christ has given a new meaning to suffering: it can henceforth configure us to him and unite us with his redemptive Passion.*
> (#1505)

Jesus also commanded his disciples to go forth and heal the sick and to cast out demons. It is a trust that the Church has sought to carry out down through the centuries.

It is no accident that the very first hospitals and refuges were founded by the Church. Congregations of men and women have been founded with the specific ministry of caring for the sick and the suffering. It is a ministry that emphasises the exquisite charity of Christ for our stricken humanity.

However, all such bodily healings point to the much more fundamental healing of the soul. Christ, *the Sinless One*, himself was not subject to the bodily infirmities that are part and parcel of humanity's fate. Yet he took upon himself the most terrible afflictions of body and soul in his Passion and Death in order to save us from the horrors of Hell and its eternal punishment.

3. The Sacrament of the Sick

The Church, as a concerned mother, follows in the healing footsteps of Jesus. She is concerned with the numberless afflictions that invade the lives of the faithful. That the early Church, in particular, was deeply concerned about this issue is evident from the letter of James:

> *Are any among you sick? They should call for the elders of the church and have them pray over them, anointing them with oil in the name of the Lord. The prayer of faith will save the sick, and the Lord will raise them up; and anyone who has committed sins will be forgiven.*
> **(James 5: 14-15)**

This sacrament is also a link with the Passion and Death of our Saviour, and draws from the agonies of our Blessed Lord the strength to face the sorrow and distress of dying. In union with the Passion it helps to strengthen the Body of Christ, and helps as St Paul writes:

> *I am now rejoicing in my sufferings for your sake,*
> *and in my flesh*
> *I am completing what is lacking in Christ's afflictions*
> *for the sake of his body, that is, the church.*
> **(Colossians 1:24)**

In churches, in both the east and the west, tradition has honoured this apostolic practice of anointing the sick. In the west and over time it came to be administered to those in danger of death, and so it was called *'Extreme Unction'* or the *'Last Rites'*. It is also called the *'Sacrament of the Dying'*. Just as the sacrament of Baptism initiates the recipient into the spiritual life and incorporates the soul into the Body of Christ, so the sacrament of the *last anointing* comforts the soul at the point of departure from this life. As the Catechism says:

> *This last anointing fortifies the end of our earthly life like a solid rampart for the final struggles before entering our Father's house.*
>
> *(#1523)*

This still survives in granting the Eucharist as *Viaticum,* on the understanding that it gives a special strength to one who is about to leave this world and go to the Father. However, Vatican II restored the ancient practice of administering the sacrament to one who is ill, whether in danger of death or not. In this more relaxed way does Holy Mother the Church, our spiritual guide, manifest her pastoral concern for the flock entrusted to her care, recalling the command of Jesus to Peter:

> **Feed my lambs! Feed my sheep!**
> **(John 21:15)**

It is evident that one of the greatest of human fears is the fear of death and the primary instinct to protest the loss of life. We recall the plaintive reproach of Martha to Jesus:

> ***Lord, if you had been here, my brother would not have died.***
> **(John 11:2)**

There is, in addition, the assault on the memory of past sins and spiritual failures. There is the inevitable danger of despair and the lack of trust in God's mercy. All this is heightened by physical weakness as well as the fear of God's judgements. To this is addressed the prayer of the priest invoking the divine mercy and the presence of the Spirit:

> *Through this holy anointing, may the Lord in his love and mercy help you with the grace of the Holy Spirit.*
> *May the Lord who frees you from sin save you and raise you up!*

++++++++++++++++++++++++++++++++++++++

Breathe on me, Spirit of God,
that I may think what is holy!
Drive me, Spirit of God,
that I may do what is holy!.
Draw me, Spirit of God,
that I may love what is holy!.
Strengthen me, Spirit of God,
that I may preserve what is holy!.
Guard me, Spirit of God,
that I may never lose what is holy!

St Augustine

Questions #16

* * *

1. What are the consequences of the disobedience of our first parents?

2. Why is there such a widespread denial of the idea of sin today?

3. What is the difference between repentance and reconciliation?

4. What are the conditions necessary for a good confession?

5. Why all this penitential rigmarole cooked up by the Church? Why can't I just fall on my knees and tell God very simply that I'm very sorry for what I've done wrong?

    What is yur response to this objection?

6. What is the importance of the sacrament of matrimony?

7. Indissolubility is a necessary component of marriage. Explain!

8. What are the effects of the sacrament of matrimony?

9. *What are the three Orders in the Church and what are their functions in brief?*

10. *Christ's death gives point to all our sufferings! What does this mean?*

11. *"In my flesh I am completing what is lacking in the sufferings of Christ." What can St Paul possibly mean by these words?*

12. *What are the effects of the Anointing of the Sick? What other names are given to this sacrament and why?*

17. THE HOLY SPIRIT— SOUL OF THE CHURCH!

* * *

(a) The Divine Promise
 —1. The Promise of the Paraclete
 —2. The Fulfilment of the Promise
 —3. The Divine Presence
 —4. The Temple of the Living God!

(b) The Authority of the 'Paraclete'
 —1. The Council of Jerusalem
 —2. The Spirit of Justification
 —3. The Work of the Spirit

(c) The Abiding Presence
 —1. The Spirit of Remembrance
 —2. The Witness of History
 —3. The Development of Doctrine
 —4. The Divine Gift

17. The Soul of the Church!

* * *

(a) The Divine Promise

1. *The Promise of the Paraclete*

At the Last Supper, Jesus in the Hour of his ministry promised his followers that he would not leave them *orphans*. They were stricken with sadness at the prospect of his leaving them. He would be replaced by *Another!* That was his solemn promise—to send the Holy Spirit.

> *When the Spirit of truth comes, he will guide you into all the truth; for he will not speak on his own, but will speak whatever he hears, and he will declare to you the things that are to come. He will glorify me, because he will take what is mine and declare it to you.*
> **(John 16:13-14)**

Jesus here promises the Spirit who will continue his message and work in *the Truth*. As Vatican II so aptly phrases it:

> Our Lord 'completed and perfected Revelation and confirmed it . . . by sending the Holy Spirit of truth'[185].

It is interesting to note that the *Spirit of Truth* mirrors the claim of Jesus to be *the Way and the Truth and the Life*. In this Jesus also reveals more of the life of the Trinity, and that in the life of the Church the Holy Spirit will take his place, not to supplant him but to confirm and glorify his work and message!

2. *Fulfilment of the Promise*

The promise made at the Last Supper to send the Holy Spirit was renewed by Jesus just before his Ascension into heaven. Nine days later that promise was fulfilled.

---

[185] *Dei Verbum* 4

> *When the day of Pentecost had come, they were all together in one place. And suddenly a sound came from heaven like the rush of a mighty wind, and it filled the house where they were sitting. And there appeared to them tongues of fire, distributed and resting on each of them, and they were all filled with the Holy Spirit.*
>
> **(Acts 2:1-4)**

The drama of the first Pentecost is but the fulfilment of the words of Jesus. Pentecost was the Jewish *Shabuoth,* the second of the major annual feasts, falling fifty days after the Passover. It was the celebration of the feast of the *First Fruits* of thanksgiving for the harvest. It was also a celebration of the giving of the Law to Moses on Mt Sinai. Jews and proselytes came from far and near, from all parts of the civilised world to celebrate and worship in the Temple.

All the liturgical overtones inherent in the situation are now invested with much profounder and more mystical meanings with the descent of the Holy Spirit upon Mary and the disciples. The *New Law* of the Spirit was now launched upon the world!

The spirit that had once rushed upon the young David in the Old Testament now rushed upon the followers of Jesus in the New. Here the apostles, who but a short time before had skulked in craven fear behind locked doors, were now transformed into intrepid apostles and proclaimers of *the Good News.* They were now ready to face martyrdom!

3. The Divine Presence

We have already noted that the *Great Commission* gave the Church the assurance of the divine presence to the end of time is a tribute to the work of the Holy Spirit. Faith in the presence of the life-giving Holy Spirit has been present in the work of the Church. This is manifest in its sacraments and in the lives of individuals ever since Christ uttered his command to evangelise the nations. This was the unfailing teaching of the fathers of the early Church. They presented the Holy Spirit as the prime indwelling principle in the Church, *the Mystical Body of Christ*. The Holy Father, Pope Paul VI touched on this profound mystery of the life of the Spirit in the Church when he said:

> *The Church lives by the outpouring of the Holy spirit, which we call grace, that is to say, a gift par excellence, charity, the Father's love, communicated to us in virtue of the redemption wrought by Christ in the Holy Spirit.*[186]

The Catechism also has this to say on the subject:

> *The Holy Spirit is the protagonist, 'the principal agent of the whole of the Church's mission'* (John Paul II). *It is he who leads the Church on her missionary paths. 'This mission continues and, in the course of history, unfolds the mission of Christ, who was sent to evangelise the poor; so the Church, urged on by the Spirit of Christ, must walk the road Christ himself walked, a way of poverty and obedience, of service and self-sacrifice even to death, a death from which he emerged victorious by his resurrection'.*
> (#852)

The Holy Spirit is, therefore, the vibrant soul, and powerhouse of the Church, an infinite, *uncreated* and *transcendent* principle ever at work in the sanctification and the salvation of souls.

> **For in the one Spirit we were all baptised into one body**
> **—Jews or Greeks, slaves or free—**
> **and we were all made to drink of one Spirit.**
> **(1 Corinthians 12:13)**

4. *Temple of the Living God!*

> *For we are the temple of the living God;*
> *as God said, I will live in them and walk among them,*
> *and I will be their God, and they shall be my people.*
> **(2 Corinthians 6:16)**

It is fundamental in the theology of St Paul that the Christian community is an *organic unity*. Despite the apparent diversity of gifts and functions manifested in its day to day existence, there exists within it an

---

[186] *Address to a General Audience. Oct. 16 1974*

overriding unity of thought and purpose. The presence of the Holy Spirit, both in the life of the Church and in the lives of its individual members pervades his letters. Although the term 'soul' is not explicitly scriptural it expresses, as far as human language can express it, the pervasive action of the Spirit in the Church, as the following quotation indicates:

> *What the soul is to the human body, the Holy Spirit*
> *is to the Body of Christ, which is the Church.*

This quotation comes from one of the sermons of that great doctor of the Church, St Augustine. Pius XII makes the following commentary on the same in his encyclical *Mystici Corporis* (1943):

> *To this Spirit of Christ, as an invisible principle, is to be ascribed the fact that all parts of the body are joined one with the other and with their exalted head; for the whole Spirit of Christ is in the head, the whole Spirit of Christ is in the body, and the whole Spirit of Christ is in each of its members.*

This thought of the Church as *the temple of the Holy Spirit* is, once again, a recurring theme in the writings of St Paul, as in the following example:

> **Do you not know that you are God's temple and that**
> **God's Spirit dwells in you?**
> **If anyone destroys God's temple, God will destroy that**
> **person. For God's temple is holy, and you are that temple.**
> **(1 Corinthians 3:16-17)**

> **In him the whole structure is joined together and grows**
> **into a holy temple in the Lord; in whom you also are built**
> **together spiritually into a dwelling place for God.**
> **(Ephesians 2:21-22)**

The Spirit ensures that the promise of Jesus will be kept, that he will be with his Church *until the end of time*. The Spirit fulfils what his very name suggests that he will never cease to *breathe* his gift of life and love into the Body of the Church. His constant presence ensures its survival, enabling it to surmount the crises and trials that are inevitably part of the Church's earthly existence. Here is how one theologian expresses it:

> *But the fundamental thought, that the Body of Christ is and must be an organic body, that it works by its very nature in a manifold of functions, and that this manifold is bound together by the one Spirit of Christ into an inner unity: this thought is native to Saint Paul, and it is the heritage and the fundamental principle of the whole Christian gospel.*[187]

(b) The Authority of the Paraclete

1. The Council of Jerusalem

It is evident that the early Christian Church was predominantly Jewish. There were thus many converts, *Judaizers*, who still insisted on the observance of the Old Law. There was a danger that the new born faith would degenerate into another sect of Judaism. These Judaizers were a thorn in the apostolate of Paul and his helpers. The latter had brought the Gospel to the Gentiles and now their apostolate was threatened as related in Acts:

> **Then certain individuals came down from Judea and were teaching the brothers, "Unless you are circumcised according to the custom of Moses, you cannot be saved."**
> **(Acts 15:1)**

This campaign to convert the newly baptised to the ways of Judaism was brought to the attention of the church in Jerusalem when some Pharisee converts insisted that circumcision and the observance of the Mosaic Law was also a necessary component of Christianity. After listening to the accounts of Paul and Barnabas of the signs and wonders that God had worked among the Gentiles, Peter and James rejected the thesis of the Judaizers. It is important to note that the Church now promulgated a directive to the Gentile converts which concluded with these words:

---

[187] *Karl Adam: the Spirit of Catholicism*

> *For it has seemed good to the Holy Spirit and to us*
> *to impose on you no further burden than these essentials:*
> *that you abstain from what has been sacrificed to idols*
> *and from blood and from what is strangled and from fornication.*
> *If you keep yourselves from these, you will do well. Farewell.*
> **(Acts 15:28-29)**

What is apparent here is that the Holy Spirit is recognised as the guiding principle of their decision. In fact, he is mentioned in the very first place. This has been the firm conviction of all subsequent Councils down to the present day.

2. *The Spirit of Justification*

The Church's doctrine of *justification* is based on the assumption that man has a spiritual destiny. It is the answer to the perennial questions: *Why are we here? What is the purpose of existence? Is this world all that there is to work for?* The Spirit comes to answer these ultimate questions. The first work of the Spirit *is initiating the soul* into the Kingdom of God. This is the process of conversion which mankind so desperately needs. This is called *justification*. It is the divine impulse by which the Holy Spirit turns a man towards God and his love and turns him away from sin. Sin is a denial of God and a rejection of his love. Here the Holy Spirit, *who convinces the world of sin,* who inspires the sinner to accept the offer of God's friendship. The sinner can either accept it or reject it. But as the Council of Trent[188] maintains, man still needs the divine help of the Holy Spirit to accept the offer. The Catechism makes this most stirring pronouncement on the Holy Spirit's work in this respect, quoting the great Augustine:

> *Justification is the most excellent work of God's love made manifest in Christ Jesus and granted by the Holy Spirit. It is the opinion of St Augustine that-'the justification of the wicked is a greater work than the creation of heaven and earth!' because 'heaven and earth will pass away, but the salvation and justification of the elect will not pass away'.*

---

[188] *The Council of Trent 1545-1563*

> *He holds also that the justification of sinners surpasses the creation of the angels in justice, in that it bears witness to a greater mercy'.*[189] (#1994)

3. The Work of the Spirit

As the guiding principle of the Church and its Soul, the Church is always at work promoting the will of the Father through the inspiration of teaching and example in Jesus' life and ministry. We see it in a special way in our own century in the work and decisions of the Second Vatican Council. This is a milestone in the Church's history that renews the assurance of the Spirit's presence, his bounty and the manifestation of his gifts in our times. It is further evidence of the Spirit, *'infinite and uncreated'*, at work throughout the Church. All this is aptly summarised in the Church's Catechism[190] : The Holy Spirit *works in many ways to build up the whole Body in charity:*

> — *by God's Word 'which is able to build you up':*
> — *by Baptism, through which he forms Christ's Body:*
> — *by the sacraments, which gives growth and healing to Christ's members:*
> — *by the grace of the apostles, which holds first place among his gifts;*
> — *by the virtues, which make us act according to what is good;*
> — *by the many special graces, called 'charisms,' by which he makes the faithful fit and ready to undertake various tasks and offices for the renewal and building up of the Church.*
>
> (#798)

Pope Paul VI summed up this teaching of the Church when he said in 1973:

> *The gift of the Spirit, conferred on all the baptised, is the foundation both of the freedom of God's children in the exercise*

---

[189] *From Augustine's commentary on the Gospel of John (In Jo.ev. 72.3)*
[190] Peter J. Kreeft: Catholic Christianity (Ignatius Press, San Francisco, 2001) p.98

of their rights in the Church, and of the charismatic gifts which he confers directly on the faithful.

(c) The Abiding Presence

1. *The Spirit of Remembrance*

> *But the Advocate, the Holy Spirit,*
> *whom the Father will send in my name,*
> *will teach you everything,*
> *and remind you of all that I have said to you.*
> **(John 14:26)**

The Spirit is the *memory* of the Church! This is a logical consequence of the Holy Spirit as the *Spirit of Truth*. It also belongs to the Holy Spirit as *Counsellor* to keep on *reminding* the Church of all that Jesus said and did. As the supreme witness of the life of Jesus and his teaching he is the *Remembrancer*, so to speak, of the Church. On the whole, we are very forgetful people! This forgetfulness breeds ingratitude for the very benefits that God constantly bestows upon us in one form or another. We need to be *reminded* of them—*constantly!* As St Augustine comments so appropriately in his *Confessions* about our misfortunes and our sins:

> *We weep and we forget that we have wept!*

The Catechism also reminds us that the Holy Spirit makes present the mystery of Christ in the liturgy of the Church. It states this solemn truth with remarkable simplicity:

> *The Christian liturgy, not only recalls the events that saved us, but actualises them, makes them present. The Paschal mystery of Christ is celebrated, not repeated. It is the celebrations that are repeated, and in each celebration there is an outpouring of the Holy Spirit that makes the unique mystery present.*
>
> (#1104)

The Eucharist, in particular, is the *Sacrifice of Remembrance*. At the most solemn moment of the consecration the priest calls upon the Holy Spirit to effect what Jesus commanded at the Last Supper: **Do this in**

remembrance of me. **(Luke 22:19)** In this respect St John Damascene (8th Century AD) reminds us:

> *You ask how the bread becomes the Body of Christ, and the wine . . . the Blood of Christ. I shall tell you: the Holy Spirit comes upon them and accomplishes what surpasses every word and thought . . . Let it be enough for you to understand that it is by the Holy Spirit, just as it was of the Holy Virgin, and by the Holy Spirit, that the Lord through and in himself, took flesh.*
>
> (#1106)

2. *The Witness of History*

It is a fact of our human experience that persons, events and institutions have a *beginning* and an *end*. Our very own existence, the very fact of our own births and deaths are striking witnesses to this sovereign truth. There are also limitations to the survival of all that touches our lives. History only serves to confirm this sovereign law of nature. Civilisations come and go; empires rise and fall; people are born and die; plants grow, and wither.

Mathematicians in fact have invented the symbol of the *bell curve* to give us a graphical expression of this *rise* and *fall* of all human institutions, of business markets, plagues and profits! One institution, however, defies this mathematical prognosis, the bell curve of growth and decline and confounds its prophets of doom. It is the *Catholic Church*! This aspect of the Church so struck a Protestant historian that he wrote what is probably the most eloquent tribute ever made to the Church's perennial youth:

> *There is not, and there never was on this earth, a work of human policy so well deserving of examination as the Roman Catholic Church. The history of that Church joins together two great ages of civilisation. No other institution is left standing which carries the mind back to the times when the smoke of sacrifice rose from the Pantheon, and when camelopards bounded in the Flavian amphitheatre. The proudest royal houses are but of yesterday when compared to the line of the Supreme Pontiffs.*

This tribute to the perennial youth of the Church only underscores the fact that the Church is not a human institution but a *divine* one. Its founder is *divine,* its message is *divine*. Its very existence bears the stamp of divinity! It has been entrusted with a mission that must endure to fulfil the Great Commission of Jesus. What other human institution can rival the longevity of Christianity? What other human institution can boast of its survival despite the lomg list of unparalleled persecutions and the testimony of innumerable martyrs?

3. *The Development of Doctrine*

The Catholic Church is often accused of '*inventing*' new doctrines or dogmas. It is not only a shallow but a baseless indictment of the teaching authority of the Church. This authority comes from Christ himself, the founder of the Church, when he said:

> **Go therefore make disciples of all nations . . . .**
> **teaching them to observe all that I have commanded you.**
> **(Matthew 28:20)**

It is the duty of the Church to *teach*. Part of the job of a teacher is to instruct its adherents and to organise the data of revelation for them. These data did not come in carefully drafted communiqués. These were not spelled out like a well written summary of beliefs, like the *Magna Carta* or the *American Constitution*. For newcomers to the faith there were summaries compiled like the *Apostles' Creed*. But the implications of many basic beliefs had still to be drawn out. It may come as a surprise to many that it took over six centuries for the full implications of Jesus as the God-Man to be worked out. And this is at the very heart of the redemptive message! Why should it be a matter of astonishment that the dogma of *Transubstantiation* was proclaimed only in 1215, or *papal infallibility* in 1870.

What is re-affirmed is what has always been there, whether *implicitly* or *explicitly*. The Church is compelled to reply and state its position when what has been handed down *(tradition)* comes under attack. There is no revealed doctrine proclaimed by the Church that is not contained *substantially* in the revelation of scripture. This means that the doctrines or dogmas of the faith are not conjured out of thin air or proclaimed on some whim of pope or Council. These truths are contained, *explicitly* or *implicitly,* in revelation. It is with the latter that work has to be done to draw out, or to tease out, whatever lies at the heart of the original message.

All this is done under the guidance of the Holy Spirit directing the teaching ministry of the Church. In a sense the Church is like a garden in which Jesus has planted the seeds of revelation. Under the influence of the Holy Spirit, *the Spirit of Truth,* these seeds grow and produce the flowers and the fruits that are necessary for the Church's survival. The harvest arrives at the time when it is most needed to combat the evils and heresies of the ages!

> *The Advocate, the Holy Spirit that the Father will*
> *send in my name—he will teach you everything,*
> *and remind you of all that I told you.*
> **(John 14:25)**

4. The Divine Gift!

Throughout the Church's history there is a Spirit that guides the Church and seeks the sanctification of all its members. In the work of the Holy Spirit there is that incessant call to holiness that comes in the wake of justification. This is realised through the sacramental system which spans the Christian's entire life. From *Baptism* to the last anointing in *the Sacrament of the Sick* we have the pledge of fulfilment of Christ's promises of our salvation and entry into eternal life. In all the important stages of our lives, from the cradle to the grave. we are accompanied by the Holy Spirit, the Spirit of *Consolation, the Comforter, the Advocate,* and our ever present *Helper.* All this gives us an insight into this sacramental penetration of our lives, which the Holy Spirit fulfills.

Moreover, Jesus left this world physically. His Passion and Death would deprive the apostles of the comfort they had known over the whole of his ministry. But he found a way to share himself with us in the institution of the Eucharist. We *eat his flesh, and we drink his blood!.* So great is the love of Jesus for his Church, that he permeates it, not merely with his blessing and his might, but with the gift of his own self! As God and Man he enters into a real union of flesh and blood with it, and binds it to his being even as the branch is bound to the vine.

> *I am the vine, you are the branches.*
> *Those who abide in me and I in them bear much fruit,*
> *because apart from me you can do nothing.*
> **(John 15:5)**

Nothing on this earth can compare with this intimate surrender of Jesus to us in the embrace of Holy Communion. For a brief moment in the Eucharistic union we are, so to speak the Ark of the Covenant carrying, not the tables of the Law itself, but the very author of that Law! Or again, for so short a while, we resemble Mary carrying the unborn Jesus in her womb as she went to visit her cousin Elizabeth!

How true it is, as Jesus assures us, that we are not left *orphans* in this world. Under the forms of *Bread* and *Wine* the Master lives amidst and in his disciples. The Bridegroom, the Lord, with his Bride, the Church, dwells in the midst of his community, until that day when he shall return in visible majesty on the clouds of heaven. In this superabundance of God's mighty love the words of the psalmist spring to mind:

> *There is none like you among the gods,*
> *O Lord, nor are there any works like yours.*
> **(Psalm 86:8)**

* * *

Sacramental Signs

* * *

> *Since Pentecost, it is through the sacramental sign of the Church*
> *that the Holy Spirit carries on the work of sanctification.*
> *The sacraments of the Church do not abolish but purify and integrate*
> *all the richness of the signs and symbols of the cosmos and of social life.*
> *Further, they fulfil the types and figures of the Old Covenant, and*
> *make actively present the salvation wrought by*
> *Christ and prefigure*
> *and anticipate the glory of heaven.*
> **(#1152)**

The Prophecy of Isaiah

++++++++++++++++++

*A shoot shall come out from the stump of Jesse,
and a branch shall grow out of his roots.*

*The spirit of the LORD shall rest on him,
the spirit of wisdom and understanding,
the spirit of counsel and might,
the spirit of knowledge
and the fear of the LORD.*

*His delight shall be
in the fear of the LORD.
He shall not judge by what his eyes see,
or decide by what his ears hear;
but with righteousness
he shall judge the poor,
and decide with equity for the meek of the earth;
he shall strike the earth with the rod of his mouth,
and with the breath of his lips
he shall kill the wicked.*

*Righteousness shall be the belt
around his waist
and faithfulness the belt
around his loins.*

++++++

(Isaiah 11:1-5)

Questions #17

* * *

1. *When and where did Jesus' promise of the coming of the Holy Spirit occur, and when was it first realised?*

2. *What is significant about the day of Pentecost in the Jewish calendar?*

3. *We are the temple of the living God! What exactly does this mean in view of its consequences in our lives?*

4. *How does the Holy Spirit figure in the Council of Jerusalem?*

5. *"The Holy Spirit is the guiding principle of the Church!" In what ways can you suggest that this is possible?*

6. *"The notion of the development of doctrine is alien to the message of Christ". What would you say to this objection?*

7. *Why do we call the Holy Spirit the Spirit of Remembrance?*

8. *How does the witness of history relate to the Church?*

9. *What do you understand by "Justification" and how does it relate to you personally?*

18. I BELIEVE IN THE CHURCH!

* * *

(a) I Believe in the Church
    —1. Its Meaning!
    —2. The Necessity for a Church
    —3. Christ in His Church!

(b) By What Authority?
    —1. The Great Commission
    —2. Tradition
    —3. Scripture and Tradition
    —4. The Magisterium & the Deposit of Faith

(c) The ROCK of the Church!
    —1. The Choice of a Leader
    —2. The "Power of the Keys"
    —3. The Gift of Infallibility!

(d) The Sacrament of Christ
    —1. The Church's 'Sacramental' Mission
    —2. The Church as 'Witness'!
    —3. The Paradoxes of the Church

18. I Believe in the Church!

* * *

(a) Belief in the Church!

1. Its Meaning!

On the face of it, to profess *belief in a Church* is an odd statement, especially when we have just professed belief in *God* and in his *Son*. It would appear evident that we cannot place *the Church* on the same level as *God* and his Only-Begotten Son, *Jesus*. God alone is the object of divine belief. Still, this same expression has been found in the Creed from the very beginning. It is a literal translation from the Greek *via* the Latin version. We can, however, understand that this expression *I believe* conveys the notion of *trust*. I *trust* that the Church is a truthful messenger of God's word of salvation. Likewise, I *trust* that she can guide me and point out to me the road to salvation, that she is the valid minister of the sacraments etc. This trust can go on to accept that the Church is a trustworthy witness, even relying on the testimony of Paul who writes to his beloved protégé, Timothy:

> *I hope to come to you soon, but I am writing these instructions to you so that, if I am delayed, you may know how one ought to behave in the household of God, which is the church of the living God, the pillar and bulwark of the truth.*
>
> **(1 Timothy 3:14-15)**

But my belief must go beyond this notion of simple trust. It must accept the Church, despite all its shortcomings and historic failings, as the divinely appointed instrument of our salvation. It is Christ's work in action here and now. More than that, it is the Mystical Body of Christ! In some mysterious way, through the power of the Holy Spirit, Christ is projected through the centuries in His Church, to which he promised his abiding presence.

2. The Necessity for a Church!

For no one ever hates his own body, but he nourishes and tenderly cares for it, just as Christ does for the church, because we are members of his body.
(Ephesians 5:29-30)

It would appear obvious, at first blush, that God in His infinite Mercy, after having made the long awaited revelation of Himself in Jesus Christ, His only Son, would make provision for the preservation of that revelation of His infinite love for all future generations. It would, likewise, appear equally obvious that those future generations would require the same certitude about the original revelation and its central message as was granted to the very first Christians who were taught by the apostles themselves. A *fallen* world was seeking redemption! If sinners needed to be rescued from their sins and from all those things that sought to destroy the very reason for their existence, then there must be some means of effecting their rescue. The mortal life of Jesus lasted only thirty-three years. When he returned to *the right hand* of his Father, certain questions needed answers:

How was his message of salvation to be perpetuated?
How was the work he had done, and died for, to be saved from dissolution and extinction?

All this would necessarily demand, even from a purely human standpoint, *organisation* and an *institutional hierarchy* to fulfil its sacramental outreach. As the Catechism points out there is a legacy that must be handed on to successive generations:

The apostles entrusted the 'Sacred Deposit' of the faith (the depositum fidei) contained in Sacred Scripture and Tradition, to the whole of the Church, 'By adhering to (this heritage) the entire holy people, united to its pastors, remains faithful to the breaking of bread and the prayers. So maintaining, practising and professing the faith that has been handed on,

> *there should be a remarkable harmony between the bishops and the faithful.*"[191]
>
> (#84)

This is very evident in the life of St Ignatius of Antioch, a martyr, who stood in direct line with the apostle John through his master Polycarp. En *route* to martyrdom in Rome in 108 AD he wrote a series of *farewell* letters which give an illuminating insight into the early Church at the end of the first century and at the beginning of the second. To the church at *Magnesia* he writes:

> *I exhort you to strive to do all things in harmony with God; the bishop is to preside in the place of God, while the presbyters are to function as the council of the Apostles, and the deacons, who are most dear to me, are entrusted with the ministry of Jesus Christ.*

3. Christ in His Church

Even before he came to be the apostle of the Gentiles, this truth of the Church as the very *Body of Christ*, was engraved on the soul of Paul. He had encountered Christ on the road to Damascus where he was going to hunt down all those who had converted to faith in the Galilean Messiah. There just outside Damascus he was knocked off his horse and heard a strange question put to him in the Hebrew language:

> *'Saul, Saul, why are you persecuting me?'*
> and when Paul queried: *'Who are you, Lord?'* The Lord answered, *'I am Jesus whom you are persecuting.'*
> **(Acts 26:14-16)**

Here from the lips of Jesus himself Paul heard this identification of Jesus with his Church. It was engraved on Paul's soul and it was an identification that appears again and again in his letters to his converts.

> *For just as the body is one and has many members, and all the members of the body, though many, are one body, so it is with Christ. For in the one Spirit we were*

---

[191] *Quotation taken from Dei Verbum (10) of the Second Vatican Council*

> *all baptized into one body—Jews or Greeks, slaves or*
> *free—and we were all made to drink of one Spirit.*
> **(1 Corinthians 12-13)**

> *But speaking the truth in love, we must grow up in*
> *every way into him who is the head, into Christ,*
> *from whom the whole body, joined and knit together*
> *by every ligament with which it is equipped, as each part*
> *is working properly, promotes the body's growth*
> *in building itself up in love.*
> **(Ephesians 4:15-16)**

What all this means is that we must reinterpret or retranslate all that concerns the Church into terms of our identity with Christ. Baptism, for example, is no longer simply a passport into the Church but a spiritual rebirth and an incorporation into Christ's Body. This gives us a title or a right to share in all the merits that he has won for us by his Passion and Death on the cross. In view of all this we can understand why one author unhesitatingly concludes:

> The fundamental reason for being a Catholic is the historical fact that the Catholic Church was founded by Christ, was God's invention not ours—unless Christ, her founder is not God, in which case not just Catholicism, but Christianity itself is false. To be a Christian is to believe that 'Jesus Christ is Lord.' To acknowledge him as Lord is to obey his will. And he willed the Catholic ('universal') Church for all his disciples, for all Christians. We are Catholic because we are Christians.[192]

(b) By What Authority?

1. The Great Commission

> *All authority in heaven and on earth has been given to me.*

---

[192] *Peter Kreeft; Catholic Christianity (Ignatius Press, San Francisco, 2001) p.98*

> *Go therefore and make disciples of all nations, baptising them in the name of the Father and of the Son and of the Holy Spirit, and teaching them to obey everything that I have commanded you. And remember, I am with you always, to the end of the age.*
>
> **(Matthew 28:19-20)**

It is unthinkable that Jesus, after his death and resurrection, would leave his followers to grope blindly in the darkness of their own ignorance. A Christian of the 21st century needs to hear the same message, and be assured of the same certainty that a Christian of the 1st century enjoyed. There had to be an authentic and acknowledged messenger of that same message and endowed with that same certainty. This messenger of authenticity and divine assurance was the *Church*.

It was precisely on this issue the First Vatican Council (1870) made this comment:

> *The eternal shepherd decided to establish his holy Church in which the faithful would be united, as in the house of the living God by bonds of the same faith and charity.*[193]

It is a *supreme* authority that has been granted to Jesus by the Father. All *authority!!* In virtue of that authority He commands his apostles and disciples to go forth in his name and convey His message of salvation to the entire world. In effect, his followers were invested with the same *divine* authority that Jesus had to carry on his work. We have, therefore, this comforting assurance that his presence would still be mediated on earth through *human* instruments.

2. *Tradition*

There is only one source of revealed truth and that is *divine Tradition*. Basically, this word means *the handing on to posterity* the message of the Good News! The apostles, responding to the Lord's command, imitated what their Master himself had done. They *preached* the Gospel. In an age and among cultures where literacy was but the prerogative of a few the

---

[193] *John Paul II in The Church, Mystery, Sacrament, Community (vol. 4 p.24)*

'living voice' of the Gospel was the only means feasible for this message to the mass of believers.

It is imperative to underscore the importance of this *tradition* from which both the *oral* and *written* messages derive. In the voice of *tradition* there resounds the authority of the Great Commission. In that voice the Church is conceived. In that voice the Gospel message springs to life. In that voice the Church has the assurance of fidelity in handing on Christ's command to make disciples of all nations! Because the original tradition was *oral* did not mean it was somehow defective, or that its hearers were short-changed! As Vatican II pointed out:

> Now what was handed on by the apostles includes everything which contributes to the holiness of life, and the increase of faith of the People of God; and so, the Church, in her teaching, life, and worship, perpetuates and hands on to all generations all that she herself is, all that she believes.[194]

Nevertheless, the *written* record of Scripture remains the *primary* pillar of Tradition. However, there are other *secondary* sources, the liturgical traditions, the writings of the Fathers of the Church and the theological treatises that have come down to us throughout the centuries. While these are not constitutive of tradition they are witnesses to it. They are family heirlooms, so to speak, that tell us their stories of loyalty and fidelity to what has been inherited from the past and handed on to the future!

3. *Scripture and Tradition*

Inevitably, the essentials of that original oral message were committed to writing. The latter was never intended to supplant the oral tradition. Its aim was to record its substance and to reinforce the essentials of its message. There is, therefore, a very intimate relationship between the oral tradition and the scriptures. This is spelled out very clearly in the Catechism:

---

[194] *Dei Verbum 10*

> *Sacred Tradition and Sacred Scripture are bound closely together and communicate one with the other. For both of them, flowing out from the same divine wellspring, come together in some fashion to form one thing and move towards the same goal. Each of them makes present and fruitful in the Church the mystery of Christ, who promised to remain with his own 'always, to the close of the age'.*
>
> (#80)

There are dangers in the written word, when divorced from the context of tradition. There is the danger of *fixation*, i.e. an obsession with a single-minded interpretation of a written word, phrase or sentence. There is also the danger of *private* judgements, or *personal* interpretations which splinter the Gospel message into countless religious affiliations. What holds the written word in balance is *Tradition*, about which one author writes:

> *Tradition is the Church's life;,,,,,,,it is the Church's faith. And because in Catholic Christianity . . . . the Spirit of the Risen Christ being present in the Church until the end of time, so quite naturally the life and faith of the Church are seen as the proper context in which to read, study and expound the Scriptures. Tradition, as the Christian religion itself, the life and consciousness of the the Church considered as a reflection of the word of God, of God's self-communication, is necessarily a reality at once larger than the Bible and inclusive of it.*[195]

4. *The Magisterium & the Deposit of Faith*

This teaching authority of the Church radiating from Christ's command to go out and make disciples of all nations, is called the *magisterium*[196]. It empowers the Church, under the leadership of the

---

[195] Aidan Nichols O.P. *The Shape of Catholic Theology* (The Liturgical Press, Collegeville, Min. 1991, p. 169)

[196] The Latin 'magisterium' comes from the original 'magister' or 'teacher' in English. It reflects the original command of Christ to his Church to go and teach 'all nations.'

successor of St Peter, to teach authoritatively and infallibly all that pertains to faith and morals in our journey towards eternity.

What is passed on in the *magisterium* is called the *deposit of faith*. This deposit is the sum of revelation and tradition given by Jesus to his apostles. This in turn was passed on to their successors. About this heritage of our faith the First Vatican Council made this comment:

> *Faith's doctrines which God has revealed are not before us as some philosophical discovery to be developed by human ingenuity but as a divine trust (depositum) handed over to the Spouse of Christ for her faithful safeguarding and infallible exposition.*

It also means that the deposit of faith cannot be *changed, altered or added to*. It must be handed on intact from generation to generation. But that does not mean, however, that our *understanding* of it is not subject to progressive enlightenment and advancement in knowledge. The Fathers and the doctors of the Church have written about it and cast fresh light upon it. The divine truth of revelation is like a brilliant jewel that throws off ever-changing spears of multicoloured light as it is turned in the light of the sun!

(c) The ROCK of the Church!

1. *The Choice of a Leader*

> *And I tell you, you are Peter,*
> *and on this rock I will build my church,*
> *and the gates of Hades will not prevail against it.*
> **(Matthew 16:17)**

We have seen that the vehicle for the authentic transmission of the message of salvation and the *authority* for its preservation lies in the *Church*. This is the burden of the Great Commission. There is one further step in this transmission of authority, the choice of a leader who could assume the special responsibility for guiding the infant Church. It would have to be someone who would take his place after his death. Jesus chose Peter! The promise for this *tradition*, or the handing on of authority, was made at *Caesarea Philippi*.

There in the shadow of a gigantic rock on which stood a temple, dedicated to *Caesar Augustus,* Peter made his supreme confession of faith in Jesus:

> *You are the Messiah, the Son of the living God.*
> **(Matthew 16:16)**

Jesus then confirmed the blessing Peter had received:

> *Blessed are you, Simon son of Jonah! For flesh and blood has not revealed this to you, but my Father in heaven. And I tell you, you are Peter, and on this rock I will build my church, and the gates of Hades will not prevail against it.*
>
> *I will give you the keys of the kingdom of heaven, and whatever you bind on earth will be bound in heaven, and whatever you loose on earth will be loosed in heaven.*
> **(Matthew 16: 17-19)**

2. The Power of the Keys!

It may be worth remarking in passing that it could be said that Jesus made the most famous pun in the whole of biblical history! In the shadow of the great rock of *Caesarea Philippi* He changed Simon's name to *Peter*. However, the actual word in Aramaic for *Peter* is *Kepha* (= rock). And upon this *Kepha* (Peter) he would build His Church. It is unfortunate that the force and subtlety of the exchange between Jesus and Peter is lost, as so often happens in translations from the original. In passing, it should also be noted that when God changes a person's name, he does so to underscore the fact that this person has been chosen for some special role in the divine plan of salvation.

But there is also a rather subtle reference in the choice of the name *Kepha* for Peter. There are synonyms for this term *rock* as a divine attribute in the Old Testament, symbolising God's *power* and *might!* There are many references to this, but that of the psalmist will suffice:

> *(God) alone is my rock and my salvation, my fortress;*
> *I shall not be shaken*
> **(Psalm 62:6)**

Moreover, the phrase *"the keys of the Kingdom of Heaven"* conveys the idea of the supreme authority that was to be conferred on Peter and his successors. This is a reference to the supreme jurisdiction that they were to exercise over the whole Church. Here it may be well to recall the relevant words of Isaiah, words which would obviously be very familiar to those present:

> ***I will place on his shoulder the key of the house of David;***
> ***he shall open, and no one shall shut;***
> ***he shall shut, and no one shall open.***
> **(Isaiah 22:22)**

The *'Power of the Keys'* denotes supreme authority of *binding* and *loosing*, as is evident from the prophet Isaiah. St Peter is often depicted with these two keys in paintings and sculptures. The symbolism becomes even more trenchant when we hear Jesus speaking to John in the Book of Revelation:

> ***I am alive forever and ever;***
> ***and I have the keys of Death and of Hades.***
> **(Revelation 1:18)**

After the Resurrection the authority of Peter is confirmed in the answer given to the triple question that Jesus addresses to Peter:

> ***Simon son of John, do you love me?***
> **(John 21:16)**

With each successive assurance of his love Peter is given the command to feed *the lambs* and *the sheep* of Jesus. These terms of *lambs* and *sheep* are the biblical metaphors for the followers and pastors of the *Good Shepherd*, and for all those who, in the future, would become members of His Church.

3. The Gift of Infallibility

One of the gifts of the continued presence of Jesus in his Church is the charism of *infallibility*. Jesus, moreover, promised the gift of the Holy Spirit who would be the teacher and guide throughout the centuries.

This means the Church *cannot err in matters of faith and morals*. But this charism of infallibility also belongs in a special way to the successor of Peter, the *Pope*. This means that in special circumstances, the Holy Father can speak with supreme authority on matters of faith and morals. Infallibility is, on the one hand, a safeguard, a preservative of the truth. On the other hand, it may be regarded as a *negative* gift. It is, in effect, a *preventative* of error! It is intended as a protection of the *Supreme Shepherd* of the Church to prevent the *sheep*—the faithful—from falling among the rocks and into the *ravines* of error and deception.

> *This is the infallibility which the Roman Pontiff (the Pope) the head of the college of bishops, enjoys in virtue of his office, when, as supreme shepherd and teacher of the faithful, who confirms his brethren in their faith* (cf. Luke 22:32), *he proclaims by a definitive act some doctrine of faith or morals. Therefore, his definitions, of themselves, and not from the consent of the Church, are justly styled irreformable, for they are pronounced with the assistance of the holy Spirit, an assistance promised to him in blessed Peter . . .*
> (Vatican II: *Dogmatic Constitution of the Church* no. 25)

(d) The Church—The Sacrament of Christ[197]

1. *The Church's Sacramental Mission*

The usual definition of *'sacrament'* as *'an outward sign of inward grace'* is applied to the Church's sacramental system. However, the Second Vatican Council also revived the original meaning of the term in calling the Church *'the Sacrament of Christ'*.

Again the Catechism spells out the meaning of the phrase:

> *The Church's mission is not an addition to that of Christ and the Holy Spirit, but is its sacrament: in her whole being, and in all her members, the Church is sent to announce to bear*

---

[197] *This issue enlarges on what we have already touched upon in the Sacraments pp14 etc.*

witness, make present, and spread the mystery of the communion of the Holy Trinity. (#738)

It then goes on to quote *St Cyril,* Patriarch of Alexandria: (412-444 A.D.)

> *All of us who have received one and the same Spirit, that is, the Holy Spirit, are in a sense blended together with one another and with God. For, if Christ, together with the Father's and his own Spirit, comes to dwell in each of us, though we are many, still the Spirit is one and undivided. He binds together the spirits of each and every one of us . . . . and makes all appear as one in him. For just as the power of Christ's sacred flesh unites those in who it dwells into one body, I think that, in the same way, the one and undivided Spirit of God, who dwells in all, leads all into spiritual unity.*

As Pope Paul VI so graphically expresses it: the church is *"the universal sacrament of salvation . . . at once manifesting and actualising the mystery of God's love for men".* Here he is simply expressing the sentiments uttered long ago by the great doctor of the West, St Augustine:

> **It was from the side of Christ, as He slept on the Cross, that there came forth the wondrous sacrament which is the whole Church.**

In these words Augustine sees the Church as symbolised by the *water* and the *blood* flowing from the side of Christ. Both the *water* and the *blood* are identified with the sacraments of Baptism and the Eucharist, the two fundamental rites in the life of the Church, the first, the bestower of life and the second its sustainer! St Bernard of Clairvaux in one of his sermons expresses in his own unique style this dual character of God's Church:

> ***O humility! O sublimity! Both tabernacle of cedar and sanctuary of God; earthly dwelling and celestial palace; house of clay and royal hall; body of death and temple of light; and at last, both object of scorn to the proud and bride of Christ!***
>
> **(#771)**

Through the abiding presence of the Holy Spirit, the Church as *the sacrament of Jesus* is perpetuated in the world. It is to be *visible* and *identifiable*, going forth with his authority to continue His work. It was to proclaim the Good News and preach His presence in every age, in every corner of the globe. In this wise it was to fulfill the Master's words so manifest in the urgency of the Great Commission:

Go and make disciples of all nations!

2. The Church as Witness

We have already seen that it is part of the sacramental mission of the Church to bear witness in contemporary society to the truth of Christ and his message of salvation. In the Book of Revelation the apostle John, writing to the seven churches of Asia, wrote of grace and peace from the father and from

> ***Jesus, the faithful witness,***
> ***the first born of the dead.*** **(Revelation 1:5)**

What is a witness? A witness is someone who is called to *testify* on behalf of another. The most common use of the term is in the judicial system, whether from the defence or the prosecution. Here it has a much wider meaning of outstanding example! John the Baptist was a *witness* to Jesus:

> **Behold the Lamb of God**
> **who takes away the sin of the world! (John 1:29)**

Jesus, in his turn was the faithful *witness* of the Father's will. Before Pilate he was at pains to proclaim his own testimony as a *witness* to the truth:

> *For this I was born,*
> *and for this I came into the world*
> *to bear witness to the truth.*
> **(John 18:37)**

This role of Jesus as *witness to the truth* has been passed on to his Church. The latter was to bear witness to Christ and his message of salvation. This duty to witness flows directly from the *Great Commission* from the command to go out out to preach the Gospel to all nations.

It is obvious that witnessing demands *conviction* in the passing on of Christ's message. This was evident in the apostles, who underscored their convictions with signs and wonders. Their ultimate witnessing was the giving of their lives for the sake of the message.[198]

This duty of *witnessing* was passed on to the successors of the apostles, who in turn gave their own witness at the expense of their lives. What is true of the apostles, the primary witnesses to Christ, and to their successors, is true also of the Church today. Its mission is to bear witness to Christ and his saving message.

This duty to witness comes from the very title of *Christian*, which means a *follower of Christ*. In fact, the committed Christian finds God and his faith meaningful in his, or her, whole life. It is this *personal* witness that is the most powerful example in a world that so often ignores, denies or even seeks to erase Christ's message of truth and love. This act of witnessing, however, does not demand a belligerent or vociferous proclamation of the Gospel to all and sundry. The quiet assurance of a life devoted to the faith is always more compelling. The words of a great man who suffered for his faith under a godless regime speaks volumes:

> *The world needs witnesses as a road needs traffic signals;*
> *though they are silent, signals speak clearly*[199]

3. The Paradoxes of the Church

The Church operates within the context of this world. It is entangled in earthly affairs; it is enmeshed in the rhythms of secular history. But beyond and beneath the facade of temporal concerns and the Church's visible reality lies an *eternal spiritual reality*. Herein is proclaimed the Church *as the bearer of the divine life* to all mankind. Hence, we have the following paradoxes embedded in the concept of the Church living in the world, but not of it:

---

[198] *It is important to note that the Greek word for a witness is 'martur' from which we get the English 'martyr', denoting one who sacrifices his or her life for the faith.*

[199] *Cardinal Van Thuan (1928-2002) former Archbishop of Saigon who spent 13 years in prison, 9 of them in solitary confinement!*

1. The church is a *visibly structured society*, while claiming to be the *Mystical Body of Christ*.
2. It is also at once a *visible society* and, at the same time, a *spiritual community*.
3. It has an *earthly existence* that promises its believers *heavenly rewards*.

All this adds up to a paradox that defies human reasoning and analysis. Its truth is only amenable to acceptance in the light of faith, a faith that is prepared to accept, in the first place, that the Church has been divinely appointed to carry on and fulfil the salvific work of Christ Himself. To the outsider the Church may appear just like any human organisation, complete with buildings and personnel. It may also put on splendid liturgical services, gilded with lights and echoing with the inspiring hymns of its congregations. But all this visual and emotional splendour is only a screen for a far deeper spiritual reality of Christ still walking amongst us, just as he did nigh two millennia ago. His message of love and his healing ministry still spill out on the congregations of the twenty-first century just as they did on captive audiences of Judea! As the Catechism expresses it:

> *The Church is essentially both human and divine, visible but endowed with invisible realities, zealous in action and dedicated to contemplation, present in the world, but as a pilgrim, so constituted that in her the human is directed towards and subordinated to the divine, the visible to the invisible action to contemplation, and this present world to that city yet to come, the object of our quest.*
>
> (#771)

The writer of the *Letter to the Hebrews* condenses all these sentiments in very apt terms:

> **For here we have no lasting city,**
> **but we are looking**
> **for the city that is to come**
> **(Hebrews 13;14)**

++++++++++++++++++++

The Catechism of the Catholic Church has this to say on the role of the Holy Spirit in the life and work of the Church. On the other hand, it also spells out that it is a Church of sinners!

> *The Holy Spirit is the protagonist, "the principal agent of the whole of the Church's mission." It is he who leads the Church on her missionary paths. "This mission continues and, in the course of history, unfolds the mission of Christ, who was sent to evangelize the poor; so the Church, urged on by the Spirit of Christ, must walk the road Christ himself walked, a way of poverty and obedience, of service and self-sacrifice even to death, a death from which he emerged victorious by his resurrection." So it is that "the blood of martyrs is the seed of Christians."*
>
> *(#852)*

> *On her pilgrimage, the Church has also experienced the "discrepancy existing between the message she proclaims and the human weakness of those to whom the Gospel has been entrusted." Only by taking the "way of penance and renewal," the "narrow way of the cross," can the People of God extend Christ's reign. For "just as Christ carried out the work of redemption in poverty and oppression, so the Church is called to follow the same path if she is to communicate the fruits of salvation to men."*
>
> *(#853)*

Questions #18

* * *

1. *What does this expression—I believe in the Church!—really mean?*

2. *Why is the Church identified with Jesus himself-?*

3. *Who said the Church is the pillar and the bulwark of truth? What does this mean?*

4. *What do these terms denote—tradition; magisterium; deposit of faith?*

5. *What are the characteristics of Christ's Church?*

6. *What is the significance of Peter as the Rock of the Church?*

7. *What is meant by the Power of the Keys?*

8. *What do you understand by infallibility?*

9. *Why is the Church called the Sacrament of Christ?*

10. *The Church came forth from the side of Christ! What does this mean?*

11. *Why must the Church be a witness to the world and what does this mean to you personally?*

19. THE HOLINESS OF THE CHURCH

* * *

(a) The Mark of Holiness
    —1. What is holiness?
    —2. An Unholy Church?!
    —3. The Primary Mark
    —4. The Basis of Holiness

(b) The Church and Holiness
    —1. The Holiness of the Founder
    —2. The Means of Holiness
    —3. Holiness 'in via'
    —4. The Witness of History

(c) Personal Holiness
    —1. God's Sovereign Will
    —2. The Purity of Heart
    —3. The Goal of Holiness
    —4. To the Glory of God!

19. The Holiness of the Church

* * *

(a) The 'Mark' of Holiness

1. What is holiness?

> *You shall be holy*
> *for I, the Lord your God, am holy!*
> **(Leviticus 19:2)**

This was God's command to Moses, the Lawgiver of the Old Law, and to his Chosen People. The perfect fulfilment of that command is to be found in Jesus, the *Holy One of Israel*.

Jesus, the new Moses, manifested the holiness of the Father as His followers are called to manifest that same holiness in their lives. But what is holiness? In its absolute sense, holiness is proper to God alone. As Mary proclaimed in her Magnificat:

> *Holy is his name!*
> **(Luke 1:49)**

Holiness is of God's very essence: it is the glory of divinity! As the prophet Isaiah, beholding the Seraphim in God's presence, heard the thunder of their song:

> *Holy, holy, holy is the Lord God of hosts!*
> **(Isaiah 6:3)**

On the purely human level, notions of *holiness* tend to be rather superficial. In general, however, a person is considered *holy*, if he or she manifests a certain dedication to religion.

St Thomas Aquinas tells us that *holiness*—also called *sanctity*—is the term used for all that is dedicated to the service of God. The word itself means *separateness*, or the *freedom from defilement*. While this would appear to be a rather negative definition, it is, nevertheless, the basic requirement for divine service. Hence it can be said that in the moral order holiness is the proclamation of God's sovereign rights in human affairs, and the fulfilment of his claim to our obedience, especially in the keeping of his commandments. This was a constant theme of St Paul in his exhortations to his converts:

> *Put off your old nature, which belongs to your former manner of life, and is corrupt through deceitful lusts, and be renewed in the spirit of your minds, and put on the new nature, created after the likeness of God in true righteousness and holiness!*
>
> **(Ephesians 4:22-24)**

2. An Unholy Church!

There are some who would dispute the Church's right to be called *'Holy'*. They claim, if Catholics were truly honest with themselves, they would see it as an obviously *sinful* Church! This, in fact was stated in the second Vatican Council! Justification is sought for this in the long history of infidelity and frailty in the life of the Church. Even in apostolic times there were warring factions within the Church. St Paul himself was compelled to write to his own converts in Galatia:

> *You foolish Galatians, who has bewitched you?*
>
> **(Galatians 3:1)**

That was one of the themes that inspired Paul's letter—the fickleness and frailty of his converts:

> *I am astonished that you are so quickly deserting the one who called you in the grace of Christ and are turning to a different gospel—not that there is another gospel, but there are some who are confusing you and want to pervert the gospel of Christ.*
>
> **(Galatians 1:6-7)**

There have been heresies and heresiarchs, such as *Arius*[200] and *Nestorius*[201], who have split the Church. There have been betrayals and desertions in the Church's long history. There have been bad Popes and unfaithful bishops, shepherds who have been *mercenaries* to their flocks. The whole scene of infidelity is described by one author:

> *The centuries of the Church's history are so filled with human failure that we can quite understand Dante's ghastly vision of the Babylonian whore sitting in the Church's chariot; and the dreadful words of William of Auvergne, Bishop of Paris in the thirteenth century, seem perfectly comprehensible. William said that the barbarism of the Church must make everyone who saw it rigid with horror:*
>
> *"Bride she is no more, but a monster of frightful ugliness and ferocity."*[202]

The whole thrust of all these objections to the Church's *holiness* is based primarily on our obvious, and very human weakness. The Church is not called *'holy'* because its members, whether taken collectively or individually, are *sinless*. They are sinners; we are all sinners. We might even say that the Church is *a collection of sinners run by sinners!* It was for *the forgiveness of our sins* that the whole plan of salvation was devised. The reason why Jesus came amongst us was to rescue us from our sinfulness.

> **For us men and for our salvation**
> **he came down from heaven!**
> **(Nicene Creed)**

Therefore, it cannot be too strongly asserted that the Church is not called *'holy'* in the Creed because all its members, either collectively

---

[200] *Arius was an Egyptian priest from Alexandria who gained widespread support for his heretical teaching that denied the divinity of Jesus.*

[201] *Nestorius of Antioch, another heresiarch who denied Mary's title as 'Mother of God'. He was condemned at the Council of Ephesus 431 AD.*

[202] *Joseph Cardinal Ratzinger (now Benedict XVI) in his Introduction to Christianity (Ignatius Press, 1990) p.262*

or individually, are holy. It does not mean its many congregations are made up of *sinless* men and women. Nor does it mean that the very guardians of the faith—from the Pope down to the lowliest parish priest—are immune to moral frailty and sin. That we should fail at times to live up to the demands of the faith should come as no surprise, when we consider the depth of our human weakness, and the frailty of our best intentions. Heaven itself was not immune to the rebellion of Lucifer and his followers. Even in the chosen group of the apostles there was a *betrayer* and a *denier,* as well as wholesale desertion by the very men Jesus trusted! Jesus knew their weakness and he still chose them to found *his* church! The answer, therefore, to the question of the Church's *holiness* must come from a totally different perspective!

3. The Primary Mark

When we speak of a a *mark* in relation to the Church we mean that she has some special sign or characteristic that enables people to identify her. The Nicene Creed identifies four marks in the Church—*One, Holy, Catholic and Apostolic.*

The Apostles' Creed, however, is content to single out two of the marks that distinguish the Church. They are *holiness* and *catholicity.* The mark of *holiness* ascribed to the Church goes back to the first and second century AD. It is the oldest and most important of those adjectives used to describe the nature of the Church. It is a constant theme, either *explicitly* or *implicitly*, of all the letters of St Paul. That of his address to the Romans is typical:

> *To all God's beloved in Rome, who are called to be saints: Grace to you and peace from God our Father and the Lord Jesus Christ.*
> **(Romans 1:7)**

As holiness is of God's very essence, it is an expression of the immutable love by which He loves His own goodness. From this flows His *moral* holiness by which He loves holiness in others and, therefore, wishes to communicate it and share it with them. From this we conclude that the Church is holy because of its *origin,* its *founder,* its *ideals,* and its *sacraments* which are the *channels* of holiness! It is obvious that the source of all holiness is God Himself.

4. The Basis of Holiness

Only God is essentially holy, all others are only holy by *participation,* i.e. by sharing in that holiness. Holiness is of his very nature. Everything else outside of the divinity can only *mirror* that holiness. So the angels *reflect* God's holiness; man *shares* in that inimitable holiness of God. The Church, therefore, is a unique organisation called into existence by God himself *to manifest his holiness*! One might say that there is no other reason for its existence. It stands or falls, so to speak on this fundamental mark of *holiness!* There is a threefold rationale for this:

a. The Church has received this obligation to promote holiness from Christ himself. Christ was sent as an exemplar from the Father, and he handed on the same commission to his followers. Jesus gave a command for them t*o go forth and make disciples of all nations and baptise them in the name of the Trinity?* (Matthew 28:16-20). This baptism was to be an initiation into the holiness of God himself!

b. Through Christ's redeeming actions in his *Passion, Death and Resurrection he* gave a structure to the Church to enable all believers to strive after and to achieve the goal of holiness in God; namely, the hierarchy, essential doctrines, sacramental rites and liturgical activity. All are devised to further the sanctification or holiness of the participants.

c. God offers himself to the faithful individually! This sublime and utterly incomprehensible gift of the Most Holy Trinity is given to all who manifest their love for God in keeping his word:

If a man loves me, he will keep my word,
and my Father will love him, and we will come to him
and make our home with him.
(John 14:23)

(b) The Church and Holiness

1. *The Holiness of its Founder*

The Church, as *Christ's* Church, is an instrument of holiness. We have already noted the identification of the Church with Christ himself.[203] The channel of this communication is Jesus himself, the founder of the Church, Jesus, the *All-Holy One*, the sinless one:

> *He committed no sin, and no deceit*
> *was found in his mouth.*
> **(1 Peter 2:22)**

The holiness of the Father shines through Jesus. Hence He is *absolutely* incapable of sin. The Second Council of Constantinople in 553 AD condemned the proposition that Christ was burdened with the unruly passions of the soul and the desires of the flesh! The Church is, therefore, holy in its Founder. It is also holy in its *origin* because that origin is God Himself. This is all too evident when He claimed it as *His* Church!

As Jesus said to Peter at Caesarea Philippi:

> *And I tell you, you are Peter,*
> *and on this rock I will build my church.*
> **(Matthew 16:18)**

And, as if to give added point to this statement, Jesus also declared the Church's identity with Himself in upbraiding the Pharisee Saul for his persecution of His followers:

> *Saul, Saul, why do you persecute me?*
> **(Acts 9:4)**

---

[203] *katharos* means free from the defilement of sin; free from wickedness. It can also denote a cleansing of the spirit. This moral freedom implied *deliverance* from the slavery of Satan and his wiles.

The holiness of Jesus radiates in His Church especially through the ministry and *indwelling* of the Holy Spirit. Through the action of the latter all Christians are called to holiness. As the Second Vatican Council affirmed:

> *Faith teaches that the Church . . . is holy in a way that can never fail. For, Christ the Son of God, who with the Father and the Spirit, is praised as being 'alone holy' loved the Church as his Bride, delivering himself up for her. This he did that he might sanctify her.*

2. The Means of Holiness

We have already alluded to the means of holiness that are available to the faithful. The means are three—the *sacraments*, its *doctrine* and its *liturgy*. They all contribute to the renewal of the Church and to the sanctification of its members.

As St Paul so graphically expresses it:

> **And all of us, with unveiled faces, seeing the glory of the Lord as though reflected in a mirror, are being transformed into the same image from one degree of glory to another; for this comes from the Lord, the Spirit.**
> **(2 Corinthians 3:18)**

The degrees of glory come to us through the liturgy and the sacraments. The Catechism is at pains to point this out:

> *In the liturgy the Holy Spirit is teacher of the faith of the People of God and artisan of "God's masterpieces", the sacraments of the new Covenant.*
> (#1091)

> *In this sacramental dispensation of Christ's mystery the Holy Spirit acts in the same way as at other times in the economy of salvation: He prepares the Church to encounter the Lord; He recalls and makes Christ manifest to the assembly. By His transforming power, He makes the mystery of Christ present here*

and now. Finally, the Spirit of communion unites the Church to the life and mission of Christ.

(#1092)

3. Holiness 'in via'!

The holiness of the Church *in time* is an *imperfect* holiness. It is holiness *in via*, that is, in a state of journeying towards the *Promised Land*. God is guiding it and bringing it closer to its fulfilment in history. The consummation comes when it is finally perfected in the *Second Coming of Christ!* The Church on earth, therefore, reflects the current status of the kingdom or the reign of God in the world we live in. Holiness, as a reality or an ideal, is a sharing in the divine nature, a free gift of the Father. Like all gifts it can be accepted, rejected or abused. We still struggle with our sinful nature. We are, as St Paul says, *'earthen vessels'* that can easily be shattered! Sin is obviously part of the life of the believers in the Church, because they have a *fallen* nature. Christ came to save us, *because* we are sinners, and *not* because we are perfect!

> ***Go and learn what this means,***
> ***'I desire mercy, not sacrifice.'***
> ***For I have come to call***
> ***not the righteous but sinners.***
> **(Matthew 9:13)**

However, our own *personal* sinfulness is not the true nature of the Church itself. The latter offers us the means to regain the divine life and assure us of redemption. It is up to us to accept it through repentance, through the Precious Blood of Christ shed for the redemption of all mankind. The Second Vatican Council summarises this reality in its *Dogmatic Constitution* of the Church:

> *While the Christ, holy, innocent and undefiled, knew nothing of sin (2 Cor. 5:12), but came to expiate only the sins of the people, the Church, embracing sinners in her bosom, is at the same time holy, and always in need of being purified, and incessantly pursues the path of penance and renewal.* (#8)

4. The Witness of History

***Like living stones, let yourselves be built into a spiritual house, to be a holy priesthood, to offer spiritual sacrifices acceptable to God through Jesus Christ.* (1 Peter 2:5)**

In its long history the Church has been blessed with countless saints drawn from every walk of life who, in one degree or another, have drawn on the inexhaustible treasures of Christ's redemption. In every age, whether in rulers or in subjects, there have never been wanting witnesses to the holiness of the Church. We have already noted that in the twentieth century there have been more martyrs to the faith than in all previous centuries! It is one of the great paradoxes of the faith that it thrives on persecution! As a great writer of the early Church, Tertullian, wrote:

> *the blood of the martyrs is the seed of the Church!*

Pope Pius XII in his immortal encyclical on the Mystical Body *(Mystici Corporis)* reiterates the point that the Church is both a visible sign of holiness and a channel for attaining it.

> It is spotless *in its sacraments by which it gives birth to and nourishes its children; in its sacred laws imposed on all; in the evangelical counsels which it recommends; in those heavenly gifts and extraordinary graces through which, with inexhaustible fecundity, it generates hosts of martyrs, virgins and confessors".*[204]

(c) Personal Holiness!

1. God's Sovereign Will

It is obvious that the mark of *holiness* in the Church should also be the distinctive character of its members. The call to holiness that echoes

---

[204] *Mystici Corporis* #65

in Paul's letter to the Romans is a call to all those who share Christ's very name as *Christians*:

> **To all God's beloved in Rome who are called to be saints!**
> **(Romans 1:4)**

The question then arises: how is this imperative of holiness to be accomplished? The answer lies in the example of Christ himself. The guiding principle of our Saviour's life was the will of his Father. In the Gospel of John this is clearly stated in the aftermath of Jesus' encounter with the woman at the well of Jacob. When he was pressed by his disciples to eat, he replied:

> **My food is to do the will of him who sent me**
> **and to accomplish his work.**
> **(John 4:34)**

This obedience to the will of his Father was the hallmark of the life of Jesus. Even in the extremity of his suffering in the garden of Gethsemane, his prayer was:

> **Not my will, but thine be done!**
> **(Luke 22:44)**

His life of obedience was consummated on the Cross, when he prayed to his Father

> **Father into thy hands I commend my spirit!**
> **(Luke 23:46)**

This example of Jesus is the signpost to sanctity. His life points the road to holiness. It is not an easy road. Conforming our lives to that of Christ is a lifelong struggle. As a member of the Body of Christ I must replicate in my life the image of the Head of that Body, Christ himself.

St Paul was at pains to stress this upon his converts in Galatia:

> **My little children, with whom I am again in travail,**
> **until Christ be formed in you!**
> **(Galatians 4:19)**

2. Purity of Heart

> **Blessed are the pure in heart,**
> **for they will see God.**
>
> **(Matthew 5:8)**

If there is one phrase in the Gospel that echoes *personal* holiness if is *the pure in heart!* The word *pure* has a much more extensive coverage of meaning than is usually associated with sexual purity. In its extended meaning the *purity* of the beatitudes might be defined as follows:

> *Blessed are those whose motives are not mixed, whose intentions are pure, whose minds do not indulge in ulterior motives, whose designs are totally single-minded, free from all duplicity or deceit, and fixed solely on God's will.*

If we accept this broader concept of purity, then this beatitude is the most demanding of all the beatitudes, since it demands absolute purity in our motives, which are usually besmirched with layers of self-seeking. We are so prone to self-deception that purity in our motives is so difficult to achieve without the special grace of the Holy Spirit. Truly blessed indeed is the man or woman whose motives are as clear as sparkling water, and whose eye is fixed on God and His glory alone. In the context of the early Church the word *katharos* [205] was closely tied to sexual morality, since it was here that the greatest battles against pagan *mores* of the age were fought. St Paul writes rather scathingly to the Corinthians on this very subject:

> *It is actually reported that there is sexual immorality among you, and of a kind that is not found even among pagans; for a man is living with his father's wife. And you are arrogant! Should you not rather have mourned, so that he who has done this would have been removed from among you?*
>
> **(1 Corinthians 5:1-2)**

---

[205] *katharos'* denotes freedom from sin and all moral defilement or deliverance from the thrall of Satan!

It was to holiness of life that he appealed to his converts. They had to renounce their former mode of living. The latter was *'akatharsia'*, the way of *uncleanness*, that was opposed to *'hagiasmos'*, the way of *sanctification* and *holiness*. It is an appeal that is as relevant today as it was then!

> *For this is the will of God, your sanctification:*
> *that you abstain from fornication;*
> *that each one of you know how to control your own body*
> *in holiness and honour, not with lustful passion,*
> *like the Gentiles who do not know God.*
> **(1 Thessalonians 4:3-5)**

3. The Goal of Holiness

During our earthly sojourn the holiness of the Church is, as we have always insisted, an *imperfect* holiness. We are constantly striving to do better, to reach out to the goal set by our founder. Apart from Christ himself, the only creature that realised the perfection of holiness is Mary, his blessed mother. She was completely submitted to God's holy will. The *Fiat* [206] of surrender at the Annunciation of the angel Gabriel was the hallmark of her entire life on earth.

All the rest of us resist to a greater or lesser extent the impulses of grace. We resist the promptings of the Holy Spirit and the sanctifying power offered so generously through the sacraments. We are sinners, not because the Church is failing in its purpose, but because of the perversity of our nature, and its deep-rooted egotism and pride! The trauma of Adam's fall lies so deeply embedded in our nature that we are scarcely aware that it exists! Our wounded nature, therefore, so often resists the healing balm of divine grace!

Only in eternity will the perfection of holiness be realised. All the visible supports offered us in this world through the Church—*the priesthood, the sacraments, the guidance of its teachings etc.*—all will be replaced by God himself. In the ultimate embrace of the *Beatific*

---

[206] *'Fiat' a Latin word meaning "Let it be done"; It echoes Mary's surrender to God's will!*

Vision will our holiness be consummated! As the Book of Revelation expresses it:

> *Behold the dwelling of God is with men. He will dwell with them, and they shall be his people, and God himself will be with them; he will wipe away every tear from their eyes, and death shall be no more, neither shall there be mourning nor crying nor pain any more, for the former things have passed away.*
> **(Revelation 21:2-4)**

4. To The Glory of God!

> *The holiness of God is the inaccessible centre of the eternal mystery. What is revealed of it in creation and in history, Scripture calls 'glory', the radiance of his majesty. In making man in his image and likeness, God 'crowned him with glory and honour', but, by sinning, man fell short of the glory of God'. From that time on, God was to manifest his holiness and by giving his name, in order to restore man to the image of his creator.*
> (#2809)

Finally, we reach the whole point of our existence and of the true meaning of *holiness* in our lives. We exist to manifest *the glory of God!* From our own point of view God's glory is manifested in our lives, in striving to fulfil his will in our regard. This is the perpetual challenge that we face in this constant striving for perfection, and fulfilling his will our obedience to his Church. It is in this way that God is glorified. This was the path that Jesus trod.

He always sought to glorify his Father. *How?* By doing his will! This point was made clear at the well of Jacob when Jesus said to the apostles when they besought him to eat:

> *My food is to do the will of him who sent me, and to accomplish his work.*
> **(John 4:34)**

The *leitmotif* of the life of Jesus was to give glory to his Father. In the final days of his public ministry he prayed:

> *Father, glorify thy name. Then a voice came from heaven.*
> *'I have glorified it, and I will glorify it again!'*
> **(John 12:28)**

St Paul urges us also to manifest this glory:

> *So, whether you eat or drink, or whatever you do,*
> *do all to the glory of God.* **(1 Corinthians 10:31)**

Our entire lives, everything about us, everything that we say or do, must promote God's glory. That is why we are here, as St Paul insists, so that everything about us should manifest God's eternal glory.

It was this profound insight that led St Ignatius Loyola to choose as the motto for the Order of the Jesuits—*ad majorem Dei gloriam*—for the greater glory of God! As Christians progress in the spiritual life and gain greater insight into the things *'of God'*, they come to realise that their own puny egotistical concerns, even their own perfection or salvation, are not the ultimate goals of their own existence. No, their sanctification and salvation must be viewed in the final context of giving *glory to the Most Holy Trinity*. In his *Priestly Prayer* as the High Priest of the New Covenant, Jesus makes the admission that is so pertinent to all his followers:

> *I glorified you on earth, having accomplished the work*
> *which you gave me to do, and now, Father,*
> *glorify me in your presence,*
> *with the glory that I had with you*
> *before the world was made.*
> **(John 17:4-6)**

* * *

> *Too late I have loved You,*
> *O Beauty, ever ancient, ever new!*
> *Too late have I loved You.*
> *And behold, You were within, and I abroad,*
> *and there I searched for You; deformed;*
> *I plunged amidst those fair forms,*

which You had made. You were with me.
but I was not with You . . . .
You called, You shouted, and You burst my deafness,
You flashed and You shone and You scattered my blindness.
You breathed fragrances, and I drew breath and I panted for You!
I tasted both hunger and thirst. You touched me
and I burned for Your peace!
from the *Confessions* of St Augustine

Questions #19

* * *

1. What do you understand by a mark in relation to the Church?

2. What is holiness? And why is it the primary mark of the Church?

3. In what way does holiness relate to the Church?

4. What is the foundation of holiness?

5. The holiness of the Church is an imperfect holiness. What does this mean?

6. Why does St Peter call members of the Church 'living stones!'?

7. "Holiness is Purity of heart!" What exactly does this mean?

8. What does Leon Bloy say about holiness?

9. *What is the ultimate end of personal holiness?*

10. *"The Church has had so many blots in its history, so many grave sins among its leaders etc., etc. How can you even talk about the 'holiness' of the Church". How would you respond to this objection?*

11. *I exist to promote God's glory! How is it possible to accomplish that?*

12. *How do you see yourself personally responding to the demands of holiness?*

20. THE CATHOLICITY OF THE CHURCH

*   *   *

(a) In Scripture and Tradition
—1. The Prayer of Jesus
—2. The Great Commission
—3. The Message of Pentecost
—4. The Witness of Tradition

(b) The Claim of Catholicity
—1. The Term 'Catholic'
—2. The Universal Call Today
—3. The Scandal of Division
—4. The Anonymous Christian

(c) The Universal Sacrament of Salvation
—1. The Second Vatican Council
—2. Ecumenism
—3. Evangelisation
—4. Restoration of the Whole Person

20. The Catholicity of the Church

* * *

(a) In Scripture and Tradition

1. *The Prayer of Jesus*

We have already alluded to Christ's priestly prayer to his Father. Here it might be well to underscore the implications of that prayer. The *catholicity* of the Church is also intimately connected, as we have seen, with the concept of *unity*. It was on the realisation of this unity that the prayer of Jesus is so relevant:

> *That they may all be one.*
> *As you, Father, are in me and I am in you.*
> *That they may be also one in us, so that*
> *the world may believe that you have sent me.*
> (John 17:21)

This priestly prayer of Jesus to the Father for unity must be heard! But we are far from it, some will say. This unity that you hanker after is just a mirage! Look at the thousands of churches and denominations all claiming to worship the one, true God and then they turn and start fighting each other. Yes, it cannot be denied that the disunity of Christendom is a scandal, a stumbling block to any seeker after truth, a serious impediment in its efforts to convert the world to Christ in accordance with the Great Commission, to go out into the whole world and make disciples of all nations.

Nevertheless, all this does not invalidate the claim of the Catholic Church to be the *one true* Church founded by Christ and entrusted to Peter and his successors. Vatican II's *Dogmatic Constitution on the Church* is emphatic on the subject:

> *His Church (the unique Church of Christ) which in the Creed we avow as One, Holy, Catholic and Apostolic subsists in the Catholic Church, which is governed by the successor of Peter and by the bishops in union with that successor.*

> *For we are what he has made us,*
> *created in Christ Jesus for good works,*
> *which God prepared beforehand*
> *to be our way of life.* (Ephesians 2:10)

2. The Great Commission

> *Go, therefore, make disciples of all nations,*
> *baptising them in the name of the Father and*
> *of the Son and of the Holy Spirit,*
> *teaching them to observe all that I have commanded you,*
> *and, behold, I am with you to the close of the age.*
> **(Matthew 28:19-20)**

The Church is *Catholic* in virtue of the *Great Commission* given to the apostles and disciples after the Resurrection. As given to us in the words of Matthew Christ's command extends *to all times, to all places and to all peoples. Catholicity,* therefore, flows from the will of Christ himself. This emerges from the full import of the *Great Commission*. Christ invokes the plenitude of authority or power he enjoys both in Heaven and on earth. In virtue of this supreme authority he commissions his disciples to go forth and evangelise all nations! This evangelical effort was to embrace the totality of Christ's work and message of salvation. Implicit in all this is both a geographical and doctrinal component:

a. *A geographical or ethnic universality as the field of apostolic endeavour:*
b. *A doctrinal universality in its message of salvation.*

The Catechism draws out the full implications of all this as follows:

> *In her subsists the fullness of Christ's body united with its head; this implies that she receives from Him 'the fullness of the means of salvation' which He has willed; correct and complete confession of faith, full sacramental life, and ordained ministry in apostolic succession. The Church was, in this fundamental sense, Catholic on the day of Pentecost and will always be so until the day of the Parousia'.*
>
> (#830)

3. The Message of Pentecost

> *When the day of Pentecost had come,*
> *they were all together in one place.*
> *And suddenly a sound came from heaven*
> *like the rush of a mighty wind,*
> *and it filled all the house where they were sitting.*
> *And there appeared to them tongues as of fire,*
> *distributed and resting on each one of them.*
> *And they were all filled wiht the Holy Spirit.*
> (Acts 2:1-4)

The geographical extension of the Church is implicit in the drama of Pentecost. The author of Acts gives a lengthy list of all those who witnessed the miracle of Pentecost. They came from all over the diaspora, and from Libya to Mesopotamia. This geographical outreach underscores the universality of Christ's message. This message of salvation was not only for the Jews, but for the Greeks and the barbarians! No one was to be excluded!

> *Are not all those who are speaking Galileans?*
> *And how is it that we hear,*
> *each of us in his own native language.*
> (Acts 2:7-8)

The action of the Holy Spirit made it amply clear that the Saviour's message was not one of *exclusion* but one of *inclusion*, embracing the whole world! Hence the Pentecostal experience bears this very distinctive mark of *catholicity*. It was a trumpet call to the world that Christ's message was for all time the message of universal salvation. St Paul, the *Apostle of the Gentiles,* makes this very clear when he wrote to the Corinthians on behalf of his protégé Timothy:

> *For this reason I sent you Timothy, who is my beloved and faithful child in the Lord, to remind you of my ways in Christ Jesus, as I teach them everywhere in every church.*
> (1 Corinthians 4:17)

Here Paul emphasises the coherence of *unity* and *catholicity* in Christ's message. It is a message that pervades all his letters, as manifested in his letter to the Romans:

> ***For I am not ashamed of the Gospel.***
> ***It is the power of God for salvation for everyone who has faith,***
> ***to the Jew first and also to the Greek[207].*** **(Romans 1:16)**

There is also the very significant encounter of St Peter with the centurion Cornelius and his kinsfolk and friends as related in chapter ten of Acts. The Holy Spirit came down upon them in what has been called the *Pentecost of the Gentiles!*.

4. *The Witness of Tradition*

What has already been said on the Great Commission needs to be re-stated in terms of *Tradition*. *Scripture* and *Tradition* are said to be the pillars of the Church's *magisterium*.[208] In a certain sense, however, there is only one *source* of revealed truth and this source is *divine Tradition*. It is by this means that the faith has come down to us, handed on from generation to generation for nigh two thousand years! The word *Tradition* itself means *to hand on* or *to hand over*. It is inspired by the words of Jesus himself when he solemnly *handed on* to the apostles the divine authority to go forth in his name to the ends of the earth:

Tradition, therefore, is the living stream of the Church's teaching and the source of its sacramental life that incorporates us into the life of the Godhead. Through the Spirit Christ assures us of his never-failing presence; it will go on to the end of time! In this sense also we call this tradition essentially *Catholic* in the all-embracing authority of its founder and the universal outreach of the divine mandate to promote his teaching *'to the ends of the earth'!* When we state, therefore, that

---

[207] *The word 'Greek' is a synonym for 'Gentile'. Greek was the 'koine' or the common language of business and communication throughout the Mediterranean.*

[208] *The 'magisterium' is the teaching authority of the Church, an authority given to it by Christ himself when he told it to go forth and teach all nations. (Matt.28:20).*

the Church is Catholic we are stating, in effect and in summary, three things:

1. The Church is Catholic because it is the recipient of the Great Commission by which Christ entrusted to the apostles and to their successors to go forth to the ends of the earth.
2. The Church is Catholic because it reaches out to the whole world with this all embracing message of salvation. No one is excluded from the saving merits of Christ's Passion, Death and Resurrection from the dead.
3. Each member of that Church is Catholic in accepting, without reservation, the full authority of the Church commissioned by Christ under the direction of its bishops, the successors of the apostles, in union with the Bishop of Rome, the successor of St Peter.

All this is summed up on what has been called the *Vincentian Canon*:

What has been believed everywhere, always and by all![209]

(b) The Claim of Catholicity

1. The Term 'Catholic'

The word *'catholic'* is a word of many meanings. The dictionary gives it the meaning of *what is of use to everybody* or *of universal concern*. We can also talk of someone having *catholic* tastes or interests, which means that he or she has an all-embracing range of sympathies or interests. Here, however, we speak specifically of a *religious* dimension, wherein we talk of *'catholic'* with a capital C! To be more specific, it is usually prefaced with the adjective *Roman*. So we get the term *Roman Catholic* which almost sounds a contradiction in terms! But it is used to denote those Catholics throughout the world that owe their religious allegiance to the Holy Father in Rome.

---

[209] *So called after St Vincent (5th century) of Lerins who lived in southern Gaul (France).*

The word comes from the Greek phrase *kath'holou*; it means *'with regard to the whole'*. This generates the adjective *katholicos* meaning *universal* and giving us *'catholic'* in English. The term is also used in reference to the *Catholic Epistles* of SS. Peter, James, John and Jude. This use is to be explained that these letters were not written to a specific church—to Rome or Corinth or Philippi—but to all the churches of the time. The use of this term *Catholic Church* can be traced as far back as the early second century, when St Ignatius of Antioch wrote:

> *Where the bishop appears, there let the people be,*
> *just as where Jesus Christ is, there is the Catholic Church.*

By the third century the term *'catholic'* had become a distinctive mark of the Church, marking it off from dissident or sectarian bodies who voiced disagreement with the Church of Rome. In the time of the Decian persecution (c.250 A.D.) one of the martyrs, Pionius, a priest of the church at Smyrna, was asked by the presiding judge: *To what church do you belong?* Pionius simply replied: *To the Catholic Church*. The answer is revealing in the sense that Pionius did not say: *To the Church of Smyrna*, but rather alluded to the communion of a world-wide church of which that of Smyrna was simply a part. Catholicity, therefore, was not solely a matter of geography, but a matter of belief. This belief embraced a commonly held corpus of doctrine inherited from the apostles of the first century. This title of *Catholic* was, therefore, primarily a matter of *unity* or *oneness*, but, by that very fact, it came also to have a *geographical* extension. In the catechetical instructions of St Cyril of Jerusalem (c.350 A.D.) we find the following statement about why the Church is called Catholic:

> *because it extends over all the world, from one end of the earth to the other; and because it teaches universally and completely one and all the doctrines which ought to come to men's knowledge, concerning things both visible and invisible, heavenly and earthly; and because it brings into subjection to godliness the whole race of mankind.*[210]

---

[210] *Marthaler: The Creed (TwentyThird Publications, Mystic, Conn. 1993) p.301.*

2. The Universal Call Today

> *In Christ we have also obtained an inheritance,*
> *.... so that we, who were the first*
> *to set our hope on Christ,*
> *might live for the praise of his glory.*
> **(Ephesians) 1:11**

The words of St Paul dealing with our universal inheritance in Christ are echoed by the Catechism in quoting from the document *Lumen Gentium* of Vatican II:

> '*All men are called to belong to the new People of God. This People, therefore, while remaining one and only one, is to be spread throughout the whole world and to all ages in order that the design of God's will may be fulfilled; He made human nature one in the beginning and has decreed that all His children who were scattered should be finally gathered together as one . . . . The character of universality which adorns the People of God is a gift from the Lord Himself whereby the Catholic Church ceaselessly and efficaciously seeks for the return of all humanity and all its goods, under Christ the Head in the unity of His Spirit*'.
>
> (#831)

It is from Jesus as its head that the Church receives the fulness of the means and message of salvation. With its rule of faith and its sacramental life it is fully equipped to carry out the mandate of its founder. Fortified by its unbroken apostolic succession that can be traced back to the day of Pentecost it will go on in its journey of faith, serene and unruffled, until the day of judgement!

3. The Scandal of Division

On the other hand, to some it might appear, that, as has been remarked elsewhere, the *catholicity* of the Church is as questionable as its *holiness!* The seamless garment of the Church, it is alleged, has been torn up, ripped apart and shredded into so many Churches. To the scandal of the unbeliever, many claim, with greater or lesser insistence, to be *alone* and in the right! For well nigh a thousand years there was one Catholic

Church! Then came the great schism of 1054 A.D. that split the Church into east—the *Orthodox*—and the west—the *Roman Catholic*. It was a division that owed more to political manoeuvring than to any genuine disagreement over doctrine. But the so-called *Reformation* of the sixteenth century split the Church still more. The fissile notion of *private interpretation* of the Bible splintered the dissident sects even more. Today it is almost impossible to count the multiplicity of denominations and the variations in dissent in the twenty-first century! The ecclesiastical landscape of the west today makes a mockery of Christ's prayer:

> *That they all may be one,*
> *even as you Father, are in me, and I in you.*
> **(John 17:21)**

It is no wonder that to any outsider seeking the truth must view the many so-called ecumenical endeavours among Christian groups and the various denominations as a mere jostling for power and battling for the allegiance of the *lost!* The same answer for this scandal of division can only be given that has been given with regard to the *holiness* of the Church. As we have said, and can only keep repeating *ad nauseam,* that the Church is *holy* not because its members are holy and sinless, but because its origin is in God and its founder is Christ, the *Sinless One!*, *and the means He gave it are conducive to the attainment of holiness and the salvation of souls.*

In the same way, the Church is *Catholic* from the inspiration and the Great Commission of Christ himself. That it is not *Catholic,* in the fullest sense of the word, is due more to man's frailty and the sinfulness of his nature than to the perceived shortcomings of the Church itself. Catholicity lies at the heart of the Church's mandate, even if it still remains as a goal in the fulfilment of Christ's prayer to the Father:

> *The glory that you have given me I have given them, so that they may be one, as we are one, I in them and you in me, that they may become completely one, so that the world may know that you have sent me and have loved them even as you have loved me.*
> **(John 17:22-23)**

4. The Anonymous Christian!

> *This is right and is acceptable in the sight of God our Saviour, who desires all men to be saved and to come to the knowledge of the truth. For there is one God; there is also one mediator between God and men, the man Christ Jesus.*
> **(1 Timothy 2:3-5)**

We are still bedevilled by the old age question that, if Christianity is still a minority faith, how can the term Christian be termed *'catholic'* or *'universal'*, when the majority of mankind is non-Christian? To add to this confusion there seems to be a resurgence of paganism in the thrust of secularism in our contemporary world. To meet these challenges there has emerged in contemporary theology the term *'the anonymous Christian'* usually associated with the German theologian, Karl Rahner. In Paul's letter to Timothy the apostle states the two basic principles of redemption:

a. God wills all men to be saved and
b. the sole mediator of redemption is Jesus.

God's salvific will embraces the whole of mankind, and the instrument of that will is the cross of Jesus. No one can be saved except through the blood of Jesus!. *But how is this possible for those who either do not recognise Jesus as Saviour, or who have never even heard of him?* We must then fall back on the primary principle that God wills all men to be saved. If that is so, then the grace won by Christ is offered in those special circumstances where men and women acting in good faith seek to fulfil God's will. It is this implicit faith manifested in good and moral living that fulfills that other principle manifested in the letter to the Hebrews:

> *And without faith it is impossible to please God, for whoever would approach him must believe that he exists and that he rewards those who seek him.*
> **(Hebrews 11:1)**

Another way of expressing it is to say this person belongs to the soul of the Church. The problem is certainly not new, although the title of "the anonymous Christian" is modern. Even in the early Church it must have cropped up, for we read of Tertullian, whose books reflect the attitude of Christianity *vis-à-vis* Roman society, writing about the *anima naturaliter christiana,* or *the soul that is naturally Christian!* He is speaking of the good pagan whose life of natural goodness would do credit even to those who profess to be Christians! Maybe, even in our own experience, we have encountered persons whose lives radiate that same virtue and goodness that we would expect of those who would call themselves *Christian*!

> *In the mind of the Lord the Church is universal by vocation and mission, but when she puts down her roots in a variety of cultural, social, and human terrains, she takes on different external expressions and appearances in each part of the world. The rich variety of ecclesiastical disciplines, liturgical rites, and theological and spiritual heritages proper to the local churches "unified in a common effort, shows all the more resplendently the catholicity of the undivided Church."*
>
> (#835)

(c) The 'Universal Sacrament of Salvation'!

1. *The Second Vatican Council*

It was in lieu of the term *Catholic* that the Second Vatican Council decided to use the term *Universal*. It was an effort to dispel the denominational emphasis of the word *Catholic* and return it to the basic meaning that underpins the Great Commission. It did so in several documents, of which the following is typical:

> *Christ, having been lifted up from the earth, is drawing all men to himself (John 12:12). Rising from the dead, he sent his life-giving Spirit upon the disciples, and through this Spirit, has established his body, the Church, as 'the universal sacrament of salvation'.*
>
> (Lumen Gentium 48)

What the Council is stressing here is that the grace of salvation comes from and through the Church. It is the channel or the medium through which grace is given.[211] This prompts the question: *How is this possible?* The answer lies in this that the Church is, first and foremost, an outward sacramental sign, an instrument of reconciliation, perpetuating the work of Christ himself. As St Paul tells us:

> *In Christ, God was reconciling the world to himself, not counting their trespasses against them, and entrusting to us the message of reconciliation. So we are ambassadors for Christ, God making his appeal through us. We beseech you on behalf of Christ, be reconciled to God!*
> **(2 Corinthians 3: 18-20)**

Once again, the question surfaces as to how the Church can exercise this intermediary role of reconciliation with regard to those people who, neither recognise it, nor have any contact with it? If we accept the Church as an extension of the Incarnation of the Word, then the Church takes on the intercessory role of the Word made flesh. Pius XII made this very point, when he wrote:

> *Dying on the Cross, he left to his Church the immense treasury of the redemption, towards which she contributed nothing. But when these graces are distributed, not only does he share the work with his Spouse, but wishes that it be due, in a way, to her activity. A true awe-inspiring mystery, and one unceasingly to be pondered: that the salvation of many depends on the prayers and voluntary penances which the members of the Mystical Body of Jesus Christ offer for this intention.*

All this gives point to the liturgy of the Eucharist in particular. In its celebration we find the unique sacrifice made for the salvation of the whole world. The Mass is said not solely for those present. Its outreach is for the whole of humanity. That is what the prophet Malachi foretold:

> *For from the rising of the sun to its setting my name is great among the nations, and in every place incense is offered to*

---

[211] *Francis Sullivan S.J. The Church We Believe In (Paulist Press 1988) p. 110*

> *my name, and a pure offering; for my name is great among the nations, says the LORD of hosts.*
>
> **(Malachi 11:1)**

2. Ecumenism

In face of the obvious disunity among Christians Vatican II sought to try and remedy this gaping wound in the Body of Christ. Through two of its decrees, the *Decree on Ecumenism* and the *Decree of the Eastern Catholic Churches* it sought to promote the restoration of unity among all Christians through the acknowledged processes of co-operation and dialogue. It was an endeavour to reverse centuries of hostility and mudslinging that was a source of scandal for the non-Christian, as well as being a violation of the very fundamental command of Christ himself *to love one another!* There are some who view these initiatives as somehow a betrayal of their faith. Even if it is not a betrayal of the faith, then it opens the door to embarrassing compromises and the threat of *syncretism*[212]. The Council denied this. The Church is now, and always was, *the Church of Christ*, the chosen instrument of God's saving will in time. There is no question of concessions on matters of faith and morals, or surrendering its historic place in the development of doctrine. There is, here and now, an historic situation that cannot be reversed. We must come to terms with the realities of the present, and not insist on re-fighting the battles of the past! We cannot deny the existence of these ecclesial communities, or act as if they did not exist! We cannot anathematise them as heretics, or demonise them as traitors. After all, do we not share the same loyalty to Christ? So why not accept what unites us, and pray for the will of Christ to be realised in our communities. In its decree, *The Restoration of Unity*[213], the Council recommended certain things to reawaken *"the desire to recover the unity of all Christians"* which is *"a gift of Christ and the Holy Spirit"*.

These are summarised in the Catechism:

---

[212] *Syncretism signifies an attempt to combine conflicting religious systems in their beliefs or practices as to present a show of unity. It has been called "papering over the cracks"!*

[213] *From the Council Decree "Pietatis Redemptio."*

— *a permanent renewal of the Church to greater fidelity to her vocation;*
— *conversion of heart of the faithful to live holier lives for unfaithfulness is the cause of division;*
— *prayer, both private and in common, for the unity willed by Christ;*
— *fraternal knowledge of each other;*
— *ecumenical formation for both faithful and priests;*
— *dialogue among theologians;*
— *collaboration among Christians in various areas of service to mankind;*

(#821).

3. Evangelisation

The duty to promote the spread of the Gospel flows from the imperatives of the Great Commission. Evangelisation, properly so-called, entails the continuous proclamation of the Good News of Christ and his Kingdom, and the promotion of God's glory everywhere in the world. If Christ died to save all men, then it is the duty of all Christians to be actively concerned about it. Vatican II made this point in saying:

> *Every disciple of Christ has the obligation to do his part in spreading the faith. Yet Christ the Lord always calls whomsoever he chooses from among the number of his disciples, to be with him and to be sent by him to preach to the nations. Therefore, through the Holy Spirit, who distributes his charismatic gifts as he wills for the common good, Christ inspires the missionary vocation in the hearts of individuals. At the same time, he raises up in the Church certain groups, which take as their own special task that duty of preaching the Gospel which weighs upon the whole Church.*

The command of Christ falls not merely on the leaders of the Church, it falls on all by virtue of their baptism. This is only reinforced by the very title that the baptised are known as Catholics. From that very title there flows an interest, if not the resolve, in the spread of the Gospel. Catholicity, as a mark of the Church, demands of its adherents

> *to strive energetically and constantly to bring all of humanity under Christ as its head.*
>
> (Lumen Gentium 13)

> *There is a logical consequence of all this. The Church can never renounce its mark of Catholicity. It is branded into its very soul! For the church ever to renounce its efforts to evangelise the non-Christian world would be to renounce the realisation of its own catholicity—and this it can never do!*[214]

Even if the statistics of conversions are not heartening, even if our expectations are not rosy or bright, Christianity cannot rest content on being the religion of one continent rather than of another. Even if the prospects of conversion are dim, even if its missionary outlook is abysmal, the Church cannot abandon its mission to evangelise! The words of Paul to Timothy are as relevant today as when they were first written:

> **In the presence of God and of Christ Jesus, who is to judge the living and the dead, and in view of his appearing and his kingdom, I solemnly urge you: proclaim the message; be persistent whether the time is favourable or unfavourable; convince, rebuke, and encourage, with the utmost patience in teaching. For the time is coming when people will not put up with sound doctrine, but having itching ears, they will accumulate for themselves teachers to suit their own desires, and will turn away from listening to the truth and wander away to myths.**
>
> **(2 Timothy 4:1-4)**

These final words are a sober warning for us all. There are always new fads and fashions, especially in the realm of the spirit. A new *'prophet'*, another *guru*, a new idea, a new slant on old problems, all such nostrums seem to attract our restless spirits as a remedy for all our spiritual ills. St Augustine's words still echo like a clarion call down the ages:

---

[214] *Francis Sullivan: op.cit. 131.*

Thou has made us for thyself O God,
and our hearts are restless until they rest in thee!

4. Restoration of the Whole Person

There is a *universal* aspect to Catholicism which has been rightly emphasised. There is a *unity* and a *comprehensiveness* in its doctrines that also has universal appeal. However, there is an inner echo of that same appeal to be found in the life and work of the individual Catholic that must not be overlooked. Our fallen nature looks to the Church and its teaching for the restoration of man's original state of grace lost in the Garden of Eden.

If in the first Adam all men fell, in the Second Adam they all arise. This applies not only to the fact of the resurrection, but to the restoration and sanctification of man's innate faculties, to the elevation of his whole being, spiritual as well as material. If the whole of nature fell in Eden then it arose in Nazareth, when **the Word became flesh and dwelt amongst us** (**John 1:14**)

> *The Church, as the Body of Christ, lays hold of all that is of God, and, therefore of man's body, his senses and his passions, just as much as of his intellect and will. And in redeeming his body and senses and passions by sanctifying grace from their earthliness and selfishness and reclaiming them for God, she not only wins them back for his Kingdom, but also ennobles and deepens them.*[215]

This ennobling of the whole of human nature involved the Church in combating many heresies that denigrated the body. Such were the Gnostics and the Manichaeans of the early Church, the Cathari and the Albigenses of the Middle Ages. The Church met these challenges in defending the dignity and worth of the human body. The body was not *"a garment of shame"*, but a gift for the continuance of the human race through the sacrament of marriage. Moreover, the body itself is destined to share in the glory of the resurrection. This same reverence for the human body, and all that we associate with it, gave rise to the immense

---

[215] *Francis Sullivan op.cit. 157.*

blossoming of art in paintings and sculpture. Catholicism, in fact, inspired generations of artists whose work in glory and magnificence has never been surpassed, Raphael, Michelangelo. and Leonardo da Vinci. The list goes on and on. The same could be said for music that has inspired countless generations, Gregorian Chant, Palestrina, Haydn and Mozart. Art is forever indebted to the Church for its original inspiration and its universal appeal.

++++++++++++++++++++++

Questions #20

* * *

1. "The mark of Catholicity is intimately connected with that of unity" Explain!

2. What is the origin of the term 'Catholic' and when did its use become widespread?

3. When you say the Church is Catholic, what exactly do you mean?

4. The Catholicity of the Church is very questionable in our world today. Comment!

5. The Anonymous Christian! What does this mean?

6. The Church is the Universal Sacrament of Salvation. Explain!

7. Ecumenism is a will o' the wisp, a pipe dream in our shattered world. Do you agree and, if not, what could be your own contribution to it?

8. *What is (i) syncretism? (ii) the Vincentian Canon?*

9. *That they all may be one! How can you help to fulfil Christ's wish?*

10. *The Restoration of the Whole Person! What does his mean?*

21. THE PEOPLE OF GOD

* * *

(a) The Household of God
 —1. The Status of the Laity
 —2. Redressing the Issue
 —3. 'Lumen Gentium'

(b) Dignity of the Laity
 —1. The Priesthood of the Faithful
 —2. A Holy Nation
 —3. A Prophetic People
 —4. A Royal People!

(c) Mission of the Laity
 —1. The Laity in the World
 —2. The Laity in the Church
 —3. "We are the Church!"
 —4. Conclusion

21. The People of God

* * *

(a) The Household of God!

1. Status of the Laity

> *Now, therefore, if you will obey my voice,*
> *and keep my covenant,*
> *you shall be my own possession among all peoples*
> *for all the earth is mine, and you shall be to me*
> *a kingdom of priests and a holy nation.*
>
> **(Exodus 19: 5-6)**

Despite the depth and clarity of scriptural quotations about the *People of God* the relationship of its hierarchical authority with its flock has had a rather checkered career. Throughout its history the Church has grappled and struggled with the *status of the laity* in the question of the latter's rights and functions, its spirituality and its mission in the Kingdom of God. There is inevitably a tension between the structures of ecclesiastical authority, on the one hand, and rights and dignity of the laity, on the other. It is a struggle endemic to human nature wherever issues of authority and individual freedom come into play.

The Scriptures of the *Septuagint*[216] use the word '*laos*' for people as distinct from their rulers or their leaders, such as priests, prophets and princes. However, there is another meaning for *laos* in the Septuagint. It is the notion of *laos* as *God's people*. It highlighted, for example, Israel, as a people chosen from among the nations, as the bearer of God's Covenant and promises.

It is this latter sense that found its way into the New Testament to affirm all Christians as chosen, called and predestined as *'citizens with the saints'* and *'members of the household of God'*.

The words of St Paul to the Ephesians are emphatic on this point:

---

[216] *The 'Septuagint' is the Greek translation of the Old Testament, sometimes referred to as the "Alexandrine Canon".*

> *So then you are no longer strangers and aliens, but you are citizens with the saints and also members of the household of God, built upon the foundation of the apostles and prophets, with Christ Jesus himself as the cornerstone.*
> *In him the whole structure is joined together and grows into a holy temple in the Lord; in whom you also are built together spiritually into a dwelling place for God.'*
> **(Ephesians 2:19-22)**

St Paul's words obviously covered the entire Church of the baptised, whatever their status either as clergy or laity. Unfortunately, this crucial notion of the importance of the *laity* in God's scheme of redemption fell by the wayside. There were historic circumstances, such as the fall of Rome and the barbarian invasions, that created a gap between the clergy and the laity. The former were the educated classes and the latter the uneducated. The so-called *Dark Ages* [217] were indeed dark for the grasping of the central truth about the true status of the laity within the Church as vital members of the Body of Christ.

Inevitably, the terms *lay* and *laity* took on *pejorative* overtones. The gap widened between the hierarchy with their religious allies, the monasteries and religious organisations on the one hand, and the *ignorant* commoners of their congregations. On the other hand, it was inevitable that the sense of election and consecration of the latter as an integral part of God's covenanted people was either forgotten or ignored.

2. Redressing the Issue!

The Second Vatican Council set out to remedy the situation. This was done in two documents:

1. ***The Decree on the Apostolate of the Laity***
2. ***The Pastoral Constitution on the Church in the Modern world.***

---

[217] *The Dark Ages is a term traditionally reserved for the period 500-1000 A.D. It reflects the utter confusion that befell Europe with the decline and fall of the Roman Empire.*

Evidently, the work of the Council Fathers was the climax of several movements that had gone on in the early part of the 20th century. The first was the *liturgical* movement that had sought to enhance the celebration of the liturgy through the active participation of the laity. The liturgy it was maintained, was a communal enterprise of the worshipping community. The laity were no longer to be considered simply as passive spectators, but as active participants in the sacramental worship of the Church.

Another aspect of this was the advance in *ecclesiology*, or the theology of the Church. This was highlighted by the seminal work of Pope Pius XII, his wartime encyclical *Mystici Corporis* or *Of the Body of Christ* (1943). This highlighted once again the importance of the laity in the divine scheme of things. The laity were living members of the Body of Christ, and not simply the object of canonical restrictions. In the light of scripture and the writings of the Fathers of the Church the encyclical highlighted the fundamental truth that *all* members of the Mystical Body had a part to play in God's work of salvation.

3. Lumen Gentium[218]

Vatican II was unique in the history of the church. Its uniqueness lay in the sense that it was not summoned to launch the customary anathemas against the heresies and errors of the day, but rather to outline the pastoral and theological dimensions of the Church's mission to the world. What emerged from the Council Fathers was a document that presented the laity to the world not just as appendages to hierarchical concerns or purely spectators of liturgical ceremonies.

Essentially, the Council affirmed the fundamental equality and dignity of all members of the Christian community as *the People of God*. This equality and dignity rested on the basic sacrament of *Baptism*. From this sacrament flowed the newly baptised's incorporation into the *Body of Christ* and the imperative of striving after holiness. The

---

[218] *Lumen Gentium (The Light of the Nations) reflects the biblical title of Jesus as the "Light of the World". It dealt with lay issues in two chapters: 'The People of God' and 'the Laity'.*

second sacrament of initiation, *Confirmation,* set another seal on the baptised empowering the recipient to share in the mission of Christ to evangelise.

In the Body of Christ its members have varying functions according to their state in life. While all share the same sacraments of Baptism and Confirmation, their roles in the world can widely differ. But whatever these roles may be, the sacramental characters authorise the recipients to accept the authority of the *Great Commission* to go forth and reflect Christ in the world.

The Council affirms the redemptive value of the daily activities of the laity in the family, workplace, school and society. The laity empowered by the Spirit of Christ, exercise their apostolate typically amidst the affairs of the world as a kind of leaven. Because of their secular character, the laity are the Church in the heart of the world, and therefore, they bring the world into the heart of the Church.[219]

(b) The Dignity of the Laity

1. The Priesthood of the Faithful

Now therefore, if you obey my voice and keep my covenant, you shall be my treasured possession out of all the peoples. Indeed, the whole earth is mine, but you shall be for me a priestly kingdom and a holy nation.

(Exodus 19:5-6)

These words were uttered by God to Moses in his journey of leading the Chosen People from the slavery of Egypt to the Promised Land. The very words and the circumstances in which they were uttered point to a future Messiah who was to fulfill the role of saviour and redeemer of a new priestly kingdom and a holy nation!

But you are a chosen race, a royal priesthood, a holy nation, God's own people, that you may declare the wonderful works

---

[219] A.A. Hagstrom's article *Theology of the Laity* (New Catholic Encyclopedia) *pp290-293.*

> *of him who called you out of darkness into his marvellous light. Once you were no people, but now you are God's people; once you had not received mercy, but now you have received mercy.*
>
> **(1 Peter 2:9-10)**

These words of Peter echo those of God to Moses, but they express more powerfully the *sacramental* identity of the laity, because of its realisation of the latter in Christ, the great *High Priest of the New Covenant*. This *sharing* of the laity in Christ's priesthood, therefore, is not an empty expression of devotion to the Church. This *common* priesthood, along with the *ministerial* priesthood, is a valid participation in the priesthood of Christ himself. This was emphasised by the Council as a logical consequence of the action of the Holy Spirit in the sacraments of baptism and confirmation.

There results from this consecration and embodiment in the Body of Christ a special witness of the laity in the world. From the very nature of the activity of the laity in the world there is a special sphere of influence open to it which is closed to members of the hierarchy and ministerial priesthood. From the quality of their lives and the power of their witness to the faith lay persons are fulfilling the *Great Commission* in teaching primarily by example, but also by word and explanation.

One author expresses all this so admirably:

> *Every Baptism is a consecration to the priesthood of Christ, for Baptism removes man from the profane world, appropriates him to Christ, and sanctifies him for the performance of those most general acts of worship which belong to the vocation of the child of God. And the sacramental character of Confirmation intensifies this priesthood, since it fits the Christian to take an active share in the building of the Temple of God equips him for the apostolate and for its evidences of the spirit and of power.... This priestly conjunction of all with the high priesthood of Christ, an utterly sacred conjunction, is the source whence springs the close fellowship of all in their prayer and faith and love.*[220]

---

[220] *Karl Adam op.cit. p 130*

2. A Holy Nation!

The words of God to Moses, as related in *Exodus*, were fulfilled in Christ. Christ's Church on earth, as *a Chosen Race* and a *Holy Nation* is a communion of the faithful led by the Vicar of Christ and by the hierarchy in union with him. This notion of the Church as a *'communion'* was strongly emphasised by the Second Vatican Council when it referred to the loss of that communion in the Fall:

> *The gathering together of the People of God began at the moment when sin destroyed the communion of men with God, and that of men among themselves. The gathering together of the Church is, as it were, God's reaction to the chaos provoked by sin. This reunification is achieved secretly in the heart of all peoples: 'In every nation anyone who fears him and does what is right is acceptable to God.*[221]

The Catechism (##782-786) also spells out the characteristics of the *People of God*, characteristics that clearly mark off the Church as wholly distinct from every other religious, ethnic or cultural groups in history:

1. *It is not confined to any particular race or people.*
2. *Membership is determined, not by physical birth, but by a spiritual rebirth, being 'born anew of water and the Holy the Spirit'.*
3. *The Head of this People is Christ, the redeemer, the Messiah, whose name they bear!*
4. *The status of this People is marked by a divine dignity in the freedom of the children of God and as Temples of the Holy Spirit;*
5. *In Christ the People of God become a kingdom of priests to God the Father!*
6. *The People of God now share in Christ's prophetic office.*

---

[221] *Lumen Gentium #9 (quoted in CCC #761). The last sentence is taken from St Peter's speech on the question of the acceptance of the Gentiles into the Church.*

7. This People also share in the the royal office of the Kingship of Christ.
8. The sovereign law of the People is the New Commandment —to love others as Christ has loved them!
9. Its mission is to be the salt of the earth and a light to the world.
10. Its destiny is to extend the Kingdom of God, initiated by God himself, until it has been brought to perfection in the Parousia, in the coming of Christ at the end of time.

3. A Prophetic People!

The Catechism spells out this aspect of the People of God as follows:

> *The holy people of God shares in Christ's prophetic office, "above all, in the supernatural sense of faith that belongs to the whole People, lay and clergy, when it "unfailingly adheres to this faith . . . . once for all delivered to the saints", and when it deepens its understanding and becomes Christ's witness in the midst of this world.*
>
> (#785)

The role of the prophet in the Old Testament was to convey God's wishes to the Chosen People in order to bring them back from their sinful ways. Almost without exception, from the days of Moses, these prophets were brought to prophecy against their will. Jonah is the classic example. In the fulness of time their work was fulfilled in the coming of Jesus.

> *Jesus fulfilled the messianic hope of Israel in his threefold office as priest prophet and king.*
>
> (#436)

The Church carries on this prophetic office, first in remaining faithful to the central message of redemption, and secondly in responding to the threats and dangers that inevitably confront her. Today this manifests itself in the numerous encyclicals that are issued by the Supreme Pontiff that arouse the faithful to be watchful for the assaults, both subtle and brazen, that are so often launched against the integrity of the faith.

This prophetic office falls to the individual Christian to make a similar stand against Satan's attacks. From the very fact of being a Christian he or she must be a prophet in fidelity to the faith. Thus fidelity is once again God's voice speaking to a faithless generation and proclaiming the message of salvation.

4. A Royal People

> *You know that the rulers of the Gentiles lord it over you*
> *and their great men exercise authority lord it over them.*
> *It shall not be so among you; but whoever*
> *who would be great among you must be your servant,*
> *and whoever would be first among you must be your slave;*
> *even as the Son of Man came not to be served, but to serve,*
> *and to give his life as a ransom for many.*
> **(Matthew 20:25-26)**

Christians are also a royal or *kingly* people! Once again the Catechism informs us that Christ *"exercises his kingship by drawing all men to himself through his death and Resurrection"*

We owe our allegiance, therefore, to Christ. The question naturally surfaces as to how we share in the royalty of our sovereign Lord. The answer comes from Jesus himself. He claimed to be *the light of the world* (John 8:12) and so he wanted his followers to shed that same light on all around them!

> *You are the light of the world. A city built on a hill cannot be hid.*
> *No one after lighting a lamp puts it under the bushel basket,*
> *but on the lamp stand, and it gives light to all in the house.*
> *In the same way, let your light shine before others,*
> *so that they may see your good works and give glory to your*
> *Father in heaven.*
> **(Matthew 5:14-16)**

When we speak of royalty, we naturally conjure up visions of majesty in the secular world. It is a world of authority and command, a world of their symbols of golden crowns, and of royal purple, a world of fawning courtiers and servile subservience. There is a very clearly marked territorial component wherein the king's wishes are enforced, usually without question. But God's sovereignty resides in his omnipotence, in that omnipotence which brought all things into existence. All earthly authority is but a pale reflex of God's. However, Jesus came to serve. The rulers of this world think that it is their *right* is to demand and command others to serve them!

This is a far cry from the kingship of Jesus. His royalty is a total inversion of worldly power. The decrees of autocrats and the tawdry symbols of earthly power have no place in the *Kingdom of God*. This is a king whose throne is the *Cross,* and whose sceptre is a *reed*. There are no armoured divisions at his command, and no police to enforce his laws. It is a kingdom wherein *love,* unconditional love, must reign supreme. Service to others is the royal command! In conclusion, let us quote the words of Pope St Leo who summarises all that can be said on this entire subject of the characteristics if the *People of God*:

> *The sign of the cross makes kings of all those reborn in Christ. and the anointing of the Holy Spirit consecrates them as priests, so that, apart from the particular service of our ministry, all spiritual and rational Christians, are recognised as members of this royal race and sharers in Christ's priestly office. What indeed is as royal for a soul as to govern the body in obedience to God. And what is as priestly as to dedicate a pure conscience to the Lord and to offer the spotless offerings of devotion on the altar of the heart.*[222]

(c) Mission of the Laity

1. *The Laity in the World*

> *You are the light of the world. A city set on a hill cannot be hid. Nor do men light a lamp, and put it under a bushel, but on a stand, and it gives light to all in the house. Let your light so shine before men, that they may see your good works, and give glory to your Father who is in heaven.*
> **(Matthew 5:14-16)**

---

[222] *St Leo the Great (see CCC #786)*

From all the foregoing it is apparent that the secular character of the laity has a unique mission. It is sometimes said, and, often with considerable justification, that the lives of Christians are no different from the non-believers who surround them.

It was Mahatma Gandhi who once made this point when he said that he would be a Christian himself, *if Christians were Christians twenty four hours a day!* While there may be a certain amount of hyperbole in his views the point he made was a valid one. So often the lives of Christians are, apparently, no different from their pagan associates! It might even be said that Christians are scarcely aware of their sacramental dignity. Perhaps it has been lost in the hurly-burly existence of life, with its ups and downs, with its joys and sufferings!

Nevertheless, because of their immersion in the affairs of the world, lay persons are uniquely qualified for being its evangelists. It is through their very status as laity that they can make the Church visible and operative in a way that is denied to clergy and religious. The Council affirms the redemptive character of the laity in the family, at work, in school and in society.

Because of their secular character,
the laity are the Church in the heart of the world and
they bring the world into the heart of the Church.[223]

2. The Laity in the Church

Here we come to a very touchy question; how far does the common priesthood of the laity touch the inner life and organisation of the Church itself? The Council did not flinch from grasping the nettle in stating that the laity can take on a direct form of active co-operation in the work of the clergy. *Lumen Gentium (#33)* clearly states that the laity can be collaborators in the apostolate of the hierarchy.

Although the Council did not specify the precise nature of this co-operation it has been suggested that it could well include certain roles, preaching, ecclesiastical administration and works of mercy etc. The laity are already the *ordinary* ministers of the sacrament of marriage and *extraordinary* ministers of baptism. They can perform *para-liturgical*

---

[223] *ibid.*

services such as a communion service where a priest is not available. There also can be direct deputation, in cases of necessity, to perform certain functions, such as blessing a marriage. It all amounts to a partnership in the Spirit in that sovereign mission of communicating the life-giving grace of Christ's redeeming sacrifice. In God's work the laity should be seen, not as competitors or challengers, but as helpmates and allies. The motivating force of all apostolates flows from the theological virtues of *faith, hope and charity*, which are sacramental gifts of a common baptism.

3. *"We are the Church!"*

Fallen nature will ever seek to intrude even into the holiest of enterprises and therein lurks the danger, in practice, of elevating the laity to the status as *the* Church as divorced from its hierarchical structure. We have heard the cry from members of the laity: *We are the Church!* It is, at times, a passionate cry resonating a cleavage between the laity and the hierarchy, even relegating the latter to a subordinate role!

Our human nature tends to oscillate between extremes. The attempts to heal the long historic divorce between the clergy and the laity can arouse considerable animosity on the part of the latter. It was against such a danger that Pope John Paul II spoke of the Church as a *communio*,[224] an organic union of both laity and clergy, devoted to the one common enterprise of fulfilling the will of Christ.

The Holy Father reiterated the *conciliar* position on the status of the laity. He highlighted the baptismal identity of the latter, emphasising their unique *secular* character and vocation. Lay people, in their own secular environment, are called to be *the salt of the earth!* There is a diversity of charisms, ministries and responsibilities. These come not from personal ambition or worldly motives but from the action of the Holy Spirit. It is from the Holy Spirit that there comes the participation of the faithful in the threefold offices of Christ. his *priestly, prophetic* and *royal* roles. It is within that context that the roles of the laity find their meaning, based on the foundation of their common sacramental identity in baptism and confirmation.

---

[224] *John Paul 11 in his Apostolic Exhortation speaks of the Church's laity as "Christ's Faithful People".*

4. Conclusion

The Church is involved, by its very existence, in a spiritual warfare of cosmic proportions. It is obvious, on a purely natural level, that this battle would be extremely one-sided, were it not for the supernatural help that comes to us through the administration of the sacraments. Through these supernatural helps there comes help from on high to equip us for battle! It is a common misconception, therefore, to view these sacraments on a purely *personal* level. Our egocentricity can debase even the most spiritual of gifts. Nevertheless, there is a fundamental truth that must be stressed and re-stressed to keep us aware of our *incorporation into the priesthood of Christ*.

Here is one of the most profound truths of the Catholic faith that, beyond the purely personal and religious relationship of our relationship with Christ, there is a much more burning reality in the sacraments that needs to be deeply underscored. This is, that quite apart from our subjective feelings and personal life in grace, there is our *incorporation into the priesthood of Christ*. It leaves an indelible mark on the soul, that no amount of sin or infidelity can ever erase. This is because the sacraments of *baptism* and *confirmation* are ultimately due to the divine action of the Holy Spirit upon the soul. They brand a seal upon it that can never be erased.

All this is summarised by the Catechism:

> *Christ, High Priest and unique mediator, has made of the Church 'a kingdom for his God and Father'. The whole community of believers is, as such, priestly. The faithful exercise their baptismal priesthood their participation, each according to his own vocation, in Christ's mission as priest, prophet and king. Through the sacraments of baptism and Confirmation the faithful are "consecrated to be . . . a holy priesthood".*
>
> (#1546)

A Chosen Race, Royal Priesthood!

* * *

This praise was given long ago by Moses
to the ancient people of God,
and now the apostle Peter rightly gives it to the Gentiles,
since they have come to believe in Christ!
As the cornerstone, he has brought the nations together
to the salvation that belonged to Israel.
Peter calls them a 'chosen race', because of their faith,
to distinguish them from those, who,
by refusing to accept the living stone,
have themselves been rejected.

They are a royal priesthood,
because they are united to the body of Christ,
the supreme king and the true priest!
As sovereign he grants them his kingdom,
and, as high priest, he washes away their sins
by the offering of his own blood.
Peter says they are a royal priesthood;
they must always remember to hope
for an everlasting kingdom and to offer God
the sacrifice of a blameless life.
They are also called a consecrated nation,
a people claimed by God as his own . . . .
In the Acts of the Apostles we read:
The Holy Spirit has made you overseers,
to care for the Church of God
which he bought with his own blood.

Thus, through the blood of our Redeemer,
we have become a people claimed by God as his own,
as in ancient times, the people of Israel
were ransomed from Egypt
by the blood of a lamb!
                               St Bede the Venerable[225]

---

[225] *St Bede the Venerable*

Questions #21

* * *

1. *What is the origin of the term laity?*

2. *How did the gulf between clergy and laity originate?*

3. *How did the Council come to grips with this issue?*

4. *What did the council document Lumen Gentium decide about it?*

5. *What characteristics of the People of God do you consider the most outstanding?*

6. *On what is the Priesthood of Laity based?*

7. *How do you consider the laity as a prophetic people?*

8. *In what ways do the laity exercise their mission as Christians?*

9. *The so-called royalty of the laity belongs to a topsy-turvy world? Any comments?*

10. *"We are the Church!" In what sense do you find this statement acceptable?*

11. *What conclusions do you draw for yourself in the light of your reading?*

22. THE COMMUNION OF SAINTS

* * *

(a) The Centrality of Christ
    —1. Introduction
    —2. The First Adam
    —3. The Second Adam!

(b) The Body of Christ
    —1. The Kingdom of God
    —2. Pius XII's Encyclical
    —3. Christ the Head
    —4. The Bride of Christ!

(c) The Presence of Christ
    —1. Christ in the Sacraments
    —2. Christ in the Eucharist
    —3. Christ in the Teaching Church

(d) Christ and the Spirit
    —1. The Spirit and the Body
    —2. The Principle of Indefectibility
    —3. The Papacy—Principle of Unity!
    —4. The Following of Christ.

22. The Communion of Saints

* * *

(a) The Centrality of Christ

1. Introduction

Ultimately, there is a profound mystery in this elusive subject of the Church as the *Body of Christ*. The roots of the subject lie deep in the divine counsels and God's purpose in creation. The thread of the unity of Christ and his Church is to be sought in that purpose. Scripture serves as our guide in the unravelling of that thread. Paul in his letter to the Colossians points the way:

> *He is the image of the invisible God, the firstborn of all creation; for in him all things in heaven and on earth were created, things visible and invisible, whether thrones or dominions or rulers or powers—all things have been created through him and for him.*
>
> **(Colossians 1:15-16)**

The whole of creation is centred in Christ. He is the *firstborn!* Everything that exists bears that stamp of its divine origin. St John, in the Prologue to his Gospel, reiterates the same theme:

> *All things came into being through him, and without him not one thing came into being.*
>
> **(John 1:3)**

It is this centrality of Christ *in all things* that must be underscored when we come to the topic in hand.

2. The First Adam

> *"Let us make humankind in our image, according to our likeness....*
> *So God created humankind in his image,*

> *in the image of God he created them;*
> *male and female he created them."*
> **(Genesis 1:26-27)**

Notice that God's intention covers not one particular individual but the whole of mankind. The Hebrew word *Adam* in Hebrew stands either for the *individual* or for *mankind* in general. God's decree of creation stands for the whole human race. Adam and Eve as the prototypal couple, represent the entire human race. All their descendants are involved in their fate. Their fateful decision to disobey the Creator's command involves us all! Their spirit of rebellion entered the very fabric of human nature! In our highly individualistic society we are at a loss to understand the communal aspect of Adam's fall. We are so inured to the demands of our own egotism that it is a stretch to consider that there is a community vision of mankind in which we are personally involved. We find it difficult to accept that somehow I shared in that primeval decision of rebellion. Nevertheless, it is imperative to grasp this notion of mankind as *community* in order to understand the role of Jesus as the Second Adam.

3. The Second Adam

> *Thus it is written, "The first man, Adam,*
> *became a living being";*
> *the last Adam became a life-giving spirit.*
> *The first man was from the earth, a man of dust;*
> *the second man is from heaven.*
> **(1 Corinthians 15:45,47**

Christ's mission was to reunite mankind to God, to reverse the primeval curse pronounced on our first parents. If we understand man or mankind, not as a collection of individuals, but as *one man*, globally disinherited, then we can grasp the core of Christ's mission as the *second Adam* come to restore the friendship with God that the first Adam had cast aside.

This brings us to the Incarnation and the question of the origin of the Church. From all that has been said we are led to the inescapable conclusion that, just as we are involved in the creation of the *first* Adam, so we are involved in the life and death of the *Second*! St Paul makes this abundantly clear:

> *For the love of Christ urges us on, because we are convinced that one has died for all; therefore all have died. And he died for all, so that those who live might live no longer for themselves, but for him who died and was raised for them.*
>
> **(2 Corinthians 5:14-15)**

If Christ is the *Head* of the Church then redeemed humanity is the *Body of Christ*, for the Body cannot exist without its Head! So, the taking of flesh from the womb of the Virgin Mary by the Word of God encompasses also the conception of the Church. Having said all this, we can understand St Paul's conclusion:

> *Just as we have borne the image of the man of dust, we will also bear the image of the man of heaven.*
>
> **(1 Corinthians 15:49)**

(b) The Body of Christ

1. *The Kingdom of God*

The phrases, the Kingdom of God or the *Kingdom of Heaven*, are often quoted in scripture as the realm of man's salvation. There are also many other terms, such as, the *vine*, the *field, the lost coin,* etc. In the New Testament expressions involving this word *Kingdom* occur over a hundred times. The imperative of seeking the *Kingdom* may aptly be summarised in Christ's command:

> ***Seek ye first the Kingdom of God!***
>
> **(Matthew 6:33)**

In time, the Church was identified as the vehicle for admittance into this kingdom. The existence of the Church as a *divine kingdom*, however, is determined, not by the value-systems of this world, but by the imperatives of the next. Nothing can compare with the prospect of an eternity of happiness with God! Nevertheless, the Church, with its eyes riveted on eternity, cannot be considered as a purely haphazard collection of individuals. It is a highly visible, easily identifiable, organisation of communities that are knitted together in terms of loyalty and allegiance to a local superior, normally the bishop, under the leadership of the *Vicar of Christ,* the Pope. There is, however, an *inner dynamic* that takes the Church beyond the realm of purely secular or earthly organisations.

If we take the analogy of the human body, we note that the *hand writes* and the *voice speaks,* but they do so under the control of *mind* and *will (the soul).* In like manner, the members of the Church respond to the demands of the faith made known to them by their leaders. It is important to note that this response does not arise from the dominance of charismatic leaders who can wow audiences with spellbinding rhetoric. No, the response comes *via* the ministry of an organised hierarchy, which has received the commission to *evangelise* and *shepherd* the flock. This commission, *via* the imposition of hands, goes back in an unbroken succession to the apostles themselves. They, in their turn receive the commission to go out into the whole world and bring it to Christ! So we can easily come to the notion of the Church as a *Body—the Body of Christ!*

2. *Pius XII's Encyclical*

This truth of the faith that the Church is *the Body of Christ,* with the latter as its *Head,* is a profound truth that is embedded in Scripture and Tradition. It also forms the subject of one of the great encyclicals of the twentieth century, *Mystici Corporis Christi,* written by Pius XII in 1943. In it he states:

> *If we would define and describe this true Church of Jesus Christ which is the One Holy Catholic and Apostolic Roman Church— we shall find no expression more noble, more sublime or more divine than the phrase which calls it 'the Mystical Body of Christ'.*

Although the term, in its fulness, dates from the ninth century, its basis lies very clearly, as we shall see, in the words of Holy Writ. To the question: *Who are the members of this Mystical Body?* the Holy Father offers this answer:

> *Only those are really to be included as members of the Church who have been baptised and profess the true faith and who have not unhappily withdrawn from body-unity or for grave faults been excluded by legitimate authority.*

Life in Christ begins in Baptism. With this gift one is destined to grow and expand in a life of holiness and submission to the divine will. Through this *life in Christ* the members of the Church should grow up into his likeness, imaging the goodness and holiness of the invisible God

3. Christ the Head!

> **He is the head of the body, the church; he is the beginning, the firstborn from the dead, so that he might come to have first place in everything.**
> **For in him all the fullness of God was pleased to dwell.**
> **(Colossians 1:18-19)**

As a visible organisation the Church has a *human* face. Beneath this earthly disguise there lies the profound supernatural reality of *grace* and *truth*. This reality is a union of *Christ* with his *Church*, a union which still preserves the identity of each. From this it is no great stretch to conclude that Christ the Lord is the real *Head* of the Church. It is *Christ's* Church, just as he made clear to Peter when he said: **Upon this Rock I will build MY Church!** Christ's redemptive blood flows through every vein of grace into the furthest reaches of the Body of the Church! It is this fundamental fact that dominates the teaching of Paul and the early Fathers of the Church.

> **And he has put all things under his feet**
> **and has made him the head over all things for the church,**
> **which is his body, the fullness of him who fills all in all.**
> **(Ephesians 1:22-23)**

> *But the fundamental thought, that the Body of Christ is and must be an organic body, that it works by its very nature in a manifold of functions, and that this manifold is bound together by the one Spirit of Christ into an inner unity; this thought is native*

to St Paul, and it is the heritage and fundamental principle of the whole Christian gospel[226].

4. The Church—the 'Bride' of Christ

It is easy to consider the notion of the Church as *the Bride of Christ* as simply a flight of fancy, a picturesque metaphor without substance. This is far from the mind of Paul as expressed in his letters. In the theology of St Paul there emerges a very clear picture of the Church and its members being identified with Christ. It is a union cemented in the Blood of Jesus on the Cross. Paul calls Christ the saviour of the Body. He likens this union of Christ with his Church to the marital union of husband and wife.

> **"For this reason a man will leave his father and mother and be joined to his wife, and the two will become one flesh." This is a great mystery, and I am applying it to Christ and the church.**
>
> **(Ephesians 5:31-32)**

This intimate relationship between Christ and his Church is is so eloquently summarised by Karl Adam as he takes this image of husband and wife to underscore the headship of Christ:

> *The Church is the Bride of Christ, for whom he gave himself. And with a like train of thought the Seer of the Apocalypse celebrates 'the marriage of the Lamb', and sings of his 'Bride' that has prepared herself.*
>
> *(Revelations 19:7-8).*
>
> *Later mystical theology wove out of these scriptural thoughts, its wondrously sweet bridal mysticism, in which Christ is the Lord, the Church his bride, and the two in closest union generate the children of life*[227].

---

[226] *Adam: The Spirit of Catholicism (Franciscan University Press 1995) pp.16-17*

[227] *ibid. pp. 40-41*

Even when we have said all this, there still remains a much more profound basis for the identification of the Church as the *Body of Christ*. The Church, as the chosen instrument of redemption, is a projection of the Incarnation through time focusing on, and perpetuating, its message and its mystery!

(c) The Presence of Christ

1. *Christ in the Sacraments*

The ultimate purpose of the liturgy is to foster that union with Christ, that great Lover of souls. All the prayers of the Church are offered to the Father *'through Christ Our Lord'!* He has won for us the right to plead with his Father for all that is necessary for our salvation. In special moments like the reception of *Baptism* Christ sends his Spirit of Life, the divine life that unites us with God himself. In Confirmation he sends his Spirit, the Comforter, the one who is to steel our resolve to be a true foot soldier of Christ. In the *Sacrament of Reconciliation* he sends the Spirit of Peace, that very same peace that he gave to his apostles on the very day of his resurrection. (John c.20) We want to hear the words of Jesus, the words that he addressed to the paralytic: **Take heart, son; your sins are forgiven. (Matthew 9:2)**

In the *Sacrament of Marriage* the love of husband and wife is united to that of Christ himself so that his love can preserve that union and render it fruitful in the lives of their children. In the *Sacrament of the Sick* Jesus once again walks the roads of Galilee with his healing hand, and where necessary, gives the grace of courage and resignation for the end.

In the *Sacrament of Ordination* he transmits the same authority that he once gave to his apostles to go and convert the nations, to bring the message of salvation and win the world to the Kingdom of God. In sum, we can only repeat what has already been expressed, so eloquently and so powerfully, by Karl Adam:

> *This is the deepest purpose of the liturgy, namely, to make the redeeming grace of Christ present, visible and fruitful as a sacred and potent reality that fills the whole life of the Christian*[228].

---

[228] *ibid.p.17*

2. *Christ in the Eucharist*

So we go to Church to breathe in the aroma of Christ's holiness and to escape the fetid atmosphere of the world. We go there to strengthen our resolves, to nourish our spirit with the Bread of Life. Our soul needs that refreshment, that union with Christ that must sustain us in the battle with all that is against him! I come to be identified with him, to be near him, like the poor woman in the Gospel who said to herself:

> *If I only touch his cloak, I will be made well.*
> **(Matthew 9:21)**

But he offers us not merely the hem of his cloak, but his *Body, Blood, Soul* and *Divinity*. Responding to his own divine we wish *to eat his Flesh and drink His Blood!* No greater manifestation of that divine love can be found than in the Eucharist, the very Sacrament of love. It is a synthesis of the life and death of Jesus and of his Resurrection from the dead. Here is the perpetual reminder of the Father's overwhelming love for us in that he entrusts his Son to us in circumstances that appear to defy even rationality itself—*to be eaten!* It is here at the Table of the Eucharist that Christians identify with Christ, uniting with him and with all those sharing in that same divine banquet. Here are fulfilled all the blessings of the New Covenant. It is this that prompts St Thomas Aquinas to exclaim:

> *In this Sacrament the whole mystery of our salvation is contained*[229].

As Jesus promised us all in his Last Supper discourse we have not been left as *orphans* in this world. He will never abandon us. He will never leave us! In the Mass we have the greatest demonstration of the presence of Christ in our midst. For a few brief moments he reaches out to us in a welcoming embrace. For a few brief moments we are an *Ark of the Covenant* carrying not merely the Tables of the Law but the very author of that Law itself. For a few brief moments, we carry Jesus as Mary carried him in her womb. What mysteries surround us and what

---

[229] *St Thomas Aquinas: Summa Theologica 3a, 83,4*

love enfolds us! Indeed, in this very Sacrament of Love is incarnated the truth of the Church as the Body of Christ!

3. *Christ in the Teaching Church*

From the very beginning man is prone to rebellion. This instinct to challenge authority is part of the legacy of Adam's disobedience. Resentment to authority is found in every walk of life so it is inevitable that it will be found in the Church itself. The demands to keep up with the times, to be *with it,* are frequently aired. We are constantly assailed with proposals for structural reform. Incessant watchfulness is demanded to ensure the integrity of Christ's message.

The command *to make disciples of all nations* entails the obligation of passing on Christ's message of salvation. Inevitably this involves teaching and responding to the challenges that the world continually utters. Jesus has passed on this authority to speak in his name:

> **Whoever listens to you listens to me, and whoever rejects you rejects me, and whoever rejects me rejects the one who sent me.**
>
> **(Luke 10:16)**

It is important to remember that when we talk of the Church's *dogmas* or her doctrines, they must not be viewed as the imperious demands of some authoritarian taskmaster, but as the revelations of Christ himself. It is the *Bridegroom* manifesting himself through his *Bride*, the Church, to an age that needs his voice. It is his *infallible authority* that flows through the decrees of his representatives here on earth. Christ and his redemptive message must be passed on to successive generations and be as clear today as it was in the very first centuries. As one author sums it up:

> *Thus all the dogmas of the Catholic Church are stamped with the name of Christ; they would express each and every aspect of his teaching, they would bring the living, redeeming, ruling, judging Christ before our eyes, according to all the dimensions of his historical manifestation*[230].

---

[230] *Karl Adam op.cit. 19*

Throughout history the various Councils of the Church have met to answer the challenges of the world and to intervene in the controversies that have at times convulsed the Church. The Holy Father in modern times has issued various encyclicals and has frequently taken up issues that need to be clarified or restated. Bishops in their turn issue pastoral letters in response to local problems that have provoked controversy. What the Catechism says about the Church's teaching or *catechesis* is so appropriate. In catechesis

> *'Christ, the Incarnate Word and Son of God . . . is taught—everything else is taught with reference to him—and it is Christ alone who teaches—anyone else teaches to the extent that he is Christ's spokesman, enabling Christ to teach with his lips . . .*
>
> *Every catechist should be able to apply to himself the mysterious words of Jesus: My teaching is not mine but his who sent me.*
>
> **(John 7:16)**

(d) Christ and the Spirit

1. The Spirit and The Body

Christ's Body is intimately joined to the Spirit. This Spirit is the life-principle, or soul, of the new economy of salvation ministered through the Church. It is the Spirit that *'animates'* the Body of the Risen Christ, and, through the latter, the spiritual life of all believers.

> *There is one body and one Spirit,*
> *just as you were called to the one hope of your calling,*
> *one Lord, one faith, one baptism,*
> *one God and Father of all.*
>
> **(Ephesians 4:4-6)**

Even in our natural bodies there is an overflow of pain whenever any limb or organ is affected. If I injure my foot, my whole body is concerned, it reacts in sympathy to the injury. Personally, I am also concerned about how it affects my life in general, my work, my recreation, my family, etc. The echoes of that injury radiate around me. Something similar happens in the life of the Church. It is through *Baptism* that this divine life is communicated. It is the foundation for the building up of the *Body of Christ*. There then comes into action the same basic principle that operates in the growth of this life. All good deeds, all acts of virtue by a single member of the Body raises and invigorates the life of the Body. Contrariwise, every sin and moral failure—the spiritual equivalent of physical injury—diminishes it! So I cannot say that what I do in the affairs of the Spirit matters only to myself. Far from it, what I do and what I say send their ripples like stones falling in a huge pond. They wash up on the farthest shores of the Church's existence!

As the poet John Donne,[231] in a famous quotation, remarked:

> *No man is an island, entire of itself;*
> *every man is a piece of the continent, a part of the main;*
> *if a clod is washed away by the sea, Europe is the less . . . .*
> *any man's death diminishes me,*
> *because I am involved in mankind.*
> *and therefore, never send to know for whom the bell tolls,*
> *it tolls for thee!*

2. The Principle of Indefectibility

Whatever might be said of the Church, from the human standpoint, it is not a *perfect* Church! It is, moreover, an *unfinished* Church, an *incomplete* Church. The perfection of the Church awaits the hereafter! As St Augustine said *'It is still night!'*

He elaborates on this by saying:

> *The Church stands in darkness, in this time of her pilgrimage,*
> *and must lament under many miseries.*

Our Lord foretold as much when he described the Kingdom of Heaven as a net that contains bad fish as well as good. He also likened it to a field in which cockle was to be found as well as wheat. He warned

---

[231] *John Donne, Dean of St Paul's Cathedral in London in 17th century was noted for his poetry as well as his sermons.*

his disciples about coveting honours and the *first* places. When Judas *betrayed* him and Peter *denied* him we can readily assume that this pattern of betrayal and denial will arise time and again in the course of the Church's history. That history, despite the succession of saints and martyrs, does not often make pleasant reading. Nevertheless, while distress and failure are part of the Church's history, Christ still promised that *the gates of hell would never prevail!*

> **And remember, I am with you always, to the end of the age.**
> **(Matthew 28:20)**

What Jesus promised is that the Church will survive until *the end of time*. What he is promising is *indefectibility*. This means that whatever is *indefectible* will be free from decay or disintegration. In the present context it means that the Church will survive *essentially* as Christ founded it. It will never fail. Like the leaven of the Gospel the message of Christ works slowly in the world. It will gradually permeate all levels of society, despite the resistance of fallen nature and Satan's unrelenting opposition. At times, it may appear that all is lost, that the Church has sunk into *'a state of torpor or even of lingering death*'[232]. But, time and again, she awakens from the apparent sleep of *winter* into the splendour of a blessed *spring*!

3. The Papacy: Principle of Unity

The Pope, as the Rock of the Church, is both a symbol and a guarantee of the abiding unity of the Church. He has a dual role. As the Bishop of Rome, he makes those recommendations and decisions that are appropriate for the see of Rome. However, as the successor of St Peter, he lays claim to speak on behalf of the whole Church. It is his duty to provide for the *lambs* and the *sheep* of the entire flock of Christians. However, in practice his words are confined to the faithful of the Catholic Church.

As *the Vicar of Christ*, he speaks, therefore, with a divine authority that commands the obedience of all the faithful. This exercise of authority does not mean that he is at liberty to preach private views

---

[232] *Karl Adam: op.cit. p. 229.*

or promote personal opinions. On the contrary, as the First Vatican Council emphatically declares, he is bound in conscience to proclaim and interpret the truths of revelation inherent in the *written* and *unwritten* mind of the Church. In the papacy there is a continuity of an authority that is rooted in *Scripture* and *Tradition*.

This authority does not rest on popular approval. Neither does it rest on any other member of the Church, whether it be the Episcopate or the laity. He is the Supreme Pastor, whose power rests on the authority of Christ himself. Still, this monumental power is a trust that must be wielded with discretion and with love, since it is a spiritual trust involving the salvation of souls and their eternal destiny.

4. *The Following of Christ!*

The logic of all this is that we cannot claim that *the Church must be brought up to date, that it is high time that the Church got 'with it', or modernised itself in accordance with the latest fashions*. This is especially true of *morality*. The logic of being a Christian is to follow Christ. The journey is often not a pleasant one. The road to Calvary led to the crucifixion! There is this relentless pressure of our fallen nature to demand that the strict demands of the Church's teaching on morality be relaxed. It demands that the Church recognise or condone *divorce* and *premarital sex*. Then come demands on behalf of *abortion* and *homosexuality*. On all sides we are urged to capitulate: *We must be broadminded and tolerant of deviance. After all, did not Christ command to love our neighbour!?* We have to keep reminding ourselves of the basic reasons for being a *Christian* in the first place. *What, after all, is the raison d'etre of the Church?* It is to make us Christians! *And what does it mean to be a Christian?* To be a follower of Christ!

It means to be a member of the Church that he founded. It certainly does not mean that I should be a follower of the latest fashion. There is only one morality, that is the morality of Christ, not the morality of *Margaret Sanger*, nor that of *Karl Marx*, nor of *Germaine Greer*, nor of *Hugh Heffner*. No, the only guide we have is the Church, no matter how unpalatable it may appear to our jaundiced eyes or our fallen natures. The only assurance that we have that Christ is speaking to us is in the Church that he founded. Human nature, unfortunately, with its incessant demands for satisfaction and capitulation, flows ever downwards. Like water, it always seeks the lowest level!

The Church in its teaching emphasises that it is *Christ* who is the heart of catechesis. The main tenet in this catechesis is to reveal Christ, to manifest his teaching and his ministry to the world. In doing so it reveals the eternal love of the Father and the sacrifice of his Son in the most horrifying of deaths for the salvation of the world.

* * *

Questions #22

* * *

1. Who wrote the encyclical Mystici Corporis Christi and when? What does it say about the Church's title of the Body of Christ?

2. Which letters of St Paul deal especially with this topic?

3. The Bride of Christ! Why is this title so appropriate for the Church?

4. Adam? What is the significance of this word and how is it relevant to our topic?

5. Why is Christ called the Second Adam? How does the Second Adam relate to the first Adam?

6. What does St Thomas Aquinas say about the Eucharist?

7. What is the relationship of the Spirit to the Body of Christ?

8. What do you understand about the principle of indefectibility?

9. *Who is John Donne and what has he to do with the present subject?*

10. *The Church is not a democracy! What does this mean?*

11. *What does it mean to be a Christian? What must be your personal response?*

23. A 'HOLY COMMUNION'!

* * *

(a) The Sharing of Holy Things
- —1. The Ambiguity of the term "Saints"!
- —2. The 'koinonia'
- —3. Inter-communion of the Saints

(b) A Holy Fellowship
- —1. A Communion of Saints
- —2. A Community of the Holy Spirit
- —3. The Testimony of Holiness

(c) A Holy Sharing
- —1. The Sacramental Sharing
- —2. The Communion of the Word
- —3. The Communion of the Liturgy
- —4. The Communion of Prayer

(d) The Sacrament of Communion
- —1. The Commands of Jesus
- —2. The Road to Emmaus
- —3. The Recognition of Jesus
- —4. The Eucharistic Sacrifice
- —5. To the Glory of the Most Holy Trinity!

23. A Holy Communion!

* * *

(a) The Sharing of Holy Things

1. *The Ambiguity of the term 'Saints'!*

It might seem superfluous to add a statement of belief in the *Communion of Saints* when we have just considered various aspects of the Church. As one author puts it:

> *What is the Church if not the assembly of the saints?*

This is really a rhetorical question. It expects the answer:

> *The communion of saints is the Church!* (#946)[233]

However, the phrase *Communion of Saints*, raises several issues. In the very first place, the English translation of the article there is the question of its fidelity to the original version of the Creed in Latin, and in its turn, the translation from the Greek. We are left with the ambiguous phrase—*'communio sanctorum'*. If we rely on the English translation alone, it can lead to an obvious criticism that there is no mention of the *sacraments*, especially the *Mass* or the *Eucharist* in the Creed. On the face of it this implicit criticism would appear to have some justification.

However, the criticism arises from the limitations of the English translation. The latter seriously restricts the meaning of the relevant words in the original language. The English translation of *'sanctorum'* as *of saints* is misleading, since the Latin *'sanctorum'* refers to *two* distinct realities, *sancti* and *sancta*. *Sanctorum* is the genitive plural of both *sancti* and *sancta*, and, therefore, means *of holy persons and of holy things!*

Here, once again, is confirmed the Italian saying, *traduttore—traditore! The translator is a traitor!* The English translation gives us a rather one-sided version of the original. The link between the two meanings, however, has been preserved in the Eastern liturgies:

---

[233] *CCC*

> *Sancta sanctis,* "God's holy gifts for God's holy people," is proclaimed by the celebrant during the elevation of the holy Gifts before the distribution of communion. The faithful (sancti) are fed by Christ's holy Body and Blood (sancta) to grow in the communion of the holy Spirit (koinonia) and to communicate it to the world.
>
> (#948)

The *sancta* (Greek *hagia*) of the early Church were *the sacraments* or *mysteries*. So the *'communio sanctorum'* was, first and foremost, a sharing in the mysteries, a participation, or a sharing, in the divine rituals of the *sacraments*, especially of the *Eucharist*.

Here the words of St Paul are very relevant, especially with regard to the Eucharist:

> **The cup of blessing that we bless, is it not a sharing in the blood of Christ? The bread that we break, is it not a sharing in the body of Christ?**
>
> **(1 Corinthians 10:16)**

2. The 'koinonia'

The Greek word for *sharing* is *koinonia*. This term denotes far more than a simple association. It is a *communion*[234], or a fraternal union of hearts, bonded in a common interest. This common interest originates in the sacrament of Baptism. The recipients of this sacrament gain the right to share in the celebration of *holy things*, again, the *mysteries* or the sacraments of the Church. They do so as newly formed members of the faithful.

As one author says:

> *(It) creates among those who benefit from it the most profound and intimate bonds and exchanges that can exist: it is the principle of a vast fraternal communion".*[235]

---

[234] Some translations prefer *'participation'* instead of *'communion'.*
[235] *de Lubac: Theological Fragments (Ignatius Press, San Francisco 1989) p16.*

The Catechism elaborates on this theme as follows:

> *We must therefore believe that there exists a communion of*
> *goods in the Church.*
> *But the most important member is Christ, since he is the*
> *head.... Therefore, the riches of Christ are communicated to*
> *all the members through the sacraments*[236].
> *As this Church is governed by one and the same Spirit,*
> *all the goods she has received necessarily*
> *become a common fund.*[237]
>
> (#947)

3. The Inter-communion of the Saints!

It is in this communion of holy things that one finds the source from which the individual Christian receives his or her personal sanctification as well as communion with his brothers and sisters in Christ. The Church is, in effect, a holy family, bonded by the Holy Spirit. The prayers and actions of the faithful, and of even one individual, are felt throughout the Body of Christ. As St Paul expresses it so succinctly:

> ***If one member suffers, all suffer together with it;***
> ***if one member is honoured, all rejoice together with it.***
> ***Now you are the body of Christ***
> ***and individually members of it.***
> **(1 Corinthians 12:26-27)**

> *Since all the faithful, form one body, the good of each is*
> *communicated to the others....*
> *we must, therefore, believe that there exists a communion of*
> *goods in the Church.*
> *But the most important member is Christ, since he is the head....*
> *Therefore, the riches of Christ are communicated to all the*
> *members through the sacraments. As the Church is governed by*

---

[236] *St Thomas Aquinas, Symbol 10.*
[237] *The Roman Catechism 1,10, 24*

> *one and the same Spirit, all the goods
> she has received necessarily become a common fund.*
>
> (#947)

(b) A Holy Fellowship

> *For just as the body is one and has many members,
> and all the members of the body,
> though many, are one body,
> so it is with Christ.*
>
> **(1 Corinthians 12:12)**

1. A Communion of Saints

We have already shared the ambiguity in the translation of the original Latin, *communio sanctorum,* as the Communion *of the saints.* Here we turn to the secondary meaning as the fellowship of *holy persons* or of the saints, as St Paul was wont to describe them. Holiness sprang from the very fact of being baptised and this was the sense that Paul used in addressing his converts. That in the introduction to his letter to the Colossians is typical:

> **To the saints and faithful brothers and sisters in Christ in Colossae: Grace to you and peace from God our Father. In our prayers for you we always thank God, the Father of our Lord Jesus Christ, for we have heard of your faith in Christ Jesus and of the love that you have for all the saints.**
>
> **(Colossians 1:2-4)**

Paul was simply addressing a *community of the Spirit* whose goal was to be *holy.* The Christian goal of sanctity arose from the imperative of their baptism. As *the People of God* and as members of *the Mystical Body of Christ* it was evident—if their sacramental life meant anything at all—that there had to be a mutual assistance and a communal striving for identification with the life and death of their Lord and Saviour, Jesus Christ.

> *I ask not only on behalf of these, but also on behalf of those who will believe in me through their word, that they*

> *may all be one. As you, Father, are in me and I am in you, may they also be in us, so that the world may believe that you have sent me.*
>
> **(John 17:20-21)**

2. A Community of the Holy Spirit

This prayer of Jesus on behalf of his followers is not merely a prayer for ecumenism, or for a union of Christian denominations, desirable as that may be, but a clarion call for a profound spiritual fellowship that was anchored in the very heart of the Trinity itself! It cannot be too strongly stated that it is God himself who is the author of *community*. The grace of the Spirit is the glue that cements all the parts together. God's dealings with mankind all involve the covenant of *community*. Whether it be with Noah, Abraham or Moses a *family* or a *people* are always involved. As the prophet Ezekiel expresses it:

> *I will give them one heart, and put a new spirit within them; I will remove the heart of stone from their flesh and give them a heart of flesh, so that they may follow my statutes and keep my ordinances and obey them. Then they shall be my people, and I will be their God.*
>
> **(Ezekiel 11:19-20)**

The Church has little meaning for its existence, if it is viewed solely as an *earthly* organisation, or even as a *charitable* institution. While money, organisation and rules play their part in its functioning, as in any human community, they are always subordinate to the overarching concerns of the Spirit. Human decisions must be seen in the context of *the salvation of souls!*

3. The Testimony of Holiness

In the course of time the term *'saint'* became more and more constricted. At first it was confined to the martyrs, to those valiant souls who, in their violent deaths, gave the ultimate witness to their faith. Then it spread to those whose lives gave evidence of *heroic* virtue and exceptional holiness. Today, it involves a canonical process that scrutinises every aspect of a prospective candidate for sainthood.

Holiness is a gift of the Spirit to the Church. The Christian needs this community of the saints and their heroic witness. And this is valid not only for today, but our concerns go back through time, century after century, to the long list of martyrs, to the saints of every age, condition and occupation. Their lives speak to us in words of encouragement and inspiration. Having achieved the palm of victory they are cheering us on, as the author of Hebrews recalls:

> *Therefore, since we are surrounded by so great a cloud of witnesses, let us also lay aside every weight and the sin that clings so closely, and let us run with perseverance the race that is set before us.*
> **(Hebrews 12:1)**

As Christians we honour them as valiant warriors of the faith and invoke their intercession. They are part of that gigantic family of the faith and they are deeply concerned that we too may one day join them.

> *Another angel with a golden censer came and stood at the altar; he was given a great quantity of incense to offer with the prayers of all the saints on the golden altar that is before the throne. And the smoke of the incense, with the prayers of the saints, rose before God from the hand of the angel.*
> **(Revelation 8:3-4)**

(c) A Holy Sharing

1. The Sacramental Sharing

> *They devoted themselves to the apostles' teaching and fellowship, to the breaking of bread and the prayers.*
> **(Acts 2:42)**

++++++

This quotation from Acts, also called *the Gospel of the Holy Spirit*, is a testimony to the deep reverence in the early Church for the sacraments, especially for the sacraments of *Baptism* and the *Eucharist*. The former was the initiation into the fellowship of the *'saints'* and the latter was the food that sustained the life of that fellowship. However, the very first element mentioned is that of *teaching. And what was taught?* The message of Jesus about the *Kingdom of God!* Here we have the communion of faith, the sharing of the divine message which Jesus wished to be communicated to the whole world:

> *Go therefore and make disciples of all nations, baptising them in the name of the Father and of the Son and of the Holy Spirit, and teaching them to obey everything that I have commanded you. And remember, I am with you always, to the end of the age.*
> **(Matthew 28:19,20)**

Teaching Christ's message enriches the faith of the Church, and as the Catechism puts it:

> *The faith of the faithful is the faith of the Church received from the apostles. Faith is a treasure of life which is enriched by being shared.*
>
> (#949)

2. The Communion of the Word

In all this, however, we must not forget that among the *sancta,* or *holy things,* is the communion of the *Word!* The veneration of God's Word parallels that of the Holy Eucharist. This is apparent also in the words of Vatican II that we give the same veneration to the Word of God as we do the Blessed Sacrament![238] This sharing in and of *'holy things'* takes us back to the actions and gestures of Jesus in the Gospels. They are invested with a timeless quality which makes them relevant to every age and to every culture. We see Jesus stepping into the Jordan and all the waters of the world are touched and blessed in that timeless gesture! They can now be used in the sacrament of Baptism and in the various blessings by Holy Water of the things we use.

---

[238] *Vatican II: Dei Verbum 21*

3. The Communion of the Liturgy

Touching and gesturing take on this timeless symbolism in the liturgy. We read that it was in the breaking of the bread that the two disciples recognised Jesus! It is, therefore, a matter for regret that such meaningful rituals are so often lightly regarded and even treated with either disdain or disrespect. Our materialistic culture and our rationalistic outlook tend to divest these sacred things of their spiritual content and outreach. On the contrary, their meaning is rich and their symbolism profound. The Holy Spirit also distributes his *charisms* or gifts within the communion of the Church. Their purpose is spelt out very clearly by St Paul:

> *Now there are varieties of gifts, but the same Spirit; and there are varieties of services, but the same Lord; and there are varieties of activities, but it is the same God who activates all of them in everyone. To each is given the manifestation of the Spirit for the common good.*
> **(1 Corinthians 12:4-7)**

4. The Communion of Prayer

This manifestation of the Holy Spirit comes, in a special way, in the charism of prayer. Prayer puts us in touch with God, just as Abraham walked in his presence and in his covenant.[239] A holy sharing entails a communion of prayers. In its liturgical prayers the Church prays for all the faithful. The Church touches not only the infinite merits of Christ but also the prayers of the saints here on earth, in purgatory and above all the prayers of the saints in glory! The very term *Communion of Saints* expresses a communal interest in which all share. It signifies a concern for the salvation of everyone. If Christ died for all mankind then the same concern should animate all his followers. In its chapter on prayer the Catechism introduces the subject with these words:

> *Prayer is the life of the new heart. It ought to animate us at every moment. But we tend to forget him who is our life and our all. This is why the Fathers of the spiritual life in the Deuteronomic*

---

[239] *see Genesis 15:6 and 17:1-7*

and prophetic traditions insist that prayer is a remembrance of God often awakened by the memory of the heart:
We must remember God more often than we draw breath![240]
But we cannot pray at all times, if we do not pray at specific times, consciously willing it. These are the special times of Christian prayer, both in intensity and duration.

(d) The Sacrament of Communion!

1. The Commands of Jesus

Scripture records many commands of Jesus but two specific *commands* to the apostles are worthy of notice. The first concerned *Baptism* and the second concerned the *Eucharist*; *Go and baptise all nations!* and *Do this in memory of me!* The first gives supernatural life and the second nourishes it. They go hand in hand; they are inseparable. St John leaves no doubt on this issue:

> **Very truly, I tell you, unless you eat the flesh of the Son of Man and drink his blood, you have no life in you. Those who eat my flesh and drink my blood have eternal life, and I will raise them up on the last day.**
> **(John 6:554)**

2. The Road to Emmaus

In the events of the day of the Resurrection of Jesus, certain events stand out and among them we find the encounter of the two disciples on the road to Emmaus. Although we have already discussed this episode several times it is still well worth exploring again. Firstly we do so because it concerns Jesus, secondly, because in that concern we find echoes of our own spiritual concerns and lessons for living the life of the Spirit! As the Gospel of Luke tells us two disciples were en route to Emmaus from Jerusalem, when they were joined by a stranger who enquired about their topic of conversation. Cleopas and his companion *(probably his wife)* spoke about the events leading up to the death of Jesus and then

---

[240] *St Gregory Naziansus*

the story of some women who had seen an angel at the empty tomb informing that Jesus was very much alive! There is a phrase in their account that may strike a chord in our lives:

> ***We had hoped that he was the one to redeem Israel.***
> **(Luke 24:21)**

The words of the disciples *'We had hoped'* speak volumes of the discouragement and disappointment that dogged them on this journey away from Jerusalem. Footsore and weary they had shared with each other the sad tale of disappointed hopes and personal frustrations. And all the time Jesus was at their side listening to their story about himself! He then upbraids them:

> *"Oh, how foolish you are, and how slow of heart to believe all that the prophets have declared! Was it not necessary that the Messiah should suffer these things and then enter into his glory?" Then beginning with Moses and all the prophets, he interpreted to them the things about himself in all the scriptures.*
> **(Luke 24:25-27)**

3. *The Recognition of Jesus*

Even then the two disciples did not recognise him! They only recognised Jesus at supper in *the breaking of the bread*. This expression, *of the Breaking of the Bread*, was a commonplace in the early Church for the celebration of the *Eucharist*. Here we have the teaching of scripture first and then the celebration of the Eucharist. This is what happens every Sunday at the celebration of the Mass. It is here that we get relief from our journeys of disappointment and discouragement, and the strength to go back to Jerusalem—in other words, to the workaday world in which we still have to toil.

This expression, *the Breaking of the Bread*, brings to mind the image of close friends sharing in a common meal. Nevertheless, this sacrament has had many other names in the course of its history. They all in one way or another reflect the depth of this profound mystery of God's love;

the Lord's Supper, the Divine Liturgy and the Sacrifice of the Mass. But one stands out, that of the *Holy Eucharist*, the Sacrament of *Thanksgiving* to the Father for this supreme gift of his love.

4. The Eucharistic Sacrifice

The Eucharist, as liturgy, is essentially a one-act drama, comprising several themes. We might single out three for particular consideration. They reflect the life of the Trinity at work within the Body of Christ and within the lives of the communicants:

1. The thanksgiving to the Father
2. The memorial of Christ (the 'anamnesis')
3. The invocation of the Spirit. (the 'epiclesis')

The term *Eucharist* is derived from the Greek *eucharistia* which means *thanksgiving*. It spells out the great debt of gratitude we owe to the Father for his gifts of creation, redemption and sanctification in Christ. As the Roman liturgy expresses it:

> *Through Christ, Our Lord, you give us all these gifts.*
> *You fill them with life and holiness,*
> *you bless them and make them holy.*

The Eucharist is also a *memorial* of the death and the Resurrection of Jesus. The Greek term, *anamnesis*, recalls the words of Revelation:

> **You are worthy to take the scroll and to open its seals, for you were slaughtered and by your blood you ransomed for God saints from every tribe and language and people and nation; you have made them to be a kingdom and priests serving our God, and they will reign on earth."**
> **(Revelation 5:9-10)**

Finally, we have the *epiclesis*, or the invocation of the Holy Spirit. This was always a prominent part of the Eastern liturgy. It was renewed in the Roman liturgy after Vatican II:

Father, we bring you these gifts. We ask you to make them holy by the power of your Spirit that they may become the Body and the Blood of your Son, our Lord Jesus Christ, at whose command we celebrate this Eucharist.

5. To the Glory of the Most Holy Trinity!

This honouring of the Most Holy Trinity takes place in the celebration of the Eucharist. Here is manifested, in a most dramatic form, the gathering of the *People of God t*o honour and worship the God who is Love itself. In honouring that love the community partakes of the *Bread of Life,* the manna that sustains them in the *desert* of human affairs and worldly concerns.

However, there is something far more profound than all that. In personally receiving Christ, we have become *one with him*! Through Baptism we enter into the life of the Church, the Body of Christ. But, this life needs sustenance; it needs to be fed and nourished. Just as our body demands constant nourishment and our mental life is sustained by knowledge and instruction, so must the life of grace within us be fed, nurtured and sustained! So we need the *Bread of Angels,* as St Thomas calls the Eucharist, to sustain our journey in the spirit. No words are more eloquent than the words of Jesus himself to illustrate this imperative of our spiritual life:

> ***This is the bread that came down from heaven,***
> ***not like that which your ancestors ate, and they died.***
> ***But the one who eats this bread will live forever.***
> **(John 6: 57)**

Questions #23

* * *

1. *What is the problem with the translation from the Latin of the phrase Communion of Saints?*

2. *What other name can be used for the word sacrament and why?*

3. *What is the meaning of the following words;*
   > *koinonia,*
   > *eucharist*
   > *anamnesis*
   > *epiclesis*

4. *Can you name two basic commands of Jesus to his apostles?*

5. *What is meant by saying that the Church is much more than an earthly organisation?*

6. *What is the significance of the encounter of the two disciples with Jesus on the Road to Emmaus?*

7. *How does this encounter relate to your own spiritual life?*

8. *What is the basic structure of the Mass?*

9. *What is meant by saying the actions and gestures of Jesus are as important as his words?*

10. *What does the phrase "Communion of Saints" mean to you personally?*

24. MARY, MOTHER OF THE CHURCH!

* * *

Introduction

(a) Predestined Soul
 —1. The Eternal Gospel
 —2. The 'Woman' of Genesis!
 —3. The Annunciation
 —4. The Angelic Greeting!
 —5. Elizabeth's Greeting!

(b) The Witness of John
 —1. The Wedding Feast at Cana
 —2. The Testament of Calvary
 —3. The Visions of Revelation

(c) The Privileges of Mary
 —1. The 'Immaculate Conception'
 —2. The Mother of God
 —3. The Mother of the Faithful
 —4. The Mediatrix of All Graces

++++++++++

Conclusion *'Intrinsic to Christian Worship'*

3. Mary, Mother of the Church!

* * *

Introduction

There are few topics of Catholic belief that so often raise the hackles of many non-Catholics as much as Catholic devotion to Mary. They argue that such devotion has no scriptural basis. Moreover, it is an *insult* to Christ, who should be the *sole* object of our worship and devotion. At best, such preoccupation with devotion to Mary is a distraction, and, at worst, wholly inimical to the worship that is due to Christ alone as our Redeemer. It is our purpose here to give the lie to these and similar objections and to show that the Catholic devotion to Mary, the mother of Jesus, has sound scriptural warranty.

It is one of the tenets of Catholic theology that any truth proclaimed by the Church is to be found *explicitly* or *implicitly* in Scripture or Tradition. There is often a fine line between what is *implicit* or *explicit* in revelation, and the limits of either have often provoked furious debates. Nevertheless, if the Church is the *Body of Christ* and animated by the *Holy Spirit*, it must grow in understanding of the *Word of God* and the message of salvation. Such growth is a sign of vitality in a Church, *ever ancient, ever new!*

This has been particularly true of the recognition due to the Mother of Jesus, the Mother of God. From the very outset it must be stated that, before God, Mary in herself, is *nothing*! An infinite distance separates her as a *creature* from her *Creator*. Both in the grace of nature and of the spirit she is totally beholden to God. Everything about her is the precious gift of the Almighty. In this respect the words of that great lover of Mary's honour, St Louis de Montfort, could not be more appropriate:

> *With the whole Church I acknowledge that Mary, being a mere creature, fashioned by the hands of God, is, compared to his infinite majesty, less than an atom, or rather, is simply nothing... However, considering things as they are, because God has decided to begin and accomplish his greatest works through the Blessed*

Virgin ever since he created her, we can safely believe that he will not change in his thoughts nor in his way of acting.[241]

Even more ridiculous is the claim of some misguided academics that devotion to Mary is a blatant borrowing from pagan rituals. The antics of the gods and goddesses of antiquity are as far removed from Christian belief as night is from day! Nothing, therefore, is so implausible, so preposterous, as to label Mary as a *mother-goddess* like some hangover from a bankrupt paganism. Mary was never worshipped in the early Church. She had the unique distinction of being one who was the *Mother of the Messiah*. This was her role in the drama of redemption and the reason for her existence, and her title of honour. In conclusion, we will endeavour to show in the following sections how devotion to Mary is rooted solidly in scripture, and that devotion to her is a natural consequence of her association with Jesus and his ministry. Her appearance in the economy of salvation, far from being an *accident* of history, as some would have us believe, is an *integral* part of God's message of salvation for all mankind!

(a) Predestined Soul!

1. The Eternal Gospel

> **Then I saw another angel flying in mid heaven, with an eternal gospel to proclaim to those who live on the earth—to every nation and tribe and language and people.**
> **(Revelation 14:6)**

Here in the very last book of scripture comes a pregnant phrase, *an eternal gospel*. What is this *eternal gospel*? With the gift of hindsight we realise that the gospel the angel is carrying is the eternal message of redemption that is coming to fulfilment at the end of time. The central character in that Gospel is Christ—*the Word made flesh*—destined to go forth at the Father's behest to bring the Good News of God's eternal

---

[241] St Louis Grignon de Montfort in "True Devotion to the Blessed Virgin" No 1.

love to a fallen humanity, **to every nation and tribe and language and people!**

But how is this *going forth from the Father* to be effected? How is The Word *through whom all things were made* (John 1:3) going to make his entry into the world?. He needs a helpmate! If God is to become *man*, he *needs* a mother! It is this eternal fact that becomes the focal point of history. A Jewish maiden called *Miriam* (Mary) becomes central to the divine plan! Hence we can say that in the *eternal gospel* the names of Jesus and Mary are inextricably intertwined.

For this very reason Pope Pius IX., in his decree on the *Immaculate Conception* in 1854, held that the names of Jesus and Mary are inseparably linked *in the one and same decree of predestination*. The same thought was reiterated in the decree of the Assumption promulgated by Pius XII in 1950, when he said that *the august Mother of God, (was) mysteriously united from all eternity with Jesus Christ* **in one and the same decree of predestination.**[242]

2. The Woman of Genesis

The fulfilment of the *'eternal gospel'* in history came about in the garden of Eden. There God lavished his love and friendship on Adam and Eve. He created them in his own image and endowed them with the preternatural gifts of freedom from *death, ignorance* and *disease*. These they lost in their disobedience to God's command.

God's quizzing of the culprits resulted in a blanket condemnation of the human race. In that primordial scene of judgement, however, in which the consequences of the original fall are spelled out, there comes this singular message of hope:

> ***I will put enmity between you and the woman,***
> ***and between your offspring and hers;***
> ***he will strike your head, and you will strike his heel".***
> **(Genesis 3:15).**

---

[242] *Encyclical"Munificentissimus Deus" of Pius XII. 1950.*

In this decree we see the woman and her offspring, Mary and Jesus, inextricably intertwined in a message of redemption. In particular *"the woman"* is singled out as the special adversary of Satan. An undying and unremitting enmity is foretold between *'the woman'* and Lucifer. *Who was this woman?* Certainly not Eve, who had fallen into Satan's clutches! It had to be *the woman* most closely associated with him who would strike the serpent's head, who would bear the future redeemer. This was most fitting, since Eve was an instrument of mankind's fall, it was equally fitting that Mary as the *Second Eve*[243] should be an instrument of its rising.

3. The Annunciation

> *But when the fullness of time had come,*
> *God sent his Son, born of a woman, born under the law,*
> *in order to redeem those who were under the law,*
> *so that we might receive adoption as children.*
> **(Galatians 4:4-5)**

Here in Paul's letter to the Galatians we get once again the reference to *the woman* of Genesis. God's ways are not our ways. He works with meticulous care over generations, over centuries, and even millennia, to achieve his purposes. Here at last, God was now prepared to step into the fulfilment of the *eternal gospel!*

In the Gospel of Luke we get an account of the most earthshaking news in the whole of history. *God is about to become man!* This encounter of an archangel with a Jewish teenager is so well known that it can be read with a certain indifference, and even with apathy. The account hardly strikes a chord of wonder, and we remain blind to its profound ramifications.

Where did it all begin? In Nazareth! It was a provincial backwater in a despised region of Palestine. *'Can any good come out of Nazareth?'* was the scathing remark that a future apostle was to make. It revealed the common contempt for this obscure village of Galilee. Yet it was here that God laid out his plan for the salvation of the world at the feet of an unknown teenager! The whole scenario is utterly mind boggling that so much would depend on the consent of a simple and obscure peasant girl

---

[243] *see Genesis 3:15 for the earliest reference to the future mother of the Messiah.*

in a remote corner of the Roman Empire! And she said in effect: *Yes! Yes, a thousand times yes! Let God's holy will be done in me! Let him do whatever is good in his sight!* What a magnificent gesture of faith and total surrender!

> **Behold I am the handmaid of the Lord!**
> **Let it be to me according to your word! (Luke 1:29)**

God steps into history! He becomes part of his own creation at a maiden's behest! This was Mary's total surrender to the divine designs. The Church celebrates this surrender in the *Advent Preface* of the Mass, when it says of Jesus:

> *His future coming was proclaimed by all the prophets.*
> *The Virgin-Mother bore him in her womb with love beyond all telling!*

4. The Angelic Greeting!

> **In the sixth month the angel Gabriel was sent by God to a town in Galilee called Nazareth, to a virgin engaged to a man whose name was Joseph, of the house of David. The virgin's name was Mary. And he came to her and said, "Greetings, favoured one! The Lord is with you."**
> **(Luke 1:26-28)**

The mystery of the Incarnation, the very pivotal truth of the faith, would suggest that the mother of Jesus was an extremely holy person. When the angel greeted her, he did not use her name, he gave her a title that would suggest as much. St Luke uses the Greek term *kecharitomene* in the angelic greeting and it has been translated *Full of grace* or *Highly favoured*, and in the present instance: *Favoured One!*

Traduttore, traditore![244] This is an Italian saying that points to the shortcomings of translations, and nowhere is this more apparent than in the present instance. The root of *kecharitomene* is the verb *charitao* which can be translated *to gift or endow with grace; to honour with blessings*. Since it is used by the angel as a mode of address it takes on the flavour of a divinely authorised identification. The angel, as God's

---

[244] *In English "Translator, traitor!".*

ambassador, addresses her with a title which, in this context, defies adequate translation.

However, from the significance of the encounter—*God seeking entry into this world!*—we would presume that the title itself is invested with the profoundest meaning, that Mary was endowed with grace to the fullest extent of her being. As one commentator explains it:

The Greek (kecharitomene) indicates a perfection of grace. A perfection must be perfect not only intensively but extensively. The grace (or favour) that Mary enjoyed must not only have been 'full' or strong or complete as possible at any given time, but it must have extended over the whole of her life, from conception[245].

5. Elizabeth's Greeting

Blessed are you among women, and blessed is the fruit of your womb. And why has this happened to me, that the mother of my Lord comes to me? For as soon as I heard the sound of your greeting, the child in my womb leaped for joy.
(Luke 1:42-44)

In the account of Luke's Gospel the context of the Visitation of Elizabeth must be noted. Mary had been notified of Elizabeth's own pregnancy and had hastened to her side. She carried within her womb the Son of God made flesh, the long-promised Messiah. As such she is the antitype of the *Tabernacle* or the *Ark of the Covenant*, bearing within her body the author of the Law itself! It is evident that Elizabeth has had a revelation of the Annunciation, and so she breaks out in exclaiming: *Blessed are you among women!* Here we must note that this is a transliteration of the Hebrew (Aramaic) superlative. In the latter there is no superlative mode as there is in English, usually expressed by the suffix—*est*, or the prefix *most*. So what Elizabeth is really saying is; *You are the most blessed of all women!*

That greeting puts Mary in the line of all the great women of the Old Testament, and as one far surpassing them all. Moreover, every woman that was to follow her could not rival her in dignity! If

---

[245] see Karl Keating:"Catholicism and Fundamentalism" (Ignatius Press, 1988) p.269.

we would list the outstanding women of the Old Law—*Eve, Sarah, Rachel, Debborah, Judith* and *Esther* etc, Mary far surpasses them all in dignity and importance. So we can here echo the words of the Song of Songs:

> *Who is she that cometh forth as the morning rising,*
> *fair as the moon, bright as the sun, terrible as an*
> *army set in battle array?*
> **(Song of Songs 6:9)**

Mother of my Lord! Here there are also echoes of the authority that was conferred in the mother of the King in ancient Israel, the *gebirah*. We see Solomon bowing before his mother Bathsheba and placing her on his right hand! Finally, at the sound of Mary's greeting the infant in the womb of Elizabeth leaped for joy! This once again recalls the Ark of the Covenant which David greeted with joy, dancing and leaping in its presence. *(2 Samuel 6:12)*

(b) The Witness of John

1. The Wedding Feast at Cana

The Gospel of John is unique in that the author only chooses *seven* signs or miracles in his account of the ministry of Jesus. Among the hundreds, nay among the thousands, of miracles that adorned the life and mission of Jesus, John chose to pick only seven! The number, a biblical number, is itself significant, but the choice itself reflects a profound spiritual message The first of these is the wedding feast at Cana. It is in this context that we first get a glimpse of Mary's importance in the economy of salvation.

> *On the third day there was a wedding in Cana of Galilee,*
> *and the mother of Jesus was there.*
> *Jesus and his disciples had also been invited to the wedding.*
> **(John 2:1-2)**

The phrase 'on *the third day*' is a typical biblical expression that heralds something of prime importance. Here it points to a *'wedding feast'* which is a symbol of *the kingdom of God*, of the Church and of Heaven itself. *And the mother of Jesus was there!* This is a statement honouring the mother of the redeemer, but, in the sequel, it is invested with much greater meaning. Mary intervenes in the celebrations when she says to Jesus, *They have no wine.* Jesus in reply addresses her as *'Woman'. This* immediately transports us back to Genesis and to the promise of perpetual enmity with Satan.

> **I will put enmity between thee and the woman**
> **(Genesis 3:15)**

One of the most extraordinary aspects of the entire narrative in John is that the bridal couple involved are never mentioned. This is precisely the point. The whole thrust of the narrative points to the manifestation of Jesus as the Messiah about to begin his ministry. The water that is transformed into wine echoes the transformation that is about to take place. The old Dispensation is about to give way to the New Covenant, the *new wine.* The latter, in its turn represents Jesus himself, both as the *Truth* that he is, and as the *Blood* that he will shed and share with his followers. In sum, we are led to the conclusion that John, in the spiritual subtext of the Gospel, wishes to present to us the true bridal couple Jesus and Mary. Mary, as the *Bride*, and symbol of the *Church*, constantly points to the Bridegroom, Jesus, and keeps repeating to us all: *Do whatever he tells you!* The Catechism summarises it all as follows:

> *The Gospel reveals to us how Mary prays and intercedes in faith. At Cana the mother of Jesus asks her son for the needs of a wedding feast; this is the sign of another feast—that of the wedding of the Lamb where he gives his Body and Blood at the request of the Church, his Bride.*
>
> (#2618)

2. The Testament of Calvary

> **When Jesus saw his mother and the disciple whom he loved standing beside her, he said to his mother, "Woman, here is your son." Then he said to the disciple, "Here is your mother." And from that hour the disciple took her into his own home.**
>
> **(John 19:26-27)**

In this historic scene on Calvary we are witnessing the last Messianic act of Jesus, the mutual entrustment of Mary to John and of John to Mary. The very circumstance of it invests the whole proceeding with profound significance. Here the *'Hour'* of Jesus reaches its climax and the fulfilment of salvation history! Here Mary, standing at the Cross and united to her Son, consummates the *Fiat* [246] uttered to the Angel of the Annunciation.

John brings Mary into two crucial points in the ministry of Jesus, at the very *beginning* and at the very *end*. She appears in the beginning as the instrument of the very first miracle of Jesus and as being thereby responsible for the initiation of faith in Jesus and his message. Here at the very end of the ministry of Jesus, in the heart of the Hour, Mary is singled out as the last gift of Jesus to his Church in the person of John. She is thereby confirmed in her crucial role as the *Mother of the Church*.

Does this diminish, in any way, the role of Jesus? Far from it! It only enhances the loving mercy of Jesus, who confides to us another powerful intercessor in our vale of tears. Moreover, it could only have been done by the will of the Father who in the first instance entrusted his Son to us through her, now entrusts us to her as well. The former is by far the more significant, so how can we possibly object to the latter? Just as Jesus is the *Second Adam*, so in the context of redemption Mary is the *Second Eve*, the earliest title accorded her even as early as the second century by the Church fathers. The woman of the first creation was called *Life (=Eve)* of the *Mother of all the Living*. Now Mary as the Mother of the New Life becomes the Mother of all those living the new life in Christ. Just as Eve had yielded to the serpent, the fallen angel of darkness, so Mary had surrendered to the angel of light.

Just as Eve stood by the tree in the garden and ate of its forbidden fruit, so Mary now stands beneath the tree of the Cross from which flows the fruit of life, the blood of Jesus. The struggle with Satan goes on in the life of each individual and she stands as the Mother ever-ready to intercede with her Divine Son.

---

[246] *This Fiat—"Let it be done"*- links the Annunciation to the Passion and Death of Jesus.

3. *The Visions of Revelation*

In Revelation, this final Book of scripture, we get apocalyptic visions of Mary's role in the economy of salvation. The imagery of Revelation is highly symbolic and replete with references to the Old Testament. Commentators see both the Church and Mary in this symbolism. As St Clement of Alexandria[247] writes:

> *Only one Virgin-Mother exists, and, according to my point of view, no better name can be suited to her than the name Church!*

In effect, the symbols are interchangeable, when viewed from different standpoints. This fact is crucial in interpreting Revelation where symbolism abounds! In general, this symbolism is both ecclesial (i.e. referring to the Church) and Marian. It is with the latter that we are primarily concerned with here. When John looked up to heaven, what did he see?

> **He saw the Ark of the Covenant in God's temple. A great sign appeared in heaven, a woman clothed with the sun, and the moon under her feet, and on her head a crown of twelve stars.**
> **(Revelation 11:19-12:1)**

The Ark of the Covenant which Moses erected in the desert contained the Tables of the Law (*the Commandments*) and the manna. This is a symbol of Mary who held in her womb, not merely the tables of the law but the very Lawgiver himself (the Word). The manna, symbol of the Eucharist, reinforces the image of Mary as the one from whom Christ took his flesh and blood, sacrificed on Calvary and given to us in the Sacrament of the Eucharist. The Marian theme of the twelfth chapter is buttressed when John continues to refer to the son *who is to rule the nations*. This is an obvious reference to Jesus. The enmity prophesied in Genesis 3:15 between the woman and the serpent, in this case the dragon, is played out once again:

---

[247] *St Clement of Alexandria noted leader and philosopher of the 3rd century.*

> *Then the dragon stood before the woman*
> *who was about to bear a child,*
> *so that he might devour her child as soon as it was born.*
> *And she gave birth to a son, a male child,*
> *who is to rule all the nations with a rod of iron.*
> **(Revelation 12:4-5)**

There is also a reference to Mary as the Mother of the Church when the dragon (Satan) goes to war with her offspring, the children of the new Eve:

> *Then the dragon was angry with the woman, and went off to make war on the rest of her children, those who keep the commandments of God and hold the testimony of Jesus.*
> **(Revelation 12:17)**

All this is but a tiny sample of the heavy symbolism that is packed into the twelfth chapter of Revelation. From the very nature of the subject we can only touch on this subject very lightly. But it will serve to show that Mary plays an integral part in the story of salvation. The role of the first Eve is now reversed. Just as Eve was drawn from the side of Adam, so now Jesus will come forth from the womb of Mary!

(c) The Privileges of Mary

1. "The Immaculate Conception"

This unique privilege was demanded by Mary's destiny to be the Mother of God. It is unthinkable that *the thrice holy* God would take flesh from a woman that had never known the slightest taint of sin even for a second of her existence. The unique intimacy that marks the relationship between a mother and her child would demand special privileges where a mother had a child *who was God!* From all that has been said about the angel's greeting there is only one legitimate conclusion that from the first moment of her existence Mary was conceived *immaculate* without the slightest stain of original sin. As the Second Vatican Council expresses it:

> *From the first instant of her conception she was adorned
> with the radiance of an entirely unique holiness.*
> (Lumen Gentium #56)

This idea of the *Immaculate Conception* must not be understood as referring to the conception of Christ. Nor does it refer to a miraculous conception in the womb of her mother Anne. Her conception was normal in the ordinary course of nature. But it was gifted with a tremendous spiritual privilege, the freedom from all stain of original sin.

But there is more. All this means that she never had the slightest stain of personal or actual sin. By a singular privilege of the divine bounty Mary was preserved from the slightest taint of actual sin. Put more positively, Mary, in her entire life here on earth, never denied God the least sign of love for him and for the fulfilment of his holy will. This would account for the title given her by the Eastern Churches, the *Panagia*—the All-Holy One!

2. The Mother of God!

> **And why is this granted to me,
> that the mother of my Lord should come to me?**
> **(Luke 1:43)**

Mother of my Lord! 'Mother of God!'
These words have echoed down the centuries. They rang in the ears of a British statesman when he once visited a church in Italy. It was John Bright, a noted statesman of nineteenth century England, who had just heard a preacher extol the virtues of the *'Madre di Dio!'* He was stunned. The phrase haunted him for over twenty years. He constantly asked himself how could any human being lay claim to such an awesome title? *How could any creature born in time lay claim to be the mother of the eternal God?*

John Bright is not alone in his concerns. This title of Mary as the *'Mother of God'* always seems to provoke considerable concern, if not outright indignation, on the part of certain Christians. It arises from the notion that it appears to place Mary on a level with the divinity itself. The concern is not new. It arose in the early Church under the heresiarch *Arius* who denied the divinity of Christ, and by extension, this title of Mary as *Mother of God*.

It arose again in the following century when a famous preacher from Antioch, Nestorius by name, was made Patriarch of Constantinople in 428 A.D. by the emperor Theodosius II. Nestorius raised the issue again when he doubted that the title of *theotokos* or *God-bearer* was appropriate for the mother of Jesus. He maintained that there were two persons in Christ, one *human* and the other *divine*. Mary was simply the mother of the human person. Therefore, Mary should be called *Christokos*—Christ-bearer, and not *Theotokos*—God-bearer! If, however, *Jesus is God*, then Mary is the Mother of God, truly *theotokos!* This impeccable logic was the belief of the early Church. One of its many martyrs, St Ignatius, Bishop of Antioch, who died in 106 A.D. is on record as saying :

> *Our God was carried in the womb of Mary!*

This title of *theotokos* was popular among Orthodox believers and especially in the Greek monasteries. On this issue Nestorius was strongly challenged by the Alexandrian church. There Cyril, the Patriarch of Alexandria (412-444), a noted theologian, denounced him in his sermons, writings and letters. At the Council of Ephesus in 431 A.D. the position of Cyril was proclaimed as the tradition of the Church and Nestorius was denounced and deposed from office. He was sent into exile and died in Egypt around the year 450 A.D. Mary's honour was finally and fully vindicated. The importance of the title *Mother of God* lies at the heart of our redemption. As Cardinal Newman so aptly pointed out:

> *We cannot refuse this title to Mary without denying the Divine Incarnation that is the great and fundamental truth of revelation, that God became man!*

The key to Mary's greatness and dignity lies in her divine maternity. She is the *Mother of God!* Everything else that can be said about this supremely privileged creature flows from that unique title. She is, as the English poet Wordsworth, depicted her, *our tainted nature's solitary boast!* Her role and her position in the economy of salvation is not simply an accident of history, but was something preordained from all eternity in God's salvific will!

3. Mother of the Faithful

We have noted right from the beginning that Mary was an integral part of God's plan of salvation. Her surrender to God's plan at the Annunciation echoes throughout the ministry of Jesus. But it does not stop there. As the Council was at pains to point out:

> *Thus the Motherhood of Mary in the order of grace, which began with the consent she gave in faith at the Annunciation and which she sustained without wavering beneath the Cross lasts until the eternal fulfilment of all the elect. Taken up to Heaven she did not lay aside this salvific duty, but by her constant intercession, continued to bring us the gifts of eternal salvation.*
>
> (Lumen Gentium 62)

The title *'mother'* has special and very human considerations. There is nothing on earth so appealing as the intimacy that unites a mother with her child. This was true also of Mary in her relationship with her son Jesus, but it went far beyond that on the spiritual plane. It is on that plane, in the order of grace, that we enter into a special relationship with Mary, our heavenly Mother. Mary's spiritual motherhood is wrapt up in her concerns for Jesus and his message of salvation. Everything that she does, everything that she thinks about, is for her Son and his glory. That message of Jesus is for us and that brings her concern to us. Our salvation is her motherly concern! As the Council summarises it:

> *Embracing God's salvific will with a full heart . . . she devoted herself totally as handmaid of the Lord to the person and work of her Son, under him and with him . . . serving the work of Redemption.*
>
> (Lumen Gentium 56)

As she is the Mother of the Church she is the mother of each individual Christian. But even more than that, as we have already said, she is the *Second Eve*, the spiritual *mother of all the living*. Her spiritual motherhood is, in effect, the human extension of the Divine. Just as the Word found a gateway into the world in Mary, so too may God find in Mary the gateway into our souls! The whole purpose of her maternal activity is to open up our hearts to the love of Jesus. And so the whole aim and effect of her spiritual motherhood finds expression in those beautiful words of one of her great servants, St Louis Grignion de Montfort:

> *Forming us in Christ and Christ in us!*

Mary has a *unique* place in the economy of salvation. This, however, is not to say that she operates *independently* of Jesus. Far from it, she is totally dependent on her Son and his saving grace. Nevertheless, as his mother, she occupies a special place in his heart, a place that far surpasses the normal human relationship that a mother shares with her son. She was chosen from all eternity for this special role, and Jesus will be forever known as the *Son of Mary!* She was the Father's choice as the instrument whereby the *Word made flesh* was clothed with our humanity.

She is the one closest to Jesus, both historically and spiritually. Mary conceived the Word of God in her heart and flesh by the power of the Holy Spirit who overshadowed her *(Luke 1:35)*. It is by that same Holy Spirit, *the very soul of her soul and the very life of her life,* that she attains this spiritual fruitfulness of being our Mother! Her universal motherhood confers upon her a unique power of intercession.

4. *Mediatrix of All Graces*

From the writings of John a very simple truth emerges, that there is a unique and indestructible truth of the union of Jesus and Mary in the work of man's salvation. The two main characters at the foot of the Cross are powerful symbols of this penetrating truth. John stands for every Christian to whom Mary is now their mother in the spirit. This is the opinion even of a Church Father, Origen, who lived from c.185-254 A.D. There is a profound error in judgement in the theological thought of those who believe that Catholics put Mary *on a par with Christ.* Hence they object to the title *Mediatrix of all graces.* This does not supplant Christ. Far from it! It enhances the role of her Son in that as she surrendered wholeheartedly to the Incarnation she became the *first mediator* between God and mankind in consenting to become the Mother of *the Word made flesh!* Her role is essentially a subordinate one to that of Christ himself as St Thomas Aquinas makes abundantly clear in saying:

> *Christ alone is the perfect mediator of God and men. in as much as, by his death, he reconciled the human race to God . . . .*

Mediation is a commonplace office in human affairs. After all, we *mediate* for others when we pray to God on their behalf for whatever will benefit them either materially or spiritually. This does not diminish the role of Christ, since all prayers go back through him and are entirely dependent on him. What we share in this way on a very human level can also be said of all the saints and especially of Mary's intercessory powers but in a far more powerful and more effective way. She is, after all, the Queen-Mother! The Second Vatican Council puts it all in perspective:

> *Mary's function as mother of men in no way obscures or diminishes this unique mediation of Christ, but rather shows its power. But the Blessed Virgin's salutary influence on men . . . flows forth from the superabundance of the merits of Christ, rests on his mediation, depends entirely on it and draws all its power from it.*
>
> (Lumen Gentium #60)

Conclusion

"Intrinsic to Christian Worship"

> *The Church's devotion to the Blessed Virgin is intrinsic to Christian worship. The Church rightly honours "the Blessed Virgin with special devotion."* [248] *From the most ancient times the Blessed Virgin has been honoured with the title 'Mother of God', to whose protection the faithful in all their dangers and needs . . . .*
>
> (#971)

---

[248] *Lumen Gentium 68*

From all that has been said it is clear that Mary has played, and still plays, a compelling, if subordinate, role in the history of salvation. *All generations will call me blessed!* The Church has dutifully fulfilled this biblical prophecy. Mary is called the *Blessed Virgin! Our Blessed Lady!* Moreover, the document explicitly states that devotion to Mary as *intrinsic to Christian worship*. What this means is that there is an inextricable link between Mary and her Son in the work of our redemption. It flows ultimately from God's sovereign will in choosing her for this role and her total surrender to that role: ***Let it be to me according to your word!* (Luke 1:29)**

Finally, devotion to Mary is far removed from the worship paid to God. The latter is *latria* or the profound adoration to be found in the divine worship that is given to God alone. The devotion given to Mary is *special*, because of her special role is called *hyperdulia*.

Hyperdulia is the special reverence or devotion accorded Mary as *the Mother of God*. This is far below the worship given to God but it far surpasses the honour *(dulia)* given to either the angels or the saints! It cannot be stressed too much that it is no accident that she was especially favoured by God himself. In honouring her we honour his choice. In honouring her we honour Jesus her Son, who was *obedient to her* in the silent years of Nazareth. *For thirty years!*

He still honours her in heaven as he did on earth and that is why we turn to her in our times of need. This does not dishonour Jesus nor diminish his power as the unique mediator of our salvation. It is for this reason that the Church in its documents records the following:

> *Holier than the cherubim and the seraphim, she enjoys greater glory (and deserves greater veneration) than all the other saints, for she is full of grace(Luke 1:28), she is the Mother of God, who happily gave birth to the Redeemer for us . . . .*

An Ancient Prayer to Mary

> *We fly to thy patronage, O Holy Mother of God,*
> *Despise not our petitions in our necessities,*
> *but deliver us from all dangers,*
> *O glorious and ever-blessed Virgin!*[249]

---

[249] *Earliest prayer to Mary recorded in the 3rd century.*

A Mediaeval Tribute to Mary

* * *

Mary and the Church

* * *

Mary and the Church are one mother;
yet more than one mother;
one virgin yet more than one virgin.
Both are mothers, both are virgins.
Each gives birth to a child of God the Father, without sin.
Without any sin, Mary gave birth to Christ the head,
for the sake of his body.
By the forgiveness of every sin,
the Church gave birth to the body,
for the sake of its head. Each is Christ's mother,
but neither gives birth to the whole Christ
without the cooperation of the other.
In the inspired scriptures,
what is said in a universal sense of the virgin mother, the Church,
is understood in an individual sense of the Virgin Mary,
and what is said on a particular sense of the virgin mother Mary
is rightly understood of the virgin mother, the Church.
When either is spoken of, the meaning can be understood of both,
almost without qualification.

Blessed Isaac of Stella[250]

---

[250] *Blessed Isaac of Stella a Cistercian monk, philosopher and theologian in 12th century.*

Questions #24

* * *

1. What do you understand by the term 'Eternal Gospel'?

2. What is the connection between the 'Woman in Genesis'? and the 'Woman in Revelation'?

3. Are there any similarities or contrasts between the angel's greeting of Mary and that of Elizabeth?

4. It is preposterous that a mere human being should be the Mediatrix of all graces. Moreover, it is an insult to the one mediator, Jesus Christ! What would you say to these objections?

5. What significance can you attach to Mary's role in the Wedding Feast at Cana?

6. Behold your mother! What did Jesus intend with these words to John?

7. Why is Mary described as the "Ark of the Covenant?"

8. *"A Woman clothed with the sun!" What does this mean?*

9. *It's an awful stretch of the imagination to call Mary 'the Mother of God'! Any comments?*

10. *Why is devotion to Mary intrinsic to Christian worship?*

11. *What part should Mary play in your own spiritual life?*

25. DEVOTION TO THE SAINTS

* * *

(a) Devotion to Mary,
- —1. A Glorious Example!
- —2. The Church's Devotion
- —3. Mary in the Liturgy
- —4. Mary's Maternal Intercession

(b) Veneration of the Saints
- —1. The Invisible Church
- —2. The Angelic Hosts!
- —3. The Intercession of Saints
- —4. One Mediator, Many Intercessors!

(c) The Church Suffering
- —1. Purgatory
- —2. The Book of Maccabees
- —3. The Teaching of Jesus
- —4. St Paul to the Corinthians.
- —5. The Teaching of the Church

25. Devotion to the Saints!

* * *

(a) Devotion to Mary

1. A Glorious Example!

Under the heading of the Church we have noted the theological and biblical foundations of Mary as *the Mother of the Church*.[251] Here, we shall confine ourselves to the consequences of those considerations, namely, the Church's devotion to Mary, and her motherly concern for the faithful.

It is obvious that Mary as the *Mother of the Church* and Mother of all the faithful, has a special interest in the eternal welfare of her children. At the same time as a mother she stands out as a shining example of a soul wholly surrendered to the will of God. The greeting of the Archangel; *O Thou who art full of grace!* is the hallmark of Mary's sanctity. That fullness of grace which characterised her entire life stands out as a beacon, drawing all souls to the light of Christ. As Pope Paul VI in his encyclical *Marialis Cultus* wrote:

> *First, the Virgin Mary has always been proposed to the faithful by the Church as an example to be imitated ... because she heard the word of God and acted on it, and because charity and a spirit of service were the driving force of her actions. She is worthy of imitation because she was the first and most perfect of Christ's disciples. All of this has a permanent and universal exemplary value.*

2. The Church's Devotion

We have already noted that Mary, as the Mother of God, is venerated with the special honour of *hyperdulia*, which places her above the angels and saints in heaven. For this reason the Catholic Church has accorded her a special place in the liturgy. Christ stands at the heart of the Church's

---

[251] *In the preceding chapter.*

liturgy. But we have emphasised that Mary's name is inseparable from that of her Son, and in honouring her, we honour the Father who chose her for his Son, we honour the Son who was obedient to her in Nazareth, and we honour the Holy Spirit who overshadowed her in the Incarnation! So the liturgical honour given her honours the Most Holy Trinity who lavished such marvels of grace upon her! Even in the very first century of our era Mary was given the titles of *the Holy One; the All-Holy (Panagia)*. Her name was inserted in the Creed. In the fourth century her name was inserted in the Canon of the Mass *(Roman Rite)*. In the Liturgy of the Hours the Church adopted the Mary's Canticle of *the Magnificat* in its Vespers as a hymn of praise to the Most Holy Trinity.

In addition, the Church finds in Mary the most perfect expression and the exemplary referent of the worship in spirit and in truth, which the Church is to render God, when it celebrates the Divine Mysteries. In this sense already, one could say that the whole Liturgy is Marian, even if the character is not always explicit.

3. Mary in the Liturgy

Pope Paul V1 in his famous encyclical *Marialis Cultus* made the point that, while the liturgy of the Church re-enacts the life of Christ, it also seeks *'to include Mary in the annual cycle of the mysteries of her Son!'* It does so to recognise the singular place of honour that belongs to her in Christian worship as the Mother of God and *'worthy associate of the Redeemer!'*

Beginning with Advent the feast of the *Immaculate Conception* ushers in the period of waiting and maternal expectancy of the birth of Jesus. This expectancy is heightened by the words of the *Advent Preface* that Mary bore our Saviour in her womb *'with love beyond all telling!'* The Christmas season is not only a celebration of the birth of Jesus but a rejoicing in Mary's 'divine, virginal and salvific motherhood'. This is emphasised when the new year is ushered in with the proclamation of the *divine motherhood* (January 1). The cycle of redemption is renewed in the season of Lent in which we find the feast of the Annunciation (March 25), celebrating Mary's crucial consent to God's request for her cooperation in the mystery of redemption!

Paul VI. also lists the unique chain of feasts that honour Mary under various titles found in various regions and in local churches, that have their own special reasons for honouring the Mother of God. All this climaxes in the Feast of the Assumption wherein the Holy Father waxes almost lyrical:

> *The solemnity of August 15 celebrates the glorious Assumption of Mary into heaven. It is a feast of her destiny of fulness and blessedness, of the glorification of her immaculate soul and of her virginal body, of her perfect configuration to the Risen Christ; a feast that sets before the eyes of the Church and of all mankind the image and the consoling proof of the fulfilment of their final hope, namely, that this full glorification is the destiny of all those whom Christ has made his brothers, having flesh and blood in common with them.*

4. Mary's Maternal Intercession

While giving honour to the Most Holy Trinity for the gift of Mary to us as our heavenly mother, these feasts of Mary also emphasise her intercessory role. If she is truly our *mother*, then she is interested in her children and their eternal welfare. Her will is united with her Son in wishing the best for all. But her favoured position in the economy of salvation also makes her an ideal intercessor on our behalf. *Intercession* differs from other forms of the prayer of petition in that it seeks some benefit or grace for another, rather than praying for oneself. The entire life of Christ was a gigantic prayer of intercession, so to speak, on behalf of all mankind. This role of intercessor does not stop now that he is in heaven.

As scripture itself relates:

> **Consequently, he is able for all time to save those who approach God through him, since he always lives to make intercession for them.**
> **(Hebrews 7:25)**

It is as *man* that Jesus intercedes for us, and prays for us. It is inevitable that his Mother shares these same concerns. In fact, the whole court of Heaven, including the angels, is united in them. The Council of Trent clearly defined this when it stated:

> *the saints reigning together with Christ offer*
> *their prayers to God for men[252].*

Our Lady's intercession, however, differs basically from that of the angels and the saints. Its basis lies in the *divine maternity—she is the Queen—Mother!* and in her unique cooperation in Christ's sacrifice. Her intercession is *truly maternal*. She pleads for all her children in every age! Her motherly concern far outstrips the poignant cry of St Paul for his Galatian converts:

> *My little children, for whom I am again in the*
> *pain of childbirth until Christ is formed in you,*
> **(Galatians 4:19)**

(b) The Veneration of the Saints

1. The Invisible Church

> *If one member suffers, all suffer together;*
> *if one member is honoured, all rejoice together.*
> **(1 Corinthians 10:26)**

It is evident that when we speak of the Church that we speak of the Church here on earth, the *visible* Church, with its many churches and a *visible* hierarchy. However, this is only a fraction of the real Church, the *invisible* Church, that reaches far beyond the cramped conditions of time and space! As the Council was at pains to point out there are three states of the Church:

> *When the Lord comes in glory, and all his angels with him, death will be no more and all things will be subject to him. But at the present time some of his disciples are pilgrims here on earth. Others have died and been purified, while still others are in glory, contemplating 'in full light, God himself triune and one, exactly as he is'.*

---

[252] see Denziger 1821 (The author was was a leading German Catholic theologian and author of a handbook of Creeds and Definitions).

These last few words are taken from the council of Florence (1439) and leads us to the conclusion that the three choirs of Heaven, Earth and Purgatory:

> *all sing the one hymn of glory to our God.*
>
> (#954)

The journey of the saints on earth leads ultimately, *via* a place of purification, to the throne of God in Heaven. However, it is not a *lonely* road, for as scripture tells us:

> ***Therefore, since we are surrounded by so great a cloud of witnesses, let us also lay aside every weight and sin which clings so closely, and let us run with perseverance the race that is set before us, looking to Jesus, the pioneer and perfecter of our faith . . .***
>
> **(Hebrews 12:1)**

That *'mighty cloud of witnesses'* are the angels and saints, especially those who have gone before us. But there are saints on earth who are praying for us; the Church is praying for us. There is a mighty confluence of prayer and grace flowing into our lives from all quarters of the Kingdom of Heaven. There is a supernatural interchange of spiritual power gushing through the Body of Christ, and we here on earth benefit from it all!

2. The Angelic Hosts!

In our self-absorbed culture, in a society bemused by science and technology and immersed in a crass materialism, the existence of angels is so often classed with the '*Easter Bunny,*' or viewed as the product of an overheated imagination! Nevertheless, the existence of angels is a matter of revelation. There are countless numbers of them in the courts of heaven. They are his special army under the leadership of St Michael. As the Catechism so succinctly puts it, quoting St Thomas Aquinas:

> *Angels are spiritual creatures who glorify God without ceasing and who serve his saving plans for other creatures.*
> *'The angels work together for the benefit of us all'.*(#350)

In scripture too we find angels as messengers of God. They are messengers of healing and of good news. They are also messengers of doom and destruction! It was an angel who brought to Mary the staggering news of the Incarnation. It was an angel that warned Joseph of Herod's murderous designs. In the Book of Revelation angels are the harbingers of a terrifying destruction at the end of time. If sainthood consists in the doing of God's will, the angels stand in the front rank of God's creation. As an English poet[253] wrote of them:

> *Thousands at his bidding speed,*
> *And post o'er land and ocean without rest!*

A special cult of devotion to the angels developed in the West under the influence of two saints, *St Benedict,* and *Pope St Gregory the Great* (590-604). It culminated in the work of St Bernard (1090-1153) who was the most eloquent promoter of devotion especially to the Guardian Angels. It is a matter of the virtue of *religion* that veneration is due to these servants of the Most High. The veneration accorded to them is the secondary veneration called *dulia*. *The Guardian Angels* are spiritual intelligences deputed by God to exercise special care of people here on earth. Their existence can easily be inferred from Our Lord's own words:

> **See that you do not despise one of these little ones;**
> **for I tell you, that in heaven, their angels always behold**
> **the face of my Father who is in Heaven!** (Matthew 18:10)

From this there also sprang the belief[254] that we each have a Guardian angel from birth to guide us through our time here on earth. This angel represents us before God, prays for us, and defends us. Devotion to one's Guardian Angel is to be encouraged. As Scripture tells us:

> **For he will give his angels charge of you to guard you in all**
> **your ways. On their hand they will bear you up, lest you**
> **dash your foot against a stone!**
> **(Psalm 91:11-12)**

---

[253] *John Milton (1603-1674) in his famous sonnet "On His Blindness".*
[254] *In theological terms this is called "proxima fidei" i.e. a very strongly held belief in the existence of Guardian Angels.*

3. The Intercession of the Saints

All this is but a prelude to the subject of the intercession and veneration of the saints in glory. The Catechism goes on to say:

> *Being more closely united to Christ, those who dwell in heaven fix the whole Church more firmly in holiness.... They do not cease to intercede with the Father for us, as they proffer the merits whch they acquired on earth through the one mediator between God and men, Christ Jesus ... So by their fraternal concern our weakness is greatly helped.*
>
> (#956)

Hence, it is that we are able to honour that concern by enlisting their help in our special needs here on earth. We can hear the same cry from so many saints as that expressed by Paul to his Corinthian converts

Be imitators of me, as I am of Christ!
(1 Corinthians 11:1)

The exhortation of St Paul is a pointer to the subject of the veneration of the saints and illuminates this thorny topic! It must be emphasised that the most perfunctory reading of the Word of God will readily reveal that certain individuals are closer to the Divine Majesty of God than others. We recall the special devotion of Noah, Abraham and Moses and the prophetic works of Elijah and Isaiah, to name but a few in the Old Testament. Moses, in particular, frequently interceded with God on behalf of his people. In the New there is a special place for *Mary*, the Mother of Jesus Christ, the twelve apostles and St Paul. Catholicism has a special place for these outstanding friends of the Almighty. We recognise God's work in their lives and we honour his choice. In honouring them we honour him who chose them in the first place, and raised them up to fulfil his will. As the liturgical prayer of the Church[255] puts it: *'Wonderful is God in his saints!'* In the *Martyrdom of St Polycarp* we find these compelling words:

---

[255] *In the Liturgy of the Hours.*

> *We worship Christ as God's Son; we love the martyrs as the Lord's disciples and imitators and rightly so, because of their matchless devotion towards their king and master. May we also be their companions and fellow disciples!*

4. One Mediator, Many Intercessors!

Nevertheless, the subject of the *intercession and veneration* of the saints is one that is sure to arouse controversy with those Christian denominations that stoutly maintain that there is but one mediator between God and men and that is Jesus Christ. And for this they usually quote St Paul:

> **For there is one God; there is also one mediator between God and humankind, Christ Jesus.**
> **(1 Timothy 2:5)**

Catholics readily agree that there is only *one mediator*, but insist that praying to the saints does not violate this unique mediation of Jesus. It is only a reaffirmation of it. What they assert is that the words of St Paul refer to the *unique* mediation of Christ.

The saints of the Old and of the New Dispensation are the special friends of God and in praying to them we seek to enlist their help in that very capacity as friends who are dear to God. We ask them to join their prayers to ours so as to give greater weight to our intercession. Moreover, it seems to Catholics highly bizarre that those who reject the intercession of the saints, our friends in heaven(!), have no scruples whatever in asking their friends here on earth to pray for them! The Catechism sums up the Catholic position by quoting the Council as follows:

> *It is not merely by the title of example that we cherish the memory of those in heaven; we seek, rather, that by this devotion to the exercise of fraternal charity the union of the whole Church in the Spirit may be strengthened. Exactly as Christian communion among our fellow pilgrims brings us closer to Christ, so our communion with the saints joins us to Christ, from whom, as from its fountain and head, issues all grace, and the life of the People of God itself.*
>
> (#957)

We erect Halls of Fame to honour athletes. We give countless awards to recognise the accomplishments of artists and those who have been of service in some capacity to the community. Can we do anything less than to give a special place of honour to those who have spent their lives in the noblest of all enterprises, the fulfilment of God's most holy will in their lives? The saints on earth have all one and the same aim—to carry out God's will in their lives. That is the goal of all their efforts. Those in heaven are all too anxious to assist them. Every soul won for Christ is a victory for them. Hence, the letter to the Hebrews gives us a picture of the hosts of heaven surrounding us and urging us on to win the race and claim the palm of victory!

> *Therefore, since we are surrounded by so great a cloud of witnesses, let us also lay aside every weight and the sin that clings so closely, and let us run with perseverance the race that is set before us.*
> **(Hebrews 12:1)**

(c) The Church Suffering!

1. Purgatory

The subject of the *Communion of Saints* cannot ignore a final word on the *Church Suffering, i.e. Purgatory.* These are those who are assured of salvation, but they still have some debt to repay to the divine justice. This debt is repaid by a process of purification, hence, the term *purgatory*, or *place of purification*! There is not a great deal in scripture about the nature of this purification from the defilements of the self-love that still remain, even when sin has been forgiven. Even a modicum of self-examination will reveal that we are very much attached to our will and the love of self. We still lack the total surrender to God that his overwhelming love demands of us. Purgatory assures us that we will reach that stage of total surrender that the *Beatific Vision* of God demands. As one author so aptly and so shrewdly remarks:

> *By nothing is self-assertion radically healed as by the acceptance of what the self shrinks from as it shrinks from suffering.*[256]

---

[256] see *Frank Sheed: Theology and Sanity (Sheed & Ward, 1960) p.248.*

What, then, has scripture to say on the subject?

2. *The Book of Maccabees*

We can find a telling reference in the history of the Maccabees:

> *But if he was looking to the splendid reward*
> *that is laid up for those who fall asleep in godliness,*
> *it was a holy and pious thought.*
> *Therefore he made atonement for the dead,*
> *so that they might be delivered from their sin.*
> **(2 Maccabees 12:45)**

These words, recorded in the aftermath of a battle won by Judas Maccabaeus against Gorgias, the governor of Idumaea, refer to the soldiers killed in battle who had manifested a certain attachment to pagan idols. He wanted to make atonement for them, and, in doing so, he manifested a belief in a life after death. At the same time he professed a belief that forgiveness of sins was possible after death. *Was he mistaken? Is it possible that there is a state where some souls suffer after death on account of their sins?*

3. *The Teaching of Jesus*

The justification for this belief he found in Our Lord's own words when Jesus spoke about the sin against the Holy Spirit.

> *Whoever speaks a word against the Son of Man will be forgiven,*
> *but whoever speaks against the Holy Spirit will not be forgiven,*
> *either in this age or in the age to come.*
> **(Matthew 12:32)**

From these words of Our Lord it is evident that there are sins that *can be forgiven* in the world to come. Since this obviously excludes Heaven, **since nothing unclean can enter there (Revelation 21:27)**, there must be another place or state for the completion of forgiveness.

On another occasion Jesus speaks of a prison from which no one can escape *'until he (or she) has paid the last penny'.* **(Matthew 5:26)** The inference is clear that there is a possibility of repayment. Otherwise, the words of Jesus become wholly pointless or redundant. The Word of God is neither pointless nor redundant.

4. St Paul to the Corinthians

St Paul has also something to say on the subject in writing to his Corinthian converts when he talks of the fire of judgement. It is a fire that will test the fabric and the foundations of one's spiritual life whether it was built on gold, silver, precious stones or straw etc. He concludes in saying:

> *If the work is burned up, the builder will suffer loss;*
> *the builder will be saved, but only as through fire.*
> **(1 Corinthians 3:15)**

We have laboured to show that the doctrine of Purgatory is firmly rooted in scripture and tradition. But apart from all that, it is a belief that would appear to be rooted in common sense. When we consider the *thrice holy* God, dwelling in inaccessible light and before whom even Moses and the prophet Isaiah trembled, it is evident that very few can fulfil the command of Jesus:

> *Be perfect, therefore, as your heavenly Father is perfect.*
> **(Matthew 5:28)**

Even in the holiest of persons there is usually some evidence of attachment to creatures and to the things of this world. The slightest fault must be purged before it can be admitted to the divine presence. There have been many martyrs to divine love in the history of the Church. But they are a relatively small group in the history of the Church. The majority of us are very much attached to our own will even though we profess to love God with all our heart and soul! We can only imagine the absolute purity that is demanded for a soul to gaze on the thrice holy God in the beatific Vision!

5. The Teaching of the Church

The Catechism of the Catholic Church answers the question for us by stating that there is a place or state of final purification:

> *All who die in God's grace and friendship, but still imperfectly purified, are indeed assured of their eternal salvation, but after death, they undergo purification so as to achieve the holiness necessary to enter the joy of Heaven. (#1030)*

The Church's name for this process of purification is *Purgatory*. Its existence has been formally expressed in the *Council of Florence (1439)* and in the *Council of Trent (1563)*. It represents a truth rooted in tradition and in scripture. Even as far back as the second century we find that great writer and thinker, Tertullian, giving witness to the early Christians who were wont to offer prayers and alms on behalf of the dead that they might find peace *(pax)*, refreshment *(refrigerium)* and eternal rest *(requies)*.

At the root of the problem lies our failure to grasp fully the consequences of our sins. It is an all too human failing on our part that always seeks justification for its moral failures in terms of what the world or public opinion says or might say. The Catechism, on the other hand, enlightens us on the subject as follows:

> *To understand this doctrine and practice of the Church, it is necessary to understand that sin has a double consequence. Grave sin deprives us of communion with God and therefore makes us incapable of eternal life, the privation of which is called the "eternal punishment" of sin. On the other hand every sin, even venial, entails an unhealthy attachment to creatures, which must be purified either here on earth, or after death in the state called Purgatory.*
>
> *This purification frees one from what is called the "temporal punishment" of sin. These two punishments must not be conceived of as a kind of vengeance inflicted by God from without, but as following from the very nature of sin. A conversion which proceeds from a fervent charity can attain the complete purification of the sinner in such a way that no punishment would remain. (1472)*

Questions #25

* * *

1. What is the basis for our devotion to Mary?

2. What are the earliest examples of devotion to Mary

3. What are the earliest feasts celebrated in honour of Mary?

4. What is the earliest prayer recorded expressing devotion to Mary?

5. What part should devotion to Mary play in my life?

6. What are the three states of the Church?

7. What is the rationale for the veneration of the saints?

8. What is canonisation?

9. Does praying to a saint take away from the unique mediation of Jesus?

10. What is the scriptural basis for Purgatory?

11. Why is its existence a matter of common-sense?

12. Why are the Souls in Purgatory called Holy?

13. And why should we pray for them?

26. THE MYSTERY OF INIQUITY!

* * *

(a) The Reality of Sin
    —1. God's Covenant
    —2. Sin and the Spirit
    —3. The 'Disappearance' of Sin!
    —4. Sin is a Mystery!

(b) The Wages of Sin
    —1. The Pride of Lucifer
    —2. The Fallout of Original Sin
    —3. The Sin of the World!

(c) The Devastation of Sin
    —1. Our Wounded Nature
    —2. Our Utter Helplessness
    —3. The Meaninglessness of Sin!
    —4. The Insanity of Sin!

26. The Mystery of Iniquity

* * *

This element on the *forgiveness of sin* in the Apostles' Creed comes so close to the end that it can so easily be viewed as an appendix to the main body of the Creed itself. As a result its position might tend to diminish its importance and consign it to the level of a minor postscript to all that had gone before. Far from it! This doctrine of *the forgiveness of sins* touches the very heart of the Creed. Not only that, it lies at the heart of the Covenant. It helps to explain the mission of Jesus which is aptly expressed in the words of the Nicene Creed:

> *For us men and for our salvation*
> *He came down from heaven!*

(a) The Reality of Sin!

1. God's Covenant

> *As for you, you shall keep my covenant,*
> *you and your offspring after you*
> *throughout their generations.*
> **(Genesis 17:9)**

Historically, God's special relationship with man is bound up in terms of what is called a *covenant*. The term *'covenant'* has the human dimension of a *contractual agreement* when related to business transactions, marriage agreements or political wheeling and dealing. Such commitments involve agreements between equals. In *biblical* terms, however, the term *covenant* has a totally different complexion, since those concerned in the covenant are far from being equals.

In the covenant the prime mover is God himself. God is the first to take the initiative; God *creates*; God *chooses*; God *makes the offer of salvation*. There is nothing on the part of the creature to warrant this choice. Hence those involved respond not as equals, but as subordinates, people willing to accept what is offered, with its challenges of wholehearted cooperation and long term fidelity. We see this in the lives of Noah and Abraham. In the life of Moses the covenant of the *Torah* or the Law[257], enters into every aspect of the entire fabric of his people's existence. Throughout their history they are constantly reminded of it by the prophets, and they are often punished by plagues, famine and invasion in their failure to observe it.

Infidelity and the abject failure to honour the covenant is what we call *sin*. The covenant is violated and the *divine-human* relationship is thereby fractured. In the incident of Moses and the Golden Calf the shattering of the tablets of stone at the base of Sinai is a powerful symbol of the betrayal of the Covenant *(Exodus 32)*. It underscores the deep ingratitude of the people who, having witnessed the signs and wonders of the Exodus from Egypt, abandoned themselves to idolatry and debauchery.

No matter how it is framed in terms of human rights or political expedience, the refusal to honour God's covenant is not only a base betrayal, but also the grossest ingratitude. It might seem surprising that *revelation* is essential for the forgiveness of sins. Man left to his own devices is incapable of comprehending the enormity of sin and the impossibility of its forgiveness follows as a result.

2. *Sin and the Spirit*

It might seem odd that the *Spirit of Love, the Paraclete the divine Comforter,* should have anything to say about sin. But the Spirit is also the *Spirit of Truth*, and *Truth* demands the exposing of the *lies* and the *deceptions* that lie hidden in the very heart of sin. We have already seen that the Holy Spirit is the *'Convincer of Sin'.* Jesus had already alluded to this crucial role of the Holy Spirit in speaking to his apostles:

> **And when he comes, he will convince the world**
> **of sin and righteousness and judgement;**
> **concerning sin, because they do not believe in me.**
> **(John 16:8-9)**

In essence, the *self-absorbed* world of Jesus' time differs little from our own world of today. No matter the change of time and circumstance,

---

[257] *The Law is summed up in the Decalogue or the Ten Commandments.*

human nature varies little. Our own world is also a self-enclosed world, locked into itself, engrossed in its own petty concerns, awash in the relentless pursuit of *money, pleasure and power*. It is a world so forcefully denounced by St John:

> *The love of the Father is not in those who love the world; for all that is in the world—the desire of the flesh, the desire of the eyes, the pride in riches—comes not from the Father but from the world.*
>
> **(1 John 2:15,16)**

All *grave* sin is basically an outright rejection of God. It is a repudiation of his salvific message, of his love, and of the Passion and Death of Jesus. The blindness, the incredulity and rejection that greeted Jesus in his own time continues to greet him today in an increasingly hostile and unbelieving environment.

3. The 'Disappearance' of Sin!

> *I am of the flesh, sold into slavery under sin!*
>
> **(Romans 7:14)**

Sin! It is not a popular word! In fact, it is considered to be out of fashion. It is deemed to be a *mediaeval hangover*, ill-suited to the temper of our *progressive(!)* times. *After all, don't we live in the 21st century, quite happy with our dazzling array of gadgets and gizmos!* The *'apple'* of technology, like the fruit of the garden of Eden, *is fair to the eyes and delightful to behold.*(Genesis 3:6). Nevertheless, like all created things they have the taste of death!

We have the hardest time acknowledging that we are really *sinners!* To bend the knee and acknowledge that we are *truly* sinners, that we stand in need of redemption, is ultimately a gift of grace! Well over a half-century ago Pius XII went so far as to say that our world had lost *the very sense of sin!* It is but natural that, when the existence of God is denied, there is the consequent loss of any feeling of offence against him. This is especially understandable where the *non-existence* of God has been legislated and actively promoted. But it is no less apparent in those cases where people live out their entire lives *as if God did not exist!* Our Holy Father, John Paul II, in his encyclical on the *Holy Spirit* points to the crucial act of rebellion on the part of our first parents that infected and poisoned our spiritual bloodstream. About it he has this to say:

> *The original disobedience presupposes a rejection, or at least a turning away from the truth contained in the Word of God, who creates the world . . . . Therefore. at the root of human sin is the lie which is a rejection of the truth contained in the Word of the Father.*
>
> (n.37)

4. *Sin is a Mystery!*

Ultimately, *sin is a mystery!* Many may be puzzled by this simple statement. They identify sin with its human counterpart, with the legal term *crime*. This is far from being *mysterious*; it is quite open and shorn of anything, either elusive or incomprehensible. *Murder* is murder and *adultery* is adultery! There is nothing complicated about the issue. True, the facts may not be disputed on the human level, but sin is a fact that must be judged on quite a different level. It is an *offence against God*; it is a violation of *his law*. That alone sheds a vastly different light on the issue. Since God is a mystery, the things that concern him partake of that mystery. It flows from the incomprehensibility of God in himself and from man's incomprehensibility of all that he owes to his Creator in the first place. St James puts all this in perspective when he says:

> **Every generous act of giving, with every perfect gift, is from above, coming down from the Father of lights, with whom there is no variation or shadow due to change.**
>
> **(James 1:17)**

However, the mystery is only compounded when we consider how man himself acts in his choices. The essence of the mystery on this level, lies in the question: *Why is it that we so often choose what is regularly inimical to our best interests not only on the supernatural level but also on the human level as well?* We are accustomed to accept instructions on how to operate what we buy. A car, for example, must be operated within the parameters of those instructions. Otherwise, we run grave risks in our driving. Likewise in living, to ignore the validity of God's laws is to court moral breakdown and even risk social and even personal disaster.

(b) The Wages of Sin!

1. *The Pride of Lucifer*

> *How you are fallen from heaven, O Day Star, son of Dawn! You said in your heart: 'I will ascend to heaven above the stars of God I will set my throne on high . . . . I will make myself like the Most High!'*
>
> **(Isaiah 14: 12, 14)**

It is customary to track the history of evil and sin back to the garden of Eden. Behind the disobedient choice of our first parents lurks the epic drama of rebel angels wholly opposed to God. It is here that *the mystery of iniquity* is at its most dramatic! It was in heaven itself that the banner of revolt was raised against the Creator. In the other world of heavenly spirits sin had already wreaked its havoc as described so eloquently in the Catechism:

> *Scripture speaks of a sin of these angels. This "fall" consists in the free choice of these created spirits, who radically and irrevocably rejected God and his reign.*
>
> *We find a reflection of that rebellion in the tempter's words to our first parents: "You will be like God. The devil has sinned from the beginning; he is a liar and the father of lies."*
>
> **(#392)**

Here the question spontaneously suggests itself: how could Lucifer, an angelic intelligence, one of the brightest luminaries of God's creation, entertain the notion of challenging the might of his Creator? It is an eternal conundrum! The poet Milton suggests the enormous pride that inspired the heavenly rebellion: *Better to reign in hell than serve in heav'n!*[258]

---

[258] *from Milton's "Paradise Lost".*

2. The Fallout of Original Sin

Unfortunately, the revolt in heaven spread to the earth! Here our first parents were no match for the deception and the guile of the *'father of lies'*. Left to himself man is incapable of warding off the onslaughts of evil. Revelation, with its promise of divine help, becomes necessary to prevent the world from spiralling downward into an orgy of self-destruction. It demands to be rescued from itself, from its own obstinacy, blindness, and stupidity!!

> *So when the woman saw that the tree was good for food, and that it was a delight to the eyes, and that the tree was to be desired to make one wise, she took of its fruit and ate; and she also gave some to her husband, who was with her, and he ate.*
>
> **(Genesis 3:6)**

What was forbidden fascinated Eve and seduced both her and her husband. There is an intensity of enticement in what is forbidden. It infatuated Eve and that still beguiles her descendants. What is forbidden becomes veiled in enticement and glamor. The virtues of self-sacrifice and self-denial appear lacklustre in comparison. The poet Swinburne so graphically depicts the contrast:

> *The lilies and languors of virtue*
> *And the roses and raptures of vice.*

The consequences of that fall led to the penalty of death, the unleashing of concupiscence and the rebellion of man's baser instincts. There was the consequent darkening of the intellect and the weakening of the will, and, above all, the loss of the loving friendship of God. Apart from the general condemnation meted out by God to both Adam and Eve, the devastation of sin worked itself out in their family with the murder of Abel at the hands of Cain. But it was not the fall of Adam and Eve alone that took place. The whole of mankind was embroiled in the consequences of the divine judgement delivered against the culprits involved. In that prototypical trial of our first parents the whole of humanity was destined to share in the judgement passed on them.

Sin, in effect, devastated the whole of creation and *it had to be rebuilt.* Today we are confronted with the physical devastation and desolation of plagues, earthquakes and tornadoes, but material disasters pale in comparison to the spiritual penalties and the internal disorder inflicted on the descendants of Adam and Eve. The poet Milton aptly summarises it all:

> *Of man's first disobedience, and the fruit*
> *Of that forbidden tree, whose mortal taste*
> *Brought death into the world, and all our woe* . . . .[259].

'And all our woe!' The whole of nature was shattered, that nature that had once rejoiced the heart of God and caused him to pronounce it *good!*

3. The Sin of the World

> **The next day he saw Jesus coming toward him and declared, "Here is the Lamb of God who takes away the sin of the world!"**
>
> **(John 1: 29)**

St John the Baptist, who heralded the public ministry of Jesus, was the one who proclaimed him as *the Lamb of God* and as the one who would destroy Satan's power over the world. John's expression about the *'sin of the world'* may appear puzzling at first, since the word *sin* is in the singular. We would normally expect him to say *'the sins of the world'!* However, it is a global expression conveying the sense of man's profound depravity and the utter sinfulness of the world.

In the sentence pronounced on the guilty couple we find this remarkable judgement:

> **Cursed is the ground because of you!**
>
> **(Genesis 3:17)**

---

[259] *John Milton op. cit.*

Man's working of the earth is cursed. All the works of his hands bear the imprint of that primeval curse. They fracture in his hands; they are destined for destruction and obscurity. Their very transience bears witness to the power of this divine judgement. It is, moreover, evident that the malaise of man's fall runs much deeper than individual or personal failure. It is customary to reflect on original sin as a fall from grace in this or that person. The fall of Eden touches our entire humanity and reaches into the very fabric of creation itself.

> *Revelation gives us the certainty of faith*
> *that the whole of human history is marked*
> *by the original fault freely committed by our first parents.*
> (#389)

Hence the liturgy of the Church speaks of *"the sin of the world"* as something far greater than the sum of its individual failures. It strikes at the very heart of all humanity. The malaise of that original fall seeps into every corner of God's original handiwork. When the crown of creation fell, the whole of creation fell. Its original goodness was corrupted and man lost complete dominion over it as well as his very self! The sacred text assures us that every kind of sin is wiped away in *the blood of the Lamb!*

(c) The Devastation of Sin

1. *Our Wounded Nature*

Because of our wounded nature, and our spiritual blindness, it is difficult to assess the corrupting influence of sin. A sick man usually finds it difficult to diagnose the root of his weakness, but he has within himself the possibility of recovery. There is a rough parallel between the ills of the body and those of the soul. Granted the inherent weakness of human nature, it cannot be said that the fundamental goodness of that nature is entirely lost. In the heated debates of the sixteenth century controversy raged around the issue of original sin and its effect on human nature. As against Luther's assertion of its *total* corruption, the Council of Trent asserted that although Adam had lost original justice of God's friendship:

> *the whole Adam, body and soul, was changed for the worse through the offence of his sin',*[260]

However, it was not *total* depravity. That change was, first of all, *'the death of the soul'* conjoined to physical suffering and, ultimately, to death. This change was inherited by all the descendants of Adam. It was passed on by propagation, from parents to their children. The result of all this is that, although man's nature is warped by a profound corruption, he still remains a creature of God. He is still made in his image and retains a basic freedom for the choice of goodness and virtue. Hence the change is not a total corruption of nature.

Nevertheless, that fundamental weakness of spirit still endures. Reason is darkened by original sin and that darkness is only deepened by *actual* sin. This in turn makes difficult any choice of what is good or best in terms of the spirit. This loss of sensitivity to goodness and virtue leads to the blight of egotism and to the immediate satisfaction of what appeals to the senses. It is obvious, therefore, that every capitulation to sin dulls the attraction of virtue and self-denial. A barrier is effectively erected to the influence of grace and the inspirations of the Spirit.

2. *Our Utter Helplessness!*

In contrast to the many panaceas offered him today, it is patent that man cannot save himself. Help must come from *without*. So God broke into the worlds of Noah, of Abraham and of Moses. Finally, he broke into the world of Mary, the sinless virgin of Nazareth. At the behest of the Father, the *Sinless One* went forth in the power of the Spirit to convince the world of its profound sinfulness. Nowhere is this more dramatically demonstrated than in his Passion and Death on the Cross! As St Paul describes it so graphically:

> **For our sake he made him to be sin who knew no sin,**
> **so that in him we might become the righteousness of God.**
> **(2 Corinthians 5:21)**

---

[260] see James E. Hanson C.S.C. *"If I'm a Christian, why be a Catholic?" The Biblical Roots of the Catholic Faith (Paulist Press, 1984) p.71.*

In the power of that same Spirit Jesus comes into our world to convince it of its utter sinfulness. Of ourselves it may be trite to say that we can denounce *sin*, until, as the popular saying goes, *'the cows come home'!* We can rail non-stop against the iniquity of our times. However, it is only the Holy Spirit who can ultimately reveal the true nature of our sinfulness, and shed his divine light on the darkness of our wrongdoing and its dire consequences.

> ***As for you, you shall keep my covenant,***
> ***you and your offspring after you***
> ***throughout their generations.***
> **(Genesis 17:9)**

3. The Meaninglessness of Sin

But sin brings its own devastation into the heart of man, into the very meaning of his existence. Since God is the author of everything, then man, without God, begins to lose the sense and significance of all around him. Without God man loses his bearings, just as a sailor loses his bearings without a compass.

> *Therefore without God everything is literally inexplicable, not only in the sense that man cannot find the explanation, but that there isn't one. Therefore again man is really doomed to live in a meaningless universe, and he can grow weary of the effort to live a meaningful life in a context that has no meaning.*[261]

A *Godless* society can be said to come apart at the seams and morality is the first line of defence to crumble. There is nothing to justify resisting temptation. The line of least resistance is the obvious course of action. Meaningless lives, like water, seek the lowest levels! The solvent of *meaninglessness* works its way through society, as Sheed goes on to say:

> *This simple principle—'I don't know why I shouldn't'—so sane, so reasonable, begins by justifying divorce and birth*

---

[261] F. Sheed op.cit. p.282

> *control; it has gone on to justify all sorts of abomination; it has not ended yet.*

These words, written over half a century ago, are sadly prophetic. Movements are afoot to justify and legitimise such things as *abortion, euthanasia, pornography* and all sorts of *sexual deviance*. As the author so rightly remarks, *it has not ended yet!* St Paul in one of his letters gives an apt description of this lamentable state of affairs:

> *Now this I affirm and insist on in the Lord: you must no longer live as the Gentiles live, in the futility of their minds. They are darkened in their understanding, alienated from the life of God because of their ignorance and hardness of heart. They have lost all sensitivity and have abandoned themselves to licentiousness, greedy to practice every kind of impurity. That is not the way you learned Christ!*
>
> **(Ephesians 4:17-20)**

4. Sin is Insanity!

No matter how much we try to understand the reality of sin and its results, we must come to the final assessment that sinning is a form of *insanity!* Insanity is a loss of touch with reality. It can be a permanent state in which persons are wholly lost in a state of unreality. We call them *lunatics* and incarcerate them for their own safety, and the safety of others.

Or it can be a temporary loss in which some act of madness occurs. So, when we take it upon ourselves to defy the very one who has created us, who suffered for us and redeemed us, who has only our best interests at heart and who wants to ensure our eternal happiness, then it can be truly said that we have lost touch with reality. We have surrendered ourselves to the possibility of eternal loss!

In this light serious sin can only be viewed as an act of utter madness! Sinning is *rampant insanity!* And still, we yield to its seduction with glorious abandon. Our reasoning is so often blinded by our imagination, and we seek immediate gratification at the expense of some future happiness offered to us in the acceptance of God's law. In addition, we offer to ourselves some rationale that apparently justifies our actions.

Everybody is doing it! I am hurting nobody! What harm is there in it? With such excuses we seek to exculpate ourselves and quieten the protests of conscience! We hear, moreover, this common complaint about some disaster, or misfortune:

> *Oh, why did God permit this to happen?*
> *Why could he not have intervened?*

God has given us all free will, and that means we have the gift of *choice*, the choice of saying either *Yes* or *No* to him. If that choice is abused we have only ourselves to thank for the disasters that result. We cannot accept the gift of free will and then complain if our choices lead to mayhem, disorder and disaster.

Here lies *the mystery of iniquity!* In the gift of free will itself is to be found the very means at our disposal to defy God himself! It caused Lucifer to challenge God; it led our first parents to disobey him. Their incomprehensible and perverse challenges to divine authority have wrought havoc in the minds and hearts of all mankind. Through our overweening pride and self-love sin is forever invested with a glamour that wreaks havoc on mankind's will and imagination.

As we survey the history of mankind and contemplate the rise and fall of civilisations we see man at war with himself as well as with his neighbours. But along with this cavalcade of collective insanity, we also witness the lesser scenes of individual murder and mayhem. Alongside this spate of evil mankind has endured the scourge of pestilence and plague and untold suffering. The drama of that primeval tragedy of Eden is re-enacted time and time again throughout the centuries and it will go on to the crack of doom! And all that torrent of calamity and distress flows from the *one* sin of disobedience.

> Disfigured by sin and death, man remains "in the image of God", in the image of the Son, but is deprived "of the glory of God", of his "likeness". The promise made to Abraham inaugurates the economy of salvation, at the culmination of which the Son himself will assume that 'image' and restore it to the Father's "likeness" by giving again its Glory, the Spirit who is "the giver of life".
>
> (#705)

Questions #26

* * *

1. *How does the biblical covenant differ from the human covenant?*

2. *Why did Pope Pius XII say that the world had lost the sense of sin?*

3. *Why should you say that sin is a mystery?*

4. *'Better to reign in hell than serve in heav'n'. Who said this? What does it mean?*

5. *What are the consequences of original sin?*

6. *What is the sin of the world?*

7. *What are the consequences of sin?*

8. *Sin is meaningless! Meaning?*

9. *Why doesn't God, if he is a good God, prevent all the evil in this world?*

10. *Sin is absolute insanity!* **Comment!**

27. THE DIVINE FORGIVENESS!

* * *

(a) The Road to Forgiveness
—1. The Necessity of Forgiveness
—2. The Price of Forgiveness
—3. The Forgiveness of Jesus
—4. Forgiveness and Peace

(b) Sacramental Forgiveness
—1. Baptismal Forgiveness
—2. Eucharistic Forgiveness
—3. Penitential Forgiveness
—4. Witness of the Early Church

(c) Receiving Forgiveness
—1. Reception of the Sacrament
—2. Repentance
—3. Giving Forgiveness!

27. The Divine Forgiveness

* * *

(a) The Road to Forgiveness

1. *The Necessity of Forgiveness*

We have already dwelt on the subject of *sin* and the modern tendency to deny its very existence. It would be well to keep in mind what has already been said on the subject, since the denial of sin strikes at the very heart of Christ's message—*forgiveness!* In an age when the existence of God was challenged and so often denied, it was inevitable that the notion of sin would slip into oblivion. *If* there is no God, then there is no-one to offend! Likewise, in an increasingly materialistic society it is very easy to assume that we are not such bad people after all, and that, in effect, we are not really sinners. If we are not *sinners*, then we do not need to pray for forgiveness! St John in one of his letters takes issue with such bizarre notions:

> *If we say that we have no sin, we deceive ourselves, and the truth is not in us.*
>
> **(1 John 1:8)**

There have only been two completely sinless persons, Jesus who was sinless by nature and Mary who was sinless by the divine gift of grace. Perhaps it is the meteoric advance of technology and the rise of education that promotes the idea of our own self-sufficiency and the odd notion that there is nothing in our lives that needs forgiveness! We are so prone to self-deception that we can readily explain away our sins and rationalise our waywardness!

2. *The Price of Forgiveness*

> *The next day he saw Jesus coming toward him and declared, "Behold the Lamb of God who takes away the sin of the world!"*
>
> **(John 1:29)**

Here for the first time in the Gospel story Jesus is given the title of *Lamb of God*. It was a proclamation of the role Jesus was to play in the forgiveness of sins. This proclamation takes us back to the Passover sacrifice of Exodus when the blood of the lamb was sprinkled and smeared on the door posts of the houses to protect the firstborn of the Israelites in Egypt:

> *The blood shall be a sign for you*
> *on the houses where you live:*
> *when I see the blood, I will pass over you,*
> *and no plague shall destroy you*
> *when I strike the land of Egypt.*
> **(Exodus 12:13)**

The sacrifice of the Passover lamb points to a future that is also foretold in prophecy. It brings to mind the prophetic words of Isaiah that reveal in a most striking fashion the future Passion of the Lamb of God.

> *But he was wounded for our transgressions, crushed for*
> *our iniquities; upon him was the punishment that made*
> *us whole, and by his bruises we are healed....*
> *He was oppressed, and he was afflicted,*
> *yet he did not open his mouth;*
> *like a lamb that is led to the slaughter,*
> *and like a sheep that before its shearers is silent,*
> *so he did not open his mouth.*
> **(Isaiah 53:5,7)**

This foretelling of the Passion of Jesus, given centuries before it came to pass, brings to mind that in the blood of the Lamb we are made *whole* again. The power of this Blood is manifest in the healing of the bruises and mortal wounds of sin. This picture of the Lamb, the very symbol of innocence, enduring the torments of the Cross, is all the more heartrending in the contrast between man's iniquity and the sinlessness of the Lamb of God.

The whole drama of the Passion from Gethsemane to Calvary spells out the price that Jesus was prepared to pay to win forgiveness from the Father. The horrors of that Passion are an eloquent demonstration of the love of Jesus for us and of the Father's deep desire to offer us anew the gift of sonship in his eternal love.

3. *The Forgiveness of Jesus*

> *For us men and our salvation*
> *he came down from heaven.*
> **(Nicene Creed)**

Salvation implies *forgiveness* and Jesus came down to offer us forgiveness! Forgiveness was a vital part of the ministry of Jesus. He forgave the adulterous woman as related in John 8:1-11. The same mercy was extended to the woman who washed his feet (Luke 7:48). and to the paralytic who was laid at his feet (Mark 2:10-11). Jesus always showed the greatest gentleness towards repentant sinners. Even to his own disciples who had deserted him and denied him he proffered the hand of forgiveness!

On the summit of Calvary God's forgiveness was sealed forever in the *Blood of Jesus*. In effect, there is nothing more searing to our sinful consciousness than to contemplate the *Way of the Cross*. There we behold the spectacle of Jesus, the *Sinless One*, the Lord of all creation, submitting to the dictates of a petty governor of an obscure Roman province, enduring the buffoonery of a brutal soldiery, treading the road to Calvary, and all the while, being subjected to a frenzy of mockery and ridicule. This journey of sorrow, which culminated in the heart-rending plea of Jesus to his Father, echoes and re-echoes down the centuries to our own times with its timeless appeal to every sinner's heart:

> ***Father, forgive them;***
> ***for they do not know what they are doing.***
> **(Luke 23:34)**

But this gift of forgiveness is a very fragile gift! It is certainly not fragile on God's part, but it is certainly fragile on man's part. The fault line of original sin runs through the heart of humanity. We have only to look at the so-called news in which man's iniquity is often colourfully displayed. As one journalist so glibly, but meaningfully, remarked: *Good news is no news!* History teems with wars and disasters and the whole gamut of mankind's overweening pride and utter stupidity. We are the victims of our own blatant injustice, insatiable greed and flagrant immorality. Even the great apostle felt the weight of that original injustice which weighs us all down:

> *For we know that the law is spiritual; but I am of the flesh, sold into slavery under sin. I do not understand my own actions. For I do not do what I want, but I do the very thing I hate.*
> **(Romans 7:14-15)**

Sold into slavery under sin. To understand Paul's metaphor we must conjure up the world in which Paul lived. It was a world in which slaves were chattels; they were things, bought and sold like cattle. Completely at the beck and call of their masters, they had no rights, except that of constant service. That was the image that came to Paul's mind in considering the plight of the sinner, wholly at the mercy of Satan! That is the curse that dogs our earthly existence. It would have been our destiny to eke out our lives in the shadow of that curse had Christ not come to our rescue. *For us men and our salvation he came down from Heaven.* (Nicene Creed)

> *But now that you have been freed from sin and enslaved to God, the advantage you get is sanctification. The end is eternal life. For the wages of sin is death, but the free gift of God is eternal life in Christ Jesus our Lord.*
> **(Romans 6:22-23)**

4. *Forgiveness and Peace*

On the evening of the Resurrection Jesus appeared to his disciples and the very first gift he offered them was *peace*. When he first came into this world at Bethlehem the angels sang of *peace to men of good will*. Peace is the gift of the Resurrection, and it is peace that is the most precious commodity that Christianity can bring to the world. We all desire peace—peace of mind, peace in our families, peace in our communities, peace among nations. Peace speaks of the presence of God, as the proverb[262] goes: *Where there is peace, God is there!*

---

[262] *see G. Herbert's Outlandish Proverbs (17th century).*

But that precious gift of peace was lost through sin. Let us never forget that it was just *one* sin that embroiled entire humanity in physical and moral confusion and the penalty of death! The fall of our first parents plunged the whole world into turmoil, and this turmoil will persist until the end of time. Jesus sought to right that wrong, and all subsequent wrongs, and offer us anew the gift of peace in bringing us reconciliation and forgiveness. Whenever we offend a person, wittingly or unwittingly, we always desire reconciliation and forgiveness. There is a natural urge to restore peace. But in offending God we offend *infinitely!*[263] That is the terrible power of our free will in defying our Creator. Still, the infinite love of the Father has sent us a Redeemer to redress the balance and offer us a means of forgiveness in the sacraments of reconciliation. Christ came to our rescue! He came to offer us peace, for he is the Prince of Peace!

(b) Sacramental Forgiveness

1. Baptismal Forgiveness

> *Truly, truly I say to you, unless a man is born of water and the Spirit, he cannot enter the Kingdom of God.*
> **(John 2:5)**

These words point to the sacrament of baptism and the cleansing role of water. There are many signs of this spiritual symbolism in scripture: the floods that cleansed the world of wickedness in the days of Noah, the escape from Egypt through the waters of the Red Sea and the crossing of the Jordan by the Chosen People into the Promised Land. It is through Christ that we have been freed from the domination of sin in our lives and reconciled with the Father. It is important to note that forgiveness comes primarily in the sacrament of Baptism. This point emerges very clearly in the Nicene Creed which states:

We acknowledge one baptism for the forgiveness of sins.

---

[263] *Again we are reminded of the dismal depths of our offences against God's infinite love!*

This a reminder of the origin of the Creed, that it was born in the questions given to the *baptizandi* in their initiation into the faith. But since moral lapses and failures are part of our lives we need the restoration of our spiritual health. At Pentecost St Peter responded to the anguished queries of his hearers when they asked: Brethren, *"what shall we do?"*

> **Repent and be baptised, everyone of you in the name of Jesus Christ for the forgiveness of your sins, and you shall receive the gift of the Holy Spirit.**
>
> **(Acts 2:38)**

The Catechism summarises the decrees of the Council of Florence on the subject:

> *By Baptism all sins are forgiven, original sin and all personal sins, as well as all punishment due to sin. In those who have been reborn nothing remains that would impede their entry into the Kingdom of God, neither Adam's sin, nor personal sin, nor the consequences of sin, the gravest of which is separation from God.*
>
> *(#1263)*

2. Eucharistic Forgiveness!

The Catechism, in its reflection on the fruits of Holy Communion, notes that the primary effect of the sacrament is to augment our *union with Christ*. However, the Catechism also notes that the *second* effect of the sacrament is the forgiveness of sins. This may sound surprising since we usually associate the forgiveness of sins with the sacrament of reconciliation. At the same time, we are reminded that we cannot be united with Christ *'without at the same time cleansing us from past sins and preserving us from future sins'*[264]

> *For as often as we eat this bread and drink the cup, we proclaim the death of the Lord. If we proclaim the death of the*

---

[264] see CCC #1391.

Lord, we proclaim the forgiveness of sins. If, as often as the blood is poured out, it is poured for the forgiveness of sin, I should always receive it, so that it may always forgive my sins. Because I always sin, I should always have a remedy.[265]

This sacramental strengthening of charity necessarily involves the wiping out of *venial sins*. By the love that we manifest in the reception of the sacrament we help to curb our selfishness and our pride, the root of all our sins. St Ambrose sums it all up so beautifully:

The Eucharist is our daily bread for our daily sins!

On the question of mortal or grievous sins the Catechism states:

By the same charity that it enkindles in us, the Eucharist preserves us from future mortal sins. The more we share the life of Christ and progress in his friendship, the more difficult it is to break away from him by mortal sin. The Eucharist is not ordered to the forgiveness of mortal sins—that is proper to the sacrament of Reconciliation.

(#1395)

3. Penitential Forgiveness

***He is the atoning sacrifice for our sins,
and not for ours only
but also for the sins of the whole world.***
(1 John 2:2.)

It is difficult, nay it is impossible, for us to grasp the enormity of sin, to gauge the infinite malice that lies at the heart of human wrongdoing. Consider how Adam and Eve, still in that state of original friendship with God, fell for the wiles of the serpent and ate of the forbidden fruit. Their fall from grace involved, not only themselves but their children and their childrens' children until the end of time. There is, moreover,

---

[265] *St Ambrose "On the Sacraments" see CCC #1391*

an endless catalogue of offences in the gravity of sin which is hinted at in the Church's Catechism:

> *The sinner wounds God's honor and love, his own human dignity as a man called to be a son of God, and the spiritual well-being of the Church, of which each Christian ought to be a living stone.*[266]

In ways far beyond our power to comprehend, Jesus took upon himself the sins of us all. There in that garden of sorrow in Gethsemane, and upon the cross of crucifixion on Golgotha, the drama of our redemption is played out. In some mysterious and self-sacrificing manner Jesus could thus satisfy the claims of divine justice on behalf of every person who is willing to accept his terms of pardon. As scripture assures us:

> *Although he was a Son, he learned obedience through what he suffered; and having been made perfect, he became the source of eternal salvation for all who obey him*
>
> (Hebrews. 5:8-9)

It was in this way that the power of satisfaction for sin was passed on to the Church through the chosen disciples who had followed their Lord in his years of ministry:

> *"Peace be with you. As the Father has sent me, so I send you." When he had said this, he breathed on them and said to them, "Receive the Holy Spirit. If you forgive the sins of any, they are forgiven them; if you retain the sins of any, they are retained."*
>
> (John 20:21-23)

This incredible gift of divine love and favour in the sacrament of Penance is so aptly described by Tertullian as "the second plank of salvation after the shipwreck which is the loss of grace."[267]

---

[266] *CCC#1487*

[267] *The Catechism is here quoting Tertullian one the greatest Christian apologists of the 2nd and 3rd centuries*

4. Witness of the Early Church

It was understood by the early Church that this power of forgiveness was active among them. Although we do not have exact accounts of the administration of this sacrament, it is evident that *self-accusation* of one's sins was a requirement for forgiveness. A century or two later we have writers that are more precise in describing the whole process of penance in which the main part is the confession of the penitent:

> *Ambrose makes things clear, saying; "This right is given to priests only". Pope Leo 1 says absolution can be obtained only through the prayers of the priest. These utterances are not taken as anything novel, but reminders of accepted belief.*[268]

The Catechism has also this to say about the sacrament of forgiveness with special reference to the power of *binding* and *loosing* given to the apostles by Jesus:

> *The words bind and loose mean: whomever you exclude from your communion will be excluded from communion with God; whoever you receive anew into your communion, God will welcome back into his.* **Reconciliation with the Church is inseparable from reconciliation with God!**
>
> (#1445)

(c) Receiving Forgiveness

1. Reception of the Sacrament

Certain conditions are obvious requirements for the validity of the sacrament. Repentance or contrition is the first essential. Then follows the actual confession of sins. First and foremost, mortal sins or grave sins must be confessed. Confession of venial sins, although they are not *necessary* matter, is strongly recommended by the Church, since it wins us grace to combat the evil tendencies of our nature. As St Augustine expresses it so succinctly:

---

[268] *St Peter Julian Eymard (1811-1868)*

The beginning of good works is the confession of evil works.
You do the truth and come to the light!

The priest suggests some form of penance, either in the form of some prayers or of self-sacrifice in order to make reparation for the faults that have been confessed. In effect, he is saying *that you should make up in some way for the spiritual damage that your sins may have caused.* This is called making *satisfaction*. In the case of theft or fraud this satisfaction may involve making restitution. So here we have the four elements that constitute the Sacrament—*Contrition* (repentance), *Confession* to a priest, *Satisfaction* and finally *Absolution*. Absolution in the words of *reconciliation* by the priest expresses the tenderness of our spiritual Mother, the Church. The priest invokes the Most Holy Trinity to grant the grace for which we all seek:

> *God, the Father of mercies,*
> *through the death and resurrection of his Son,*
> *has reconciled the world to himself, and sent the Holy*
> *Spirit among us for the forgiveness of sins; through the*
> *ministry of the Church may God give you pardon and*
> *peace, and I absolve you from your sins in the name of the*
> *Father, and of the Son, and of the Holy Spirit.*

2. Repentance

> *For you, O Lord, are good and forgiving,*
> *abounding in steadfast love*
> *to all who call on you.*
>
> **(Psalm 86:5)**

However, this saga of redemption is only one aspect of salvation. The gift of the *Blood of the Lamb* must be accepted. A gift does not become a gift until it is accepted! We must first accept what is offered. How do we accept this gift without price? It is only in repentance for our sins that acceptance is made manifest. This was the answer made by Peter in that first Pentecostal sermon when he made answer to the query made by those who were stricken by his reproaches for the death of Jesus:

> *"Brothers, what should we do?"*
> *Peter said to them, "Repent, and be baptised every one of you in the name of Jesus Christ so that your sins may be forgiven; and you will receive the gift of the Holy Spirit."*
> **(Acts 2:37-38)**

Simply said, repentance is *sorrow for sin committed*. It is a constant theme in God's dealings with his Chosen People in the Old Testament. Through the ministry of the prophets there was a constant call to repentance for their idolatries. But true repentance meant *metanoia* or a *change of heart*, a turning away from the ways of sin. The very word *conversion* means a turnabout in life which proclaims: *I am turning my life back to God!* The prophet Joel expressed this inner transformation when he said:

> *Yet even now says the Lord, 'return to me, with all your heart.*
> *with fasting, with weeping and with mourning:*
> *and rend your hearts and not your garments!'*
> **(Joel 2:12-13)**

Repentance is the gateway to conversion. This conversion is first manifested in Baptism. However, conversion is an ongoing process. It must continue in any life worthy of the gift of salvation. Conversion is part and parcel of daily living in the constant struggle to live a life worthy of a Christian. As the Catechism is at pains to point out:

> *Christ's call to conversion continues to resound in the lives of Christians. This second conversion is an uninterrupted task for the whole Church, who . . . . follows constantly the path of penance and renewal. This endeavour of conversion is not just a human work. It is the movement of a contrite heart, drawn and moved by grace to respond to the merciful love of God who loved us first.*
>
> (#1428)

3. Giving Forgiveness!

Forgive us our trespasses

> *as we forgive those who trespass against us!*
> **(Matthew 6:12)**

The fifth petition of the Our Father is a plea for *the forgiveness of our sins*. The basis of our plea lies in God's loving nature. If *God is Love,* as St John defines him in one of his letters,[269] then it follows that *forgiveness* must play a sovereign role in the many manifestations of that love. God's sovereign plan of salvation is itself a plan of forgiveness. As St John in his Gospel so graphically expresses it:

> *For God so loved the world that he gave his only Son, so that everyone who believes in him may not perish but may have eternal life. Indeed, God did not send the Son into the world to condemn the world, but in order that the world might be saved through him.*
> **(John 3:16-17)**

The Catechism has also this to say about this particular petition of the Our Father:

> *This petition is so important that it is the only one to which the Lord returns and which he develops explicitly in the Sermon on the Mount.*
> **(#2841)**

So important is this theme of forgiveness that Jesus in giving us the Our Father touches on this need to forgive *three times!* In fact, the only petition in this prayer to which a condition is attached is that of forgiveness. It is a chilling condition when we consider the full import of the words, namely that God extends his forgiveness to us *conditionally*. And that condition is that we extend the same forgiveness to those who have offended us! *If* we forgive others, he extends his forgiveness to us! That condition should give us pause for reflection! But in case you did not got the message the first time, Jesus goes on to say:

---

[269] *Karl Keating" Christianity and Fundamentalism" (Ignatius Press) 1988 p.185.*

*For if you forgive men their trespasses, your
heavenly Father will also forgive you;
but, if you do not forgive men their trespasses,
neither will your Father forgive you your trespasses.*
(ibid. vv 14-15)

PSALM 51

* * *

*Have mercy on me, O God,
according to your steadfast love:
according to your abundant mercy
blot out my transgressions!
Wash me thoroughly from my iniquity,
and cleanse me from my sin!
For I know my transgressions,
and my sin is ever before me.
Against you, you only, have I sinned,
and done what is evil in your sight,
so that you are justified in your sentence,
and blameless in your judgement.
Create a clean heart within me, O God,
and put a new and right spirit within me!
Cast me not away from your presence
and take not your holy Spirit from me!
Restore to me the joy of my salvation
and uphold me with a willing spirit!
Then I shall teach transgressors your ways,
and sinners will return to you.
Deliver me from blood guiltiness,
O God of my salvation
and my tongue will sing aloud
of my salvation!*

* * *

King David lusted after the wife of his officer Uriah. To conceal his adultery he had Uriah killed in battle. The prophet Nathan reproached him for his sins, and revealed God's displeasure. David repented and expressed the depths of his remorse in the immortal plea for mercy in Psalm 51 (2 Samuel chs 11,12)

St Jerome's commentary on this episode is worth repeating:

David sinned, as kings are wont to do,
David repented as kings are not wont to do.

Questions #27

* * *

1. *What is forgiveness and why do we need it?*

2. *What do you understand about the 'Price of Forgiveness'?*

3. *The entire ministry of Jesus was one of forgiveness. Comment!*

4. *What is the connection, biblical or otherwise, between forgiveness and peace?*

5. *What are the differences between Baptismal and Eucharistic forgiveness?*

6. *When and how did Jesus confer this power of forgiveness on his Church?*

7. *What is the witness of the Early Church to the transfer of this power?*

8. *What are the conditions for the reception of the Sacrament of Reconciliation?*

9. *What do you understand by metanoia?*

10. *Sold into slavery under sin! What precisely did St Paul mean?*

11. *Forgiveness must be given, before it is received! What exactly does this mean?*

12. *"I would never confess to a man! What would you say to this objection?"*

The Resurrection of the Body

28. I SHALL RISE AGAIN!

* * *

(a) The Resurrection Puzzle
      —1. A History of Rejection
      —2. Affirming the Resurrection
      —3. Crux of the Issue

(b) St Paul and the Resurrection
      —1. Heart of the Faith
      —2. Paul and the Corinthians
      —3. Baptism and the Resurrection
      —4. Conclusion

(c) The Risen Body
      —1. The Same Body?
      —2. The Glorified Body
      —3. Qualities of the Resurrection

28. I Shall Rise Again!

* * *

(a) The Resurrection Puzzle!

1. A History of Rejection

On this thorny subject St Augustine goes so far as to say in his Commentary on the Psalms:

> *No doctrine of the Christian faith is so vehemently*
> *and so obstinately opposed*
> *as the doctrine of the resurrection of the flesh.*[270]

Even in Christ's own time there were Jewish leaders, the Sadducees, who were resolute opponents of the whole idea of resurrection. They were the *liberals* who argued with Jesus on that score, and later did the same with Paul. Unfortunately, they were tainted with the ideas of the Greek philosophers such as Epicurus and the Stoics. Even Aristotle considered death as the final act of the human drama. It was the same opposition that Paul encountered when he preached to the Greeks in the Areopagus in Athens arousing their mocking laughter,

> **when they had heard of the resurrection of the dead.**
> **(Acts 17:18,32)**

To a certain extent we can understand the vehement opposition that this doctrine provokes, when we consider the nature of the body. The question automatically surfaces:

> *How can a substance so perishable and so changeable, so immersed*
> *in matter, be the recipient of an everlasting transformation such*
> *as is involved in the resurrection of the body entails?*

---

[270] *1 John 4:6*

It is evident that those who deny the *immortality* of the soul are natural enemies of the whole idea of resurrection. The early Church encountered the opposition of the *Gnostics*, the *Docetists* who looked upon matter as evil, and were, therefore, either incapable or unworthy of resurrection. They seem to have their counterpart in every age.

There appears to be a puritanical streak in society which reacts against the flesh and all its works. The Middle Ages saw the rise of neo-Manichaeism in the Albigenses, who repudiated marriage, attacking the sacramental life of the Church, as well as the secular authorities. In our own times we have a whole slew of materialists, rationalists and atheists who reject all notion of a life hereafter and, and, as a result, decry any possibility of the resurrection of the body.

2. Affirming the Resurrection

> *I am the resurrection and the life.*
> *Those who believe in me, even though they die, will live,*
> *and everyone who lives and believes in me will never die.*
> **(John 11:25-26)**

On the occasion when Jesus was gently rebuked by Martha for his absence during the illness of her brother, Lazarus, Jesus replied: *Your brother will rise again.* (John 11:23)

To which Martha rejoined:

> *I know that he will rise again*
> *in the resurrection on the last day.*
> **(v.24)**

From this account it is patent that belief in resurrection was widespread in the later years of the Old Dispensation. We also read in the Book of Daniel:

> *Many of those who sleep in the dust of the earth shall awake, some to everlasting life, and some to shame and everlasting contempt.*
> **(Daniel 12:2)**

However, Jesus taught this belief expressly on a number of occasions. It might easily be said that this doctrine of the resurrection was one of the cardinal themes of his teaching, since it related so clearly to his own resurrection from the dead. When he healed the man who had lain for 38 years paralysed by the Pool of Bethsaida, he delivered a lengthy speech in which he remarked:

> *Do not be astonished at this; for the hour is coming when all who are in their graves will hear his voice and will come out—those who have done good, to the resurrection of life, and those who have done evil, to the resurrection of condemnation.*
> **(John 5:28-29)**

Since the issue of the resurrection deals with the future there has been so much speculation on the subject. There has been considerable interest on the Second Coming. It has excited much controversy and even scepticism. However, the most solemn affirmation of this doctrine comes in the description of the Last Judgement. This terrifying scenario is described in Matthew's Gospel:

> *When the Son of Man comes in his glory,*
> *and all the angels with him,*
> *then he will sit on the throne of his glory.*
> *All the nations will be gathered before him, and he will separate people one from another as a shepherd separates the sheep from the goats.*
> **(Matthew 25: 31-32)**

The final judgement—*there is no appeal in this court!*—lays its seal on all the questions and answers that are relevant to this apocalyptic scenario wherein Jesus delivers sentence against the wicked:

> *Truly I tell you, just as you did not do it to one of the least of these, you did not do it to me.*
> *And these will go away into eternal punishment, but the righteous into eternal life.*
> **(Matthew 25: 45-46)**

3. Crux of the Issue

The crux of the question on the resurrection from the dead is anchored in the Resurrection of Christ himself. Christ, as the Second Adam, has redeemed the curse of our mortality in his own rising from the dead. The resurrection of Jesus is a reversal of the curse inflicted on the human race by God for the disobedience of our first parents. The latter forfeited the gift of immortality in yielding to the seductions of the Evil One. Since body and soul were involved in that reversal both must be involved in the resurrection, whether it be the resurrection either to everlasting life or everlasting death! The soul being a spirit is immortal; it cannot die. Hence its destiny would be incomplete if it were denied a union with its body.

The rising from the dead is the proclamation of our victory over death. This notion of a triumph over the last enemy of mankind is most definitely a biblical one. As the ultimate destiny of the just it had already been proclaimed centuries before by the prophet Isaiah:

> *Your dead shall live, their corpses shall rise.*
> *O dwellers in the dust, awake and sing for joy!*
> *For your dew is a radiant dew,*
> *and the earth will give birth to those long dead.*
> **(Isaiah 26: 19)**

(b) St Paul and the Resurrection

1. Heart of the Faith!

> *For if the dead are not raised, then Christ has not been raised.*
> *If Christ has not been raised, your faith is futile and you*
> *are still in your sins. Then those also who have died in*
> *Christ have perished.*
> **(1 Corinthians 15:16-18)**

It is well to stress this subject of the *Resurrection*, for it lies at the very heart of the Christian faith. It involves an answer to the question as to why we are here at all on this earth. We are constantly bedevilled by concerns about the ultimate meaning of our existence. That is why St

Paul was so eloquent on this subject. It cannot be stressed too much that in the resurrection of Christ Paul saw the very cornerstone of our faith. From this we can easily reach the conclusion that it is in the resurrection of Christ that we have the certainty of the resurrection of the dead when he comes again.

It would appear to be self-evident that something would be 'missing' in the final judgement, if the soul was to remain disembodied. The soul by its very nature demands embodiment! So, in the final analysis, the restoration of our bodies for everlasting bliss or woe would appear to be a natural consequence of that judgement! There was, however, an air of uncertainty about the end times that led many in the early Church to entertain the notion that the *Parousia*, or the Second Coming, was imminent, just as today there are many observers convinced that the apocalyptic signs of the Synoptic Gospels are being played out before our eyes!

2. Paul and the Corinthians

St Paul seemed to share some of these concerns and was the first to attempt a *theology* of the resurrection. The Corinthian converts, influenced probably either by the prevalent Greek philosophy, or by the views of Gnosticism, raised doubts about this central and Christian belief. Paul thought these doubts foolish but still they had to be acknowledged and answered:

> *But someone will ask, "How are the dead raised?*
> *With what kind of body do they come?"*
> *Fool! What you sow does not come to life unless it dies.*
> *And as for what you sow, you do not sow the body that is to be,*
> *but a bare seed, perhaps of wheat or of some other grain.*
> **(1 Corinthians 15:35-37)**

Here Paul compares the resurrection to the growth of a flower emerging from the seed that dies in the ground. This echoes the teaching of the Master himself with regard to growth in the spiritual life. Nevertheless, the resurrection is a mystery of faith. That is why we profess our belief in it. With God all things are possible. It has been promised and we accept that promise unhesitatingly.

3. Baptism and the Resurrection

By the very fact of receiving the sacrament of Baptism, the seed of the resurrection has already been planted in the soul. The grace of the sacrament gives us this title of participation in the death and resurrection of Jesus. St Paul is emphatic on this subject

> *When you were buried with him in baptism,*
> *you were also raised with him through faith in the*
> *power of God, who raised him from the dead.*
> **(Colossians 2:12)**

It is highly significant for *the Apostle of the Gentiles* that the resurrection of the body is intimately bound up with the resurrection of Jesus himself. For us the resurrection is the pledge of our conquest over death. Jesus, our brother in faith, has led the way, and we are to follow. It is the resurrection of Jesus himself that is the key.

> *But in fact Christ has been raised from the dead,*
> *the first fruits of those who have died.*
> *For since death came through a human being,*
> *the resurrection of the dead has also come*
> *through a human being;*
> *for as all die in Adam, so all will be made alive in Christ.*
> **(1 Corinthians 15:20-22)**

4. Conclusion

That there will be, at the end of time, a general resurrection of both the good and the evil is a dogma of the Church. It is a dogma expressed implicitly by Christ himself when he said:

> *The hour is coming . . . .*
> *when the dead shall hear the voice of the Son of God . . . .*
> *And they who have done good shall come forth*
> *unto the resurrection of life; but they who have done evil*
> *unto the resurrection of judgement.*
> **(John 5:25-30)**

For Paul it is evident that human existence, whether in this life or the next, was to be an affair of the whole person. Just as both *body* and *soul* had worked out the message of salvation in this life, they needed to share that same relationship—albeit a transformed one—in the world to come. Redemption did not consist, as both the *Greeks* and *Gnostics* believed, in the liberation of the soul from the body. The *whole person* needed redemption, for the body *needed* to share in the liberation of the soul. The *how* of it all is still a great mystery of the faith. To this Paul gives eloquent testimony:

> *For the trumpet will sound,*
> *and the dead will be raised imperishable,*
> *and we will be changed.*
> *For this perishable body must put on imperishability,*
> *and this mortal body must put on immortality.*
> *When this perishable body puts on imperishability,*
> *and this mortal body puts on immortality,*
> *then the saying that is written will be fulfilled:*
> *Death has been swallowed up in victory."*
>
> **(vv. 51-54)**

(c) The Risen Body

1. *The Same Body?*

The crucial question naturally arises:

In the resurrection do we have the same bodies as we had on earth?

The answer to that question was attempted by the *Lateran Council of 1215* in saying that Christ will come at the end of time

> "and all will rise with their own bodies which they now have
> so that they may receive according to their works,
> whether good or bad".

It is obvious that Jesus arose with the same body that died on the Cross. *But do the dead in general have the same body in the resurrection as when they were alive?* How this identity is established has been a matter of discussion throughout the centuries. What is meant by the expression *the same body*? Some would question the very possibility. Bodies wear out and decay; they crumble to the dust. Some are blown apart in horrific explosions, and some are devoured by wild animals!

With God nothing is impossible! All our questions and answers can never solve the riddles of something wrapped in God's will and almighty power. That is why it is an article of faith to which all human judgements must bow! There is a profound mystery here that evades all human reasonings, and even our wildest imaginings. We can only add what the Catechism has to say in seeking to respond to this very question:

> *How? Christ is raised with his own body: 'See my hands and my feet that it is I myself; but he did not return to an earthly life. So, in him, 'all of them will rise again with their own bodies which they now bear', but Christ 'will change our lowly body to be like his glorious body' into a 'spiritual body';*
>
> *But someone will ask, 'How are the dead? With what kind of body do they come? You foolish man! What you sow does not come to life unless it dies. And what you sow is not the body, which is to be, but a bare kernel . . . What is sown is perishable, what is raised is imperishable . . . The dead will be raised imperishable . . . for this perishable nature must put on the imperishable, and this mortal nature must put on immortality.*
>
> (#999)[271]

2. The Glorified Body!

**Then the Lord GOD will wipe away the tears
from all faces, and the disgrace of his people
he will take away from all the earth, for the LORD has spoken.
(Isaiah 25:8)**

Here we are concerned primarily with the *glorified* state of the just. Much that can be said about the qualities of the risen bodies are educated guesses and inferences from the hints supplied by scripture especially

---

[271] *In Psalmis 88 sermo n.5.*

from what we see in the appearances of Jesus in his glorified state after the Resurrection. First of all, the *just* rise *with Christ:*

> *For since we believe that Jesus died and rose again,*
> *even so, through Jesus, God will bring with him*
> *those who have died.*
> **(1 Thessalonians 4:14)**

The resurrection is, as it were, *a new creation.* It is God's handiwork of renewal, a restoration of all things by the same hand of omnipotence that wrought the first creation.

> *And the one who was seated on the throne said,*
> *"See, I am making all things new."*
> **(Revelation 21:5)**

This amazing restoration of all things is the fruit of the work of the Second Adam who triumphed over death. Death is the last enemy to be conquered in this titanic battle with evil. Death can only be truly conquered if our bodies share in the resurrection from the dead. It is this triumph over death that St Paul celebrates when he exclaims in exultant tones:

> *Where, O death, is your victory? Where, O death, is your sting?*
> *The sting of death is sin, and the power of sin is the law.*
> *But thanks be to God, who gives us the victory*
> *through our Lord Jesus Christ.*
> **(1 Corinthians 15:55-57)**

3. *Qualities of Resurrection!*

It is important to note that Christ's Resurrection is the *mainspring* of the resurrection of the Christian to glory. It is also its model. While the Resurrection and the state of glory are mysteries of the faith, we can attempt to describe that state since we have before us the example of Jesus, who is *the first born of many brethren.* Hence we do not hesitate to say that all those who share in the victory of Christ's resurrection are endowed with four transcendent qualities or characteristics. They are *impassability, glorification, agility and subtlety!*

a. Impassability

> *So it is with the resurrection of the dead.*
> *What is sown is perishable,*
> *what is raised is imperishable.*
> **(1 Corinthians 15:42)**

Impassability! This is a term inherited from the mediaeval Schoolmen. It implies the reversal of all that the body had to endure in its mortal life—*pain, suffering and death*. This quality puts the body beyond the reach of all human woes and disasters. The body is no longer subject to assaults either from within or without. As Jesus himself taught there is neither marrying nor giving in marriage. There is no vegetative life that depends either on food or sleep. Does this mean that we can neither eat nor drink? It has been suggested that this is possible since life in heaven has been compared to a wedding feast, where eating and drinking are part of the festivities. But such things are not essential to the quality of life there!

b. Glorification

> *Then the righteous will shine like the sun*
> *in the kingdom of their Father.*
> **(Matthew 13:43)**

This is the quality of brightness of glory by which the bodies of the saints shall *shine like the sun*. Glorification does not necessarily imply dematerialisation, since we are talking about the resurrection of the *body!* Here again, we are confronted with a mystery of faith, since glory would appear to imply the suspension of all earthly or material operations. We are guided here by the example of Christ himself in the post-Resurrection period of his life.

While there are no degrees of *impassability,* there are different degrees of glory according to the capacity in which the just *"put on Christ"* in their lives while they were here on earth. From the *Book of Revelation* we gather that there is some form of hierarchy in Heaven. There is evidently a hierarchy among the angels themselves, the highest being the *Cherubim* and the *Seraphim*.

> *And round the throne, on each side of the throne,*
> *are four living creatures, full of eyes in front and behind . . . .*
> *and whenever the four living creatures give glory and honour*
> *and thanks to him who is seated on the throne,*
> *who lives for ever and ever, the four and twenty elders*
> *fall down before him who is seated on the throne,*
> *and worship him who lives for ever and ever!*
> (Revelation 4:4,9)

c. *Agility:*

This is the quality by which the body is no longer hampered in its ability to get around. It is endowed with the capability of moving with the greatest of ease from one place to another, even with the speed of thought!

> *It is sown in dishonour, it is raised in glory.*
> *It is sown in weakness, it is raised in power.*
> (1 Corinthians 15:43)

d. *Subtlety:*

> *It is sown a physical body, it is raised a spiritual body.*
> *If there is a physical body, there is also a spiritual body.*
> (1 Corinthians 15:44)

Through *subtlety* the body becomes now wholly subject to the dominion of the soul. There will be no more harassment of the soul by unruly emotions or fevered imaginations. This can be inferred again from St Paul's own words. This *subtlety* has sometimes been identified with the ability to pass through other bodies, such as going through walls or closed doors. This is inferred once more from the example of Jesus when he appeared to the disciples in the Upper Room. However, some of the Fathers of the Church believe this was a special manifestation of divine power and not necessarily the property of a risen, glorified body. St Thomas Aquinas suggests that this quality is rather the total subjugation of the body to the desires of the soul. It is supernatural subjugation of all material desires and impulses to the higher impulses of the spirit.

* * *

If then you have been raised with Christ,
seek the things that are above,
where Christ is seated at the right hand of God.
Set your mind on things that are above,
not on things that are on earth,
for you have died and your life is hid with Christ in God.
When Christ, who is our life appears,
then you will appear with him in glory!
(Colossians 3:1-3)

* * *

The truth of Jesus' divinity is confirmed by his Resurrection. He had said:
"When you have lifted up the Son of man, then you will know that I am he. The Resurrection of the crucified one shows that he was truly "I AM", the Son of God and God himself. So St. Paul could declare to the Jews: "What God promised to the fathers, this he has fulfilled to us their children by raising Jesus; as also it is written in the second psalm, 'You are my Son, today I have begotten you.' Christ's Resurrection is closely linked to the Incarnation of God's Son, and is its fulfillment in accordance with God's eternal plan.

(#653)

Questions #28

* * *

1. Who were the opponents of the Resurrection in the time of Jesus and in the time of St Paul?

2. Why did the Greek hearers at the Areopagus laugh at Paul?

3. I am the Resurrection and the Life! What do these words of Jesus mean?

4. Why did St Paul consider the resurrection from the dead as the very heart of the Christian faith?

5. What is the connection between Baptism and Resurrection?

6. Do we have the same bodies in the resurrection as we had on earth?

7. What do you understand by the Glorified Body?

8. The triumph over death inevitably means the resurrection of our bodies! Discuss!

9. *What do these terms mean:* ***impassability***
   subtlety
   agility

10. *What does the Resurrection mean to you personally?*

29. ETERNAL HAPPINESS!

* * *

(a) Eternal Life
   —1. Our Immortality!
   —2. The Meaning of 'Eternal'.
   —3. The Credo of the People of God.

(b) The Vision of God
   —1. The Destiny of the Soul
   —2. The Union of the Finite with the Infinite!
   —3. The Beatific Vision
   —4. The Ultimate Fulfilment

(c) The Eternal God
   —1. The God of Revelation
   —2. The God without a Name!
   —3. The God of Unlimited Perfection
   —4. The God of Infinite Love

29. Eternal Happiness!

* * *

(a) Eternal Life

1. Our Immortality

> *And this is what he has promised us,*
> *eternal life.*
> **(1 John 2:25)**

This pregnant phrase—*Eternal Life!*—is an *eschatological*[272] formula that does not denote simply an existence without end. *Eternal life*, in the eyes of all the opponents of immortality, would represent an infinitely *boring* existence! There is a caricature that sees the saints sitting on the clouds and strumming their harps for ever!! Definitely a rather boring existence! On the contrary, it is an endless existence in the plenitude of intimacy with the divinity in supreme joy and consummate happiness. It is a world in a totally different dimension. Words fail to convey the reality that awaits those who do the will of the Father. St Paul makes this very clear:

> *What no eye has seen, nor ear heard,*
> *nor the human heart conceived,*
> *what God has prepared*
> *for those who love him.*
> **(1 Corinthians 2:9)**

When we speak of *everlasting life* in a purely human context we mean that the *soul* will never die. We are going to live forever! The soul has been *created* and, therefore, has had a beginning, but, as a spirit, it is intrinsically immortal; it cannot die; it will live forever! However, we know full well that death is part and parcel of our human existence. The separation of body and soul at death means that the body is left

---

[272] *see CCC Article 10 "I Believe in the Forgiveness of Sins."*

behind and disposed of. It is buried or cremated; it ceases to exist. But what we express a belief in now is that, when the body rises from the dead, it will be united to the soul and both will go on to live forever!! It is a conclusion that flows from a belief in the resurrection of the body.

2. Meaning of 'Eternal'

The term *'eternal life'* is frequently used in the Gospels. Like God himself the concept of eternity is a mystery. *Eternity is an eternal now!* There is no concept of *past* or *future* in what is eternal. Since we are rooted in time and space, we seek to understand it in those terms, for they are the only terms available to us! So John in Revelation begins his work in these words of greeting as from God himself:

> *Grace to you and peace from him who is and*
> *who was and who is to come*
> **(Revelation 1:4)**

There is, however, a paradoxical use of the term in John's Gospel where he says:

> *The Father loves the Son and has placed all things in his hands.*
> *Whoever believes in the Son has eternal life;*
> *whoever disobeys the Son will not see life,*
> *but must endure God's wrath.*
> **(John 3:35-36)**

The paradox lies in this that we speak of something that lies in the future, but St John speaks of eternal life as something that begins here and now! It flows from faith in the Son and in his message. **Whoever believes in the Son HAS ETERNAL LIFE!** The same idea is repeated in John's Gospel where Jesus in his discourse on the Bread of Life is very emphatic on the subject:

> *Very truly, I tell you, whoever believes has eternal life.*
> **(John 6:47)**

The key to the resolution of the paradox is to be found in the evangelist's use of the notion of seed in the first of his letters:

> *Those who have been born of God do not sin,*
> *because God's seed abides in them; they cannot sin,*
> *because they have been born of God.*
>   **(1 John 3:9)**

3. The Credo of the People of God

A question that arises here can be a very personal one: *how does all this affect me?* Or to phrase it in more theological terms: *how does the question of eternal life affect the eschatology[273] of souls?* The answer to the latter can be framed in *the Credo of the People of God*:[274]

> *We believe in life eternal. We believe that the souls of all those who die in the grace of Christ, whether they must still be purified in purgatory or whether, from the moment they leave their bodies, Jesus Christ takes them to paradise, as he did the Good Thief, are the People of God in the eternity beyond death, which will be finally conquered on the day of the resurrection, when these souls will be united with their bodies.*

What the Credo affirms is that there is an intermediate eschatology or state of purification of the People of God that will survive until the end of the world or the *'day of resurrection'*. Those whose lives are such that they do not have to endure the purification of the *Church Suffering* in purgatory will enter immediately into eternal life. Such was the destiny of the Good Thief, who entered into the life of the Church Triumphant. The Catechism summarises this life as follows:

> *The perfect life with the Most Holy Trinity—the communion of life and love with the Trinity, with the Blessed Virgin, the angels and all the blessed—is called "heaven". Heaven is the*

---

[273] *Eschatology, i.e. the theogical concerns approppriate to the end times and the Last Judgement.*

[274] *see note p.528*

ultimate end and fulfilment of the deepest human longings, the state of supreme and definitive happiness.

It adds a quotation from St Ambrose

> For life is to be with Christ, where Christ is there is life, there is the king.
>
> (##1024,1025)

(b) The Vision of God

1. The Destiny of the Soul

> For now we see in a mirror, dimly,
> but then we will see face to face.
> Now I know only in part; then I will know fully,
> even as I have been fully known.
>
> **(1 Corinthians 12:13)**

Once again the Creed returns full circle to its beginnings, the issue of faith.

> *What purpose does faith serve? What is its goal?*

The Catechism once again supplies the answer:

> Faith makes us taste in advance the light of the beatific vision, the goal of our journey here below.
> Then we shall see God 'face to face', 'as he is'.
> So faith is already the beginning of eternal life.
>
> (#163)

It then goes on to quote one of the *Cappadocian*[275] fathers, St Basil the Great:

---

[275] "The Credo of the People of God" composed by Pope Paul VI to commemorate the sixteenth centenary of the Creed attributed to the Council of Nicaea-Constaninople, 381 A.D..

> *When we contemplate the blessings of faith even now,*
> *as if gazing at a reflection in a mirror, it is as if*
> *we already possessed the wonderful things*
> *which our faith assures us we shall one day enjoy.*[276]

2. The Union of the Finite with the Infinite

There are naturally people who question the possibility of our seeing God at all. There are others who seek answers as to how God can let us see his very essence. Some like the *Palamites*—a group of eastern theologians—maintain that the divine essence cannot be seen either in this life or in the next. Others, like the Beghards and the Beguines of the 14th century, maintain that such a vision is well within our natural capabilities, that we can behold God *even in this life!*

Nevertheless, such opinions conflict with the evidence of scripture that, after death and in some mysterious way, God's infinite power will enable us to glimpse his very essence and see him *face to face*,

> **then I will know fully, even as I have been fully known.**
> **(1 Corinthians 13:12)**

To know fully entails dealing with God's action on the human soul. This in turn involves in one mystery after another, the innate incomprehensibility of God on the one hand, and the natural limitations of his creatures on the other. The reconciliation of these apparently incompatible elements must be ultimately left to God's omnipotence:

> **For mortals it is impossible,**
> **but for God all things are possible.**
> **(Matthew 19:26)**

---

[276] *The so-called "Cappadocian Fathers" (4th century) viz. Basil the Great, Greegory of Nyssa and Gregory of Nazianzus. They came from Cappadocia (Eastern Turkey today).*

3. The Beatific Vision

The question, however tantalising, still remains: *What is the Beatific Vision?* This very question was put to Benedict X11 by the University of Paris in the fourteenth century. In their reply they said:

> *After the passion and death of Our Lord Jesus Christ (the just) will see, and do see the divine essence in a vision that is intuitive, and also facial, no mediating creature offering itself in the manner of an object seen; but the divine essence showing itself to them immediately, nakedly, clearly and openly, and so seeing they enjoy the divine essence.*

This heavy philosophical and theological language struggles once again with something that defies all human expression. There is no parallel in our human experience that can convey the essence of the soul's vision of God, who is infinite and eternal. What Pope Benedict is endeavouring to say here is that it is not a normal mode of *knowing* or *seeing*. As St Paul describes it, it is *'face to face'*. There are no intermediaries, no shadows, nothing to intervene in the act. It is an *immediate* illumination of the mind imposed by God himself, in the special intimacy of divine love and friendship.

4. Ultimate Fulfilment

In this vision the soul reaches its final destiny. It satisfies every desire. The fulness of life has been attained. This is the goal to which the soul has aspired throughout its existence. Here is fulfilled what St Augustine expressed so beautifully:

> *Thou has made us for Thyself, O God,*
> *and our hearts are restless until they rest in thee!*

All the trials and pains of life, all the labours and toil of existence are swallowed up in the transcendent beauty and the overwhelming love of the divinity. There is no human vocabulary that is adequate to describe the divine ecstasy of the *Beatific Vision*. As was said right at the beginning of this volume, we struggle with the inadequacies of human speech to convey the depths of God's mysteries. Even in the words of

Holy Writ itself the author of Revelation has to resort to the picturesque metaphors of our earthly existence in his efforts to bring home the incomprehensible depths of divine love!

> *And I heard a loud voice from the throne saying,*
> *"See, the home of God is among mortals.*
> *He will dwell with them as their God;*
> *they will be his peoples,*
> *and God himself will be with them;*
> *he will wipe every tear from their eyes.*
> *Death will be no more; mourning and*
> *crying and pain will be no more,*
> *for the first things have passed away."*
> **(Revelation 21:3-4)**

(c) The Eternal God

1. The God of Revelation

> *Praise the LORD! Praise God in his sanctuary;*
> *praise him in his mighty firmament!*
> *Praise him for his mighty deeds;*
> *praise him according to his surpassing greatness!*
> **(Psalm 150)**

God is the goal of all our efforts. It is ironic that the Creed almost ends on the very same note where it began—with *God*! Then it may have appeared to be a rather *impersonal* God, a God that was a part of salvation history, the God of revelation who came to us in the revelation of his beloved Son, Jesus Christ. Here, however, he is identified with *eternal life*, a life that he wants to share with me, with us, in the most intimate of all embraces! The term *'life'* is difficult to define, since any definition will vary according to the scientific discipline in question. In general, whatever is capable of *immanent* movement is said to be alive or living. In religious terms, life is taken in its *transcendent* form, i.e. a life that far surpasses all forms of biological or botanical existence.

The highest form of this transcendent life is the divine life of God, the Creator and *Prime Mover* of all creation. He is *Pure Act* in terms of philosophy. In terms of divine revelation he is *the living God*, the God Immortal, who cannot die. As the Psalmist cries out:

> *My soul longs, indeed it faints for the courts of the LORD;*
> *my heart and my flesh sing for joy to the living God.*
> **(Psalm 84:2)**

2. The God without a Name!

Although in the course of mankind's history, people have accepted the existence of a God, they have usually invested him with human attributes in trying to understand him. The very term *'God'* is a human term by which we to seek to grasp what is far beyond human understanding; he is utterly incomprehensible! As theologians are wont to say: *God is ineffable or unspeakable* i.e. he is far beyond the power of words either to describe or to understand! Revelation was necessary so that his creatures might get to know him better. As the Catechism states:

> *In the decisive moments of his economy God reveals his name, but he does so by accomplishing his work. This work, then, is realised for us and in us only if his name is hallowed by us and in us.*
> (#2808)

When it says *'God reveals his name'* this must be understood in the light of what follows. He is identified by what he does in *'accomplishing his work'*. One of these decisive moments of *'work'* came when God spoke to Moses from out the burning bush. It was then that Moses asked God for his Name:

> *God said to Moses, "I AM WHO I AM." He said further, "Thus you shall say to the Israelites, 'I AM has sent me to you.'"*
> **(Exodus 3:14)**

This *I AM* is the key to God's existence; it means that God is *existence* itself, that his very nature is *to be!* It is difficult for us to comprehend any Being living in an everlasting NOW! We have nothing in our armoury of comprehension, reasoning or expression of language that can, in any meaningful way, convey an understanding of a Being that has *neither beginning nor end*, but simply exists! We struggle with the essential *contingency* of language in an effort to express the *Absolute*. The greatest thinkers have all struggled with this task.

3. The God of Unlimited Perfection

According to St Thomas Aquinas we attribute a number of perfections to God. They are

> *simplicity, omniperfection, goodness, infinity, immensity, unchangeableness, eternity, unicity, invisibility and ineffability,*

To these we have already alluded. However, at the core of it all is God's utter *holiness!* About this the Catechism states:

> *The holiness of God is the inaccessible centre of his eternal mystery. What is revealed of it in creation and history, Scripture calls 'glory', the radiance of his majesty.*
>
> (#2809)

This mystery of God only deepens when it is revealed that in the inner life of the Godhead there is not one but *three* persons! God is a Triune community, three distinct persons in one nature! One of these persons, the Second Person of the Trinity became one of us:

> **and the Word was made flesh and dwelt amongst us!**
> **(John 1:14).**

Finally, *in Jesus the name of the Holy God is revealed and given to us, in the flesh, as Saviour, revealed by what he is, by his word and by his sacrifice. This is the heart of his priestly prayer:*

> **Holy Father . . . for their sake I consecrate myself,**
> **that they also may be consecrated in truth.**
> (#1812 quoting John 17)

4. The God of Infinite Love

The Catechism comments on this topic by quoting the prophets, Isaiah and Jeremiah:

> *God's love is everlasting. For the mountains may depart and the hills be removed, but my steadfast love shall not depart from you. Through Jeremiah, God declares to his people: I have loved you with an everlasting love; therefore, I have continued my faithfulness to you. (#220)*

John the Beloved goes still further in giving us the final message of God's secret life in an *Unconditional Love* that continually astounds us. First in his Gospel:

> **For God so loved the world that he gave his only Son,**
> **so that everyone who believes in him may not perish**
> **but may have eternal life.**
> **(John 3:16)**

And then in his letters, John gives us a definition that no amount of philosophical or theological reasoning can better. It is the culmination of the revelation that began with the utterance of God's name to Moses: I AM! God's essence is *existence* itself, and the heart and soul of that existence is LOVE!

> **Beloved, let us love one another,**
> **because love is from God;**
> **everyone who loves is born of God and knows God.**
> **Whoever does not love does not know God,**
> **for God is love!**
> **(1 John 4:7-8)**

+++++++++++++++

Questions #29

* * *

1. *"The prospect of eternal life seems to me to be an awfully boring existence!" How would you respond to this objection?*

2. *What is the Credo of the People of God? And what does it say about this subject?*

3. *What is eschatology?*

4. *Who are the Cappadocian fathers?*

5. *What do you understand about the soul's destiny?*

6. *It is impossible for the finite to be united to the infinite! It's like oil and water, they don't mix! How do you respond to this objection?*

7. *What do you understand by the term the Beatific Vision?*

8. *What is God's name?*

9. *When you say that God is ineffable, what do you mean?*

10. *How, and in what ways, do you relate to God personally?*